Death
by
Laughter

FILM AND CULTURE

FILM AND CULTURE

Edited by John Belton

A series of Columbia University Press

Hollis Frampton: Navigating the Infinite Cinema, by Michael Zryd

Perplexing Plots: Popular Storytelling and the Poetics of Murder, by David Bordwell

Horror Film and Otherness, by Adam Lowenstein

Hollywood's Embassies: How Movie Theaters Projected American Power Around the World, by Ross Melnick

Music in Cinema, by Michel Chion

Bombay Hustle: Making Movies in a Colonial City, by Debashree Mukherjee

Absence in Cinema: The Art of Showing Nothing, by Justin Remes

Hollywood's Artists: The Directors Guild of America and the Construction of Authorship, by Virginia Wright Wexman

Film Studies, second edition, by Ed Sikov

Anxious Cinephilia: Pleasure and Peril at the Movies, by Sarah Keller

For a complete list of books in the series, please see the Columbia University Press website.

Death by Laughter

Female Hysteria and Early Cinema

Maggie Hennefeld

Columbia University Press

New York

Columbia University Press
Publishers Since 1893
New York   Chichester, West Sussex
cup.columbia.edu

Copyright © 2024 Columbia University Press
All rights reserved

Library of Congress Cataloging-in-Publication Data
Names: Hennefeld, Maggie, 1984– author.
Title: Death by laughter : female hysteria and early cinema / Maggie Hennefeld.
Description: New York : Columbia University Press, [2023] |
Includes bibliographical references.
Identifiers: LCCN 2023043315 | ISBN 9780231213288 (hardback) |
ISBN 9780231213295 (trade paperback) | ISBN 9780231559812 (ebook)
Subjects: LCSH: Laughter in motion pictures. | Hysteria in motion pictures. |
Women in motion pictures. | Comedy films—United States—History and criticism. |
Motion pictures—United States—History—20th century.
Classification: LCC PN1995.9.L39 H46 2024 | DDC 791.43/617—dc23/eng/20231201
LC record available at https://lccn.loc.gov/2023043315

COVER DESIGN: Elliott S. Cairns
COVER IMAGE: The cover image features silent film star Colleen Moore laughing hysterically at a television broadcast of her 1926 comedy *Ella Cinders*, which is a backstage Hollywood parody of Cinderella. In this scene, Ella Cinders practices her "cross eyes"—enhanced by trick photography—rehearsing "eye exercises" from a screen acting manual. The photograph was taken in Moore's home in Chicago in 1963. It encapsulates the division and collision between madness and pleasure—automatism and paroxysm—that envelop female laughter. Many thanks to Joseph Yranski for his help identifying this image and to Moore's daughter Judy Hargrave Coleman for her permission to reprint it.
Courtesy of Judy Hargrave Coleman, daughter of Colleen Moore.

To Léontine (whoever you are)

Contents

Acknowledgments ix

Introduction 1

PART I
Death by Laughter

1. Hysterical Laughter on the Brink of Enjoyment 23

2. Female Death by Laughter (Beyond Enjoyment) 47

3. An All Too Brief History of Laughter and Death 75

PART II
Female Hysteria

4. Gaslighting the Libido: Feminist Politics of Madness, Laughter, and Power 93

5. Laughter: The Forgotten Symptom 123

6. Mass Hysteria, Collective Laughter, and Affective Contagion 141

PART III

Early Cinema

7. Laughter Unleashed: Hysterical Women at the Movies 179

8. The Visual Cure? Moving Pictures as Neurotic Trigger and Therapeutic Instrument 215

9. From Mouth to Screen: Laughing Heads in the History of Film 251

Conclusion: Laughter, Hysteria, Power—Then and Now 279

......

Notes 283

Index 337

Acknowledgments

This book would not have been possible without the support of my friends, colleagues, students, and intellectual and archival film communities. It was initially provoked by a peculiar obituary column from 1902 that I found in a rabbit hole of the World Newspaper Archive in 2014: "LITERALLY LAUGHED HERSELF TO DEATH." As the story goes, a woman allegedly died from laughing too hard at an irresistibly funny joke. I immediately shared this fishy tidbit with Jennifer Bean and Shelley Stamp, who both encouraged me to focus less on the literality of death and more on what such stories revealed about women and their perceived relation to the physicality of laughter at the time. In that spirit, I began scouring the digital archive for every relevant example I could dig up, which were astoundingly numerous. I'd initially hoped to shoehorn these reports into my previous book about slapstick comediennes in early silent cinema, but it soon became clear that my archival ragpicking would escalate into its own project. Ten years later, here we are.

I am deeply grateful to everyone who has offered me feedback and motivation by reading chapter drafts, article adaptations, or attending talks (both actual and virtual). Nicholas Baer, I feel extraordinarily lucky to have you as a close friend and daily interlocutor. This book would not have been possible without your measureless insight, hysterical wit, and incredible warmth. Alison Griffiths, thank you for your incisive feedback, friendship, and continuous support. You have been a generous mentor and I always feel energized by our expansive conversations. James Leo Cahill, your riotous intellect and epistemological mastery of all possible theoretical implications of the movie adaptation of *Cats* have fueled my own senses of play and mischief through the completion of this work. Karen Redrobe, exchanges with you routinely explode what I believe to be possible to bring to the table as a feminist scholar and teacher. Philip Rosen, I remain singularly grateful to have had such an insightful and amusing Ph.D. advisor. Our discussions blow my mind but always leave me with solid ground to stand on and a renewed appetite for critical adventure! Jennifer Bean, you are a whirlwind of brilliance, generosity, action, and creativity— I truly cannot imagine the field of feminist film historiography or the trajectory of my own escapades without you (since that time I "fangirled" you at a conference as a graduate student in 2010). Laura Horak, my partner in crime on *Cinema's First Nasty Women* (and many other projects!), the whole field is better for all that you do, share, and give. I feel lucky to have you as a collaborator and friend. Shelley Stamp, your generosity as a feminist mentor and archival researcher/curator has been endlessly inspiring to me and to so many others. Your work is a lifeline. Cesare Casarino, whose capacity for joyous comradery is paralleled only by his commitment to collective critical thought, thank you for your extensive support over the years as my colleague, co-editor, mentor, and friend. Enrique Moreno Ceballos, Pamela Hutchinson, Elif Rongen-Kaynakçi, José María Serralde Ruiz, Kate Saccone, and Jay Weissberg, when I think of what inspires me to engage with silent film culture today, all I hear are your voices! The field is alive because of the passionate work that you all do.

I feel superlatively lucky to have had mentorship and encouragement from scholars whose writings have deeply inspired my own and laid the foundations for critical pedagogies in media studies today. I am especially grateful to Mary Ann Doane, Jane Gaines, Charlie Keil, Linda Mizejewski, Patrice Petro, Matthew Solomon, and Patricia White. At the crossroads of film historiography, comedy studies, and feminist theory, this book was multifariously shaped by conversations and encounters with Richard Abel, Mark Lynn Anderson, Claudia Breger, Mark Garrett Cooper, Joan Copjec, Timothy Corrigan, Donald Crafton, Tom Gunning, Bambi Haggins, Lynne Joyrich, Alexandra Juhasz, Anton Kaes, Kathleen Karlyn, Rob King, Lynne Kirby, Beck Krefting, Judith Yaross Lee, Joseph Litvak, Anne Nesbet, Susan Ohmer, Laurie Ouellette, Anca Parvulescu, Dana Polan, B. Ruby Rich, Nicholas Sammond, Mark Sandberg, Amy Villarejo, and Linda Williams.

I am immensely grateful to my friends and interlocutors (whose uplifting comradery and evocative insights I wish I had space here to kvell about in unfiltered detail): Caetlin Benson-Allott, Annie Berke, Mireille Berton, Annie Fee, Doron Galili, Franciszka Heller, Gunnar Iversen, Sarah Keller, Kristina Köhler, Katharina Loew, Dolores McElroy, Jennifer Peterson, Girish Shambu,

Kyle Stevens, Jocelyn Szczepaniak-Gillece, Julie Turnock, and Tami Williams. My community of friends from graduate school will always be my family. You all make me smarter by osmosis, Kenny Berger, Eugenie Brinkema, Michelle Cho, Josh Guilford, Hunter Hargraves, Nathan Lee, Aniruddha Maitra, Rijuta Mehta, Brandy Monk-Payton, Matt Noble-Olson, Sarah Osment, Pooja Rangan, and J.D. Schnepf. This project has been intellectually fueled and humorously enlivened by wide-ranging conversations with Kristen Anderson Wagner, Diana Anselmo, Clara Auclair, Meredith Bak, Courtney Baker, Alix Beeston, Stephanie Brown, Alex Bush, Liz Clarke, Allyson Nadia Field, Katherine Fusco, Jenny Horne, Lisa Jacobson, Alison Kozberg, Kiki Loveday, Lorenzo Marmo, Ross Melnick, April Miller, Debashree Mukherjee, Hayley O'Malley, Renée Pastel, Karen Pearlman, Ariel Rogers, Elyse Singer, Seth Soulstein, Aurore Spiers, Yiman Wang, Althea Wasow, Genevieve Yue, and others whose names my "Swiss cheese memory" already regrets forgetting to include.

Thank you to my two manuscript reviewers, who provided incisive, generous, and often uproarious feedback that took the project's goals to heart and invaluably guided my revisions. Thank you to my wonderful, dedicated, and insightful editors at Columbia University Press: Philip Leventhal and John Belton—and to Ben Kolstad, Susan Pensak, and all the editorial teams and staff at CUP. Immense gratitude to my research assistants Vanessa Cambier and Matthew Tchepikova-Treon, whose prodigious labor and eagle eyes for detail are behind the endnotes and citations of this manuscript.

The research involved in this project was made possible by the archivists, projectionists, and staff at the Library of Congress (Washington D.C.), the EYE Film Museum (Amsterdam), the Fondation Jérôme Seydoux-Pathé, the Cinémathèque Française, the British Film Institute, the Royal Belgian Film Archive, the New York Public Library's Billy Rose Theatre Division, and the Museum of Modern Art (New York). During the long months of pandemic lockdown, archive workers were heroically generous in digitizing materials and making them accessible to the public. I would particularly like to acknowledge Bryony Dixon, Elif Rongen-Kaynakçi, Dave Kehr, Mariann Lewinsky, Mike Mashon, Steve Massa, Stéphanie Salmon, and Marcia Tucker. Digitized databases were further invaluable, especially the Media History Digital Library, the World Newspaper Archive, and Gallica. A million thanks to my film festival comrades for always sharing their deep love, quirky knowledge, and contagious passion for silent cinema at gatherings such as the Giornate del Cinema Muto and Il Cinema Ritrovato. Shoutout to Stefanie Benz, Neil Brand, Mark Fuller, Valerio Greco, Michelle Facey, Oliver Hanley, Eva Hielscher, Uli Ruedel, and our whole "Virtual Druid" family. You all mean the world to me!

This book is so much richer for all the people I was lucky enough to cross paths with at the University of Toronto during a Mellon Post-Doctoral Fellowship on "Humour, Play, and Games" in 2014–2015. Many thanks to the incredible staff and to my cohort of fellows at the Jackman Humanities Institute: Matt Cohn, Pete Jones, Louis Kaplan, Oisín Keohane, Katie Larsen, Katie Price, Bob Gibbs, Pamela Klassen, and Kim Yates. The School of Historical Studies at the Institute for Advanced Study at Princeton University and the Institute for Advanced Study at the University of Minnesota both provided me with vital time and resources to undertake my strange research and begin to draft my manuscript. The UMN Imagine Fund, the UMN Grant-in-Aid program, the McKnight Foundation, and the Mellon Foundation offered me financial support to visit film archives and attend silent film festivals. In Fall 2016, I particularly benefitted from conversations at the UMN IAS with Jennifer Gunn, Susannah Smith, Karen-Sue Taussig, Barbara Welke, Joshua Page, Christopher Roberts, Eva von Dassow, and later with Julie Schumacher. In 2018–2019, the pieces all came together through continuous exchange with faculty fellows in Historical Studies and Social Sciences at the Princeton IAS, especially Joan Wallach Scott, Yve-Alain Bois, David Bond, Daniel Aldana Cohen, Munira Khayyat, Rima Majed, and Clara Mattei.

Material for this book has been adapted from prior publications in journals or volumes. A very preliminary version, "Death from Laughter, Female Hysteria, and Early Cinema," appears in *differences: A Journal of Feminist Cultural Studies* (27.3, Winter 2016). Thank you to Ellen Rooney, Elizabeth Weed, Denise Davis, and my peer reviewers for your support and feedback on those initial efforts. A substantially updated synthesis of the larger framing for the project, "Affect Theory in the Throat of Laughter—Feminist Killjoys, Humorless Capitalists, and Contagious Hysterics," appears in a special issue of *Feminist Media Histories* (7, no. 2, "Affect," May 2021), edited by Jennifer Bean and expanded from a virtual conference hosted by The University of Washington, Seattle in May 2020. Chapter 6 on mass hysteria and affective contagion emerged from a virtual conference on the theme of "Collectivities" hosted by the Jackman Humanities Institute and organized by Sara Saljoughi in April 2021. I am further grateful to all the centers, departments, and programs that invited me to present my research over the past decade and whose organizers and participants gave me vital feedback and encouragement. Warm gratitude to all my wacky fellow travelers in the SCMS Comedy & Humor Studies Scholarly Interest Group.

Thank you to my colleagues and PhD students in Cultural Studies & Comparative Literature at the University of Minnesota; to Kristen St. Michel and the staff of CSCL; and to my co-editors and Assistant Editors at the journal *Cultural Critique*. Awe and admiration for all my brilliant students in various courses I have taught while writing this book, namely the graduate students in "Theory on the Brink of Laughter" in Fall 2019 and undergraduates and TAs in various iteration of the comedy class at UMN. My local community in the Twin Cities keeps me going through the long Midwest winters and *too short* patio summers. Cheers to Morgan Adamson, Michelle Baroody, Ainsley Boe, Vivian Choi, Danielle Dadras, Lorenzo Fabbri, Joe Farag, Sugi Ganeshananthan, Atilla Hallsby, Christine Marran, Jason McGrath, Candace Moore, Sonali Pahwa, Bryan Pekel, Jennifer Row, Palita Sungchaengchan, Emily Winderman, and all our LHH comrades—past, present, and future!

My family has been heroically supportive throughout this whole shebang. I am profoundly lucky to have, in fact, "the best feminist mom in the world": Marianne DeKoven is my role model, fearless ally, and hilarious friend. I have my father, Julien Hennefeld, to thank for my sense of humor. (Thanks a lot!) Dan Hennefeld, thanks for being a cool big brother. Much love also to my wonderful sister-in-law, Jivelle Callender, my funny and brilliant niece, Sidney Mazie Hennefeld, the Tollesons for their unconditional warmth, and the incredible Abeel and Knoop families (Erica, Maud, Neilson, Kate, Stuart, Otis, and Jasper). Praise be to our indomitable cats Schmutz and Kibbutz, the family canines, Mia and Lani, and in memory of Sammy and Phoebe, my best pal.

Most of all, thank you to Alex Tolleson. You are the best one and I love you so much.

Death by Laughter

Introduction

Imagine being so hilarious that your jokes, impressions, or other repartee literally caused someone to laugh themselves to death.[1]

—"Does Your Stand-Up Act Need Death by Laughter Insurance?,"
Trusted Choice, insurance web advertisement, August 10, 2019

Imagine being so wild and free that your laughter literally killed you. The funniest comedian's worst nightmare betrays humor's ultimate utopian wager: to die laughing—to take flight from the world in the throes of unbearable pleasure and outrageous ecstasy. "Though extremely rare, even laughter can be a killer," warns *Trusted Choice*.[2] Death-by-laughter insurance dates back to the early 1900s (in their telling), when "a group of giggly (yet timid) cinemagoers" hired the firm Lloyd's of London "to issue a policy that would cover them in the event they actually died laughing. Now that's pretty funny."[3] What film could provoke such dangerous mirth? Was it *Tickled to Death* (1909) in which a woman brings her dead husband back to life by tickling his feet with a hat feather? Or perhaps *That Fatal Sneeze* (1907), an unorthodox comedy about nasal catastrophe? Although preposterous, death-by-laughter insurance would have been a perfectly sensible precaution at the time.

From 1870 to 1920, hundreds of women reportedly died from laughing too hard. Bertha Pruett was "Killed By A Joke" in 1893 when a young man (and "noted wit") made a risible remark at a dinner party that "threw Miss Pruett into

FIGURE 0.1 "Does Your Stand-Up Act Need Death by Laughter Insurance? (Just in case your comedy *really* kills)," Trusted Choice web advertisement for insurance, August 10, 2019.

a violent fit of laughter" that "suddenly changed to a cry of pain and she fell to the floor . . . Dead."⁴ The unnamed jokester was not a professional comedian, unlike the thespians whose riotous performance on opening night at the theater caused Mrs. Charles S. Stuber (age thirty-three) to die of acute indigestion incited by excessive laughter.⁵ Mrs. Polly Ann Jackson "had not laughed so hard in months as at the story told her which caused her death" in Kentucky in 1906.⁶

Movie exhibitors gleefully exploited fatal anxieties about *risible mortis* in their devilish gambits, offering to insure all patrons against "loss of life" due to "unrestrained laughter."⁷ For example, The Ontario Equitable Life and Accident Insurance Company issued a policy to "every man, woman, and child" attending *Lord Chumley in Canada* (1925)—advertised as "THE JOLLIEST BANG-UP COMEDY IN YEARS!"—with a "proviso that death [must] occur during the performance."⁸ (Viewers who laughed themselves to death after the last shot would be sadly out of luck.) The stunt made a killing and reaped an "immediate profit" as people flocked to test their enjoyment against the postmortem promise of $1,000 cold hard cash. "Life insurance for death by laughter is another exploitation stunt which has caught on," opined *The Exhibitors Trade Review* in 1923 in a recurring section titled "Exploitorials."[9]

Liability hazards engulf the comedy industry today, but the target has shifted from laughing spectator to edgy practitioner. Comedians face litigious backlash for everything from plagiarism to gender bans to mother-in-law jokes, exemplified by the 2009 "MOTHER-IN-LAWSUIT" against Sunda Croonquist whose outraged in-laws sued her for "making too many mother-in-law jokes" in her stand-up act.[10] In contrast, Charlize Theron absolved Sacha Baron Cohen in 2019 after she "was hospitalized for five days" from "laughing too hard while watching 'Borat.'"[11] (She had a herniated disk but *Borat* was "the straw that broke the camel's back."[12])

There is something truly utopian about the spirit of death-by-laughter insurance, which prizes the unbearable pleasures of laughter over the injurious cruelty of comedy. How extraordinary? After all, one can buy insurance for nearly any absurdity—Loch Ness monster attacks; alien abduction; poltergeist invasion; the bad luck of getting "cold feet" before nuptials ("cold feet coverage"); or the risk of devaluing a lucrative body part, such as Marlene Dietrich's smoky voice, Gene Simmons's long tongue, America Ferrera's teeth, Heidi Klum's legs, Tom Jones's chest hair, and the taste buds of various sommeliers and food critics.[13] More than a crude capitalist gimmick (which, of course, it is also), death by laughter insurance takes pleasure as a contagious, euphoric wager—a burst of jouissance—rather than a selfish possession or self-isolated feeling fueled by bitter resentment and culture war hostility.

I am not a professional comedian, but I felt enticed by this unwieldy indemnity. Naturally, I called Trusted Choice, who referred me to several brokers in my area (Minneapolis, Minnesota), all of whom declined to offer me a price quote for death by laughter insurance. Perhaps they assumed it was a prank call; when I explained that it was for research purposes, they said they had more important things to do with their time than speculate about "atypical policies" that would not increase company profits and they had never heard of such a thing anyway. When I tried again—this time posing as a "comedy entrepreneur," they further insulted me by raising doubts about my company's projected gross revenue and unlimited liability cap. A service representative at Trusted Choice named Isabelle B. laughed out loud as I read from the ad: "for those equipped with the skills to induce sidesplitting guffaws, death-by-laughter insurance might actually be a viable option."[14] She then wished me "prosperity" with my research project. (Thank you, Isabelle!) Death by laughter insurance is simply too beautiful for this reality.

THE WAGES OF DEATH BY LAUGHTER

> *So few reports of laughter-related deaths actually exist that the very thought of taking out an insurance policy for it is, in and of itself, a bit comical... Regardless of death by laughter's credibility, there's coverage for it.*[15]

It is unsurprising that a $5.36 trillion industry would want to cast a wide net by pandering to common dangers and outrageous hazards alike.[16] Laughter insurance is the logical conclusion of a capitalist economy driven by the desire for unending enjoyment and the exploitation of apocalyptic despair. "Our politics, religion, news, athletics, education and commerce have been transformed into congenial adjuncts of show business," observed Neil Postman in 1985. "The result is that we are a people on the verge of amusing ourselves to death."[17] In his best-selling book, *Amusing Ourselves to Death*, Postman pathologizes the popular addiction to television that reduces our public discourse to "dangerous nonsense."[18] Unlike fatal laughter, enjoyment of mass culture is not physically lethal: "death by amusement" serves as a metaphor for the collective tolls of pervasive commoditization. Several decades later, as dark corporate money fuels the "reality-TV-to-electoral-politics pipeline"[19] and QAnon evangelists orchestrate online scavenger hunt games for the "truth-to-come"[20] (that the deep state is controlled by a Satanic cabal of cannibalistic, child sex traffickers), the metaphor of "amusing ourselves to death" has become all too literal. It encompasses the slow-burn catastrophe of environmental collapse, neofascist resurgence, permanent war, ordinary violence, and obscene inequality. Addiction to enjoyment is ever to blame when knowledge proves futile in the face of belief, as the comforts of passive pleasure supersede the vital politics of social change.

But comedy and amusement are not the same thing, and their conflation threatens to defang humor's sharp bite in the name of subverting a relentless "imperative to enjoy."[21] Laughter grows hollow when everything is supposed to be funny. "Feminist killjoys" and "humorless" rabble-rousers thus wage battle royale against a droning chorus of laugh tracks, canned laughs, "rolling on the floor laughing" emojis, and other epiphenomena of late capitalism's "medicinal bath" of "wrong laughter," to invoke those notorious fun-crashers Max Horkheimer and Theodor Adorno.[22] What can critical comedy do in the face of so much meaningless pleasure? Humor has always held a special power to disrupt consumer culture's free fall into thoughtless conformity, whereby corporate rule and social alienation pave the way to class warfare, toxic resentment, and emboldened white supremacist misogyny. From anti-Nazi satires like Charlie Chaplin's *The Great Dictator* (1940) and Ernst Lubitsch's *To Be or Not to Be* (1942) to Ziwe Fumudoh's anti-racist parody "Stop Being Poor" (2021) and Nuotama Bodomo's Afro-Surrealist musical *Everybody Dies!* (2016), radical comedy jams the wheels of laughter's effortless adherence to passive enjoyment.

Wild laughter gives voice to unspoken taboos. It liberates dangerous desires, risky impulses, and inconvenient thoughts, unleashing an extremity of feeling that spreads through your whole body and sparks new sensations of community and solidarity. But comical laughter has lost its disobedient edge, hog-tied by the "cruel optimism" through which we compulsively "amuse ourselves to death."[23] As Lauren Berlant and Sianne Ngai incisively put it, "Both the world and comedy change when there's a demand for permanent carnival."[24] In other words, comedy no longer offers a holdout or exception to the icy embrace of "permanent carnival," as public discourse is pervaded by a ghoulish sideshow of empty hot takes, cynical-satirical memes, and ludicrous conspiracy theories. Ever hungry to eat its own tail, comedy itself has been tasked with filling the void, which it can achieve only by upping the ante on its righteous cri de coeur. Even escapist humor is now irresistibly politicized, often as a substitute for the impotence of sober, earnest, or merely uninteresting forms of protest and debate.

In critical humor studies, recent books have taken up this intense politicization of all comedy, ranging from hopeful collections on the importance of "Stand-Up Comedians as Public Intellectuals" to clarion calls exposing the actual violence of bigoted jokes (see: Raúl Pérez's *The Souls of White Jokes*) and deep dives into the ideological abyss of far-right humor (read, if you dare, *That's Not Funny!: How the Right Makes Comedy Work for Them*).[25] Comedic allegiance has become a letter of faith, causing the *why* of laughter to eclipse the contagions of humor, as male "edge-lords" lament that their genius is being censored by so-called cancel culture and feminist comics routinely receive death threats for being in any way funny, outspoken, erotic, or political.[26] This is the volatile climate in which we commit the potency of our laughs to the satirical voice of our social in-group or ideological tribe.

Under such conditions, where laughing at the right critical object might feel just as meaningful as (or no less so than) voting, attending a protest, participating in a consumer boycott, or picketing outside the house of a Supreme Court justice, it is very difficult to imagine grappling with laughter on its own terms. What is laughter if not a ratification of humor? And what is humorlessness if not a refusal of the other's enjoyment?

And yet many laughs defy any possible connection to comedy. But this is precisely the location of their renewed catharsis and disruptive radicality.

Glenda Carpio calls it "laughing fit to kill," which erupts from "the double bind of distance and nearness" to ungrievable traumas of American slavery.[27] In a similar vein, Danielle Fuentes Morgan explores the double-voiced absurdity of Black media satire as a vortex for "laughing to keep from dying"—from Georgina's uncanny "No, no, no, no" burst in Jordan Peele's *Get Out* (2017) to Maya Angelou's spoken word poem with the existential refrain: "I almost laugh myself to death. I laugh so hard HA! HA!"[28] In the absence of easy release, laughter takes on fraught emotional meaning, heavy with bottomless grief, fiery with insuppressible joy, and layered with the unresolvable anguish of living in a homicidally ridiculous world. We strip laughter of its nuanced absurdity, its minoritarian irony, and its archival afterlife when we only hear its echoes in reference to comedy and humor. To analyze the joke, in other words, is not to resolve the meaning of its laughter.

LAUGHTER WITHOUT COMEDY

This book is an experiment to embrace laughter on its own terms. I focus on the tensions between joyous laughter and nervous hysteria as these two sensations collided in the raucous bodies of pleasure-seeking women around the turn of the twentieth century. Prior to that time, to "laugh hysterically" meant to suffer from mixed feelings, such as passion and shame, hope and futility, or excitement and disgust. The stigma was typically reserved for the mirthless pathos of emotional women, whose irrational sensations were routinely hystericized as beyond the realm of knowledge, understanding, or representation. Deprived of cathartic outlets, women retreated into their bodies, unleashing torturous symptoms—from somnambulism, amnesia, phantom paralysis, and hallucinations to uncontrollable barking, yawning, hiccupping, and tongue clacking. As a somatic "conversion disorder," female hysteria offered a "proto-language" for parlaying unspeakable words into an enigmatic carnival of the flesh, paving the way for a feminist imaginary to come.[29]

But that firewall between nervous laughter and jubilant comedy collapsed by the end of the nineteenth century. Hysterical laughter was let loose upon the masses! The feverish spread of alluring spectacles (by which we now "amuse ourselves to death") invested the powers of laughter with the licensed madness of hysteria. With the rise of early cinema and its interlocking attractions (variety shows, burlesque revues, musical extravaganzas), women were widely incited to laugh louder and more convulsively than ever before. As one film trade magazine declared, "You are compelled to laugh, you cannot control yourself, you cannot resist the contagion!"[30] No recreational venue, however, was as hysterical as the cinema: "Don't you know one of the first missions of the motion picture is to GET YOU TO LAUGH? Then help the picture's mission!"[31] As women's pleasure became the gold standard for commercial profit, a crisis of deadly enjoyment preyed on the emancipation of their voluble laughter—quite literally.

Between 1870 and 1920, I repeat, hundreds of women reportedly died from laughing too hard. These bizarre obituaries proliferated in American local dailies and national newspapers alike, mourning the unforeseen deaths of women who were "Killed By a Joke," who "Had Not Laughed So Heartily In Months," and who "may have been about the first to see anything in Colorado to laugh at."[32] Amid the consecration of feminized fun by consumer capital, flippant obituaries attempted to strip laughter of its vital relation to the social politics of wild joy. Women were ruthlessly mocked for laughing themselves to death over nothing. Any taboo obscenity or unthought dissent had to be read between the lines. For example, in 1907, a woman named Barbara Barr allegedly laughed for eight hours at a terrible pun about dentistry (I disclose the punch line in chapter 2).

Georges Bataille once posed fatal joy as "ecstatic contemplation and lucid knowledge *accomplished in a single action* that cannot fail to become risk,"[33] while Hélène Cixous conjured endless laughter that exudes from "all our mouths . . . we inspire ourselves and we expire without running out of breath, we are everywhere!"[34] In contrast, Mrs. A. Fox laughed for two hours at an "amusing incident that happened at the circus," although the gag itself was withheld from print due to concerns about public safety.[35] Ernestina Nehring laughed herself to death at her young son's confusion between eggplants and chicken eggs, and Rosa Walker did the same when her husband accidentally salted the pork meat with granulated sugar. Glib hyperbole or spun from whole cloth entirely, these sad reports of women's risible deaths proceeded from comedic triggers that fell woefully short of their threshold for laughing jouissance.

DEATH FROM JOY; OR, CACHINNATING CHRYSIPPUS IN THE DEPTHS OF WIKIPEDIA

The idea of death by laughter is not so incredible. It has a documented history that dates back to antiquity. In 464 BC, the ancient Greek artist Zeuxis died from laughing "immoderately at a picture of an old woman that he himself had painted," according to *The Lexicon of Festus*.[36] "There are nine cases of death

FIGURE 0.2 Viral tweet by @depthsofwiki about the Stoic philosopher Chrysippus, who allegedly died laughing at his donkey eating his figs and drinking his wine.

from joy in Rabelais' listing," notes Mikhail Bakhtin, who admiringly surveys the body count of François Rabelais's *Gargantua and Pantagruel* (1693–1694), a multivolume saga about the satirical exploits of two grotesque giants.[37] For Bakhtin, joyful death exemplifies the utopian spirit of the carnivalesque, epitomized by ancient saturnalia and medieval folk festivals where "the people play with terror and laugh at it; the awesome becomes a 'comic monster.'"[38] Death from joy is the ultimate wager of defeating terror with uproarious laughter.

A parody Twitter account dedicated to sharing weird Wikipedia entries caused a furor over Chrysippus of Soli, the Stoic philosopher who fell into "so exorbitant a fit of laughter, that the use of his spleen took his breath away utterly, and he immediately died" on witnessing his donkey eat his figs and drink his wine.[39] On May 17, 2022, @depthsofwiki posted an image of Chrysippus with the caption, "just had to be there": the tweet quickly went viral and garnered over 379,000 likes.[40] More recently than 206 BC, a British television fan met his risible demise watching an episode of the sketch comedy show *The Goodies* (BBC, 1970–1982) in which an Englishman and Scotsman fight a duel armed with black pudding and bagpipes, respectively, and in 1989, a Danish audiologist named Ole Bentzen died laughing at a gag about Friedrich Nietzsche in the satirical jewel-heist film *A Fish Called Wanda* (1988). When the old world is dying and the new one has yet to be born, no rupture offers greater hope than the absurd leap of faith into fatal joy—giving up the ghost in laughing extremis so the stillborn future can attain a spark of life. Death by laughter makes way for tomorrow.

An Autohistoriographic Aside

Chrysippus and his male cohort of merry cachinnators were well-known to me when I came across my first (of many) "death by laughter" obituaries in 2014. A postdoctoral fellow of "Humour, Play, and Games" at the University of Toronto, I'd been finalizing research for my first book, *Specters of Slapstick and Silent Film Comediennes*, which tells the history of early silent cinema from the vantage point of feminist comedy studies. I already felt seized by too many ghosts: Laura Bayley, Little Chrysia, Sarah Duhamel, Lea Giunchi, Mabel Normand, Bertha Regustus, Wanda Treumann, Florence Turner, and an unnamed comic miscreant known as Léontine or Betty (we still haven't found her real name![41]), who starred in her own French film series from 1910–1912. As Léontine flooded her house to sail her toy boat indoors and electrocuted the police with a high-voltage battery, a woman identified as Mrs. Joe Palmer allegedly *"Died Laughing at Joke of Husband."* The obituary goes on to clarify that it was a joke *told by* her husband and not that he was a joke of a husband (although the counter-reading is irresistible) that caused Palmer to laugh so "violently" that she "could not stop" and finally "keel[ed] over dead" in 1911.[42]

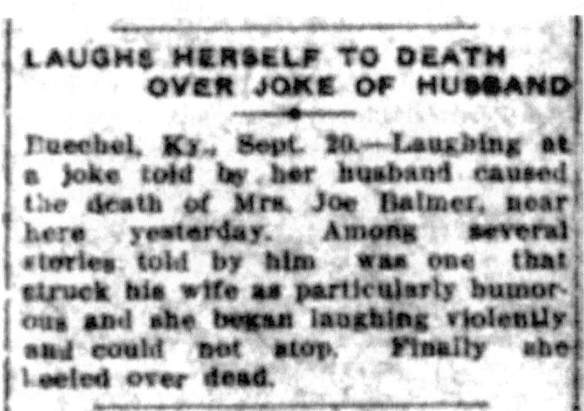

FIGURE 0.3 Mrs. Joe Palmer "LAUGHS HERSELF TO DEATH OVER JOKE OF HUSBAND," according to *The Columbus Enquirer-Sun* (Columbus, Georgia), September 21, 1911, 2. Image courtesy of the World Newspaper Archive.

DON'T KILL THE GOLDEN GOOSE

Death by Laughter: Female Hysteria and Early Cinema follows in the wake of the crisis of enjoyment that bedeviled female laughter amid the spread of cinematic modernity. Women quickly became the prized patrons—coveted, ticket-paying customers—across a vast expanse of fun-making diversions: the pleasure park, variety theater, roof garden, department store, traveling show, but most of all the moving pictures! "By the end of the '20s, one estimate is that over 80 percent of movie audiences were female," notes Shelley Stamp, whose book *Movie-Struck Girls* charts a "deep ambivalence about the escalating visibility of women at the cinema" during the silent era.[43] I focus on the volubility of women's raucous exuberance, further building on crucial feminist scholarship about the gender, racial, and class politics of early film spectatorship by Jennifer Bean, Alison Griffiths, Miriam Hansen, Patrice Petro, Lauren Rabinovitz, Laura Isabel Serna, Vanessa Schwartz, Jacqueline Najuma Stewart, Zhang Zhen, and many others.

The golden goose of an exalted mass industry and Trojan horse of decorous, morality-bound society, female revelers burst into laughter at the crossroads of contradictory designations of women's place: *domestic angel* versus *hot-to-trot consumer*. Women's laughter echoed the driving conflicts of industrial capitalist development, which at once enthroned the economic elite and undermined their traditional entitlements to cultural power.

The discourse of "death by laughter" represented the last gasp of a humorless patriarchal order that fantasized about asphyxiating female joy under the auspices of elegiac mockery. "Are American humorists heartless?" inquired *The Springfield Daily Republican*. "Just now they are making jokes about the woman who laughed herself to death at a joke."[44] The woman in question was named Anna Sperber, who reportedly dropped dead while "laughing loudly" at a funny story in 1911.[45] Or as Margaret Atwood has put it, "Men are afraid that women will laugh at them. Women are afraid that men will kill them."[46] Public panic about the lethal dangers of female enjoyment killed two birds with one stone.

Indeed, when I found Palmer's obituary in 2014, I felt loathe to take on another ghost. I was haunted by hundreds of unjustly forgotten silent film comediennes whose hysterical historicity I'd hoped to cement in a brief epilogue to *Specters* on women's laughter at the movies, which now appears as chapter 7 of this book. The year of our lord 1911—as Léontine bulldozed across Nice with a bouquet of helium balloons and a Kentucky woman's rhapsodic death "scored one for the pessimists"— the film critic Margaret I. MacDonald finally caught the *fou rire* ("crazy laughter") in a New York movie theater, which she recounts in *Moving Picture News*.[47] Her seat neighbor's euphoria in watching a film comedy—about a disgruntled housewife who crashes through the walls while test-piloting a motorized armchair—made MacDonald herself laugh "so hard at her enjoyment of the thing that the tears actually trickled down my face."[48] Lacking uproarious outlets, laughter becomes something other than itself: a compulsive tic, a sickening feeling, a pothole in one's memory, or a disturbing bodily symptom. It is a thesis of this book that the alternative to dissociative hysteria erupted from the unrepressed celebration of women's jubilant laughter, the surplus value of which drove the whole world mad.

Simply put, laughter over comedy! As we know, laughter at subversive jokes can be irresistibly political. But where does that leave senseless enjoyment with no apparent connection to radical or even perceptible humor? What Madeline Lane-McKinley calls comedy's "utopian impulse" and "anti-capitalist longing" live on in the laughter that misses the point of the joke entirely, which used to be grounds for commitment to a madhouse.[49] In the absence of insurgent humor, let us double down on the runaway pleasure of hysterical laughter. Above all, I pursue an intensity of hilarity that eludes episodic attachment (to manipulative, disappointing, cruel objects) by finding inspiration in the archive for alternative ways to live in the present.

Toward that end, I entertain an extravagant quantity and range of citations. They give texture to the wayward plenitude of the archive. I favor playful, one-off examples over sustained close readings. This approach is key to what I call hysteria-historiography, which is a collective project to wrest film history from its abandoned fragments and sneaky missing links.

The scale of my intervention is necessarily (although unevenly) transnational—we might say, disproportionately intersectional.[50] Speaking of whom, I use the "we" voice not as a comprehensive pronoun but as a collective call to any readers/ laughers who feel similarly interpellated by an impulse at hand. The ultimate wager of laughter is to liquidate all historical and identity-based divisions, even if just in a flash. I amplify relevant anecdotes with glorious exclamation marks! They signify the unresolved meaning that this book sublimates into critical writing and collectivizes via Medusan contagion. Why hoard thoughts and feelings for oneself when we can laugh them into power?

A ROAD MAP TO NINE CHAPTERS OF DEADLY, DANGEROUS, HYSTERICAL LAUGHTER!

This book consists of three parts, each with three chapters: nine chapters in total, not including this introduction and a brief conclusion. The trifecta of tripartite sections is divvied up as follows: Part 1: Death by Laughter, Part 2: Female Hysteria, Part 3: Early Cinema. These topics are not mutually exclusive, but they provide autonomous frames for exploring the suppression of women's laughter, the exploitation of female hysteria, and the transformative euphoria of early cinema through a half-century of hotwired gender politics—with vast implications for the present moment.

"Hysterical girls," Dr. Feilchenfeld, a cardiac physician, warned in 1898, "are often given to immoderate laughter."[51] Feilchenfeld related an "instructive case" involving an eighteen-year-old "girl" who suffered from "very definite cardiac symptoms after immoderate laughter."[52] She had been "free from any sign of heart disease," he claimed, until all of a sudden a friend told her a funny joke that provoked her to laugh "on and off for nearly an hour," whereby she "suddenly felt stabbing pains in the chest and was seized with fits of coughing, followed by cardiac dyspnea."[53] Feilchenfeld summons the bugaboo of hysteria (from "hystera": uterus, the medical symptom of a wandering womb). Yet most of the cachinnation obituaries I've found pull back from the brink of uterine madness. For instance, when Josephine Hochardel "laughed her last laugh" in 1907, she did not succumb to "uncontrollable hysteria, but just naturally overtaxed herself in the enjoyment of good spirits and merry jokes and stories," as per the *Anaconda Standard*.[54] The *New York Tribune* mourned Ida Bolley's supposed death by laughter in 1897: "she might have died under circumstances not so pleasant."[55] As long as women gave up the ghost to motivated enjoyment (dentistry puns, millinery gags, baking mishaps, mother-in-law jokes), their risible deaths were merely viewed as occupational hazards of female fragility, not symptoms of medical hysteria or diagnosable deviance.

Part 1: Death by Laughter

This book opens on the cusp of hysteria's risible turn. In chapter 1, "Hysterical Laughter on the Brink of Enjoyment," I trace a cultural etymology of "hysterical laughter" before it implied easy pleasure or raucous amusement. Prior to the late nineteenth century, "hysterical laughter" was the last thing you would ever want to experience with your body. It was primarily something that afflicted emotional, ambitious, and/or frustrated women on the cusp of a nervous breakdown. Above all, it arose from the sudden, simultaneous sensation of unresolvable mixed feelings. For example, the title character of *Isabel de Barsas* (1823) envisions her lover drowning and in rapid succession confirms that he is still alive: "'Ha! ha! ha! ha!' and with a violent hysterical laugh, she fell like a corpse upon the floor."[56]

(She does not really die—shortly afterward, she's revived by her maid.) Like deadly laughter (or any variant of comic laughter), hysteric outbursts of this sort were precipitated by intense, temporary excitations.

All merry laughter is "satanic," "grotesque," "monstrous," an "attribute of madness," a "symptom of lunacy," and evidence of unsettling doubleness, claimed Charles Baudelaire in his 1855 essay "On the Essence of Laughter," which never once describes it as "hysteric," "hystérique," or "hysterical."[57] Such signifiers were reserved for the gendered misery of sentimental emotion, confined to the circuits of women's sensation novels such as *Lady Audley's Secret* (1862), *The Woman in White* (1860), and *Held in Bondage* (1863). Female ambivalence debarred women's wild convulsions from the aesthetic horizons of comical genius or zany imagination. I conclude chapter 1—which traverses the history of evangelical revivals, photographic electrotherapy, zoological ethnography, sentimental biopolitics, and separatist populism—with a new genealogy of "hysterical laughter." The *Oxford English Dictionary* (OED) dates the adherence of "hysterical" to hilarious comedy to 1925, but the OED is over two decades too late. To set the record straight, I go rag-picking through the "Amusements" sections of periodicals from the 1870s to 1890s, as mirthless ambivalence gave way to hysterical exuberance on the altar of capitalist mass politics. With the rise of multifarious public pleasures, women's solicitation to indiscriminate jubilation needed new words, and where better to source them than in the affective recesses of pulp sensation novels?

From isolated misery to contagious hilarity, "hysterical laughter" maintained its grip on misogynistic repression into the early twentieth century, when female laughers became the prized targets of a rapidly ballooning culture industry. Chapter 2, "Female Death by Laughter (Beyond Enjoyment)," draws on feminist theories of jouissance and Medusan writing to resurrect the spirit of women who allegedly choked on their own laughs. When pleasure becomes *too much*—uncontrollable, all-consuming, even fatal—it amplifies radical humor's dangerous gambit to provide a new frame for possibility, solidarity, and action. At the heart of this chapter are hundreds of surreal obituaries for women who were "killed by a joke," who "went to a comedy and furnished a tragedy," or "who knew they would die laughing if they didn't stop," and so forth. I read these obituaries with a sizable grain of salt, providing further context with recourse to the anatomy of tight-laced corsetry; etiquette manuals instructing women on "how to laugh" in front of the mirror and in the correct vowel pitch; as well as Black feminist writings on laughter, social death, and the lethal absurdity of white supremacist capitalism. Above all, I hope to recharge the feminist project of comedic refusal with the madness of jouissance, which likewise seeks to shatter the limits of social isolation and affective conformity.

Modernist critical philosophy has had a burning love affair with the wager of dying from joy. In chapter 3, "An All Too Brief History of Laughter and Death," I take a detour through the Rabelaisian canon of saturnalia and medieval carnival, from the sexist painter Zeuxis who "killed himself with laughing at the sight of the antique jabbernowl of an old hag drawn by him"[58] to Bataille's fantasy of "a woman screaming, her head in flames" in his mystical "Practice of Joy in the Face of Death."[59] Traversing Nietzsche's "gay science" (or "joyful wisdom"), Sigmund Freud's reconciliation of jokes with the death drive in his postwar essay on gallows humor, André Breton's *Anthology of Black Humor*, and Jean-Luc Nancy's extremely strange discursus on "Wild Laughter," I ask, How would the history of laughing philosophy have been different if Bertha Pruett, Rosa Walker, Josie Leisslie, Louise Speetzen, and their cohort of fatal female cachinnators were taken as its subjects (instead of Chrysippus, Widenostrils, and Nietzsche's eternal madman)? I assert the universal feminist critical stakes of wild laughter in the jaws of death.

Part 2: Female Hysteria

The midsection of this book flips the metaphor of "hysterical laughter" on its head by exploring the unwritten history of laughter as a wayward symptom of female hysteria. What was female hysteria? Now a long debunked diagnostic category, the mysterious ailment ran roughshod over nineteenth-century psychiatric medicine. Symptoms of the disease ranged from ordinary exhaustion, boredom, fatigue, and nervousness to epileptic orgasms, uncontrollable hiccupping, superhuman acrobatics, and trans-species metamorphosis. A muse to later surrealists like Max Ernst and Louis Aragon and a firebrand celebrated by Hélène Cixous, Catherine Clément, Juliet Mitchell (and many others), the female hysteric gave tangible flesh to her own inadmissible desires and impossible words. Hysteria was understood as a conversion disorder that incarnated broken language in a spectacular pageant of amorphous bodily signs.

In part 2 of this book, I come to grips with the unthought connection between dueling variants of "hysterical laughter" as a gaslit symptom and a joyful convulsion. Chapter 4, "Gaslighting the Libido: Feminist Politics of Madness, Laughter, and Power," begins by reclaiming all symptoms of female hysteria as unrealized eruptions of exuberant laughter. Hysteric symptoms, unlike comical laughter, take hold once it's already too late for playful language to give voice to alienated emotions. In that state, Jean-Martin Charcot hypnotized neurodivergent women before a live audience of medical peers and curious tourists, compelling them to exhibit epileptic seizures, erotic hallucinations, and "clownist" acrobatics. From 1882 to 1893, his rectangular *amphithéâtre* overflowed with "a multicoloured audience drawn from tout Paris," enthused Axel Munthe, while Charcot plastered the walls of his Salpêtrière clinic with Albert Londe's photographs of Blanche Wittmann (hailed as the "Queen of the Hysterics"), Augustine Gleizes, Geneviève, and Rosalie Lerroux.[60]

Although irrefutably exploitative, the iconography of hystero-epilepsy has fostered the vast creativity of twenty-first-century feminist art, theory, activism, and psychiatry spanning the filmmaking of Zoe Beloff, the curatorial projects of Johanna Braun ("The Hysteric as Conceptual Operator"), and the multimedia spirit conjuring (or "gHosting") of writer/performer Laura González. "Hysteria IS feminist activism," proclaims *Hysteria*, a London-based feminist collective that "pleasurably challenges capitalism" with "hysterical solidarity."[61] Like Cixous, who declared Freud's patient Dora to be "the true 'mistress' of the Signifier" in 1975,[62] Anna Furse excavates "the female malady's" shadowy iconography in her 2020 collection, *Performing Nerves: Four Plays, Four Essays, On Hysteria*, which re-presents her earlier pieces, including *Augustine (Big Hysteria)* (1991) and *SHOCKS* (2018).[63] A new wave of experimental artists and Medusan activists have found abundant inspiration in the medical archives of female hysteria.

I further pursue a theory of *hysteric comedy* that lingers on the precipice of symbolic recognition and anarchic explosion. Feminist comedians (stand-ups, sketch comics, gag writers, improv performers, and so forth) have yet to embrace what Cecily Devereux calls "The New New Hysteria Studies": a sequel to the "New Hysteria Studies" of the 1990s.[64] For example, a recent FX documentary on women in stand-up comedy, *Hysterical* (2021), opens by separating informal uses of "hysterical" (as in "very funny") from its Greek etymology of "suffering in the womb." The thesis of the film is that feminist comedic empowerment and archival hysterical inheritance are like oil and water—they just do not mix. Against this partition of "good" and "bad" connotations of "hysterical" (MeToo movement versus the archive), I chase after the hysteric fugitivity of wayward feminist laughter, from the stand-up comedy of Michelle Wolf, Hannah Gadsby, Wanda Sykes, and Margaret Cho to the libidinal malfeasance of a woman named Esther Wakefield, who allegedly went on a laughing rampage across Chicago in 1899 after having been bit by a "kissing bug" while lounging in a hammock.

Hysteric symptoms flare up when the discharge of anxiety lacks a lifeline into the symbolic: the signs that legitimate shared reality over cynical lies uttered in bad faith. Chapter 5, "Laughter: The Forgotten Symptom," focuses on laughter's omission from nineteenth-century psychiatric research on hysteria. The ailment's leading practitioners (Freud, Breuer, Charcot, Janet, Binet, et al.) gave pride of place to any other symptom than laughter—from fugue states, motor impairments, and double vision to sneezing, yawning, barking, and hiccupping. In the case of jokes, we have an "indefinable feeling" that correlates with an unsettling sense of "absence," observed Freud, and "then all at once the joke is there," licensing a "sudden release of intellectual tension."[65] In contrast, hysteric symptoms proceed from the failure of inadmissible memory to sneak its way to the surface of rational thought. *Fou rire* at once epitomized the malady but disqualified itself from further interpretation. It was viewed as too much like any other habitual tic or gesture to unlock that dissociated "second self" whose repressed fancies and unbearable mental yearnings gave vital material to the rising scientific fields of neurology, alienism, and psychoanalysis.

But there was always a thread, however tenuous, between the spark of comedy and the explosion of laughter. I further draw on twenty-first-century neuropsychiatric studies of *moria* ("pathologic giddiness"), *witzelsucht* ("joking addiction"), and "pseudobulbar affect" that have been allegorized to depict crises of masculinity in recent anticapitalist film satires such as *Parasite* (2019) and *Joker* (2019), contrasting their hysterics to the abjection of jouissance across popular genre cinema from *Fatal Attraction* (1987) and *Single White Female* (1992) to *Black Swan* (2010) and *Benedetta* (2021). Decoding the gender politics of unwilled and unwanted laughter, I argue, holds the key to its deeper emotional expression and enigmatic cultural value.

I conclude this section on female hysteria with the promise and danger of its uncontrolled transmission. Chapter 6, "Mass Hysteria, Collective Laughter, and Affective Contagion," seeks to revive what Walter Benjamin once unhyperbolically described as "the most international and revolutionary affect of the masses": their laughter.[66] Early twentieth-century crowd psychologists denigrated the impulsive spread of contagious sensations whose "power acts like those of microbes," wrote Gustave Le Bon, "which hastens the dissolution of enfeebled or dead bodies."[67] Any crowd in his account, whether revolutionary or reactionary, represented a destructive threat to orderly society. What remains today of utopian collective laughter and its evocative potentials to create generous outbursts of solidarity and commitment across ideological and identity-based divisions?

I disentangle the collective wager of hysterical contagion from the viral transmission of thoughtless conformity, traversing the history of public panics, gynocidal witch hunts, dancing plagues, twitching epidemics, and authoritarian conspiracy theories. From medieval tarantism (look it up!) to the Great Clown Panic of 2016, I bring this rogues' gallery of anxious outbreaks to bear on the present conjuncture, in its declining powers of reason, apocalyptic environments, and weaponized culture war politics. I further enlist the insights of feminist comedy studies, speculative theories of "communist affect," experimental mad manifestos, and modernist tactics in avant-garde absurdism to envision a new way forward. Hysteric-contagious laughs give voice to festering impulses already turned into flesh, collective conversion symptoms—and might yet reveal openings toward a less cruel and exploitative, possible world.

Part 3: Early Cinema

The final part of this book rekindles the flame of cinematic modernity with (what else?) the entry of hysterically laughing women into public life and mass culture. Chapter 7, "Laughter Unleashed: Hysterical Women at the Movies," compiles hundreds of accounts of female laughing spectatorship, culled from the trade press, memoirs, scrapbooks, periodicals, publicity ads, early film theory, and surviving archive footage. There was no greater selling point for a hilarious comedy than the sheer acoustics of female enjoyment, blared from phonographic "laugh records" by barkers and spielers outside movie and variety show theaters. Films like *Sandy McPherson's Quiet Fishing Trip* (1908) were celebrated as "425 feet of non-stop laughter,"[68] while newspapers accused traveling vaudeville comics of conspiring with local corset stringers after too many women broke their corset staves in the throes of uncontrollable laughter.[69] So preached *The Nickelodeon* to film exhibitors in 1909, "Play to the Ladies."[70]

I revisit the feminist/modernity spectatorship debates of the 1990s and early 2000s, which looked to the pleasure garden of early cinema to disrupt the postmodern spectacle machine and passive consumerism endemic to late capitalist subjectivity, thereby conjuring "different futures that may be buried in the past," as Miriam Hansen suggests.[71] In that spirit, I call upon Madame Medusa: a fictive, allegorical film spectator who laughed obstreperously, kibbitzed volubly, writhed convulsively, adorned her chapeau with screen-blocking fruit baskets, but the industry kowtowed to her whimsies all the same. For example, she was the "girl in front of me" at the Julius Tannen act "who laughed so loud everyone looked around at her."[72] But the movies were her true milieu, where she was hoisted "along on a gale of laughter" while watching comedies like *The Dull Knife* (1909), in which a woman named Maggie raves about town with a large knife (because she was chasing after the knife grinder!).[73] By reviving the undead ghosts of early film pleasure while focusing on the ever-fraught relation between laughter and hysteria, I hope to incite leaps of faith into the throat of unruly hilarity in the apocalypse-mongering present. I call this method "*hysteria-historiography,*" which understands cinema as a somatic language and proxy reality for spectators on the cusp of having a powerful voice in the world.

Silent film's phantasmagoria of wayward experience has vividly shaped the field's "*neurological* conception of modernity," referring to the nervous shocks, fragmented sensations, and fleeting encounters that found aesthetic relief in fantastic screen images.[74] Chapter 8, "The Visual Cure? Moving Pictures as Neurotic Trigger and Therapeutic Instrument," takes the metaphor of "neurological modernity" all too concretely. From 1904, when the Dunning Asylum in Chicago adopted the so-called "Biograph Insanity Cure," the federal government threw money at mental asylums—which were riddled with scandals of abuse, overcrowding, and negligent care—to install film projection equipment. "Motion Pictures, the latest and best cure for insanity!" boasted Charles Gibson in 1910.[75] Slapstick comedies such as *The Mad Musician* (1908), *An Auto Maniac* (1909) and *Ham in the Nut Factory* (1915) had pride of place over all other genres. Film's "visual cure" assumed a certain reciprocity between madcap illusions and the mental life of neurodivergent spectators, allegedly calming "excitable patients" and appeasing "those suffering from chronic melancholia" to let go of "their brooding over imaginary wrongs."[76] Meanwhile, neurologists such as Theodore Weisenburg, Camillo Negro, and Arthur Van Gehuchten seized on moving images to capture fugitive symptoms for the purpose of research and teaching.

This chapter tells the history of cinema's institutional deployment as a recreational cure for diagnosable madness, bringing disability studies scholarship and mad rights methodologies to bear on early film's uses, abuses, and multifarious representations of neurodivergence. As Mario Masini and Giuseppe Vidoni warned in 1915, the spread of cinema especially afflicted "those predisposed to sensory disorders."[77] From "nutty" comedies that burlesque the contagions of neurasthenia to multireel melodramas that envision cinema as a miraculous cure for female hysteria, moving pictures reflected on their own "profound and intense impact on psychic life."[78] Ambivalence about media's jarring effects on nervous spectator experience, apparently, remains unresolved in our current conjuncture of nonstop spectacle, crisis-ridden politics, permanent carnival, and mad rights awakening.

While chapters 7 and 8 center on hysterical spectatorship—laughing enjoyment versus psychiatric treatment, respectively—we finally arrive at the rhapsodic surface of the image. Chapter 9, "From Mouth to Screen: Laughing Heads in the History of Film," establishes the foundational importance of women's "laughing heads in the history of film." From 1903 to 1915, it was common practice to conclude a short comedy with a close-up or medium close-up of the lead performers laughing, winking, spasming, and making silly faces at the camera. Now known as "the emblematic shot," these frontal displays of animated portraiture were both separate from the diegesis (the narrative world of the film) and essential to framing its meaning for the audience. I outline a genealogy of hysterical emblematic shots, spawned from the short-lived popularity of funny "facials," such as *Scandal Over the Tea Cups* (1900), *Grandma Threading Her Needle* (1900), and *At Last! That Awful Tooth* (1902). Female close-ups were caught in the headwinds of obsolescent "facials" and film's institutional drive to discipline wayward enjoyment by banishing its Medusan miscreants to the outer limits of the reel.

In my "Conclusion: Laughter, Hysteria, Power—Then and Now," I delve into the contemporary theater of endemic madness and feminist pleasure. From Desiree Fairooz's arrest for laughing out loud at Jeff Sessions's cabinet confirmation hearing to Christine Blasey Ford's emotional testimony about Brett Kavanaugh's "uproarious laughter" that became "indelible" in her "hippocampus," the power politics of enjoyment often turn on the gender dynamics of the very perception of humor. This is precisely why Hannah Gadsby defied her audience to dare to laugh at her self-triggering jokes about her own sexual trauma in *Nanette* (2018). As the line between sense and nonsense utterly collapses, comedy no longer offers a special zone for exceptional unreason, further fueling the weaponization of aggressive, tendentious, humorless, and combative forms of laughter. Yet again the angel of history beckons, only this time she has a head full of snakes. Where we perceive a long chain of cruelties, she would like to smash up the differences that have falsely been made whole. The other's enjoyment is upon us. Take heed of her unbearable jouissance! Or soon enough, we will indeed have *amused ourselves to death*—that is, if climate catastrophe, permanent war, unlivable inequality, gynocidal violence, neofascist will to power, and viral pandemics do not catch up to us first.

BUT FIRST...

Again, try to "[i]magine being so hilarious that ... your comedy REALLY kills."[79] Just imagine.

PART I
Death by Laughter

1

Hysterical Laughter on the Brink of Enjoyment

In January 2017, a Canadian woman's hysterical laughter became a viral internet sensation. Caroline Charter recorded a video of her mother exploding in wild enjoyment while witnessing her younger daughter, Suzanne, slip and fall on the slick terrain of their icy driveway in Ontario. The video "Canadian Driveway Ice Hysterics" quickly received over 1 million views and Mrs. Charter's laughter is now a patented ringtone available for purchase from iTunes. As one reporter observed, the video reveals a woman trying "to get into her car" while "her mother breaks out into hysterical laughter as she watches her daughter scramble in the snow."[1] Although slightly cruel, there is nothing unusual about the experience of laughing uproariously at the temporary misfortune of a loved one. Suzanne was not permanently injured—just a bit ruffled—and her mother no doubt vented some pent-up holiday angst at this impromptu scene of family slapstick pratfalls. As she pointed out, "We are a very close family, so we laugh a lot and don't think twice about mocking each other out of love."[2] Most important, her hysterical laughter provoked waves of joy across the internet, as users festively debated "what is funnier—the woman struggling on the ice or the person laughing in the background. OMG. Brilliant."[3]

But when did "hysterical laughter" come to be associated with enjoyment and pleasure rather than madness and suffering? It is an ordinary turn of phrase to describe joyful laughter as "hysterical"—a gesture of the throaty excess, collective contagion, and full-body convulsion at the heart of the burst. Who would ever imagine that it could be unpleasant or painful? Yet it was not until the end of the nineteenth century that this now familiar expression carried any lighthearted connotations whatsoever. Prior to that time, "hysterical laughter" was the last thing you would ever want to experience with your body. It was primarily something that afflicted emotional women on the cusp of a nervous breakdown.

FIGURE 1.1 "Canadian Driveway Ice Hysterics—MUST WATCH WITH SOUND UP!!" YouTube video posted by Caroline Charter on December 29, 2016.

For example, in the serialized print melodrama *The Balance of Life* (1850), a heart-struck young woman must break from her impoverished secret lover so that he can take a seafaring position with a colonialist speculator in the West Indies. Just upon his departure, however, she receives unexpected good news that she has inherited a small fortune, at which she "throws back her head" and "bursts into convulsions of hysterical laughter" while "uttering a scream so wild, and shrill, and long as to terrify the hearers."[4] Her laughter is neither an indication of excess pleasure nor a signal of abject suffering, but an affective implosion incited by their irreconcilable confrontation: romantic loss (the pathos of colonialism) and financial gain (a windfall of inheritance). It verged on joyful laughter's earthquake of self-partition but firmly disqualified women from the ecstasy of raucous humor. In other words, the hysterics of "hysterical laughter" excluded women's mixed feelings from the licensed madness of comedy.

Of course, all merry laughter results from "a double or contradictory feeling," claimed Charles Baudelaire in *On the Essence of Laughter* (1855), "and it is for this reason that a convulsion occurs."[5] Beyond its ordinary excitation, "laughter provoked by what is grotesque" can easily drive us to "excessive fits and swooning" of "wild hilarity."[6] (Baudelaire cites familiar aesthetic examples to illustrate these devilish extremities, such as Molière's *The Hypochondriac*, E. T. A. Hoffmann's *Princess Brambilla*, and the stock characters of the Italian commedia dell'arte.[7]) Baudelaire never once here uses the word "hystérique" or "hystérie," nor do their cognates ("hysterical," "hysteric," "hysteria") appear in key English translations.[8] He invokes laughter as "satanic," "grotesque," "monstrous," an "attribute of madness," a "symptom of lunacy," and an explosion of self-contradiction—but never "hysterical," an explicitly gendered signifier that reserved immoderate affect for the total absence of humor. Female ambivalence debarred women's wild convulsions from the aesthetic horizons of comical invention.

Instead, they evoke what Sianne Ngai has cheekily described as "ugly feelings": powerful sensations that dwell in "affective gaps and illegibilities" where they fester and deplete "one's power to act."[9] Irritation, envy, anxiety, paranoia, and "stuplimity" (shocked tedium) have pride of place in Ngai's compendium of sticky, trivial emotions.[10] Stuplimity is an especially instructive category: "a concatenation of boredom and astonishment," it brings together "what 'dulls' and what 'irritates' or agitates."[11] When a "spunky female" walked into a store in New Jersey demanding that the clerk refund the rotten eggs she had purchased, and he refused, she hurled those rotten eggs at his face: "The suddenness of the action and the phosphoric odor of the contents of the damaged [avian] ovaries" provoked "the hysterical laughter of a number of women who were [there] at the time," according to one local report.[12] There is an apparent slippage from bird womb to uterine mood encircling this impromptu scene of female laughing hysteria.

A placeholder for ordinary disaffection, shock-and-boredom solicits the sensorium shy of the tipping point for decisive action. Raw "hysterical laughter" detonated from a similar deadlock but eclipsed "stuplimity" in its tempestuous self-abandon. For example, Isabel de Barsas hears her lover's voice, fears it will be his last breath, and then abruptly learns he is absolutely fine: "'Ha! ha! ha! ha!' and with a violent hysterical laugh, she fell like a corpse upon the floor."[13] It "was long before" her maid succeeded in restoring her "to her senses."[14] De Barsas's outburst does not arise from her suffering as such but from its swift contradiction by unforeseen reality (she only *imagines* his death): an affective crisis resulting in laughter and tears. A woman also named Isabel laughed hysterically at her own foiled marriage plot in *The Albigenses* (1824): "and this laugh continued so long and so wildly, that the damsels began to tremble for reason. It was succeeded by a burst of tears copious and agonizing."[15] In contrast, Mrs. Thomas D. Crowe filed for divorce in 1870 on the grounds that she'd been in a prolonged "STATE OF HYSTERICAL LAUGHTER" all through her wedding ceremony (because her groom had drugged her).[16]

What emotion has precedence upon the simultaneous eruption of laughter and tears? "I have seen with English people, especially women" that "in hearing of some distressing case of death, or in telling the same to another, they often go into a hysterical fit of laughter," remarked Robert Swinhoe to Charles Darwin.[17] Note how the women in Swinhoe's anecdote recount their news secondhand, as if to transmit its affective incommensurability. But what if confronted by death directly? The male narrator of "Unwritten Music" (1829) keeps watch as his friend slowly dies, until suddenly the clock strikes: "I fell back in my chair in a paroxysm of hysterical laughter! I . . . have been in situations far more calculated to excite terror, but nothing ever overcame me like that."[18] The punctual reminder of time against its ghoulish contingency incited "a fit of hysterical laughter," as though he "had been a weakly woman."[19] Again, hysterical laughter exceeded pure suffering, giving voice to the contradictory presence of mutually exclusive realities, which is incidentally also the formula for incongruous comedy. "If Oedipus had been there," Captain Somers thought to himself, he "would have defied him to solve the riddle of Miss Maud Hasbrouk's inordinate, excessive, hysterical laughter."[20] An emblem of unsolvable mystery and symptom of affective rupture, hysterical laughter missed the mark of perceptible humor, which could likewise be jarring, violent, unexplainable, and grotesque. (Somers meditates on the absence of the comic to provoke such a "cachinnatory" "species of hysterics," reassuring himself that "there was apparently nothing in the world to laugh at."[21]) Stripped of its symbolic legibility, Hasbrouk's laughter "broke forth anew, and peal on peal of [it] rang through the room," until Somers begins to fear she "might yet die of hysterics."[22]

Lauren Berlant would perhaps diagnose Somers with the comic malady of "humorlessness," a will to "aspirational sovereignty" that hinges on the stone-cold deflection of another person's right to enjoyment or fun. "What constitutes humorlessness is someone's insistence that *their* version of a situation should rule the relational dynamic," explains Berlant, who sees it as a withdrawal of overstretched affect amid the "permanent carnival" of information-driven capital.[23] (From "politically correct" killjoys to alt-right edgelords, intractable affect is the new horizon of comedic power games, which arise from "the uncertainty of the event's solidity" in a crisis-ridden, dystopian climate.[24]) The archives of hysterical laughter reveal the formations of risible humorlessness: the withering of comedic pleasure from the scene of affective rupture.

Beyond mirthless hysteria, women's joyful laughter was censored and suppressed in the nineteenth century. Women were even terrified into believing that they could die from laughing too hard, whether due to overly tight corsets, calcified arteries, or sheer physical exhaustion. (I present this untold history of female death by laughter in the next chapter.) They were thus denied access to the universal human experience of laughter as a "perception of the incongruous" (James Russell Lowell), "a sudden evaporation of expectation to nothing" (Immanuel Kant), a "break between the person and their body" (Helmuth Plessner), "the victory of knowledge of perception over thought" (Arthur Schopenhauer), or even "the last stage of existential awareness before faith" (Soren Kierkegaard).[25] Sydney Smith (1850) invoked the famous example of a corpulent gentleman suited in "ostentatious habiliment" who disastrously slips and falls in the mud, provoking the onlooker to explode in a "sudden and racking revulsion from one state of feeling to another."[26] In contrast, female laughers got caught in the headwinds of their conflicting states of feeling, suspended in the throes of "racking revulsion" rather than gliding pleasurably along it, which is the utopian promise of comical joy.

HYSTERICAL LAUGHTER IN THE THROES OF SENSATION LITERATURE

There was no ground more fertile for the eruption of torturous, hysterical laughter than nineteenth-century sentimental literature. It especially garnished the plots of female-authored, wildly popular sensation novels such as *Lady Audley's Secret* (1862), *The Woman in White* (1860), *Held in Bondage* (1863), and *East Lynne* (1861).[27] Mirthless laughs burst out when women are confronted with the grotesque contradictions between their assigned social roles and their impossible ambitions. As Joan Wallach Scott reminds us, "gender is a primary field within which or by means of which power is articulated."[28] Hysteric affect offered a fragile script—cryptic, volatile, and often inscrutable—for voicing suppressed complaint and rising disaffection.

For example, in *Fortune Hunting: A Novel* (Margracia Loudon, 1832) the protagonist Elizabeth Bellevue "laughs hysterically" when she learns that her marital aspirations are unreciprocated by a man named Colonel Trump. A widow, Elizabeth's mother-in-law from a previous marriage had herself died in a paroxysm of "hysterical laughter" that was incited by a mixture of "desire," "fear, and hopelessness." Upon reading Trump's letter:[29]

> Elizabeth was perfectly pale; her lips were white, yet parched, and she seemed to gasp for breath; a tear or two forced their way and fell; a curling of the lip, and a smile of scorn, ending in an hysterical laugh, followed; then, powerful indignation mastering every feeling but shame, a universal glow rose over her neck and face and settled in burning blushes over her cheeks, while her dark eyes flashed fire.

It is important to emphasize the status of Elizabeth's vividly conflicting emotions here, like those of her mother-in-law. The joy of anticipation upon receiving Trump's letter swerves too quickly into anger, shame, scorn, rage, and disappointment.

FIGURE 1.2 "Zoe Beloff, *Alphabet of the Passions* in "Emotions Go to Work," International Museum of Surgical Science, https://imss.org/zoe-beloff-emotions-go-to-work/."

Because women's anger is "generally 'not well received,' " notes Sara Ahmed (via the philosopher Marilyn Frye), it is often camouflaged as nervous ambivalence, with vehement laughter as its detonation device.[30] In Elizabeth's case (questionable taste in suitors notwithstanding), her affective experience of hope and optimism is too abruptly displaced by anger, despair, and humiliation. Laughter marks the head-on conflagration of all the above. It was a sensorial placeholder for combustive affect to do tangibly reparative and/or politically incendiary work.

Emily Steinlight places its "calamitous surplus" at "the heart of the domestic sphere," which a new genre of "sensational novels" began to spotlight around the mid-nineteenth century.[31] "Nothing boring about the sensation novel," observes D. A. Miller, adding that it "offer[ed] one of the first instances of modern literature to address itself primarily to the sympathetic nervous system."[32] At the same time, it unleashed the "the magnetic force" of "female sexuality" onto public life, causing "worlds to collide and blend" but also maintaining "a classed and gendered hierarchy" that hinged on valuations of style and taste.[33] (H. L. Mansel condemned the genre in 1863 as "unspeakably disgusting" with "ravenous appetite for carrion" and inferior to literary realism.[34]) If the marriage plot was the backbone of the sensation genre—policing gender norms through formulaic tales of aspirational matrimony—shocking themes of lust, adultery, scandal, deceit, murder, and obscenity revealed the trouble simmering beneath the surface.

These novels have been widely recuperated as formative texts for the field of feminist affect studies, from Ann Cvetkovich's *Mixed Feelings* (1992) and Lauren Berlant's *Female Complaint* (2008) to Sara Ahmed's frequent return to George Eliot's *The Mill on the Floss* (1860) and *Silas Marner* (1861) in compiling her archive of "unhappy objects."[35] What's not received due consideration, however, is the singularity of *laughter* as a force field for the collision of individual-affective and social-biopolitical crises. Alternating with tears, laughing hysterics burst forth when new feelings strike without adequate warning and before prior emotions have the chance to recede.

Characters in sensation novels are constantly scrambling to hide their past lives and realize upward mobility through devious seduction. *Eleanor: The Spectre of St. Michael's* (1821) opens with the scene of a laughing suicide in the aftermath of an unwanted pregnancy.[36] A serialized, multivolume saga that anticipated the sensation genre's hell-raising appeals, *Eleanor* sets the stage outside a steeple where ringing church bells vie acoustically with (what else?) the "hysterical laughter" of an "interesting female," whose "whole demeanor bespoke the extreme agitation of her mind."[37] This unnamed woman is characterized by the following epithets: "mental derangement," "disorder of her dress," "wildness of her air," "the delirium of insanity," and "wretched mania" revealing an "agonized soul" that has "lost all sense of feeling, save those dreadful ones which had deprived her of reason."[38] Naturally, the cause of her misery is a handsome devil named Lord Arthur: the illegitimate father of her newborn child (Eleanor) and groom-at-the-altar to a decidedly nonhysterical woman, Georgina, who is generally admired (and resented) for possessing a certain air of "*hauteur*."[39]

Like *Jane Eyre*'s cachinnating, Jamaican Creole, gothic attic-dwelling doppelgänger, Bertha Mason (who jumps off the roof toward the end of the novel), this unnamed woman falls to her death: with a "hysterical laugh" and "convulsive scream," she cuts her feet on the jagged rocks from which she hurls herself into the sea.[40] In a gender reversal (of female falling), Lady Audley pushes her first husband down a well to sanctify her subsequent marriage to a much wealthier man after her first husband had returned unexpectedly from a gold-prospecting expedition in Australia. *Lady Audley's Secret* (by Mary Elizabeth Braddon), a lurid saga about a female homicidal bigamist of angelic countenance, was one of the most widely read novels of the nineteenth century. It was insanely popular.[41] "Sexuality, represented as a contagious disease, is the force that draws the narratives together and causes them to lose distinctness," argues Pamela K. Gilbert.[42] But its discontent takes "the form of psychic disturbance, rather than material deprivation," notes Ann Cvetkovich, "manifesting itself as anxiety, hysteria, depression, or madness."[43]

When Sir Michael Audley first proposes to Lucy, she laughs at him with "a strange laugh that jarred upon his feelings."[44] At the same time, there was an "undefined something in her manner," a "passionate vehemence," that filled him "with a vague alarm."[45] Eventually, Lucy is forced to divulge her titular secret (that she's an adulterous murderer), upon which she breaks into "a tempest of hysterical sobbing" and warns her husband that he "will laugh at" her if she reveals the cause of her tears.[46] From portent to paroxysm, her laughter erupts in response to the cosmic joke of Victorian domesticity and the legal prison of patriarchal matrimony. After faking her own death, assuming a false identity, murdering her spouse, and attempting to kill her cousin, Lucy Audley is finally banished to an insane asylum in Belgium, where she dies of a mysterious illness. Whatever malaise her laughter forebodes, its morbid surplus finally destroys her.

Berlant often points to the bizarre recurrence of slapstick in nineteenth-century melodrama, describing their genre "conjuncture" as a kind of "realism wrought from the absurd demands of power."[47] A precursor to present-day "genre flailing," as our "mode of crisis management" for navigating a world that crushes one's "confidence about how to move in it," sentiment has long flailed into the pratfalls of slapstick.[48] Confusion between these two genres reveals the "desire for a new vernacular... a new realism" that "speaks to the thinness of common sense," claims Berlant in *The Female Complaint*.[49] Updated for the twenty-first-century absurdity of ordinary crisis, they observe: "We genre flail so that we don't fall through the cracks of heightened affective noise into despair, suicide, or psychosis. We improvise like crazy, where 'like crazy' is a little too non-metaphorical."[50] Genre flailing charts a new frontier for inappropriate slapstick, while righteous "humorlessness" (again, the stone-cold denial of play, even if posed playfully) has a strange echo with sentimental melodrama.

"The slapstick of survival" pervades ordinary scenes of abject racial suffering in abolitionist melodramas, epitomized by *Uncle Tom's Cabin* (1852). An urtext for "sentimental biopower," as Kyla Schuller describes it, *Uncle Tom* deploys racial pathos to gift enslaved subjects with the weepy stamp of Western humanism.[51] "Thus, the marginalized do not have the luxury of being unsympathetic," Xine Yao concludes, "without forfeiting the provisional acceptance of their capacity for affective expressions, and, therefore, the conditional acceptance of their humanity."[52] Yao focuses on queer, racialized, and gendered sensations of "unfeeling" and "disaffection" in nineteenth-century literature, medicine, and culture.

Whose disaffection is allowed to become legible or audible, even if only in peals of hysterical affect that preface imminent ruin and probable suicide? Yao theorizes unfeeling as a "quotidian tactic of survival," an "index of the underacknowledged spectrum of dissonance," and an "insurgent potential that may not be... instrumentalized toward resistance."[53] Disaffection threatens a "break from affectability" and "disrupts reading practices that crave affective excess."[54] It might have the cadence of humorlessness, but it is all about genre flailing. Schuller glosses "sentimental biopower," in contrast to "unfeeling," as a "capacity of impressibility" to become part of the national body through emotional contagion. Those who lack purchase in "transparent" subjectivity (the unmarked "I" of white male reason) make corporeal claims to an "affectable I" through sentimental impressibility: the "network of sympathetic nerves" through which women and people of color stake their belonging in the nation-state. Impressibility paves the way to social control (with a Lamarckian twist of "acquired inheritance"), affording a perfect weapon for biopolitical governance over heterogeneous, messy populations.

Cassy in *Uncle Tom's Cabin* exhibits her hysterical disaffection and becomes a foil for Tom's attachment to "dishonest" sentimentalism (to invoke James Baldwin's scathing critique of Harriet Beecher Stowe's novel).[55] The abused sex slave of a cruel profiteering tyrant, Cassy laughs hysterically at Tom's suggestion that she seek spiritual uplift through religious faith in a higher power.

"While an insane light glanced in her heavy black eyes . . . A wild, long laugh rang through the deserted room, and ended in a hysteric sob; she threw herself on the floor in convulsive and sobbing struggles."[56] Despite its initial glimmer of absurdity, Cassy's laughter turns to rage and despair. (Unlike her ill-fated white sisters, however, Cassy reunites with her lost child when they escape together to Liberia—in the ultimate wish-fulfillment of abolitionist sentimentalism.) As Ann Douglas critiques it, sentimentalism "provides a way to protest a power to which one has already in part capitulated."[57] *Uncle Tom's Cabin* solicits the reader to intermingle a "witnessing of pain" with the pleasurable consumption of "moral self-satisfaction," remarks Berlant, and to imagine that "these impulses will lead, somehow, to changing the world."[58]

In the flailing genres of soft-boiled suffering, hysterical laughter explodes when separate realms collide: male and female domains, sprawling migratory demographics, contested class relations, impressible versus unpliable bodies, and so forth. Hitching the isolated madwoman to the swelling population, uncontrollable affect provided a makeshift container for the revelation of otherwise dangerous thoughts. "Like a flash the giddy intoxication is upon us, it is in the air, we breathe it in, it fills our lungs, and sends the blood coursing through our veins," declared Baudelaire of "the absolute comic," by which brave clowns prepare to meet their "tumultuous fate."[59] Steamrolled by pervasive pathos, women's hysterical laughs stuck in the craw of a lugubrious genre rather than thrusting them "forcibly into a new life" (as with triumphant absurd comedy).[60] To the titillated reader, their corrective intention was clear: beware mixed feelings because they can and will lead to your emotional unraveling. At the same time, ambivalent outbursts of hysterical laughter sparked vital flashes of affective self-rupture (an escape hatch from sentimental impressibility). We can therefore embrace them as placeholders for grotesque, absolute comedy in nineteenth- century women's writing.

HYSTERICAL LAUGHTER AT LARGE: LOCOFOCOS, COYOTES, AND HOLY ROLLERS

Beyond the sensation genre or archives of female ambivalence, "hysterical laughter" intensified as an imprint of all the absurdity that had yet to find affective-symbolic form. To that end, I will briefly describe the other minor contexts in which this slippery phrase surfaced before its meaning succumbed to the contagions of uproarious laughter. First, anti-elite political factions were accused of "hysterical laughter" as an oratory demerit and symptom of their uncouth decorum. Few people remember the laughing Locofocos: a separatist, anticorruption wing of New York City's Democratic Party. Founded in 1835 as the Equal Rights Party, they opposed economic plutocracy and machine corruption (that is, Tammany Hall), and aligned themselves with the labor rights movement.[61] (Their platform bears traces of libertarian ideology, such as the abolition of taxes and separation of banking from government. But their aim at the time was to strengthen labor rather than to consecrate capital.) A portmanteau of "crazy" (in Spanish) and firebrand (from the Italian for "fire," *fuoco*), the Locofocos allegedly once used friction matches to prolong a meeting after their opponents turned off the gaslights—an intriguing flicker of a now notorious signifier that was popularized over a century later. To gaslight someone means to drive them insane by causing them to doubt the reality of their own mind.

The *Boston Globe* accused the Locofocos of rhetorical delirium, comparing their "hysterical laughter" to involuntary seizures induced by forced electrocution.[62] "We think," one reporter opined, "that all the laughter, done by the Locofocos during the present canvass, will be caused by the passage of Whig lightning through their midriffs."[63] If sentimental hysterics symbolized women's emotional chaos, Locofoco laughter converged on the group's anti-elitist politics. "Deceit is her form—disorder her costume," protested the *Boston Courier*, which maligned the "hysterical, popular Locofocoism" as a consequence of excess democratization.[64]

In a similar spirit, the British novelist Henry Cockton caricatured the democratically elected House of Commons as a hotbed of zoological hysterics in his popular novel, *The Life and Adventures of Valentine Vox, the Ventriloquist* (1839–1840). Its members "cough and sneeze with unspeakable violence," they howl, yell, wail, and clap, and their "loud and apparently hysterical laughter" devolves into such "hideous sounds, to which nothing could be comparable save those which might proceed from a den in which five hundred maniacs were battling with a corresponding number of Very wild beasts."[65] Laden with repulsive tropes of British colonialism, the Commons' affective animality contrasts sharply with the stately composure of the House of Lords. Howling hysterical laughter always erred on the side of the people, emitted by the elected representatives of an unruly, feminized populace.

One degree further on the spectrum of emotional contagion, Locofoco "lightning" was eclipsed by the laughing rituals practiced at Presbyterian religious revivals.[66] Fomented by the Second Great Awakening, Baptist and Methodist camp meetings spread like wildfire across the Appalachians during the nineteenth century. Impassioned preachers led exuberant congregants in feats of bodily possession by the Holy Spirit. Robert Davidson describes these revivals in his *History of the Presbyterian Church in the State of Kentucky* (1847) in a section titled "Extravagances and Disorders." "Under paroxysms of feeling," he recounts, "persons fell down, and this was called 'the falling exercise.' There were also 'the jerking exercise,' 'the 'rolling,' the 'running,' the 'dancing,' and the 'barking exercises,' besides 'visions' and 'trances.' "[67] But it was not until 1803 that the "Holy Laugh" was "introduced systematically as a part of worship," according to Davidson.[68] The preacher's sermons provoked "whoops, cries, hysterical laughter" and barking ("bow, wow, wow") "interspersed with pious ejaculations and quotations of scripture."[69] "Hysterical" hounded what the church ordained as "Holy" when assigned by the ear of an ethnographic outsider.

Last but not least, implications of animality ("bow, wow, wow," the "Very wild beasts," and so forth) did not appear out of thin air. The term frequently referred to the howls, gobbles, barks, clucks, squeaks, and honks emitted by a variety of species. For example, "the pompous turkey-cock" broke into "hysterical laughter in his pharisaical pride at having got up earlier than his master."[70] A rancher marveled at the "spirit of eternal silence" of the Range Canyons in Utah, where "all animate nature is voiceless save the . . . hysterical laughter of the coyotes, the call of the crow and talking of the magpies."[71] When a hunter shot a loon in the middle of a storm, "a loud quack from the loon" recurred "spasmodically as roar after roar of hysterical laughter came pouring out, following the discharge."[72] From avian pride to idle magpie chatter to curdling death throes, zoological hysterics encompassed an incoherent range of meanings that were onomatopoeic and thus dependent on context.

At the London Zoo in 1897, our phonic excavation of multispecies "hysterical laughter" comes full circle with the affective soundscape of women's sensation novels. A "gallant professor" rushed to the aid of "a woman in distress," cued by her "hysterical laughter," which he describes as "a delicious abandon of unhinged reason" that caused the hairs on "my arms to assume a semi-perpendicular pose" and made "my nerves . . . suspicious of every sound for several days to come."[73] As it turns out, the unseen source of this "ungodly racket" was not a woman at all but four caged hyenas! (There's a reason why they're called "laughing hyenas.") The "hysterical laughs" of myriad species—caged in a zoo, pent up in a barnyard, or hunted in the wild—encroached on the imaginary space occupied by volatile feminine emotions.

To summarize, who were the "hysterical laughers" of the long nineteenth century? They included nervous women, morbid men, rabble-rousing populists, ecstatic gospel congregants, talkative animals (hyenas, loons, turkeys, coyotes), and affectively shattered female literary characters.

ON THE ORIGIN OF A HYSTERICALLY LAUGHING SPECIES

Is laughter a hard-wired response to the sensation of joy? Certainly not for Elizabeth Bellevue, who smiled with scorn, laughed hysterically, and flashed fire with her eyes in longing shot through with exasperation.[74] Across its expansive contexts—from talkative zoology to revivalist ecstasy to affective impossibility—the "hysterical" of "hysterical laughter" held contradictory designations of nervous stimulation and instinctive animality.

Its semiotic complaint intersected with evolutionary debates about the adaptive malleability of the species and the universality of our primordial emotions. What does it mean when gestures become other than they first appear? "Laughter seems primarily to be the expression of mere joy or happiness," remarked Darwin in *The Expression of Emotions in Man and Animals* (1872).[75] Yet "the subject is extremely complex."[76] In his version, people laugh at "something incongruous or unaccountable," in response to excitable surprise and gratified self-superiority, when "in a happy frame of mind," and (invoking Herbert Spencer) in release of "a large amount of nervous energy."[77] Barring any of those criteria, according to Darwin, we are in the realm of infantile expression and/or developmental abnormality. He invokes young children, "idiots," traumatized soldiers, victims of extreme tickling, subjects of experimental electrocution, Chinese people "suffering from deep grief," and duplicitous women as examples of laughter's immoderate expression in the absence of joy.[78]

Nineteenth-century interpretations of Darwin were widely filtered through a Lamarckian lens, as Schuller argues in *Biopolitics of Feeling*. It was believed that civilized subjects could escape atavistic inheritance by molding themselves toward hereditary perfection. "Heredity marks a key interface that differentiates and conjoins the milieu, individual, and population," Schuller explains.[79] Feelings paved the way to evolutionary progress, exploiting the "impressible" body as a biopolitical loophole to eugenic heredity. In particular, sentiment afforded a "regulatory technique" for "reconciling the impressible body to its role in a biological population" by lording over its "vital capacities" to exert "state power" and foster "capitalist development."[80] Against this Lamarckian exception, Darwin sought to establish the universality of primordial emotions common to both "civilized" and so-called "primitive cultures." An expression was "true" and "instinctive" whenever it appeared across "all the races of mankind, especially . . . those who have associated but little with Europeans."[81] As he claimed, "the far greater number of the movements of expression, and all the more important ones . . . are the same throughout the world."[82] For example, laughter expresses joy, trembling conveys fear, tears arise from sadness or suffering, blushing betrays shyness or modesty (often deriving from shame), and a reddening of the skin indicates rage or disgust.

The problem with laughter beyond its threshold of joyful excess (which some might call "hysterical") is that it then becomes indistinguishable from tears of grief, anger, or frustration. "Hence," deduced Darwin, "it is scarcely possible to point out any difference between the tear-stained face of a person after a paroxysm of excessive laughter and after a bitter crying-fit."[83] Even joyless laughs do not register as "hysterical," which Darwin quarantines to an asylum, as when "hysteric patients alternately cry and laugh with violence" due to their madness as well as the spasmodic proximity between those two expressions.[84] If the "impressible body" was an "open door" (for biopolitical domination), to paraphrase Horace Bushnell's sermon on *Unconscious Influence* (1846), then hysterical laughter shattered the evolutionary mirror between innate emotion and acquired inheritance.[85]

Darwin drew extensively on the photographic experiments of the French neurologist, Guillaume Duchenne de Boulogne. Duchenne attempted to isolate the unique muscle behind every facial expression in order to purify "true emotions" (instinctive, universal, sincere) from their false pretenders (voluntary, acquired, deceitful). Of all methods, he used facial electrocution! He applied electrified metal probes to his models and then photographed them in the grips of involuntary seizures.[86] Through these sadistic means, he claimed to reveal facial expression as a "universal language" always "composed of the same signs" and triggered by the same "muscular contractions."[87] Sentimental impressibility be damned: true expressions were "immutable, a condition without which [they] could not be universal," he declared.[88] He did allow that skillful comedians—but *not* tragedians—possessed the power "of marvelously feigning emotions," but he insists that even the most mimetically artful clown would be exposed by the hard evidence of his electrocuted mug shot.

In his rogues' gallery of "primordial expressions," there is no true laughter absent of joy. According to Duchenne, it's all in the eyes, which with just "a moment's attention" will prove when one's "gaiety is false."[89] The zygomaticus major (extending from the cheekbone to the mouth) is "the only muscle that expresses *joy* to all its degree and in all its nuances, from the simple smile to the raucous laugh."[90] Without the complicity of other facial muscles, however, it becomes the seat of "feeble false laughter."[91] Only in concert with the "parebral part" of the *orbicularis oculi* (located in the eyelid, which "does not obey the will") does the zygomaticus major yield the simple expression of laughter.[92] He further elaborates the mechanisms of "ferocious joy," "sensual delirium,"

FIGURE 1.3 "Électro-Physiologie Photographique," Plate 9 demonstrates different facial expressions induced by electric currents. Published in Guillaume-Benjamin Duchenne (de Boulogne), *The Mechanism of Human Facial Expressions* (1862).

"lubricious pleasure," "agreeable reflection," and "ecstasy" in his synoptic table—they all enlist the zygomaticus major: the engine of joy in its multifarious guises.[93]

Despite his nuanced taxonomy of innate emotions, sexual difference gave the lie to universal expression, which becomes visible in media res. Among his principal models was a woman whom he described as a "seductive wanton," who one day was very sad so he proceeded to "make her gay."[94] He staged the following scenario: a mother's infant dies while the other child, also in the throes of mortal illness, miraculously survives. "Such are the expressions of maternal pain and joy that I have tried to" convey and which "I managed to obtain."[95] He did so, first, by soliciting her "natural joy" in "making her gay" (through unspecified means), and second, by abruptly electrocuting the left half of her face to activate the "muscle of pain" (*corrugator supercilii*). In this way, he molded her countenance into a canvas for expressive montage: a split screen of earnest emotion and electroshock theater.

If only Duchenne had read more sensation literature of his time! (He was, after all, very fond of the arts and frequently turns to aesthetic examples from painting, sculpture, and literature.[96]) An uncannily similar scenario occurs in *The Ages of Female Beauty* (1838), when a grief-stricken mother loses her young daughter to inflammation of the lungs. Although heartbroken, she thinks at the same time of her two surviving sons, which brings her a dash of joy and relief. At this impossible conflict, "wild hysterical laugh burst" from "her lips" and "for many days afterward the ravings of delirium alone gave a clue" to the frenzy of her thoughts.[97] As Duchenne would have commented, her zygomaticus major and corrugator supercilia (frowning eyebrows) crossed wires amid the impossible conflict between miraculous fortune and maternal bereavement.

Motherhood and childbirth recur as Duchenne's primary examples of "pain mixed with joy," a "discordant expression" that he claims "cannot be borne for long without wounding the emotions."[98] This is why its fleeting appearance on the human face (upon "countless occasions!") has yielded "so few" traces in the history of art, with Nicolas Poussin's *The Resurrection of a Young Japanese Girl* (1641?) and Domenico Zampieri's *The Martyrdom of St. Agnes* (1619) as rare outliers.[99] At last, the fugitivity of "discordant expressions" was rendered permanent by the technologies of plate photography and facial electrocution. Other mixed gestures include the grimace, the scowl, the smirk, the cruel smile, and the evil eye. They arise—briefly or at length—from the joy muscle's physical proximity to the zygomaticus minor (the muscle of crying), but they do not cause much mischief for Duchenne's universal syntax.

Excess laughter is never a far cry from uncontrollable tears for Darwin, but this slippage is merely due to their physiological similarity. In her critique of Darwin, Sara Ahmed associates the abhorrence of affective excess with the fear of becoming "less white" and "more feminine," which "would involve moving backwards in time, such that one would come to resemble a more primitive form of social life, or a 'lower and animal like condition.' "[100] Where Darwin sees primordial inheritance, Ahmed reveals the devil of "cultural politics" that complicate the language of universal emotions.

Most of Darwin's examples point strikingly to the joyful tears of nonwhite women. (As Anca Parvulescu notes, Darwin sent questionnaires to functionaries of the British Empire to gather anecdotes about the tearful laughter of "different races of men."[101]) Bornean women frequently weep from laughing, according to Darwin, who hears "from the Rajah C. Brooke that it is a common expression with them to say 'we nearly made tears from laughter.' "[102] Malay "women of a wild tribe . . . sometimes shed tears when they laugh heartily."[103] So do Kaffir tribes in South Africa, "especially . . . the women, their eyes often fill with tears during laughter" and Sir Andrew Smith has even "seen the painted face of a Hottentot woman all furrowed with tears after laughter."[104] Although Darwin lists these examples to assert the commonality of tears from joy, he has little to add about their bearing on excess laughter in the absence of pleasure, let alone his brief mention of crying/laughing hysteria.

Doing so would deliver us into the realm of sentimental biopolitics, or even Lamarckian impressibility, to invoke Schuller. As a "regulatory technique," sentimentality sought to correct species heredity by uplifting discordant joy to the white benchmark of pliable suffering. Hysterical laughter marked a breaking point between biopolitical sensibility and raw affective sensation—absent of any grotesque-comedic outlets. Laughter past the brink of tears—laughter in the throes of pain—laughter to the abyss of madness and unreason: "hysterical laughter" was the gift of civilized white modernity for its weepy madam of the species.

HYSTERICAL OTHERS: RACISM, COLONIALISM, AND WHITE NERVOUSNESS

"This world divided into compartments, this world cut in two is inhabited by two different species," wrote Frantz Fanon in *The Wretched of the Earth* (1961).[105] In his call for instrumental violence to counter the endemic barbarity of extractive colonialism (amid national liberation movements and wars of independence across Africa), Fanon imagined the material struggle in terms of "species" partition: the white agential human versus its dehumanized racial other.

Decolonization thus necessitates the "absolute substitution" of "a whole social structure . . . from the bottom up" (beyond economic reparations for "enormous disparities in lifestyle"); otherwise, it will fail to liberate the "consciousness and . . . lives of the men and women who are colonized."[106] It must replace "a certain 'species' of men by another 'species' " in a "meeting of two forces, opposed to each other by their very nature" that transforms "spectators crushed with their inessentiality into" revolutionary actors "with the grandiose glare of history's floodlights upon them."[107] Yet the mere "possibility of [such] change" forebodes "a terrifying future in the consciousness of another 'species' of men and women: the colonizers," who would burst into horrific screams of hysterical laughter at the mere inkling of their dethronement.[108]

To laugh hysterically in the throes of sentimental impressibility, as we know, marked a developmental achievement, according to white eugenicists and experts in the mushrooming field of nervousness studies. The American nerve specialist George Beard applauded women's "impressible, susceptive organization" as a bellwether of thriving capitalist industry—a sensitivity index for the onward march of civilized progress.[109] Their violent suspension in a state of "hysterical laughter"—at the affective crossroads of joy and despair—was collateral damage from the shaky housing of a body that soaked up feelings like a sponge. In contrast, "hysterical laughter" from the "warm latitudes" (an obvious dog whistle) stripped people of their basic entitlement to self-contradiction. The eugenicist George Preston (who shared Beard's esteem for female nervousness) condemned the "wild laughter" and "contagious hysteria of the uncivilized" as by-products of their "emotional nature," "impressionability," and "intensity of the passions."[110] (Note the sharp distinction between "impressible" and "impressionable.") In contrast to what Preston describes as the "purely mental form" of white hysteria, its spread "among uncivilized or semi-civilized peoples" conceals nothing: "fear, anger, love, reverence, are all visibly depicted on the countenance, and graphically represented by gestures."[111] To deny one's reality of self-contradiction is part and parcel of wholly negating their claim to humanity.

Preston's hysterical map did not confine itself to the borders of equatorial geography but to "the fact of belonging to or not belonging to a given race, a given species," to invoke Fanon's language.[112] The white colonizer's fantasy of "hysterical laughter" diverged from its feminized variants in sentimental literature. To laugh hysterically as a nonwhite body implied a lack of "cause for restraint" rather than an unresolvable excess thereof.[113] For example, a British ethnographer visited a gambling den in colonized Hong Kong in 1884, decrying its "noise as of bedlam": "the air is full of wild imprecations, terrible oaths and hysterical laughter."[114] A reporter in Mobile, Alabama, passively observed an Indigenous girl fight an older man in her (unspecified) tribe over the remains of a bottle of whiskey: "When the girl at length obtained possession of the bottle, it was empty, and she was left sitting in the road, lamenting discordantly in sounds which one would hardly know whether to call howling or hysterical laughter."[115] The familiar scene of hope shot through with despair—a staple of the sensation novel (and lightning rod for Duchenne's facial electrocution)—is swallowed up by the symbolism here of animality and other repugnant tropes. "The native knows all this and laughs to himself every time he spots an allusion to the animal world in the other's words," remarks Fanon.[116] (Further omitted was the ongoing, genocidal trauma of Indigenous displacement from the American South along the Trail of Tears.[117]) Again, the hysterical laughs of the colonized other were reduced to their barest contradictions, denied the nuanced affective conflict that encircled white women's humorless sentiment.[118]

The golden goose of rapturous dualism, that glorious "feeling of joy at [one's] own superiority and the joy of man's superiority over nature," remained the property of white male colonizers. I do not mean this glibly. As the apex of the "absolute comic," Baudelaire returns to "those Chinese grotesque figures which we find so highly diverting, and which have much less of a comic intention than is . . . believed," as he explains: "A Chinese idol, though an object of veneration, scarcely differs from a tumble-over, or a pot-bellied chimney ornament."[119] In order for the comic to explode as an emanation from another realm, there must exist "two beings in the presence of each other" distilled through the "dual nature" of the civilized fun-maker.[120] Without license to doubleness, laughter converges on the urgencies of bare life, which run counter to its lack of any evolutionary purpose, as Spencer argues in his influential essay "On the Physiology of Laughter" (1875).[121]

Yet a kind of metaphysics of doubleness attends to the broad ethnography of hysterical laughter. A white South African correspondent observing Hindu funeral rites in Bengal dissected the women's "hysterical laughter" (or ululation) as they prepared corpses for cremation: they "begin a sort of 'wake' by bitter cries and awful lamentations. Then tearing of the hair, the smiting of the breast, and hysterical laughter are resorted to."[122] His recourse to dehumanizing stereotypes (which I do not see the need to quote further) betrays a crisis of fascination with the ritual value of their excess, uttered in order to ward off undead ghosts. "Hysterical," of course, was the white reporter's word, an effect of his ear. Beyond its tonal designation of unjoyful volubility, it tended to hover around the gateway to alternate corporeal realms.

In his 1877 African travelogues, Emilius Albert de Cossonde invokes the "hysterical laughter" of the "laughing hyenas" he encountered in Abyssinia.[123] In his version of local mythology, the villagers believed that certain animals were possessed by blacksmiths "who have the power of transforming themselves into hyenas, in order that they may devour women and children."[124] There is, of course, a self-serving economic logic to how this tale circulates: the white reader gobbles up details of the laughing blacksmith-hyena who supposedly eats his wife and children. (We must also recall that Abyssinia [now Ethiopia] was devastated by the hellscape of colonialist resource extraction, forced labor, and captive slavery—occupied by both Britain and Italy amid the "Scramble for Africa."[125]) The slippery slope from "eating the Other" in the materialist sense (exploiting their labor, consuming their resources, negating their humanity) to the metaphorical sense (appropriating their mythology) leads right to the throat of "hysterical laughter"—as a portal to bodily possession and digestive magic.[126]

"Did any of these figures exist as objects of knowledge and discourse in the nineteenth century without a racially erotic counterpart," asks Ann Laura Stoler, or "without reference to the libidinal energies of the savage, the primitive, the colonized?"[127] As postcolonial feminist scholars have argued, European white individuals and colonized racial subjects were libidinally co-constitutive bodies.[128] Stoler aims her rhetorical query at Michel Foucault's four sexed bodies: masturbating children, perverse adults, hysterical women, and the teeming population.[129] To the third term (hysterical women), we must add the special exception of laughter: where does the magic/horrific laughter of the colonized other fit in connection with the momentary insanity of nervous or ambivalent white women? The military neurologist William Hammond hazarded that Black women were becoming increasingly susceptible to nervous diseases due to their "attempts to imitate" in dress, in work, and "in lifestyle" their "American white sister."[130] If impressibility democratized "hysterical laughter" (as sentimental crisis), the flip side of that wager threatened to unleash nervous white women from their humorless corsets.

On the brink of enjoyment but not yet at that threshold, "hysterical laughter" flickered at the precipice of excess pleasure. Its arousal further anticipates our driving question in this chapter: how did "hysteria" and "laughter" became etymologically intertwined and then mutate in meaning, from emotional unraveling (due to mixed feelings) to uproarious pleasure? As we will see, it had everything to do with the consumerist fever dream of never-ending enjoyment.

HYSTERICAL HILARITY: CONTAGIOUS FUN AND MASS ENJOYMENT

When did "hysterical laughter" come to imply contagious fun? As Donald Fleming argues in *Attitude: The History of a Concept* (1967), dictionaries "are merely tantalizing" for "the historian's ultimate question *why*. Why should this word arise in this sense at this time, why exfoliate into different forms of speech, and explode into radically new meanings; why flourish or dwindle?"[131] The Oxford English Dictionary (OED) dates the adherence of "hysterical" to hilarious comedy to 1925, citing the example of a film advertisement: "Five Reels of Hysterical, Hilarious Merriment."[132] But the OED is over two decades too late: "hysterical" meant "funny" as early as 1900; for example, the *Boston Daily* praised the vaudeville comedienne May Irwin as "hysterical" and "excruciatingly funny" for her burlesque role in *The Belle of Bridgeport* (1900).[133] The Online Etymology Dictionary reveals that "hysterical" (literally "of the womb, suffering in the womb," from the Greek *hysterikos*) denoted "funny" in 1939, deriving from "the notion of uncontrollable fits of laughter."[134]

No etymological source that I have consulted offers a precise date or example of when "hysterical" acquired these connotations of enjoyment in the context of laughter. OED refers to the plural "hystericals": "a bout or display of overwhelming, uncontrollable emotion or agitation, esp. as a result of acute distress."[135] It contrasts incidents from 1797 and 1930 (both of which signal madness and distress) to a 2014 Tweet by @JackPhillips333: "Seeing the guy in the pub, absolutely smashed and singing and dancing has made my day. In hystericals."[136] There is no explanation for this extreme rupture in meaning—other than the implicit suggestion that social media liquidates all exasperating affects into weaponized forms of enjoyment. Similarly, the third adjectival entry in OED—"characterized by excessive, unrestrained emotion or agitation"—references two examples of emotional suffering (from 1862 and 1919) and then cuts to the *Daily Telegraph* (2000): "If I hadn't been about to cry, I probably would have collapsed in hysterical laughter."[137] The Online Etymology Dictionary notes that this "general sense of 'unhealthy emotion or excitement' " was pervasive "by 1839," offering no further insight into the next century as its meaning meandered toward "very funny" by 1939.[138]

Again, it was the collective social body—not the isolated nervous individual—who laughed hysterically in this exhilarating new sense of the phrase. Yet we start to see a glimmer of its forthcoming signification already in the 1870s, perhaps even among those hysterically laughing women in the New Jersey shop where a "spunky female" pelted a beleaguered clerk with "damaged" chicken "ovaries."[139] (In Yiddish, that would make her the schlemiel and the shop clerk the schlimazel.) The smell of rotten eggs, however, could have tipped the scales from excitation to disgust. In 1873, there was reportedly "more exhibition . . . than was expected" at the comic opera house in Stockton, California, during the premiere of *Don César de Bazan* (by Jules Massenet).[140] A male eccentric of uncanny resemblance to Horace Greeley (who had just lost his U.S. presidential bid) cavorted around the theater shaking hands with random people and wearing "a long linen coat that was a comical sight in itself."[141] When he rose to clap with both hands that "sounded like two large boards coming together with almost superhuman force," the audience "was convulsed with laughter and applauded the old gentleman."[142] ("Convulsive" was a common descriptor for joyful laughter at the time.) It was not until the second act (as Don Jose attempts to cuckold the king) that our good friend "hung his head, and in a tone audible throughout the auditorium, exclaimed: 'I knew he'd do it!' (More hysterical laughter on the part of the audience)."[143] *There it is*: an innocent aside announcing a seismic semantic turn.

A Google Ngram (of "hysterical laughter," "laughed hysterically," and "hysterical laugh") reveals that all three phrases increased exponentially in their frequency between 1870 and 1900, which of course does not say anything of their meaning.[144] My keyword searches of digital databases including the World Newspaper Archive, Internet Archive, online periodicals of Victorian literature, and various English-language journals yield few traces of "hysterical laughter" (or its relevant permutations) to signify comedic enjoyment before the mid-1880s.[145] By then, "[s]tanding room was early at a premium" at the Bijou Theatre in Boston in May 1884 to see the "very, very, very funny," gag-laden play *Skipped by the Light of the Moon*, which kept "the audience in a condition ranging from a quiet smile to loud and hysterical laughter."[146] The audience at Funke's opera house in Lincoln, Nebraska, "was an appreciative one" upon Bill Nye and James Whitcomb Riley's comic debut: "Frequent demonstrations, and in some instances almost hysterical laughter, proved the entire success of the entertainment," raved the *Daily Nebraska State Journal* in 1889.[147]

Go rag-picking through the "Amusements" sections of late nineteenth-century dailies, where promises of "hysterical laughter" firmly overpowered any sense of nervous ambivalence or affective torture.[148] "It was a season of side-splitting, hysterical laughter, in which everybody" joined: from the Grand Opera House in Boston to the Margaret Playhouse in Anaconda, Montana—blared the *Herald* and the *Standard*.[149] Then to what do we owe this joyous flourishing of hysterical meaning? The explosion of mass commercial enticements—variety shows, comic operas, pleasure centers, moving pictures, amusement parks, traveling carnivals—all paved the way for the hystericization of enjoyment, which let loose an artillery of uproarious signifiers in trade reviews and advertisements: convulsive, screaming, howling, side-splitting, corset-busting, vest-ripping, and so on and so forth. (The special place of early cinema at the center of these bankroll-bloating hysterics is the subject of Part 3 of this book.)

Laughter became pleasurably and democratically "hysterical" when its excess excitation could offer surplus value for the ruthless expansion of recreational capital. As isolated literary readers flooded the theaters (and other amusing spaces), their hunger for visceral thrills needed new words. And where better to go fishing than in the affective recesses of the sensation genres? I view this slippage from nervous catastrophe to delirious hilarity as unconscious, gradual, and largely unintentional. Most forms of symbolic rupture concretize processes of social change that have been underway for quite a while. Above all, the promise of "hysterical laughter" was a commercial hook: an imperative call to the carnival or extravaganza or fun-making spectacle that raised capital from the leisure time of an expanding middle class and from the affective desperation of laborers with unspent wages to burn. "At the same time that factory work exhausts the nervous system to the uttermost," warns Karl Marx in *Capital* (1867), "it does away with the many-sided play of the muscles, and confiscates every atom of freedom, both in bodily and intellectual activity."[150] All "the less, therefore, [the worker] enjoys it [their work] as something which gives play to his bodily and mental powers."[151] Not only did hysterical enjoyment offer an antidote to the nervous exhaustion of alienating work, true to form, it transposed that vital deficit into a magical source of further surplus value.

As Marx reminds us, "If commodities, or commodities and money, of equal exchange-value ... are exchanged, it is plain that no one abstracts more value from [them] than he throws into [them] ... There is no creation of surplus-value."[152] Capitalism dies without the constant generation of surplus value, which comes first and foremost from the cheapening of wage labor relative to the value it produces, and then further preys on that value in the commodity market for unequal (or nonequivalent) exchange. The hystericization of enjoyment converted off-the-clock recreation into human fodder for more capitalist domination. "Hysterical" was the missing semantic link between nerve-deadening work and value-adding fun. As Andrew F. Jones details, in the context of the commodity market for gramophone recordings of human laughter in colonial Shanghai, their merchants "laughed [themselves] all the way to the bank."[153] Simply put, the rampages of twentieth-century capitalism made "hysterical laughter" fun: from excessive emotion to surplus enjoyment.

Exuberance of this ilk was not yet something one experienced alone but as part of a collective, contagious, and uproarious crowd. (Residual meanings still prevailed when one's hysterics flared up in private, as we will see in the next chapter about death by laughter.) The phrase also retained its unpayable debt to white supremacy, extractive colonialism, and racial dehumanization. At the scene of a lynching in Kansas in 1901, a violent mob broke out in "hysterical laughter" while "yelling in a manner that perhaps had never before been heard in the city of Leavenworth."[154] Their rhapsodic bloodlust took cover in the "same shameless falsehood that 'Negroes are lynched' " to defend white womanhood, as Ida B. Wells testified in her 1909 address on lynching as "color-line murder."[155] Fred Alexander, a Black man, had been falsely accused of assaulting and murdering a white woman. In yet another "gruesome tribute the nation pays to the color line," eight thousand "irresponsible, bloodthirsty, [white] criminals" stormed into his jail cell in Kansas, maimed his body, and burnt him at the stake.[156] Alexander maintained his innocence the whole time, enduring hours of threats to extract a confession of his presumed guilt. But the hysterically laughing mob was unmoved by "either education or agitation."[157]

Vainglorious laughter always carries the specter of homicidal violence (as humor "superiority" theorists have warned us—from Plato to Descartes to Hobbes, and onward).[158] But the use of this expression ("hysterical") to describe it (murderous laughter) arose in tandem with emergent connotations of commercial fun and rapacious enjoyment. Bloodthirsty hysterics of the unruly mob were flipsides of the law-abiding hilarity unleashed by pleasure-seeking crowds. Whether for surplus vitality or for extralegal barbarity, hysterical laughter was no longer "Lady Audley's Secret," to paraphrase Steinlight's argument that sensation novels "incorporate specters of mass population into an ungovernable female body."[159] Cutting out the middle-woman, hysterical laughter was let loose upon the masses. It became the property of both the vigilante clan and the mushrooming population, tenuously contained and commoditized by so many, new, fun, and invigorating spaces of leisure and entertainment.

Whether their visceral explosions—widely felt as pleasurable—derived from joy or anxiety, or surprise, or anger, or fear, or disgust, or any of the other supposedly innate, universal emotions, their effects were unmistakably "capital": lucrative and barbaric (from the Latin *caput*, meaning "head," as in "off with their head," which is how prisoners were commonly executed). Amid these semantic upheavals, women held sticky positions between contagious laughter and its mortally destructive consequences. They could now laugh along with the chorus—but sometimes they were told, it would kill them.

2

Female Death by Laughter (Beyond Enjoyment)

Can you really die from laughing too hard? From 1870 to 1920, hundreds of women allegedly suffered such a fate. In this bizarre and mostly untold chapter of U.S. history, women laughed themselves to death while doing housework, playing bridge games, having dental work, or going to the theater. If a joke could be indicted for manslaughter, it would have been convicted on evidence of women's laughter. For example, on April 23, 1902, in Louisville, Kentucky, Catherine Maude Rice "was visiting some friends when one of them told her a funny story." As the sensationalist headline claimed: "LITERALLY LAUGHED HERSELF TO DEATH: Lesion of the Brain Caused by Kentucky Girl's Violent Fit of Mirth."[1] The sudden turn from pleasure to pain—and from vigorous life to unforeseen death—was always the hook in these reports.

Women enjoyed their laughter extravagantly, that is, until they no longer enjoyed it at all. Bertha Pruett was "Killed By a Joke," Polly Ann Jackson "Had Not Laughed So Heartily In Months," and a woman in Denver "may have been about the first to see anything in Colorado to laugh at," according to the *Dallas Morning News*.[2] In 1897, a woman "went to enjoy a comedy and furnished a tragedy" when she laughed herself to death at a theater in Pittsburgh.[3] Female amusement offered a setup for the grizzly punch line of death by enjoyment, as these perversely pithy obituaries reveal. But women themselves were mocked for giving up the ghost to such a ludicrous killer, as if constitutionally unfit for uproarious humor. "Pegasus generally feels inclined to pace toward a graveyard the moment he feels a side-saddle on his back," joked the writer Mary Mapes Dodge in 1885.[4] Long confined to the sidelines of sentiment, women exploded into laughter with equally hazardous consequences.

FIGURE 2.1 "A woman laughed herself to death in a Pittsburg theatre," according to the *Wheeling Register* (Wheeling, WV), November 10, 1897, 4. An image of this headline is pasted over a frame enlargement from the French silent slapstick comedy, *Rosalie et Léontine vont au théâtre [Rosalie and Léontine Go to the Theater]* (Pathé, 1911). Courtesy of the British Film Institute and The World Newspaper Archive.

Pruett, for instance, was in laughing fits over a wry remark uttered by her sweetheart (a noted wit) when she rapidly lost control and "blood gushed from her nose and mouth."[5] Like Pruett, Anna Ferrer had been laughing at an old joke at a party when she made the ominous remark, "I know I shall die laughing if I don't stop!"[6] But the lighthearted saying, "I'll die laughing," has been a familiar idiom since antiquity.[7] No one was very worried until Ferrer had to be "lifted back on a chair, gasping for breath" and "the horrified guests could realize" she was actually dying.[8] Similarly, Ellen Lake stumbled into a bakery demanding, "Give me a drink of water please, I have been laughing so hard I am almost dead."[9] Lake fell to the floor a corpse when the glass was just at arm's length. The precise cause of her mirth was unknown, but witnesses speculated that she must have "seen something ridiculous" prior to entering the bakery.[10]

It is very doubtful that these stories are true—at best, they're wildly exaggerated. They tended to circulate as curiosity items in local dailies such as the *Kalamazoo Gazette*, the *Anaconda Standard*, and the *Salt Lake Telegram*, but also in major newspapers including the *Boston Herald* and the *New York Times*. They often refer to (or simply reprint) incidents that occurred elsewhere, such as the South Carolina paper that commented on the Oklahoma woman who "laughed herself to death over a funny story," adding that she "must have heard one we haven't."[11] Names, locations, tone (which pivoted from somber mourning to icy mockery), and other key details mutated in the telling as these surreal obituaries transmitted unaccountably from paper to paper across the country. Their proliferation also coincided with a crisis of "fake news" (a widely used term at the time) that bedeviled any standards for fact-based objectivity.[12] The *Kalamazoo Gazette* wanted to titillate its readers as much as the *New York Journal* or the *New York World*—two papers vying for center ring of the "yellow journalism" circus.[13] Beyond their profit margin, but inextricable from it, the contents of these obituaries prick our gazes over a century later.

As we know well, the rumored stories that "go viral" or spread uncontrollably reveal something incredibly powerful about what readers want to believe. "WHAT WAS THE JOKE?": alas "we are left in the dark" as to the "fatal jest" that caused a "lovely woman" in New York to die laughing before physicians could "save her . . . from the grave," lamented a small daily newspaper from Emporia, Kansas.[14] The burning wager of death from *too much enjoyment* enflamed national anxieties about women's mushrooming access to full-throated fun. Ladies were warned to check their mirth or face untimely death, just as they had found increasing opportunity to delight themselves at many raucous new venues around the turn of the twentieth century. They made merry in every possible context—variety shows, moving pictures, traveling carnivals, dance halls, pleasure parks, burlesque revues—but always at their own peril!

THE SOCIAL POLITICS OF GENDER AND ENJOYMENT

These death from laughter obituaries—bizarre, uncanny, outlandish archives—reveal the contradictory social politics of how female enjoyment was simultaneously feared and solicited. Feminist cultural historians such as Jayna Brown, Anne Friedberg, Miriam Hansen, Kathy Peiss, Vanessa Schwartz, and

Zhang Zhen have established that women's pleasure was instrumental to the growth and expansion of twentieth-century consumer capital. The rabid incitement to female fun laid the groundwork for America's rising, hegemonic entertainment industry. At the same time, women infiltrated the workforce; lobbied for social rights and political enfranchisement; and sought to defy their domestic lot of housework, pregnancy, and child-rearing.

Laughter, in particular, represented a promise and a threat for mainstream society—the promise of capitalist profit but the threat of irreversible political change and cultural decline, fomenting vicious backlash and moral panic. As I argued in chapter 1, it was right around this time that "hysterical laughter" shifted in meaning: from female nervous suffering to collective, contagious hilarity. Prior to the 1880s, hysterical laughter was viewed as a condition of women's "excessive emotionality" provoked by the simultaneous sensation of sharply conflicting feelings (such as grief and relief, horror and surprise, or despair and ambition).[15] The experience was far from pleasurable. Hysterical laughter seized its victim, suspending her in an agitated state of emotional disaster, and often terminated in a nervous breakdown.

Just when hysterical laughter threatened to swing from pathos to fun, death marked a cold hard limit to the threshold of pleasure. For example, Josephine Hochardel was "probably the prettiest, gayest, and most popular student in the high school."[16] One day in 1907, however, she laughed herself to death, "not in an uncontrollable hysteria, but just naturally overtaxed herself in the enjoyment of good spirits and merry jokes and stories."[17] After all, "there are many ways ... of having too much of a 'good time,' and not infrequently death levies its grim toll on the innocent forms as well as the more sinful indulgencies [sic]." Obituaries such as Hochardel's conjured women's bodies as too fragile to savor the assorted enticements that now lay at their feet. Jolting stimuli and sensorial attractions—urban crowds, street traffic, animated billboards, moving pictures—gave "women access to a spectacle from which they traditionally had been excluded," argues Miriam Hansen, and became "emblem[s] of the simultaneous liberalization and commodification of sexuality that crucially defined American consumer culture."[18] Like sexuality, laughter cut both ways, dangerously threatening to outstrip its own instrumental value.

Women's laughs, as much as anyone else's, were now inestimable forms of commodity capital. "Laugh? Why, you'll have to tie them to the seats so that they won't roll all over the house in fits of convulsive laughter," declared the *Moving Picture World* in 1912.[19] Movie theaters even advertised free life insurance policies for the occupational hazard of dying from laughter at "dangerously funny" comedies (a morbid gimmick that I discuss in chapter 7).[20] However hyperbolic, at least that risk of death would have been remotely proportionate to slapstick's violent extremity of humor. Grotesque comedy exists to solicit the catharsis of affective liberation in a dystopian, often soul-crushing world. But "make no mistake: this transfusion will be brutal . . . its *job* is to detonate, to touch off tiny explosions at the limits of 'the thinkable,' " as D. Diane Davis summons the absolute ends of feminist laughter in *Breaking Up (at) Totality*.[21] Danielle Fuentes Morgan conjures it as an "earthquake" of "the unsaid" in *Laughing to Keep from Dying*, which explores thresholds of horror and travesty in satirical media about anti-Black racism and the afterlives of slavery.[22] Cynthia Willett and Julie Willett invite us to join in their uproarious, contagious laughter that they theorize via feminist stand-up comics who lambaste the everyday gender "absurdities that call us to action."[23] In contrast, A. Fox laughed for two hours at an "amusing incident that happened at the circus," although the gag itself was allegedly withheld from print due to concerns about public safety.[24] Barbara Barr laughed for eight hours at a corny pun related to dentistry, Ernestina Nehring laughed herself to death at her young son's confusion between eggplants and chicken eggs, and Rosa Walker did the same when her husband accidentally salted the pork meat with granulated sugar.

Mrs. Perry was exchanging merry anecdotes with old friends at teatime when "she literally laughed herself to death . . . convulsed with laughter . . . and before she could recover sank back in her chair and died."[25] The rising calamity of mild pleasantry (at bad puns and nutty mishaps) left much to be desired from its corresponding object. Jokes and gags are the symbolic fields in which laughter "break[s] up the truth" and "make[s] room for new sensations and new potential futures," as Davis puts it.[26] While she focuses on language games in philosophy and rhetoric, humor scholars embrace wild laughter as a tactic to amplify the unthought absurdities that incisive feminist comedy makes momentarily concrete. Loud, raucous, convulsive, even dangerous laughter delivers on humor's vital capacity to provide a new frame for possibility and action—to break from ordinary habits and their foothold in oppressive material conditions.

The hysterical climate of early twentieth-century enjoyment was a double-edged sword, as ruthlessly exploitative as it was socially transformative—as future chapters will detail in depth. For now, let us stick to the obituaries, which alternately ridicule and mystify their incitements to fatal cachinnation. And which one was it this time? "Was it some newly imported variation of the veteran mother-in-law jest?" asked the *Boston Herald* in its mocking eulogy for "The Unique Heroine" in Kentucky, a woman who sacrificed herself on the altar of her husband's unspecified witticism.[27] "I'll die laughing yet," remarked Mrs. Charles A. Arndt just seconds before she "passed away . . . in a fit of laughter" while visiting with her neighbor.[28]

In a telling example, the teenage daughter of a well-digger in Wicksburg, Alabama, "DIED LAUGHING" at her older brother's mishap after he fell over in his chair. It started off innocently enough: "the young girl began to laugh at his misadventure and continued to do so for about twenty minutes."[29] When "she endeavored [and failed] to control herself," she started to make signs "that she was in pain." The convulsions "caused all the muscles of her body and limbs to twitch in a shocking manner" while she rolled on the floor "screaming and shouting." She reportedly "expired" from overexertion before the physician could arrive. (A nearly identical version of this incident allegedly took place in Nashville, Tennessee, where the girl's father was a prosperous farmer—not a well-digger—and her brother had drunkenly stumbled out of his car instead of falling over in his chair.[30]) The point is that women could not even be trusted to moderate their modest indulgence, let alone raucous hysterics epitomized by that wild lady at the Empire Theatre in 1911 who "laughed so hard she scared her infant in arms until it cried."[31]

Popular obituaries pathologized all female joy as a life-or-death wager. I cannot overstate the degree to which these outbursts differed from prior imaginations of that shattering limit, when it was not the excess but the absence of enjoyment that plagued women. This distinction is extremely significant. The floodgates of ambivalent affect had been opened. But thresholds of fun needed to remain pliable for social control. If not through forcible suppression or morbid sentimentality, then how? Women's sensations—joys, desires, anxieties, mixed feelings—once unleashed, for better or for worse, became targets of capital accumulation. Hysterical laughter erupted at the crossroads of freewheeling enjoyment and misogynistic repression. The message was clear: *Ladies will please laugh at whatever you like, just not too much! Otherwise, it might kill you.*

CAUSES OF DEATH: MALADY OR FUN?

There was no scourge more eye-popping than female death by laughter, as these obituaries make clear. Bizarre fatalities were routinely milked for their newsworthy value, parlaying untimely tragedy into morbid curiosity. The medical causes of death (when mentioned at all) were buried deep beneath the headlines. For example, the article "LAUGHS HERSELF TO DEATH: Taken ill while laughing during a funny scene at the theater" eventually reveals that Mrs. Charles S. Stuber, in fact, succumbed to acute indigestion.[32] In many cases, underlying illnesses were probably triggered to crisis by laughter, which then resulted in heart attacks, strokes, calcified arteries, asphyxiation, prolonged fatigue, and so forth. (I have obtained several coroner's reports that correspond to individual obituaries, but curiously none of them mention laughter.[33])

Some obituaries specify causes of death, along with details of their risible contexts, but rarely connect the dots between the two. For example, hearty laughter led to "heart disease," the official blight cited in Annie Maher's 1898 autopsy, as she had reportedly been enjoying "some funny stories . . . immediately before she gave the last death groan."[34] A widow's laughter at the joke of a gentleman caller incited a fatal hemorrhage "which could not be checked" in Tulsa, Oklahoma, while a young married woman's laughter turned into a "paroxysm of coughing" that "ruptured a blood vessel" in Fresno, California.[35] The Victorian antilaughter evangelist, George Vasey, warned in 1875 that "in the paroxysm of laughter . . . blood cannot be transmitted freely and naturally through the lungs."[36] If this passage "be impeded for more than a few seconds, the brain becomes congested, apoplexy ensues, and in very many cases ends fatally."[37] It is a slippery slope, in Vasey's account, between feeling and physiology—from the wild abandon of jokes to the reckless palpitations they might unleash.

Mary Trelkald suffocated on her unchecked joy upon "playing the winning card in a bridge game." She "started to laugh and died still laughing before physicians could arrive."[38] (As the *Boston Herald* added, Trelkald was a very competitive player, "often anxious to win."[39]) Josie Leisslie gave up the ghost to an out-of-tune organ, but also to cardiac failure after she fell "over backward in her chair in a fit of laughter" while playing her keyboard.[40] Ladies' laughs were supposed to conjure "a ripple of music—sweet, clear, harmonious and not an incongruous medley of shrieks, cackles, giggles, and snorts," as Eloise Beaumont counseled in her column on "How to Laugh."[41] Leisslie's obituary did not comment on the melody of her laughter, but Beaumont expressed regret that "we couldn't all laugh into a phonograph" and then listen to it afterward to learn how much "torture" our friends had endured from our throats.

The Miserable Tax for a "Wasp-Like Waist"

None of these reports mention corsets, which could easily turn an abrupt convulsion of the diaphragm into a lethal proposition. We are safe to assume that Louise A. Speetzen was wearing a tight corset in 1896 when her "long," "vociferous,"

FIGURE 2.2 "Reducing the Surplus. 'Now Pull Hard!'" Scanned from stereoscope card, copyright 1899 by T. W. Ingersoll. USA copyright expired. Image courtesy of Wikimedia Commons.

and "prolonged" enjoyment of a humorous anecdote quickly caused "her merry laughter [to] change into a shriek of pain."[42] Speetzen reportedly declared, "I feel a sharp sticking pain in my side, as though a knife had been run into me." She died the next morning, due to a ruptured blood vessel in the abdomen according to the doctor who examined her.

The miserable tax for a "wasp-like waist" was well noted, confessed Margaret Briggs, whose friend, "when she was going to theatre or reception, would draw her corset even a little tighter. By and by she began to have pains in the side, which seemed almost unbearable."[43] They came "when she should have been enjoying herself," but soon they "were always there—even when she did not don the corset at all."[44] To paraphrase Thorstein Veblen's *Theory of the Leisure Class*, the "mutilation" perpetrated by female corsetry went rib-cage-in-whalebone with the ostentations of "conspicuous leisure," lowering one's "vitality" and rendering them unfit for work, but apparently also for fun.[45] Women of "the poorer classes" who "have to work hard," Veblen notes, gain "little in the way of a pretense of leisure to so crucify the flesh in everyday life."[46] But mass culture was for "'Everyone!' Young and old, rich and poor, intelligent and ignorant": a universal "source of enjoyment," proclaimed the *Moving Picture World* in 1908.[47] If capitalist fun democratized wild enjoyment, it also lethalized the "contrivances" of conspicuous leisure, namely, the corset.

Was it a corset or a "comedy performance" that became "fatal" to Mrs. George D. Baker, "a well-known summer resident of New London" in 1906?[48] The *Salt Lake Telegram* did not disclose the program that caused a "stylishly dressed" (i.e., corseted) woman to convulse herself "with mirth a moment before she expired" in 1902, except to note that her corpse still awaits identification in the morgue.[49] Mrs. Charles A. Stuber, Nellie Williamson, Mary Armisted, and Margaret Leathers all reportedly died in the throes of laughing spectatorship, according to obituaries that unmistakably indicate their affluent status. A token of "honorific leisure," to invoke Veblen, the corset's exclusion from physical labor converged on middle-class women's incursion into raucous recreational pleasure.

The (Low) Wages of Fun

Although no direct link was ever asserted between fatal laughter and tight-laced fashion, corsetry notoriously led to asphyxiation, convulsive seizures, heart disease, and lung congestion. It gave rise to chronic health problems, especially when compounded by choking collars, compression girdles, and other treacherous signals of wealth. Suffragettes and women's rights advocates decried the "endless train of evils" that mangled their vital organs and "made [them] a slave to . . . artificial supports."[50] It was not a compression corset but a miniature doll hat that killed Elizabeth Courtney in 1894. A low-wage sweatshop worker at a New York hat factory, Courtney told a derisive joke about her boss, provoking contagious laughter that "echoed through the room, where 70 girls are employed."[51] She had been sewing a toy hat onto the head of a doll, when she remarked, referring to her male boss: "I wonder how this cap would look on his head?" At that, she laughed "for five minutes and then fell from the seat dead."[52] Another report claimed that "the girls stood gathered in awe around the body of the woman who a few minutes before had been in such happy spirits."[53] This obituary is overdetermined in its social import, mixing stone-cold gender politics (don't laugh at your patriarchal superior) with anxieties about mechanized labor (playing at work undermines productivity).

There's historical precedence for this encroachment between gendered enjoyment and economic production. Women inundated the professional workforce just as their risible deaths were rapidly increasing. In 1870, women accounted for just 6.4 percent (91,963) of the nonagricultural workforce, which rose to 13.3 percent (992,638) by 1920. Similarly, according to Karen Graves, "the number of women in the United States who worked in mills and factories grew from 252,702 in 1870 to 966,167 in 1900 to 1,777,022 in 1920," also revealing the instrumental role of women workers in processes of swift industrialization.[54] By 1920, women constituted 21 percent of the overall workforce and the majority of consumer-enjoyers in the United States.[55] Even paltry wages could gain women admission to cross-class leisure spheres, such as the variety theater, amusement park, and cinema. If middle-class housewives laughed in excess as a symptom of their access to material surplus, working-class women's fatal cachinnation was implicated in a different economy of productivity and enjoyment. They laughed to death on the job.

Speaking of Courtney, it has been well established that employees of hat factories suffered severe medical complications due to mercury exposure. These included muscular tremors ("hatters' shakes"), blurred vision, and far higher rates of mortality due to pulmonary disease and tuberculosis than the national average. The U.S. Bureau of Labor and Industry compared the hat factory to a "death producing enclosure" in 1889,[56] where it was "universally acceptable . . . [to] ignor[e] the delayed consequences of toxic exposure."[57] If these poisonous labor conditions hadn't killed Courtney, perhaps she simply worked herself to the bone, and her pithy snipe against her boss was an attempt at gallows humor: one last laugh before dying. Like the corset-wearing cachinnators at the theater, women laughers of the workforce leave us to speculate about their true causes of death in the absence of definitive evidence. To that end, one wonders: what *would* the tiny doll's cap have looked like on Courtney's boss' head? Her irreverent curiosity lives on.

"THE NEW LAUGH": ALL FUN BUT NO TEETH!

As female laughers exploded onto the public stage, a vast range of popular discourses sought to regulate their immoderate joy. In 1898, the *New York Herald* promoted something called "The New Laugh," which they described as "not so much a laugh, but a vocal ripple of merriment." Young girls today are "making altogether too much noise" with their "unsubdued gaiety," the shrieks of which could "be heard from porches and piazzas.[58] The "smart" fashionable girl should "make no noise at all" with her laughter. She "keeps her mouth closed, her lips well together," and her humor "is fun and amusement personified, but . . . all in silence." It is truly the best laugh, "all but the sound, all but the opening of the mouth and the showing of the teeth."[59] What's left of a laugh when you strip it of any physical or audible basis in the body—teeth, tongue, larynx, lungs, diaphragm, belly, zygomaticus major, and so forth?

Other advice columnists encouraged women to master their "management of the mouth" by practicing their laughter in front of a mirror.[60] For example, if you have a small mouth and "even, pretty teeth," you should stretch your lips and keep your teeth slightly shut; if you have a large mouth, you should laugh under your lip, with teeth closed; but if you have protruding gums, "always open your mouth in laughing and keep your teeth well apart." With rigorous training and diligent practice, any woman can "not only laugh sweetly, but she [can] look pretty when she does it."[61] Or else, warned the sadistic etiquette guru, Loretta, you are no better than "the female for howl," whose "cachinnation . . . is a shock to the system of a human being with normally developed sense of hearing."[62]

Loretta had many harsh words for the "Girl Who Howls"—along with "The Girl Who Giggles," "The Girl Who Squeals," "The Girl Who Contradicts," "The Girl Who Orders More Than She Can Eat," "The Girl Who Is a Toady" (who sucks up to rich women), "The Girl Who Conducts a Left-Handed Courtship" (who befriends the sister to get to the brother), "The Intellectual Girl," "The Girl Who Chatters," and, of course, "The Girl Who Reflects the Failings of Humanity."[63] At the giggler, Loretta raved: "Girl, you giggle! Look at your face contorted with the meaningless muscular contractions and expansions that accompany your chorus of cachinnations."[64] Loretta further impugns the giggler as an "imbecile," "the storm-center of silliness," a "carnival of spasmodic vocalization," a "nerve-wracking, patience-killing fiend," and "one of the worst pests into which a human being can degenerate," with the final caution: "you will stifle that giggle if it takes you to the point of strangulation."[65]

Indeed, "expanded giggles may prove fatal," advised the *Tampa Morning Tribune* after a Florida woman expired from a bad case of merriment.[66] The anxious modulation of laughter parroted campaigns for public noise control, dictating that women's laughs be "soft," "sympathetic," and "merry" but never "disagreeable," "rasping," or "ironical."[67] For example, observed one etiquette columnist, "Miss Z—" has the "most exasperating cachinnation" because she is constantly interrupting herself midsentence with a grating rattle that "puts a caustic construction upon her remark."[68] Did you know that "every woman unconsciously betrays her character every time she laughs, and that she laughs in one of the vowel sounds?"[69] According to an unnamed but highly respected French specialist of the throat, voice, and eyes, "to study your sweetheart's cachinnation is to probe the recesses of her mind."[70] The difference in vowel or pitch had decisive import.

The woman who laughs in the vowel "A," for instance, "who emits a hearty 'ha-ha' is frank, loyal." But she who laughs in "E" (he-he) is "phlegmatic . . . even melancholic," and only "the timid, the irresolute, the naïve and pliable laugh in 'I'" (hi-hi), which is reserved for "children and foolish young women."[71] Because "the smile and laugh is the very window of your soul" [sic], she who laughs in "O" (ho-ho) betrays "boldness and brutality": "Never a villain in a melodrama but who mocked his victim with a 'ho-ho!' "[72] Similarly, "those who laugh in 'U' [hu-hu] are misanthropes, and the hateful noise they utter when they grin should warn their fellow creatures against them." The specialist whose research provided the basis for this study had not yet catalogued the character of the persons who laugh in 'Y' [hy-hy], but we can leave their conclusions to our imagination.

The Perils of Dentistry

Anxieties about teeth loomed large in these etiquette discourses, which debated the question of how much was "too much" (like ankles or shoulders).[73] There were, of course, other concerns than decorum at play. Oral hygiene in the late nineteenth century, like today, signified class status—good teeth meant you had enough money to visit the dentist. It was implied that the "new laugher" could very well afford to see an excellent dentist, but still she covered her teeth—except of course *at* the dentist, where women were routinely given nitrous oxide (aka laughing gas) to ease their discomfort. Jane Truman was high as a kite when she almost laughed herself to death during a tooth extraction in 1910.[74] Mrs. Abelarde McGinnis burst into a fit of laughter that "dislodged a dental bridge which dropped into her throat and choked her to death."[75] From cachinnation to suffocation, the hazards of choking provided a physiological basis for pathologizing the toothy laughter of women.

It was not a tooth but another indigestible object that asphyxiated Wilma Wade. "If there is any lesson to be drawn from [her] experience, it would seem to be that laughter is dangerous."[76] Wade had been enjoying a "hearty outburst" when she accidentally inhaled a safety pin, which had to be removed surgically from her bronchial tubes. "If Miss Wade had been taught not to laugh, but only to smile," a *Morning Oregonian* columnist scolded, "she never would have found herself in this perilous dilemma."[77] There is no mention of how a safety pin managed to penetrate Wilma's bronchial tubes during her outburst, but the author is very decisive that "preceptresses of young ladies' schools" agree "laughter is vulgar . . . unlady-like . . . [and] cruel."[78] (And don't forget, added Eloise Beaumont: "A grin is always disgusting."[79])

In a nonfatal incident in 1907, a woman named Barbara Barr allegedly laughed nonstop for eight hours at a corny joke about dentistry. Here it goes:[80]

> A man went to the dentist to have a tooth pulled. It was pulled and it hurt.
> "Oh doctor," said the patient, "What a blessing it would be to be born without teeth."
> "But my dear man," said the dentist, "we are you know."

At this, Barr laughed uncontrollably for eight hours. "Her laughter could be heard for a square," according to the *Times-Picayune*. "All kinds of things were tried to end her cachinnations, but it took two doctors 8 hours to stop them ... They threw water in her face, put keys down her back, endeavored to make her angry by insults—but still she laughed."[81] Eventually she had to be anesthetized. She awoke the next morning with no memory whatsoever of the joke (and, fortunately, no one repeated it).

Did she really forget the joke, which makes memory itself into a punch line? Barr continued to recite the setup (if only humans were "born without teeth"), pulling back from the brink of the frame-breaking wisecrack: "We are you know"! Her incompletion of the joke sustained the unending duration of her laughter. But Barr's deferral of its punch line (that we are indeed born without teeth) bears further interpretation. Sigmund Freud notoriously associated anxiety about losing teeth with a fear of castration and dread of sexual difference. It all goes back to the scene of genital revelation, according to Freud, when the little girl's discovery of the little boy's penis poses a "wound to her narcissism" and causes her to develop, "like a scar, a sense of inferiority."[82] Of course, it was Freud's own anxiety dream about women's teeth that pushed psychoanalysis from its foundations in female hysteria to the hermeneutics of dream interpretation. "Irma's Injection," Freud's enigmatic dream in 1895, involved a "recalcitrant" patient who keeps her mouth closed (like the "new laugher") as Freud is attempting to investigate inside her throat, which specifically reminds him of "women with artificial dentures."[83] After Irma finally relents, Freud finds inside her throat "a big white patch" and "extensive whitish grey scabs ... evidently modeled on the turbinal bones of the nose."[84] His nasal analogy later provoked his friend Max Schur to identify "Irma" as Emma Eckstein, a brilliant woman and Freud's former patient whose botched nasal surgery at the behest of Wilhelm Fliess had utterly traumatized Freud just two months earlier.[85] (Fliess's operation almost killed Eckstein and left her permanently disfigured.)

If only humans were born without noses! To that point, what does it mean to laugh excessively at a joke whose form is left in ruins? "Some jokes are tears in the fabric of our beliefs," writes Rebecca Krefting, because they "challenge the myths we sustain . . . and the behaviors and practices we enact to maintain that fiction."[86] Krefting emphasizes the politics of "charged humor" that fosters new spaces and networks for enacting cultural citizenship by way of feminist and antiracist laughter. Charged jokes "punch up" against oppressive power and spark communal sensations of belonging through intentional humor. Barr's dental avoidance (let alone Freud's nasal hysteria) would hardly seem to fit Krefting's criteria. But jokes can tear holes in the social fabric independent of their content by exposing what Alenka Zupančič calls (in her book on jokes) "the leak in human finitude," which spills out from the gag to create a ripple in the forcefield of the symbolic.[87] Whether a "whitish grey scab" or a latent baby tooth, the object of humor rarely means what it says it does, slipping from one signifier to another along the merry tidal wave of laughter.

Of course, by "leak *in* human finitude," Zupančič does not simply mean the leak *of* human finitude (such as anxiety about death or fear of mortality) but the absurd excess produced by its necessary incomprehensibility. "The stuff that comedies are made of is precisely this hole in finitude," claims Zupančič, whose examples of "failed finitude" range from Christian Incarnation to liberal representative democracy (or instances when "the universal itself is precisely as idiotic as its concrete and individual appearance").[88] Evangelist preachers and elected politicians variously leap to mind. The universality of being born "without teeth" further exemplifies "failed finitude" as it turns on what Zupančič calls comedy's "materialism of the spirit," whereby lofty ideals and philosophical abstractions muddy themselves in comedic filth. Indeed, the gag of toothless natality finds apt expression in Barr's butchering of the joke (which she hacks to bits), thus fomenting the furies of her unstoppable laughter.

Barr's sweetheart reportedly fled the scene in mortal anger after she'd had at it for over ten minutes. (He assumed she was mocking *him*.) As the etiquette expert Florence Hartley warned her disciples, "She laughs at the foibles, supposed or real, of her admirer: she plays a dangerous game."[89] Or as Margaret Atwood has famously put it, "Men are afraid that women will laugh at them. Women are afraid that men will kill them."[90] Bad teeth make for leaky jokes because teeth portend decay: they turn yellow and brown, form cavities from bacteria (that constantly need to be filled and refilled), and eventually rot out of your head. So Barr repeated, "I wish we were born without teeth"—as if the antecedence of birth could override all the decrepitude that proceeds from it. What's the latency of a corny wisecrack to the recurrence of an unresolvable longing? (Punch line: teeth will come soon enough, so laugh your head off, Barbara!)

OF JOUISSANCE AND TOOTHED VAGINAS

Humans may be born without teeth, but vaginas are not always so lucky. Myths of the vagina with teeth "are extremely prevalent particularly in the East, India, North America, South America, Africa, and Europe" (i.e., pretty much everywhere), notes Barbara Creed in *The Monstrous-Feminine*.[91] Antiphallic symbol par excellence, the vagina dentata wards off the evil eye of male sexual predators. In his seminar on sexual subjectivity (Seminar XVII), Jacques Lacan compares Queen Victoria to "a toothed vagina of such exceptional size."[92] Against such gynophobic malaise, Hélène Cixous embraces the toothed vagina, aligning it with the jouissance of endless female laughter in "Castration or Decapitation?"—because those are the only two options. Cixous revisits the Chinese legend of General Sun Tse, who attempted to command his 180 wives in the art of war. Defiantly, the wives started laughing, so Sun Tse decapitated two of them to set an example. "Women have no choice other than to be decapitated," argues Cixous, "and in any case, the moral is that if they don't actually lose their heads by sword, *they only keep them on condition that they lose them*—lose them, that is, to complete silence, turned into automatons."[93] As the suffragette Mary Livermore put it, "we treat the boys as though God knew how to make them, but the girls as though He were a bungler . . . tortur[ing] their heads" with constant crimping and curling.[94]

Zupančič would laugh at Livermore's joke because it points to the hole in patriarchy's finitude (maligning God by enshrining the physical inferiority of women), while Anca Parvulescu circles back to the "gaping mouths" of Ancient Greek mythology. "The Goddess of Mirth" Baubo sang obscene songs and once roused Demeter from her depression by flashing her exposed vulva. Baubo "uncovers her secret parts and exhibits them to the goddess. Demeter is pleased at the sight . . . delighted by the spectacle!"[95] Parvulescu further invokes Luce Irigaray's metaphor of the "two lips in continuous contact," which signify the fluidity and plurality of female sexuality, reminding us that "laughter is of the mouth, and the female body does not have only one mouth."[96] (To that point, neither do male or gender-nonconforming bodies.) In feminist theories of sexuality and difference, the toothed vagina is a mythological vestige of the desire to enjoy oneself deliciously in extremis. "The New York man who related a funny story at which a woman of eighty-four laughed herself to death [in 1903] will never dare to be so funny again."[97] In other words, death from laughter had teeth.

On the question of gender and excess enjoyment, however, there is surely no text more foundational or evocative than "The Laugh of the Medusa" (1975).

62 DEATH BY LAUGHTER

FIGURE 2.3 "Baubo." Statuette of female vulva from Priene, Asia Minor, fourth century BC. Image courtesy of Wikimedia Commons.

Cixous turns not to Baubo but to Medusa: the abject, snake-haired Gorgon of ancient Greek myth whose horrifying looks could petrify men to stone. (In Ovid's version, Medusa had been raped by Poseidon in Athena's temple, who then punished her with those horrifying, serpentine tresses.[98]) Cixous proclaims: "You only have to look at the Medusa straight on to see her. And she's not deadly. She's beautiful and she's laughing."[99] An urtext for a feminist counterpolitics of antipatriarchal enjoyment, Medusa's "writing," according to Cixous, "threatens to smash everything, to shatter the framework of institutions, to blow up the law, to break up and shatter the 'truth' with laughter."[100] As Todd McGowan has it in *Enjoying What We Don't Have*, nothing produces greater anxiety for the desiring subject than enduring "the other's 'excessive and intrusive *jouissance*.'" When we do so, therefore, "we acknowledge the other in its real dimension."[101] In contrast to recognition, which "is an infinite struggle," notes McGowan, the obscenity of excess enjoyment suffices entirely.[102] Laughing Medusa exemplifies authentic jouissance because she quite literally did not need to be seen (her recognition was fatal to all lookers), and so she laughs without end: "without ever reaching an end," as Cixous celebrates her indulgence.

Defined as "an excess of life" or "enjoyment beyond the pleasure principle," jouissance marks the point at which euphoric sensation becomes disarticulated from desire, which feasts on perpetual lack, the hole in finitude, being born without teeth, and so forth. (Lacan distinguished between "phallic jouissance," which is a mere compensation for lack, and "feminine jouissance," which is entirely "of the body" and "beyond the phallus."[103]) It is a highly debated concept in psychoanalysis, positing an enjoyment that can only exist for its own sake, but that in doing so dangerously overspills the threshold for easy, lack-filling pleasure. Cixous proclaims: "Laughs exude from all our mouths; our blood flows and we extend ourselves without ever reaching an end; we never hold back our thoughts, our signs, our writing; and we're not afraid of lacking."[104] An affective vortex for *écriture féminine* ("writing women"), Medusan enjoyment wrests writing from the stranglehold of the symbolic and liberates it into the body (somewhat like hysteria, as we will explore in chapter 4).

In contrast to jouissance, jokes exploit the inevitability of lack—they're not necessarily filling a hole (which is the task of anxious enjoyment) so much as they are revealing its unseen borders and then permitting the anxious subject to enjoy briefly in spite of that knowledge. For example, *there are two types of people in the world: those who divide the people in the world into two types, and those who don't.* A logical contradiction is the wheelhouse of witty jokes. Many jokesters make a gimmick of excess enjoyment, claiming to "kill," "slay," "slaughter," and so forth, with deadly material. But authentic jouissance enjoys in the shadows—not in the limelight. That is why the historical experience of death by laughter (the topic of this chapter) will always elude and exceed its (sketchy) archival remainders: the ludicrous obituary records. Jouissance lingers in the void, not in "the tight five": the stand-up comic's unfailing joke set.

Our archive's mayhem of obituary misattribution leaves the door open to retroactive jouissance. In 1911, the *Charlotte Daily Observer* reported that "*The Washington Post* says that a New York woman laughed herself to death at a joke and 'evidently subscribed to a paper we don't get.' It is certain that she did not subscribe to *The Post*."[105] In other words, the *Post* makes only unfunny jokes. Three months earlier, a daily newspaper in Tampa claimed that a woman in Kentucky "laughed herself to death at one of her husband's jokes," adding that "doubtless some Tampa husbands wish their wives would develop such a sense of humor."[106] To riff on Margaret Atwood, it is the ultimate patriarchal wish fulfillment to combine comic gatekeeping with unaccountable femicide: two birds, one stone. Indeed, one wonders why Daniel F. Shimp decided to rouse his sickly wife at midnight to tell her a very funny story, but the amusing anecdote "proved too much for her weakened heart. She was laughing as she died."[107] The humorist Helen Rowland remarked wryly in 1922: "A man will forgive his wife for committing robbery, or murder, or breaking the Ten Commandments, yet threaten to leave her for laughing at the wrong moment."[108] Shimp made her exit by laughing at the right one.

Violet Adams fell out of a window in stitches at a friend's description of a funny scene in a play, and Helen Priest died of laughter in her home while discussing the unfortunate millinery choices of one of her schoolmates.[109] Polly Ann Jackson "became so hysterical as to cause her death in a few minutes . . . while listening to a story about a 300-pound woman" at an ice skating rink whose "frequent falls were a serious menace to the building."[110] The glib inclusion of silly triggers (pratfalls, hat fails, dentistry gags, unprintable jokes) was clearly meant to skewer and lambaste a deceased woman's motivation for excess enjoyment. (The only thing worse than telling a joke that falls flat on its face is laughing hysterically at one everyone else agrees is a dud.) But the derisive reader of fatal-female-cachinnation obituaries laughed just a little too loudly. He may not have died from it, but he probably would have enjoyed himself more if he had. Nothing causes the defensively joking subject greater anxiety than encountering the other's enjoyment for its own sake—without lack, in the face of unbelievably bad jokes, and rapturously spreading through the whole body.

Capitalist mass culture had untethered women's "hysterical laughter" from the corset of pervasive sentimentality, giving rise to a new means and a new language for female enjoyment. How far would it go? Polly Ann Jackson had reportedly "not laughed so heartily in months as at the [ice skating] story told her which caused her death" on the spot.[111] Obituary mockery tried to place a guardrail around the third rail of female jouissance.

FIGURE 2.4 "The Joyous Smile of Friendly Recognition." Illustration in George Vasey's *The Philosophy of Laughter and Smiling* (1875). Image courtesy of The Library of Congress.

SOCIAL DEATH BY LAUGHTER: MINSTRELSY, SUGAR, JOYLESSNESS

In most of these death from laughter obituaries, whiteness is implied. Unless otherwise noted, it was primarily white women who gave up the ghost to their surfeit of mirth. In contrast, Lucy High, a Black female care worker, was consumed by excess grief and "gradually faded until death" after the white children she had nursed from their infancy each moved away to a big city in 1905.[112] Death from a "broken heart" (sadness, pathos, mourning, unbearable loss) especially afflicted poor women and people of color whose social status and existential purpose depended disproportionately on their reproductive intimacy with white families.

The depth and exasperation of what Bambi Haggins calls "laughter of emotional survival" did not register in these zany records of affective implosion (at circus gags and tooth jokes).[113] Raucous excess in the face of harrowing trauma has long been a motif of Black radical joy, whose convulsive tremors open onto the semiotic impossibility from which they derive.[114] Glenda Carpio compares such laughter to the sound of ululation (funeral peals) in *Laughing Fit to Kill*, invoking Samuel Beckett's example of the *risus purus* ("the laugh laughing at the laugh . . . in a word the laugh that laughs—silence, please!—at that which is unhappy") in her analysis of Suzan-Lori Parks's 1990 play, *The Death of the Last Black Man in the Whole Entire World*.[115] Its text hums with "the bitter, the hollow, the mirthless laugh against the complete betrayal of justice that the slave trade represented," writes Carpio. *Death*'s figures "howl at the consequences of racism . . . their expressions are true ululation: loud, mournful, protracted, and rhythmical expressions of grief."[116] But there was no trace of grief detected in Margaret Leathers's last laugh when she "laughed so heartily at a local performance" in 1909 "that she became unconscious and died before she could be taken from the place."[117] In a rare exception to the rule of whiteness in these obituaries, Leathers was marked as a "negress" whose "violent enjoyment" could then be exploited by the producer's exhortation: "Book that show at which a New Orleans woman laughed herself to death!"[118] In a similar vein, two comical Black performers Conroy and Pearl refused any disclaimer: "this team *will* be responsible . . . if more than one death from laughter occurs at the Empire Theatre next week," boasted the *Morning Oregonian* in 1903.[119]

Beyond the ad gimmick but short of the mirthless howl, Black laughter in extremis has a profound existential texture that both converges on death and grasps at affective survival. Danielle Fuentes Morgan calls it "laughing to keep from dying" (against Black social death and disproportionate rates of fatality), which she associates with fugitive humor whose threatening meanings take cover in plain sight. "When those jokes are [made] effectively, it's revolutionary and *they can give you life*; when there's a misfire, the results are potentially disastrous," Morgan remarks.[120] As we know, these obituaries did not exactly entertain the comical nuances of cosmic absurdity that might yet set a body on edge to laughing for dear life.

They implored: what was the joke . . . that so tickled Mrs. Charles Mohr, the woman who "laughed six hours, death coming this morning" at the soggy wit of her bereaved spouse? Mohr went "'to more violent extremes to flatter a man than any woman we ever heard of,' thinks the Duluth Herald," reported the *Augusta Chronicle* in 1914.[121] Black women were not eulogized for excess laughter at ordinary humor because then where would white female jouissance find relief (short of cachinnating suicide) from the rigors of its racial superiority, let alone its multifarious corsetry? For example, women-only minstrel shows invited ladies to "forget delicate face powders and fine dresses" and "use burnt cork, from an inch to three inches deep, and tog out in outlandish minstrel costumes."[122] In 1911, the Young Women's Christian Association of Trenton, New Jersey, revamped its annual minstrelsy extravaganza "with every effort to make this one a scream, where the preceding one was a shriek."[123] Even Loretta would call a moratorium on her embargo against "the female howler"—blackface gave the lie to the etiquette guru's laryngitic complaint. It provided white women safe haven for ecstatic catharsis without fear of ghoulish escalation.

The pageantry of white excess enjoyment, as many scholars have established, holds pride of place in the exploitative history of American blackface theater—comical variety shows, usually performed by white actors in burnt cork or shoe polish, that stereotyped Black Americans as zany, buffoonish, lazy, hypersexual, superstitious, and happy-go-lucky. Blackface became formative to the explosion of U.S. popular culture (as one of its earliest pastimes), indelibly shaping the conventions of musical variety shows, stage burlesque, and comic cartoons that provided essential material for theater, film, radio, and television. Unrestrained cachinnation flowed freely among stock characters: Zip Coon, Sambo, Mammy, Sapphire, Jezebel, Uncle Tom, and Mandingo. According to minstrelsy historian Eric Lott, these disturbing caricatures reveal "how precariously nineteenth century white people lived in their own whiteness."[124] They at once dehumanized Blackness and epitomized the burning fantasy of total escape into the body of the racial other.

Archiving Joylessness: "Sober Sue" Versus "Maggie Jolly"

Lauren Berlant suggests that the opposite of jouissance is not gloom or heartache or even depression but humorlessness: a neoliberal symptom of the constant imperative to enjoy oneself and be funny all the time. The humorless subject withholds their enjoyment as a gambit for affective power: the sober judge in a barrister wig, the predatory internet troll hijacking a lesbian vulva meme, or self-proclaimed feminist killjoys who refuse to be pleasant in accordance with the script of white supremacist heteropatriarchy. Reserving humor does not pose any real threat to the inescapable excess of toothless comedy (a hallmark of "cruel optimism"), Berlant argues, but it does exemplify a symptom of it. To be humorless is to hoard comicality and thus weaponize its communal appeals in a zero-sum game of feckless individualism versus collective solidarity. The humorless subject is the one who gets to decide what is funny—when to laugh, how loudly, and toward what conceivable ends. Humorlessness has no time for "laughing to keep from dying" and it lacks the infinite absurdity of Beckett's *risus purus* (howling at that which is unhappy).

Of all the figures we've discussed, the most humorless (in Berlant's sense), would definitively be our dear friend Loretta: the sadistic etiquette columnist who was equally appalled by "the female for howl" as she was by "The Wife Who Is a Kill-Joy." Loretta fittingly opens her antikilljoy column with a sexist joke:[125]

> A burglar was going through a man's trousers.
> The man's wife called her husband: "Wake up: there's a thief going through your pockets!"
> The man turned over and answered, "You two fight it out!" Then went to sleep.

In other words, the wife is no better than the thief who goes rummaging through her husband's trouser pockets for loose change. (Unlike the wife, the burglar would not spend that money on groceries to cook the husband his dinner—or then wash the dishes, scrub the floor, put the kids to bed, and on and on.) While Mrs. Daniel F. Shimp, Annie Maher, and Mary Bofano allegedly laughed themselves to death at their spouses' unspecified gags, "the killjoy wife" neglects to do anything of the sort. "Your husband is telling this joke and enjoying it," Loretta reprimands, but you observe "'I read that in the paper' . . . as if that killed the humor of the story. Your remark certainly kills your husband's enjoyment of it anyway."[126] To the wife who is a killjoy, Loretta humorlessly commands: you will laugh at that joke even if it kills you! *Better you die than kill my enjoyment.*

Black laughter in the United States has always walked a razor-thin line between coercive solicitation and fatal suppression. "Laughing to keep from dying" consists of barely surviving on the fumes of renegade joy. It bursts out from the recognition that systemic, inhuman evil repeatedly takes the guise of outlandish, foolish nonsense. In the face of "quotidian absurdity," as Rebecca Wanzo puts it, taboo joy protects the possibility of hope and "celebration despite the recurrence of trauma."[127] Unlike humorlessness, which holds all the cards, risky laughter wrests precious life from the death trap of joylessness.

If the humorless subject cynically leverages their alienation in a bid for supremacy, joylessness signifies abyssal disaffection stripped of any subjective entitlement. This distinction between humorless will-to-power and joyless subjugation has been thoroughly racialized by the relations of consumer capital. For example, in 1907, Hammerstein's Roof Garden headlined a "freak" performer named "Sober Sue": "a highly colored person of an ebony shade" who "will defy the populace to make her laugh during intermission . . . She was guaranteed to sigh at a vaudeville show . . . while circus clowns lull her to sleep."[128] According to *Variety*, William Hammerstein offered a $500 reward to any entertainer who could "cause Sue to break her rule," as "all the humorists from the Hotel Metropole have 'tried out' on the negress without success."[129] I repeat: Sue was not humorless but joyless, an affective affliction rooted in her biographical trauma, which *Variety* editorialized: "While [her] mother was working, the 'pick' was hangin' round the tub, and the future appeared so dreary to the young one that she lost all interest in material things."[130] Despite Sue's rainmaking popularity, "proven a good advertiser for the Roof," Hammerstein insisted on keeping her salary at $15 per week "to prevent the sober one from becoming inflated with importance."[131] Hammerstein's profit margin thus depended on Sue's wage deflation and was further increased by it: should Sue feel less miserable, she might then become remotely joyful, which would kill the spectacle. (Also, it saves the boss money to stiff his workers.)

While volatile forms of female fun played hide-and-seek with the racist tropes of minstrelsy, Black laughter (and its negation) were mined as sources of fungible capital. From the zany vaudeville stage to the humorless bail bondsman, a Black woman in Macon, Georgia, was nearly beaten to death in 1917 for "being too jolly." She was then arrested for "disorderly conduct" and sentenced to twenty days or $25 by a judge who warned her to "restrain her joy and not get any jollier."[132] (Of all things, her name was Maggie Jolly.) She told the judge that she "was only having the usual jolly time," appealing to racist expectations of compulsory joviality.[133] Maggie Jolly paid for her joy, unlike Sober Sue, who was underpaid for her joylessness.

Black Mask, White Sugar

Other than Margaret Leathers (the fatal cachinnator in a New Orleans theater), I have found only one instance of a Black woman whose death was attributed to excess joyful laughter. In 1878, a woman in Rhode Island named Rosa Walker was doing housework. Like Ernestina Nehring, who died laughing at her young son's naïve "eggplant" pun while baking rhubarb pies, Walker's risibility was aroused by an unexpected culinary accident.[134] Her husband Joshua had mistakenly salted the pork meat with granulated sugar. The following details have a familiar cadence: "She laughed, and laughed, and laughed, her merriment getting more boisterous each moment. Finally the husband became alarmed . . . witnessing in a few minutes the poor woman's departure . . . She had positively laughed herself to death."[135]

Walker's obituary noted the couple's middle-class status. Joshua Walker was described as "a respectable colored man" who had recently married Rosa, "a young woman of excellent character, and who was not quite twenty years of age."[136] Although one paper mocked her as "too funny to live," most accounts repeated the closing line from the *Providence Journal*: "The husband's horror at this extraordinary result of his innocent mistake can be better imagined than described."[137] Her risible death was thus wrapped in pathos, an "impressible" horizon for cross-racial humanism that swapped out political struggle for universal sentimentality.[138]

It is worth lingering on the guilty joke itself. Walker's trigger was not a bad dentistry pun but an accidental substitution gag about sugar masquerading as salt. A lucrative cash crop, sugar was instrumental to the rise of the African slave trade; more than half of the Africans who were trafficked across the Middle Passage landed on sugar plantations in the Caribbean or the southern United States, where life was absolute hell. For "every pound of sugar," remarked the Quaker abolitionist William Fox, "we may be considered as consuming two ounces of human flesh."[139] Sugar production was the most brutal form of slave labor, with extremely high rates of mortality. It required workers to toil in coffles to reap the tall, fibrous plants or to huddle confined inside "boiling houses" where the cane juices were then converted into raw sugar. (The Thirteenth Amendment, which abolished slavery, had been ratified in 1865, only thirteen years before Rosa "set to laughing.")

The genocidal history of sugar has a vivid metaphorical resonance in Black vernacular culture, from folk slave songs to Ava Duvernay's television series *Queen Sugar* and Kara Walker's installation art in a Domino Sugar factory.[140] It further reverberates in Maya Angelou's spoken-word poem, "The Mask," adapted from Paul Laurence Dunbar's "We Wear the Mask." Both Dunbar and Angelou open with the same lines: "We wear the mask that grins and lies. It shades our cheeks and hides our eyes ... With torn and bleeding hearts, we smile and mouth with myriad subtleties."[141] From Dunbar's collective "we," Angelou switches voices, signifying "our" tortured smile with "my" choking laugh: "When I think about myself, I almost laugh myself to death. I laugh so hard HA! HA! I almost choke, When I think about myself."[142]

"Sugar" echoes through the poem as both a cloying epithet for Black woman and a specter of slavery and social death. "They say, but sugar, it was our submission that made your world go round," repeats Angelou. By the second "sugar," her poetic allusion to savage violence ("withered flank" and "flesh ... gnarled like broken candles") is displaced by direct images of "the auction block, The chains and slavery's coffles, The whip and lash and stock." Playing on the duality of "the mask" as a cover for pain and a signal of forced joviality, "sugar" twice punctuates the self-serving "white" lie that slavery was not an inhuman evil but a capitalist economic necessity—as if the two were divisible. Chattel slavery founded an "economy of enjoyment" at the "convergence of violence and pleasure," as Saidiya Hartman elaborates in "The Formations of Terror and Enjoyment," policing the "affect, gesture, and ... vulnerability to violence [that] constituted blackness."[143] Renegade Black joy rebounded between the kiss of social death and the promise of surplus enjoyment.

Angelou closes with the lines: "From living on the edge of death, They kept my race alive, By wearing the mask! Ha! Ha! Ha! Ha! Ha!"[144] Her final laughter is double-voiced and densely layered. Could these have been her last laughs, after protesting: "I almost laugh myself to death," "I almost choke" and "split my side"? Or do they revive her ancestors who "wrote the blues in screams" and whose meaning she comes to understand "derive[s] from living on the edge of death." The poem is essentially about the proximity between enjoyment and terror, or affective survival and dehumanizing enslavement. A token of "submission" and a tenor of defiance, "sugar" playfully signifies the dangerous double entendre that lives in Black laughter, from "laughing to keep from dying" to the bittersweet taste of a white condiment that one might accidentally mistake for salt brine.

DEATH TO JOY!

If life-preserving, near death from laughter did not sustain them, women living on the edge of joylessness might have perished from less promising feelings. Mrs. Bailey Johnson of Augusta, Georgia, was "literally frightened to death" after a "voo-doo doctor" visited her home and informed her that her head was "filled with lizards," according to the *Dallas Morning News*.[145] In 1890, Mrs. Pope expired from anxiety, precipitated by "emotional hydrophobia," after she had been bitten by a rabid dog. Her body started mimicking symptoms of rabies and "weakness took mastery of her nerve."[146] Myrtle Stanley "became a maniac" in paranoia that her estranged father would kidnap her, and she died in anticipation of this "imaginary attack."[147] Mary Hendrickson, a high school student in Brooklyn, was petrified by a bad dream: she "uttered a piercing shriek . . . an expression of terror disfigured her face . . . Then she ceased to breathe—she was dead."[148] Fear "sometimes kills perfectly healthy people," claimed the *New York World*, "by arresting their action of the heart . . . [any] powerfully depressing emotion . . . such as great and sudden sorrow, could cause death in the same manner."[149] In some cases, "post-mortem examinations have found the heart actually broken," so pressured by "agony of mind" as "to cause its rupture," reported *The World*.[150]

Ida Bolley's cardiac arrest in 1897 gave "some jolly people uneasiness," but readers were reassured that "anger is the more dangerous form, tension of blood vessels being greatly increased by it."[151] In all my archival rag-picking, however, I have found only one case of a woman whose death was allegedly brought on by *anger*. In 1858, a widow in Pennsylvania became so "exasperated" with a cow that she ruptured an internal blood vessel and bled to death, succumbing to "the insanity of her passion" after the cow had broken into her garden "for the forty-seventh time."[152] Narrated in a familiar tone of glib mockery, the exceptional status of this obituary makes one wonder why exactly there weren't others like it. (There were plenty of deaths from anger involving men who killed each other—along with their wives and children—in fits of hot temper and jealous rage, often under the influence of liquor.) "Doctors say," warned Loretta, "there is an actual poisonous element, a real chemical constituent, which anger introduces into the blood. And the constant presence of such a malignant poison must wreck and ruin any constitution. You won't have ANY health left," she raved in her column on "THE MAN HATER."[153] But her suspicion of feminine anger left no trace in the hyperbolic obituary columns.

EPITAPH: DEATH BY LAUGHTER POSTMORTEM

Why did these reports of women's death by laughter escalate around 1870 and then abruptly desist half-a-century later—vanishing from historical memory (with only sketchy remainders)? By 1920, women in the United States had gained the right to vote; massively increased their presence in the professional workforce; and infiltrated the public sphere as pleasure-seeking patrons at moving pictures, amusement parks, variety shows, and other leisure-based, consumerist venues. War was the other tipping point: after the United States declared war on Germany on April 6, 1917, there were hardly any more reports of women dying from laughter.

Perhaps such obituaries would have appeared unpatriotic, when fatalities numbered in the tens of thousands, France and Germany had weaponized "laughing gas" on the battlefields, and anything less than upbeat morale was potentially treasonous under the Espionage Act.[154] Meanwhile, over twenty thousand women enlisted as army nurses and navy staff, and the mass deployment of male workers to war overseas irreversibly altered the sexual division of labor on the home front. Or perhaps the sudden cessation of deaths by laughter was also due to the U.S. War Industries Board's proclamation in 1917 that women must stop buying corsets to free up metal for military production (the suffocating corset went out of fashion soon after the armistice).[155]

The Jazz Age's footloose appeals and fancy-free zeitgeist further defanged the hazards of excess cachinnation—save as an off-color joke now and again. One Midwestern humorist quipped that Virginia Rappe "must have laughed herself to death," referring to the actress/model whose tragic death was notoriously triggered by an incident at a Hollywood party in the comedian Roscoe "Fatty" Arbuckle's hotel suite in 1921.[156] (Rappe actually died of peritonitis and a ruptured bladder, but Arbuckle was accused of her murder and stood trial for sexual assault and manslaughter.[157]) In other words, Rappe "must have laughed herself to death" because her alleged killer was a famous, laugh-making comedian.

By the 1930s, however, the specter of female death by laughter reared its ugly head and upped its body count, fomented by moral backlash against sinful enjoyment amid the tunneling economic crises of the Great Depression. In 1931, Ida Guzzle "literally laughed herself to death ... after a paroxysm of laughter during a round of merriment at a party."[158] Later that year, Mary Armisted laughed herself to death at a film comedy.[159] (The movie title was not disclosed, as one newspaper joked, because then "too many people would doubt the story," implying that the film was not very funny.[160]) Another paper wryly observed that the accident had taken place in Salem, Massachusetts: "That's where they burned witches."[161] (The *Times-Picayune* did not elaborate on the connection between these two things.)

Similar cases recurred through the 1930s and 1940s, sometimes at the movies or the theater, but also while listening to the radio, riding in an automobile, or even participating in a séance.[162] Above all, female death by laughter was a symptom of the capitalist contradiction between surplus enjoyment and moralistic repression. As such, it paved the way to the existential crises that imperil us today, as we merrily laugh ourselves to planetary extinction.

3
An All Too Brief History of Laughter and Death

What is the funniest joke in the world? According to *Monty Python*, it would certainly kill you within seconds of laughing at it. In their 1969 television skit, "The Funniest Joke in the World," the titular joke strikes down the writer who invented it, his mother, and a Scotland Yard inspector before it's weaponized by the British Army, which translates it into German one word at a time (hospitalizing an interpreter who accidentally reads two words in a row).[1] Although an unlikely method for encoding wit, the German version turns out to be even deadlier than the British one; it utterly decimates the Nazi Army (stupefied by uproarious laughter) and ultimately wins the war for the Allies. Of course, the joke's contents are never revealed in English—only parodied in a nonsensical rendition of German: "Wenn ist das Nunstück git und Slotermeyer? Ja! Beiherhund das Oder die Flipperwaldt gersput!" (If you type this phrase into Google Translate, it will respond: "[FATAL ERROR]."[2])

The meta-joke of the skit, however, is that nothing could be funnier than the premise itself. And even if such a joke did exist, it would clearly be catastrophic to air on broadcast television. The ghoulish wisecrack will have to settle for its proxy gag of watching sober men meeting their fates in the most ridiculous way (they are all men—even the mother is played by Eric Idle in drag). Abandon hope all ye who dare to incarnate its immortal punch line. Yet there's a method to *Monty Python*'s madness. The conceit of achieving transformative insight through terminal laughter has long obsessed Western philosophers: from Calchas (1100 BC) and Chrysippus (200 BC) to Pietro Aretino (1500 AD) and Ole Bentzen, the Danish audiologist who died laughing at a scene about Friedrich Nietzsche in the satirical jewel-heist film, *A Fish Called Wanda* (1988).[3]

How differently, then, would we view the history of Western culture and philosophy if women had taken center stage in the entanglement between critical thinking and deadly laughing? This brief chapter considers the vital history of death by laughter—from ancient Greece to the present day—focusing on the fascination of several modernist writers with the metaphor of laughter as death, the wager of laughing in the face of death, and the politics of laughing oneself to ego-shattering revolution in spite of death.

As we know, dozens of women allegedly died from laughing too hard during the half-century from 1870 to 1920. To name just a few: Mary Bofano, Ida Bolley, Elizabeth Courtney, Anna Ferrer, Margaret Leathers, Josie Leisslie, Ernestina Nehring, Bertha Pruett, Louise Speetzen, Mary Trelkald, and Rosa Walker were pleasantly enjoying themselves until their "merry laughter" turned suddenly into piercing "shriek[s] of pain."[4] These peculiar obituaries, as I argue in chapter 2, revealed the contradictory social politics of how female pleasure was simultaneously feared and solicited. Women were invited to let loose but terrorized not to take their Medusan excess too far.

There is a long, no less bizarre but perversely celebratory history of "death from joy" that excludes women's fatal laughter from the canons of critical thought. It was during the very years when women were giving up the ghost to "deadly cachinnation" that Friedrich Nietzsche first proposed "the gay science" (as a vindication of "the death of God").[5] Shortly thereafter, Sigmund Freud theorized laughter "beyond the pleasure principle," Georges Bataille practiced "Joy in the Face of Death," and Mikhail Bakhtin affirmed "death caused by happiness" as a hallmark of carnivalesque social renewal.[6]

I will unpack these dense references, but the crucial point is that they all seek existential redemption in the flickering insights unleashed by exorbitant laughter. Reckless joy provided a third way—an unlikely escape hatch—between nihilism and fatalism, or cowardly resignation and metaphysical blind faith. That sudden turn from playful amusement to agonizing convulsion, they exclaimed, was not tragic at all but an imperative philosophical gamble.

PREGNANT MONSTERS ARE SLAIN BY CARNIVALESQUE LAUGHTER

Women do not really get to partake in this carnival of "gay science" or "laughing philosophy."[7] (They have to hold their breath for radical jouissance or else risk being gaslit as deviant hysterics.) However, they often became the butt of the joke

FIGURE 3.1 "The Fight Between Carnival and Lent," oil painting by Pieter Bruegel the Elder (1559). Image courtesy of Wikimedia Commons.

of someone else's death by laughter. For example, Bakhtin admiringly recounts the history of "deaths from joy" compiled in François Rabelais's *Gargantua and Pantagruel* (1693–1694). In one instance, the ancient Greek artist Zeuxis died laughing "immoderately at a picture of an old woman that he himself had painted."[8] As the story goes, she had offered herself as a model for Zeuxis' portrait of Aphrodite, but the artist burst into hysterics at his own rendition of the unlikely muse. "My question is simply," as Mary Beard incisively poses it, "why would we imagine that Zeuxis would find a painting of an elderly lady so laughable? And so very laughable that it killed him?"[9]

In Bakhtin's version, there is really nothing funnier than the collision between morbid decrepitude and vital rejuvenation—when "old age is pregnant, death is gestation, all that is limited, narrowly characterized, and completed is thrust into the lower stratum of the body for recasting a new birth."[10] Joy defeats fear with laughter, rallying the people to dare to imagine a better world rather than clinging defensively to the old, failing order. Meanwhile, "death is the necessary link in the process of the people's growth and renewal. It is the 'other side' of birth."[11] The junction of feeble decline and hopeful delivery—death and birth—is precisely what allows for resistance against oppressive authority and potentially radical forms of collectivity to take root.

Bakhtin characterizes such hybrid utopianism as "carnivalesque," a genre category that he derives from the popular medieval folk festivals that European peasants celebrated for up to three months per year. During carnival "the people play with terror and laugh at it; the awesome becomes a 'comic monster.'"[12] Despite its all-empowering spirit, however, carnivalesque laughter has a malignant underbelly, as it were. Bakhtin is obsessed with parturition metaphors: "Carnival's hell represents the earth which swallows up and gives birth," he writes, "the monster, death, becomes pregnant."[13] (The old woman of Zeuxis' scornful laughter is clearly a death monster—her fatal incitement to mockery makes way for tomorrow.)

This "umbilical cord" between pregnancy and monstrosity is borne out in yet another carnivalesque scene from *Gargantua and Pantagruel*, when Gargantua's wife dies in agony while giving birth to their son Pantagruel. For a moment, Gargantua is torn: "A terrible doubt racked his brain: should he weep over the death of his wife or rejoice over the birth of his son?"[14] Such an impossible conflict between unbearable grief and miraculous life would have flung nineteenth-century women into the throes of agonizing "hysterical laughter." In contrast, it's an easy decision for Gargantua, who proclaims: "Ho, ho ho, ho, how happy I am! Let us drink, ho! And put away our melancholy!"[15] Out with the old and in with the new: Badebec dies; Pantagruel is born; Gargantua laughs.

By Bakhtin's count, there are precisely nine cases of "death caused by happiness and joy" in Rabelais's annals.[16] For example, the Stoic philosopher Chrysippus of Soli fell into "so exorbitant a fit of laughter, that the use of his spleen took his breath away utterly, and he immediately died."[17] According to Rabelais, he had observed that "a straggling well-hung ass got into the house, and seeing the figs on the table, without further invitation soberly fell to."[18] After the donkey had also helped himself to a swig of the philosopher's wine, Chrysippus was "so excessively pleased" that he followed the fate of Zeuxis, who (as we know) "killed himself with laughing at the sight of the antique jabbernowl of an old hag drawn by him."[19]

It does not appear to be Bakhtin's intention to render maternity or female aging abject—although such implications leap out of the pages of his prose. Rather, women's fluid corporeality (pregnancy, fertility, menstrual cycles) offers a convenient cipher for him to assert the cosmic interconnection among all the people. Carnivalesque bodies "could not be considered for themselves," Bakhtin argues, "they represented a material bodily whole and therefore transgressed the limits of their isolation."[20] It was only in the eighteenth century that the "bodily lower stratum of grotesque realism . . . cut off the umbilical cord which tied [it] to the fruitful womb of earth," according to Bakhtin.[21] The historical context for this antifestive partition is essential. It symptomatized the breakneck rise of an emergent capitalist economic order fueled by the primitive accumulation of raw resources that anointed the defensive individual and his law of greedy possession.[22] Laughter followed suit as common lands were enclosed and peasants stripped of their bare means of subsistence to ensure a surplus labor force. Such violent transformations were already well underway by the end of the seventeenth century. With the stone-cold rupture between feudalism and early capitalism, the "material bodily principle" celebrated by carnival was swiftly dethroned by the "biological individual" and his "bourgeois ego."[23] Carnival's collective ethos of raucous rebellion against feudalist monarchy then withered away in Bakhtin's social and materialist history of laughter.

This wicked interregnum has vivid implications for gender and reproductive labor. As Silvia Federici incisively critiques Karl Marx's version of primitive accumulation, brutal transitions from feudalism to early capitalism were staked on the altar of female monstrosity. Witches became "the embodiment of a world of female subjects that capitalism had to destroy: the heretic, the healer, the disobedient wife, the woman who dared to live alone" all fell prey to the rampages of gynocidal witch hunts.[24] Amid the fever pitch of primitive accumulation, the "pregnant hag" mutated into a demonic witch, tortured to death or driven out of her mind. No more carnival for female grotesquerie.

Feminist cultural scholars have found traction in reviving the carnivalesque—but not without reservation. "There are especial dangers for women and other excluded or marginalized groups within carnival," Mary Russo warns, stemming from the "ambivalent redeployment of taboos around the female body as grotesque (the pregnant body, the aging body, the irregular body), and as unruly when set loose in the public sphere."[25] She further notes that "much of the early work on carnival in anthropology and social history dates from the late sixties, [as] enactments of popular protest, counterculture, experimental theater, and multimedia art were all together suggestive of the energies and possibilities of unlimited cultural and social transformation."[26] But when visibility alone (of antinormative or unruly bodies) has to carry the mantle of political liberation, it is a slippery slope from transgressing taboos to merely exploiting them.

What kind of power do women enjoy within the life world of carnival, given the historicity of how their bodies have been made expendable for birth—whether to a child, to the spark of terminal laughter, or to a revolutionary new social order? These are the roles to which pregnant Badebec and Zeuxis' aging model were consigned. Meanwhile, female laughers at large were cast out from the stag chorus, unable to partake in the "life-giving womb of laughter" enjoyed by Zeuxis, Chrissipus, Janotus de Bragmardo, Ponocrates, Eudemon, Crassus, Chilon, Widenostrils, and their ecstatic fellow travelers.[27]

LAUGHTER'S SATANIC TURN

In Bakhtin's timeline, it was around the end of the eighteenth century that grotesque laughter became truly "satanic." As Charles Baudelaire famously put it in 1855, "Laughter is satanic," because "it is at once a token of infinite grandeur and an infinite misery."[28] Under the influence of Romanticism, according to Bakhtin, that "gay, liberating and regenerating element of laughter, which is precisely the creative element," vanished, and in its place, the comic-grotesque "acquire[d] traits of mockery and cynicism."[29] For example, we might think of the Kentucky woman who laughed "herself to death at one of her husband's jokes" in 1911. "Doubtless some Tampa husbands wish their wives would develop such a sense of humor," taunted the *Tampa Morning Tribune*, serving up her festive tragedy as an occasion for cynical ridicule.[30]

Whether carnivalesque "death from joy" accomplished the utopian, liberating work that Bakhtin says it did—and at whose expense—remains up for debate. It is apparent, however, that laughter's satanic turn colluded with the femicidal witch hunts ravaging Europe and North America from the mid-fifteenth to eighteenth centuries—and during which women were executed, among other things, on evidence of their infernal laughter.[31] Like *Monty Python*'s funniest joke, laughter became a weapon of war, not to be unleashed indiscriminately among all the people. It offered an affective shield for isolated subjects, who, as Freud put it, learned to "dread" external objects (anything outside their own ego) as much as they feared death itself.[32]

The element of mockery or cruelty alone did not make laughter satanic because these dynamics were already at play in the carnivalesque. Rabelais depicts them postfestum in *Gargantua* when a crowd laughs itself to death at the awkward speech of a Latin Sophister. They all laughed "so heartily, that they almost had to split with it."[33] Even the unfortunate orator eventually joined in their jubilation. This laughter was for everyone, and it persisted until "their eyes did water by the vehement concussion of the substance of the brain . . . [and their] lachrymal humidities, being pressed out, glided through the optic nerves."[34] In the end, they all died from effusive, contagious laughter.

This scene is quintessentially carnivalesque, "express[ing] the point of view of the whole world," because "he who is laughing also belongs to it."[35] In contrast, "the pure satire of modern times" destroys "the wholeness of the world's comic aspect," Bakhtin argues, "and that which appears comic becomes a private reaction."[36] While Ponocrates, Eudomon, and Janotus laughed until their lachrymal humidities poured out of their optic nerves, Ida Bolley's "calcified" arteries snapped like rubber bands when she died in isolation while snickering at her husband's inefficient farmwork.[37] A marker of affective power, laughter—despite its potential collectivity and irresistible contagion—became the individual's tactical edge but also their lonely burden.

THUS SPAKE ERNESTINA

What happened to the revolutionary, utopian potentials of laughter after its so-called satanic turn? For Nietzsche, the decline of communal life was collateral damage from the fall of religiosity, which he pronounced in *The Joyful Wisdom* (or *Gay Science*): "God is dead! God remains dead! And we have killed him! How shall we console ourselves, the most murderous of all murderers?"[38] It is, of course, the madman who proffers this wisdom, while all the people gather round to laugh at him. In aphorism 125, "*The Madman*" storms the marketplace shouting, "*We have killed him*,—you and I! . . . Do we not dash on unceasingly? . . . Do we not stray, as through infinite nothingness?" But his neighbors merely mock him, and with "a great deal of amusement," they taunt: "Why! is he lost? . . . Has he taken a sea voyage? Has he emigrated?"[39]

For Nietzsche, nothing is more sacred than the simultaneous avowal of nihilism and embrace of joyful wisdom. Satanic laughter alone exposes the fool's errand of sober empiricism, which vapidly complains that "where there is laughing and gaiety, thinking cannot be worth anything."[40] I superimpose the term "satanic" over Nietzsche's own constellation of signifiers, which include "Dionysian,'" Saturnalian," "Bacchic," "orgiastic," "convalescent," "decadent," and so forth. The Dionysian is a particularly crucial concept that he places in opposition to the Apollonian; whereas the latter represents rationality, order, self-discipline, the Dionysian (from the God of wine and dance) unleashes chaos, emotional passion, and unrepressed enjoyment.

As he puts it in *Birth of Tragedy*, "If someone were to transform Beethoven's *Ode to Joy* into a painting, and not restrain his imagination when millions of people sink dramatically into the dust, then we would come close to the Dionysian."[41]

The encounter between death and joy—nothingness and gay science—is the ultimate philosophic stake of knowledge in the wake of God, whereby "only after our death shall we attain to *our* life and become living, ah! very living! we posthumous men!"[42] But it is man (if not "superman") who gets to laugh posthumously. In contrast, woman always dies in earnest.

Nietzsche's aphorisms are littered with sexist epithets, among the most notorious of which appear in *Thus Spake Zarathustra*, XVII: "Old and Young Women":[43]

> Everything in woman is a riddle, and everything in woman hath one solution—it is called pregnancy.
>
> A plaything let woman be, pure and fine like the precious stone, illumined with the virtues of a world not yet come.
>
> Let man fear woman when she hateth: for man in his innermost soul is merely evil; woman, however, is mean.
>
> The happiness of man is, "I will." The happiness of woman is, "He will."
>
> Are you visiting women? Don't forget your whip!

In reference to that last line about not forgetting the whip, Frances Nesbitt Oppel defends Nietzsche against his feminist critics, asserting in *Nietzsche on Gender*: "The whip," however, "ends up in the reader's hand."[44] In other words, according to Oppel, sexist utterances pose further riddles in his cryptic verse, ultimately deconstructing gender binaries by playing with the limits of colloquial misogyny. As many other feminist scholars have argued, however, this would at best reduce women to ciphers, or to textual enigmas, for appealing to misogyny under the pretense of ironizing it.[45]

Mawkish maidens or Dionysian devils, women are far from the point of Nietzsche's joyful wisdom. *All frill and no will*, to paraphrase Ruth Abbey, "Nietzsche claims that women use new knowledge to adorn themselves: they do not value learning in itself, but only in so far as it ornaments them."[46] Their laughter is merely "of the herd," if not ultimately the butt of the herd's scorn. But it does not ascend to Zarathustra's "laughter of the height," which John Lippitt aligns with eternal recurrence. Such laughter arises from "self-overcoming," Lippitt explains, by he who "could make his life so joyous that he would be perfectly happy to live the same life over and over again, for all eternity."[47]

In Zarathustra's verse, "If I have ever laughed with the laughter of the creative lightning... Oh, how could I not be ardent for Eternity, and for the marriage-ring of rings—the ring of return... [But] never yet have I found the woman by whom I should like to have children, unless it be this woman whom I love: for I love thee, O Eternity!"[48] Thus implied Zarathustra: laughter is a more dependable eternal bedfellow than a woman, who merely reproduces life without affirming it.

If only Ernestina hadn't been so earnest, in a very different context, then perhaps her deadly laughter could also have struck "creative lightning," for it too was provoked by the absurd question of recurrent origins. Like Barbara Barr, who laughed for eight hours at a bad pun about dentistry (see chapter 2), Ernestina Nehring gave up the ghost to "heart disease, brought on by the fit of merriment over the innocent joke of her youngest son."[49] More of a naïve observation than an intentional witticism, little Freddie inquired:

> Mamma, if you can make a rhubarb pie out of a pie plant, could you make a chicken pie out of an egg plant? [sic]

But which came first: the chicken pie or the egg plant? In *The Wit of Women*, Kate Sanborn critiques the claim "that 'women cannot make a pun,' which, if true," she adds, "would be greatly to their honor."[50] (Nietzsche, unlike Freud, preferred Dionysian dithyrambs to sexual double entendres.) The real punch line behind this fatal malapropism sparks from the friction between eternal recurrence and maternal reproduction: doing housework, raising one's child into the symbolic—despite his linguistic confusion about the progeny of vegetables—and then dying of laughter.

Would Zarathustra have loved Ernestina for all eternity? Does it even matter? When confronted with the vital decision between "laughter of the herd" (maternal mockery in the service of social reproduction) and "laughter of the height" ("If ever I have played dice with the Gods at the divine table of the earth, so that the earth quaked and ruptured, and snorted forth fire-streams:—"), Ernestina found a loophole. And her whole "body shook and peal after peal of hearty laughter issued from her lips."[51] To invoke Lippitt, she who "could make [her] life so joyous that [s]he would be perfectly happy to live the same life over and over again, for all eternity" has never spent all her life doing housework.[52]

COMING IN THE THROAT OF DEATH

After World War I, women were granted a reprieve from their fatal cachinnation. At least in the United States, there were no reported female deaths by laughter between 1920 and 1931 (as I explain in chapter 2). The traumatic aftermath of global war—shell shock, mass casualties, and the punitive economic reparations that sowed the seeds of state fascism—ignited philosophy's obscene fascination with practices of joy that confront death: gallows humor, black comedy, rogue mysticism, and existential absurdism. In response to the traumas of war, Freud took his theory of laughter "beyond the pleasure principle," adding to the end of *Jokes and Their Relation to the Unconscious* (1905) a brief essay, "On Humour" (1927). If smutty jokes slip one past the censor of libidinal repression, ghoulish gags defensively fortify the ego against "suffering" and provide vital "escape from [harrowing] reality."[53] For example, the hangman about to be executed on a Monday spoke his last words: "Well, the week's beginning nicely"—and caput!

"To take part in the black tournament of humor," writes André Breton, "one must in fact have weathered many eliminations."[54] Breton compiled his formative *Anthology of Black Humor* in 1939, as the Nazis invaded Czechoslovakia and Poland, prompting Britain and France to declare war on Germany. In this historical context, Breton, in his preface "Lightning Rod," invoked Pierre Piobb: "There is nothing that intelligent humor cannot resolve in gales of laughter, not even the void ... Laughter, as one of humanity's most sumptuous extravagances, even to the point of debauchery, stands at the lip of the void, offers us the void as a pledge."[55] To come to grips with eternal death from the embodied constraints of mortal life—such as it appeared "on the dust-clouded road of the future" in 1939—meant conjuring a laughter that abandoned all risk, certainty, safety, sentimentality, reassurance, or comfort.[56]

Inspired by both Freud and Nietzsche, Breton's collection also includes excerpts from Baudelaire, Jonathan Swift, the Marquis de Sade, Franz Kafka, Alfred Jarry, and thirty-nine others—but only two women: Leonora Carrington and Gisèle Prassinos.[57] The lack of female voices "in the void" is not incidental but essential for reasons that flash up vividly in Max Ernst's surrealist photomontages of *The Hundred Headless Woman* (prefaced by Breton) and that later crystallize via the comic philosophies of Georges Bataille and Jean-Luc Nancy.[58] Like Breton and Nietzsche, Bataille pursued the abyss of laughter that could encompass "the totality of life—ecstatic contemplation and lucid knowledge *accomplished in a single action* that cannot fail to become risk."[59] These grandiose musings, Bataille titled "The Practice of Joy in the Face of Death," announcing himself as "the mystic" of joy.

Bataille proclaimed: "I am joy in the face of death ... Joy in the face of death annihilates me ... I slowly lose myself in an unintelligible and bottomless space ... I imagine the Earth hurled into space, like a woman screaming, her head in flames ... I laugh when I think that my eyes persist in demanding objects that do not destroy them," and so forth.[60] "Joy in the face of death" is not a far

FIGURE 3.2 Max Ernst, *The Hundred Headless Woman (La femme 100 têtes)*, 1929, p. 81. This image is accompanied by the caption, "This monkey, would he be catholic by any chance?"

cry from either black humor or Nietzsche's "laughter of the height." All three concepts seek to convert reckless ecstasy into existential salvation by abandoning metaphysical faith along with secular humanism. Their wagers, of course, are not without pitfalls, which differ from "voids." Many have critiqued Bataille's epistemology of unknowing (or nonknowledge) as a bit shallow, given the philosopher's own inability to die while repeatedly staking his claims on a mystical encounter with death—although he did allegedly offer himself multiple times for sacrificial decapitation in his secret "headless" society.[61]

To be without a head oneself was a tactical advantage in the process of dismantling philosophy's disciplinary mastery of instrumental reason—along with any other conventional or institutional mode of thinking and practice. But the void in question, that euphoric abyss of transformative insight, too often materialized as a vagina or a severed female torso or any other such orifice that could double for the impossible, philosophical task of decapitated critique. Bataille's short stories especially teem with anecdotes about violent sex, carnal degradation, and nonconsensual pursuits of philosophical ecstasy.[62] In his philosophical writings as well, violence against women recurs as a prelude to pronouncements of intellectual breakthrough—foreplay to joy in the face of death?

For example, Bataille imagines a woman falling on the sidewalk, then throwing herself from a window, and then being crushed at your feet in "a sudden and terrifying destruction."[63] (This scene appears in *Inner Experience*, one of his three books written amid the atrocities of World War II, along with *The Guilty* and *On Nietzsche*.[64]) Whereas the first fall provokes shared laughter (à la Bergsonian mockery or "laughter of the herd"), and the second induces superficial anguish, the third moment solicits a depth of laughter that "breaks the barriers of isolation."[65] It moves the herd "*From Anguish to Glory*," Bataille claims, because it makes the laugher into an "accomplice of a destruction of what you are," so "you then confuse yourself with this wind of destructive life that leads everything without pity to its end (and whose disheveled joy carries away the partitions that separate you from others)."[66] Joyful self-rupture forces the individual from their defensive solitude, further evoking the carnivalesque. Again, the people did not merely perform carnival: they *lived in it*—like a pageant without footlights that "does not acknowledge any distinction between actor and spectator."[67]

There is a specter of medieval carnival haunting Bataille's anguished laughter of terminal glory. Before the Romantic turn to a satanic laughter of self-containment, when "death from joy" was "pregnant" with playful birth and social regeneration, carnivalesque laughers could be part of "a material bodily whole" that "transgressed the limits of their isolation."[68] Like Chrysippus, Zeuxis, and Gargantua, Bataille's reveler pursued a total "loss of self" to the breaking point of radical collectivity—"a hysterical body that hoots and dances in the shadow of death, silently snickering at mortality as it glides to the chaosmos that awaits us all," as David Sterritt has put it (in reference to Donald Sutherland).[69] Epitomized by the funniest punch line, the "chaosmos" (chaos and cosmos) further reveals itself in catastrophe (of war, fascism, and economic collapse), which alone can propel revolutionary new social relations to emerge: when endured in the throes of impossible laughter.

Although seductive, Bataille's theory of social transformation, which intermingles morbid destruction with unbridled enjoyment, would be unthinkable

FIGURE 3.3 Max Ernst, *The Hundred Headless Woman (La femme 100 têtes)*, 1929, p. 305. This image is accompanied by the caption, "The Eternal Father tries vainly to separate the light from the shadows."

without the presence of erotic female suffering. It's the spectacle of violence against women that arouses this would-be headless philosopher to push his own joy across the finish line—to the void, the abyss, the face of death, and so on. As Nancy declared in "Wild Laughter in the Throat of Death," loosely paraphrased, female decapitation is the only way for the male artist to achieve true immortality. Nancy asks, "How can desire laugh? How can presence come into laughter? And what does it mean for presence *to come*?"[70] Evidently, if not in the "face of death," Nancy's "infinite joy" should just be taken in "the face, which is part of the body . . . [it] consists only of caverns and holes, like the eyes themselves, through which the illumination comes."[71] The illumination in question refers to that of the model: "She is illumination itself, without body."[72] No torso, all light, radiating through the various holes in her head.

The essay proceeds as an extended address to an absent dead poet, Baudelaire, whose fetishistic description of the woman who "consume[d]" him with a "desire to paint" provides the source text for Nancy's own analysis—which spans questions of mortality; anality; intermediality; and, not least of all, the sublime (or "the bursting joy of the deep throat" that Baudelaire once made "bloom on volcanic soil").[73] The model's laughter, according to Nancy, represents "the divine and feminine knowledge of the mystery of art as the mystery of life," but the male artist's (Nancy's? Baudelaire's? Zeuxis'?) joy alone rises to the height of "immortal pleasure. He *comes in* death."[74]

The female model clearly allegorizes both fatal attraction and epistemological fascination for Nancy, who inherits a philosophical genealogy of laughter and death handed down from Nietzsche to Breton to Bataille. But it remains unclear whether the artist merely comes (in an intellectual mind meld with his own libido) or achieves something like the affirmation of "eternal return" in the Nietzschean sense. If Bataille's existential hysterics (despite their predatory libido) harkened back to the communal life of mythic antiquity and medieval carnival, Nancy's politics of laughter is, at best, full of holes.

LAST LAUGH BEFORE THE FALL

In a legendary incident that the philosopher Hans Blumenberg has described as a "protohistory of theory"—or, for our purposes, a birth pang of critical thought—the early Greek astronomer, Thales of Miletus, was so absorbed in gazing at the stars that he lost his footing and fell down a well. A Thracian servant girl who witnessed his fall found it extremely hilarious and laughed out loud at his misfortune. "No consensus emerges about whether it is better to fall or to laugh," argues Blumenberg, citing Hannah Arendt's thesis in *The Life of the Mind*, which he summarizes: "Intellectuals learn quickly that time does not wait for them to think."[75] In other words, the Thracian girl's laughter tempered the absentminded philosopher's desire to abandon the reality on the ground for a retreat into the life of the mind.

That to Study Philosophy Is to Learn to Die, wrote Michel de Montaigne in 1580, citing Cicero, and adding: "What a ridiculous thing it is to trouble ourselves about taking the only step that is to deliver us from all trouble!"[76] Laughing philosophers par excellence, the fatal female cachinnators of the late nineteenth century also portended the death of a certain ideal of traditional femininity: the angelic Victorian, the swan-corseted Gibson Girl, the subservient domestic, the dutiful wife, the modest child-bearer, and so forth—even "the new laugher."[77] Women asphyxiated by a deadening social routine—consisting of domestic drudgery, exploited labor, punitive clothing, difficult childbirth, sexual submission, and the repeated denial of mental stimulation or political empowerment—no longer had a satisfying place in their rapidly changing, often catastrophically transformative modern world.

Gasping for one last lungful of pleasure, they took a cue from the Thracian woman, who provoked the question: better to fall or to laugh? Mrs. Lawrence of Brooklyn, New York, chose to do both when she threw herself into the rapids of the Niagara cataract in 1889, committing "suicide in the most sensational fashion" by "laughing herself to death."[78] She was reportedly a refined, attractive, and respectable young woman, who wore a dark bottle green or blue dress. "She laughed, but not insanely, so the eyewitnesses say . . . All the way down she had smiled and laughed and waved her hands, and this she kept up even when going headfirst over the falls."[79] Many bystanders at the scene gathered around to witness and gawk at the morbid spectacle. A photographer even "tried to take a view of the suicide but the torrent was too quick for him, and Lawrence's death smile will only last in the minds of those who saw her die," all of whom, by now, are long dead.[80]

It is unlikely that Nietzsche was there on the scene because he'd just been institutionalized after suffering a severe mental breakdown due to a combination of syphilis, overwork, and "vascular dementia."[81] Likewise, Bakhtin, Bataille, Breton, and obviously Nancy had not yet been born, and even if they had, why would they be off sightseeing at Niagara Falls when they clearly had more pressing agendas in France and Russia (not yet then the Soviet Union)? Had any among them witnessed Lawrence's suicidal laughter, as Bataille would have put it, breaking free "in a sudden and terrifying destruction," one doubts that it would have made the same impact on the subsequent history of laughing philosophy as that of Thales of Miletus.[82] But had there been a feminist laughing philosopher there to witness the fall, what would she have thought? Would she have laughed along with Lawrence's joyful death, her communion perhaps giving birth to the spark of a new social order?

When the old ways fail to give all the people a satisfying place, morbid symptoms such as death by laughter appear in the interregnum between horrific catastrophe and whatever fresh hell comes next.

PART II
Female Hysteria

4
Gaslighting the Libido

Feminist Politics of Madness, Laughter, and Power

What was female hysteria? Now a long debunked diagnostic category, the mysterious ailment ran roughshod over nineteenth-century psychiatric medicine. Symptoms of the disease ranged from ordinary exhaustion, boredom, fatigue, and nervousness to epileptic orgasms, uncontrollable hiccupping, clownish acrobatics, and trans-species metamorphosis. Its origins defied scientific understanding—arising from nowhere and then vanishing without a trace—and its symptoms assumed such a perplexing range of extremes that it was often disparaged as a mere wastebasket for any inexplicable affliction.

Only three things are certain about female hysteria: (1) it was a hotly gendered condition that primarily bedeviled women; (2) it reached its peak in a long, rambling history during the mid-nineteenth and early twentieth centuries; and (3) its scientific study was exploited as a total sideshow—but one that became formative to unraveling the entanglement between sexuality and identity, empirical truth and cynical spectacle, possible lives and alternate selves.

Before he analyzed dreams, Sigmund Freud viewed hysteric symptoms as royal roads to the unconscious. Jean-Martin Charcot turned his psychiatric lectures into a three-ring circus, where sexually traumatized women would orgasm on cue and then assume physically impossible, acrobatic positions. In the aftermath of these bizarre scientific developments, feminist theorists from Hélène Cixous and Catherine Clément to Sara Ahmed and Lauren Berlant have recuperated the hysteric's muffled complaint as a defiant gesture of her simmering social protest. Deriving from intellectual boredom or inhuman suffering, hysteric symptoms converted political insurgency into corporeal mystery. They offered women a coded script for expressing that which could not be communicated openly but helped pave the way for the collective politics of feminist art and uprising.

Unlike the history of women's laughter, however, the hysteria chronicles have been written, rewritten, debated and contested, theorized, performed, closed and reopened by generations of feminist scholars, artists, authors, and activists: it is a colossal field to enter. The politics of female sexuality and antipatriarchal language loom large in the discourse on this topic, as I will discuss. What has not been given its due consideration, however, is the colloquial outgrowth of the word itself: "hysteria," from the ancient Greek hystera ("uterus") to a casual modifier for uproarious laughter. As we know from Part 1 of this book, the notion of laughter as "hysterical" did not imply rollicking enjoyment until the end of the nineteenth century. Clinical studies of female hysteria have remained rigorously quarantined from mass celebrations of "hysterical laughter," like two ships in the night—one a disorder, the other a euphemism, despite their evocative etymological overlap.

I therefore claim all symptoms of female hysteria as unrealized eruptions of exuberant laughter. Squeezed into overly tight corsets, discouraged from laughing uproariously by etiquette manuals and alarmist obituaries, women were denied access to laughter as a nervous outlet or provocative gateway to envisioning topsy-turvy scenarios of social upheaval. If not toward that outburst of voluble merriment, where did their risible energy go? I see women's hysteric symptoms as laughs cut off at the knees—mutated into uncontrollable barks, meows, yawns, hiccups, facial tics, limb spasms, epileptic seizures, fugue states, somnambulism, and too many other offshoots to name.

HYSTERICAL LAUGHTER AND ITS RELATION TO FEMINIST COMEDY

Those wonderful hysterics, who subjected Freud to so many voluptuous moments too shameful to mention, bombarding his mosaic statue/Law of Moses with their carnal, passionate body-words, haunting him with their inaudible thundering denunciations.

—Hélène Cixous[1]

No feminist theorist has had more faith in the subversive powers of female hysteria than Hélène Cixous, who further proclaimed Freud's patient Dora (Ida Bauer) to be "the true 'mistress' of the Signifier"—a "poetic body" that "cannot be tamed."[2] Dora suffered from severe aphonia (loss of voice), among other documented "symptoms" (including false appendicitis and heavy vaginal discharge), but tangoed with Freud in a contest for narrative mastery over the meaning of her somatic conversion. She eventually walked out on the father of psychoanalysis and repeatedly laughed or coughed in his face, in defiance of his will to dictate the interpretation of her wayward desires—to gaslight her libido. Was Dora "the witch's daughter" of an emergent feminist consciousness or a mere pawn in the analyst's ascendant science of ascribing Oedipal sexual meaning to the chaos of the hysteric's corporeal insurgence?[3]

For Cixous, hysteria's radical dissemination of fragmented language all over the body is essential to its metaphorical alignment with laughter. In her terms, there is no tangible boundary between laughter and hysteria because both eclipse the straightjacketed confines of the patriarchal symbolic order. The laughing hysteric, like the snake-haired Medusa, "doesn't hold still, she overflows... She has never 'held still'; explosion, diffusion, effervescence, abundance, she takes pleasure in being boundless, outside self, outside same," and so forth.[4] This collision between antisymbolic laughter and enigmatic hysteria climaxes in jouissance: endless enjoyment for its own sake, "beyond the pleasure principle" (i.e., toward the death drive), and certainly in excess of the phallus.[5] If hysteria stood a fighting chance to jam "all the little adulterous wheels" of the family, Medusan laughter would be its ace in the "hole."[6]

Cixous's feminist contemporaries—although likewise fascinated with hysteria—did not always share her exuberant faith in the anti-Oedipal mischief of the ailment's libidinal politics. Catherine Clément checks Cixous's enthusiasm in their coauthored experimental text, *La jeune née/The Newly Born Woman*: "Raising hell, throwing fits, disturbing family relations," Clément claims, "can be shut back up ... always reclosable, always reclosed."[7] In psychoanalytic terms, libidinal tantrums do not reach the threshold of symbolic inscription, which is necessary for any unconscious emanation to permeate (let alone agitate) general structures of language and meaning. As Jane Gallop pithily paraphrases Clément, "Dora's outbursts burst nothing."[8] In other words, they were containable as domestic theatrics, or "at best a private, ineffectual response to the frustration of women's lives," as Elaine Showalter puts it.[9] In order to escalate the hysteric's alienated affect into public-facing activism, something more emphatic was necessary than the sheer spectacle of somatic conversion transmuted into cryptic disturbance.

Hysterical Feminist Comedy

The hysteria chronicles, in many ways, map onto long-standing debates about the subversive potentials of disruptive feminist comedy. The bone of contention cuts to the power of transgression. Can women's defiant laughs at antimisogynist punch lines have tangible effects on the social order, or are they mere outlets for blowing off steam—at best, emotional catharsis, at worst, complacent substitutes for real activism? Of burning interest is the capacity for "unruly," "uproarious," "nasty," and "hysterical" feminist jokes to parlay private affects into furious catalysts for social change and collective solidarity.

Feminist comedy evangelists reclaim deviant symptoms that have long been hystericized by psychiatric medicine and misogynistic backlash alike, asserting them as political speech. Raunchy jokes and rebellious gags liberate women's gaslit libido and unleash it onto the symbolic order. Bridget Everett's *Gynecological Wonder*, Tiffany Haddish's "Coochie Hygiene" set in *Black Mitzvah*, Jacqueline Novak's existential monologue about fellatio in *Get on Your Knees*, and a bouquet of viral vulvar memes are just the tips of the iceberg (to mix metaphors).[10] In their book *Uproarious*, Cynthia Willett and Julie Willett emphasize the powers of feminist comedy to commute negative affect into biosocial catharsis through an erotic politics of joy. If hysteria drowns language in enigmatic symptoms, then feminist jokes resuscitate those festering signifiers from the reservoir of the body through the ecstatic gateway of laughter. "Cathartic processes can transform shame and fear," they write, "reshap[ing] the contours of social space" and demonstrating how "laughter can allow us to take back our lives."[11] In a similar spirit, Bambi Haggins embraces mad laughter (or "laughing mad") as a "liberatory act," particularly in the context of Black satire where collective reckonings with the traumas of slavery and racism briefly license the cathartic refusal to suffer in their wake.[12] In the digital realm, Jenny Sundén and Susanna Paasonen broach raunchy feminist gags that "attract or repel, entice or annoy us" and thereby rewire the "affective circuits of anger, outrage, shame, and shamelessness that fuel resistant activities."[13] They ask, "How can laughter be an answer to something as serious as sexism?"[14] Although "hysteria" is not their keyword, they dwell in the danger zone of unresolvable ambivalence—once a telltale trigger for nervous disaster—that now inspires bold action through the digital virality of antisexist and queer feminist laughter.

Across these interventions, the spark of madness is what gives laughter its power to escalate inner emotion to political expression. The prose of these writings is fueled by contagious affective energy—from palpable rage to playful defiance—taking a page from Cixous's own Medusan laughter and ruckus-raising hysteria. As Cixous riffed, hysteria is a "rising, insurrectionary dough kneading itself, with sonorous, perfumed ingredients, a lively combination of flying colors, leaves, and rivers plunging into the sea we feed."[15] Unlike her antisymbolic verse, however, feminist humor (and its attendant critical scholarship) aims to reintegrate affective and bodily excess into the linguistic economy of risqué joke telling. For example, Linda Mizejewski and Victoria Sturtevant explore the double meanings of feminism's most overdetermined signifier in the introduction to their edited volume *Hysterical!*, which compiles wide-ranging essays on women in American comedy. "Despite its history as repression and misreading," they write, "the doubled meaning of hysteria is a provocative model for women's comedy because it's also a history of performance and female spectacle—women acting out and acting up."[16] But feminist comedy should also distance itself from the outmoded ailment, they warn, out of fear of "*misreading*" or "undercutting the intentionality and intelligence that are at the core of good comedy . . . [via] negative stereotypes of hysterical feminine behavior."[17] It is a fine line between incisive satire and antifeminist fodder when the performance of transgressive gender excess is at stake. To amplify hysteric tropes (that deride women as shrill, flighty, irrational, and so forth) risks further reinforcing them in the very gesture of critical appropriation.

If hysteria is sometimes a third rail for feminist comedy, laughter (in its relation to humor) has not been a pivotal concern for feminist theorists of hysteria. Even amid the resurgence of what Cecily Devereux calls the "New New Hysteria Studies" (a sequel to the "New Hysteria Studies"), comedy and laughter are routinely eclipsed by smoldering affects of anxiety, depression, rage, annoyance, and shame.[18] In prolific excavations of the ailment—which traverse academic writing and multimedia experimental performance (as I will discuss)—the specter of laughter uniquely adheres to the direct citation of Cixous's "Laugh of the Medusa" but rarely seeps into the present zeitgeist.

It is my wager that there are missed opportunities for pleasurable, forceful modes of protest that entangle intentional laughter with hysteric unrepression. When does the descriptor "hysterical" go beyond comedic hyperbole and get at the treasure trove of structural meaning at stake in somatic conversion? There is room for play in that murky void between hysteria's comedic euphemism (e.g., "she's hysterically funny!") and its psychogenic gaslighting (e.g., "her ramblings are hysteric nonsense!"). What we might call *hysteric comedy* lingers on the precipice of symbolic recognition and anarchic explosion.

Filling the Void

Witty jokes, like hysteric symptoms, hold a special power to convert affective alienation into volcanic bodily sensation in the absence of other symbolic vehicles. This is a common project shared by feminist scholars of both comedy and hysteria. In the case of comedy, will the joke congeal into a schtick or cliché before it has the chance to explode into radical new consciousness? That is always the gamble when asking so much (perhaps too much) of laughter to provide a salve for emotional suffering. "Punch lines need trauma because punch lines . . . need tension, and tension feeds trauma," Hannah Gadsby asserts in her antilaughter, feminist stand-up special, *Nanette*.[19] Gadsby recounts her discomfort serving up her memories of coming out and surviving sexual abuse as happy punch lines: "And what I had done, with that comedy show about coming out, was I froze an incredibly formative experience at its trauma point and sealed it off into jokes . . . But unfortunately that joke version was not nearly sophisticated enough to help me undo the damage done to me in reality."[20] For Gadsby, the polemical refusal of laughter within the format of stand-up outstrips the power of comedy itself to combat homophobia and misogyny. Sometimes jokes simply lack the bandwidth to parlay fraught somatic memories into joyful affective catharsis.

Michelle Wolf attempted to do just that in her notorious roast at the 2018 White House Correspondents' dinner. Unlike Gadsby, who withheld reparative laughter from an ostensibly sympathetic audience, Wolf leveraged hysteric jokes to solicit outrage and disbelief in an explicitly unfriendly environment. Her punch lines provoked palpable discomfort in the room and divisive waves of celebration and condemnation across the internet. Wolf delivered a sizzling, seventeen-minute monologue that consisted primarily of raunchy zingers about sexism, racism, cable news journalism, Wall Street corporatism, and the Trump administration's buffoonish corruption. These were epitomized by: "You guys are going through Cabinet members quicker than Starbucks throws out black people" and "I did work at Bear Stearns in 2008, so although I haven't been sexually harassed, I've definitely been fucked."[21] Wolf closed her scorched-earth joke set with an equally firebrand mic drop: "Like an immigrant who was brought here by his parents and didn't do anything wrong, I've got to get the fuck out of here. Good night. (Flint still doesn't have clean water.)"[22] Raising the specter of mass deportation and lead contamination of public drinking water, Wolf's neurotic, cringeworthy, out-of-place affect invested her forceful, humorous critique in a scandalous roast that I'd argue exemplifies *feminist hysteric comedy*. When contested meaning collides headlong with unanchored nervous energy, its whiplash could go anywhere. In Wolf's case, the echo chambers of social media's outrage machine played a repressive role in containing the cathartic ambiguity of her hysteric joke telling.

Hysteria is now a feminist comedy genre in itself, a feisty brand for stand-up specials such as Margaret Cho's *Psycho*, Wanda Sykes's *Not Normal*, Lynne Koplitz's

FIGURE 4.1 *Hysterical*, directed by Andrea Blaugrund Nevins (2021; Saint-Bruno-de-Montaville, Quebec: FX), official movie poster.

Hormonal Beast, and the FX documentary *Hysterical*, which opens by reclaiming informal uses of "hysterical" (as in "very funny") from its Greek etymology of "suffering in the womb."[23] *Hysterical* features celebrity interviews with Margaret Cho, Fortune Feimster, Marina Franklin, Kathy Griffin, and Sherri Shepherd and vast archival footage (from Moms Mabley and Phyllis Diller to Jean Carroll and Joan Rivers); it proceeds from the thesis that the popularity of feminist comedy provides a direct antidote to the gaslighting of affective and libidinal hysteria.

Each comedian is then called on to testify to how stand-up fills "some sort of void" (Feimster) and gives them a voice to tell their tale: "I have control, and I'm a storyteller," declares Rachel Feinstein. "We're just trying to fill this hole," Jessica Kirson explains, "and get the attention that we've always wanted . . . always wanting to be seen and heard and not feeling acknowledged." Whatever the emotional hole, stand-up supplies it with meaning—and the frontal immediacy of the comedians' interviews (interspersed with recent footage of their laugh-making sets) contrasts vividly with the distance of the archive, as grainy footage reminds us just how far "hysterical" feminism has come. "I can't even imagine doing stand-up at the time," Judy Gold confesses. "I don't know how Joan [Rivers] did it . . . she was hysterical." The film further analogizes the affective distance of the archive to biographical relics from each woman's childhood, prompting the comedians to recount their formative struggles with stress, depression, anxiety, eating disorders, sexism, racism, family trauma, death, loss, and professional inequity. But "once I got on that stage, it's like life was all good. There was a peace that settled in me," offers Shepherd in the context of having been called the N-word as a child.

"Hysterical" comedy thus overwrites the unconscious script of "hysterical" trauma, whereby all women fall prey to their unresolved feelings but lack any narrative or material recourse to do something about it. Stand-up is the *it* that fills the void, proving the reality of social change by the sheer popularity and ubiquity of funny women's access to the stage—forget the phallus, grab the mic!

At the same time, *Hysterical* is a commercial documentary produced for a niche audience that now streams in the demographic echo chambers of Hulu. Its conventional format forces the spectator to decide between incompatible meanings of "hysterical": excitable or excited, painful or cathartic, inscrutable or hilarious, and so forth. Its aesthetics simply do not leave room for play in the void itself because that void exists to be filled (by stand-up). In contrast, hysteric symptoms emanate from what remains incommunicable, gaining bodily power from the ludicrous rupture between inner feeling and its social articulation. "That separation cannot be wished away by an act of consciousness or analysis; it can only be altered by material and social transformation," argues Ann Cvetkovich in *Mixed Feelings*.[24]

Is it really the task of comedy (whether "hysterical" or "cringe" or simply satirical) to enact change itself, or does the most potent comedy demand an encounter with dissonance rather than promise a direct path to its vindication? The sweet spot of hysterical laughter's political potential thrives in its momentum toward self-contradiction, to short-circuit ordinary perception and its reproduction of hegemonic power: heteropatriarchy, class domination, and colonialist white supremacy. Like hysteric symptoms, comedic laughter cannot really fill the void, but it can reveal potholes in the smooth surface of the system that preys on maintaining that void. Or, as *Hysterical* implies (but does not attempt to resolve), what about all those laughing spectators who enjoy watching the documentary? Do they too take to the stage, or is seeing the film enough?

Feminist Hysteric Laughter

If feminist laughter (or any transgressive laughter) is to have a fighting chance of upsetting the social order, it has to be at least somewhat hysterical, beyond its colloquial usage: unreasonable, a scandal to common sense, and rather unhinged—if not altogether mad. While rebellious laughter benefits from proximity to hysteria (even though it then risks being discarded as hysteric), it remains unclear what it would entail for hysteria to become more like laughter.

Laughter, of course, was a common symptom of hysteria, but it rarely received isolated attention as such and was notoriously unreadable. "You see,"

Charcot declared, "the patient has been taken, during our examination, with convulsive laughter which she cannot moderate, and which will soon be followed by a shower of tears."[25] This was an utterly typical observation about hysteric laughter in the context of psychiatric diagnosis—that it would quickly give way to sobbing and was therefore not significant on its own terms. Emptied of its symbolism, hysteric laughter provided ambient noise for exploiting the ailment as a fascinating visual spectacle—as Charcot and his interlocutors did quite ruthlessly.

The bodily convulsions unleashed by hysteric laughter were extracted from their audible dimensions. The former, as I will explain, Charcot referred to as "clownism." In contrast to the vocality of hysteria, which he mostly ignored, Charcot pursued every gestural tic or spasm of the disorder as both rigorously classifiable and empirically meaningful. Indeed, the medical legitimacy of his whole taxonomy depended on giving scientific method to hysteria's madness. After his death in 1893, the psychoanalytic "talking cure" dethroned the visual theatrics of Charcot's neurologic amphithéâtre. Likewise, as an iteration of "talking," laughter was tenuously afforded a sliver of reparative value to restore meaning to anarchic utterance.

But hysteric laughter never enjoyed the nimble autonomy of laughter at jokes to intermingle bewildering nonsense with comprehensible reason.[26] In Freudian psychoanalysis, jokes broker a compromise between mental repression and silly horseplay by provisionally uniting two (or more) disparate entities. (A relevant example would be the pun "hystory," which points to a larger argument about the entanglement between gendered madness and feminist narrative that the world itself only teases.) The problem was precisely that hysteric emanations could never become *enough* like hysterical laughter. They failed to walk that semiotic tightrope between rational sensemaking and unruly absurdity, which is the lingua franca of sneaky but incisive jokes.

LAUGHING DOPPELGÄNGERS OR AFFECT ALIENS? THE PECULIAR HYSTERIA OF ESTHER WAKEFIELD

The contention is made that no stranger malady than this has ever undergone the attention of physicians.[27]

—*Anaconda Standard* (Anaconda, Montana), August 13, 1899

In the spirit of imagining hysteria as a misalignment of laughter, I'd like to turn now to Esther Wakefield, an unknown woman from Chicago whose pageantry of uproarious symptoms reportedly gave "a black eye to science" and left the country's medical physicians "all at sea" in 1899.[28] Wakefield had been lounging in a hammock outside her home on West Monroe Street in Chicago when she was unceremoniously "assaulted" by "some flying insect" that stung her on the lips. The melanolestes picipes (or "kissing bug") sent her into a "state of hysteria," characterized by raging fits of boisterous laughter and a "spasmodic desire to embrace and kiss those about her."[29] Wakefield had been described as "modest, refined, cultured—the last person in the world to give way to ... femininely nervous impulse."[30] Yet the pestilent sting contorted her personality into just that—beyond nervousness, her "hysteria assumed a tone of such violence" that she had to be anesthetized by doctors and "given over" to ether for twelve hours.[31]

Like Barbara Barr, the woman who allegedly laughed for eight hours at a corny dentistry pun (see chapter 2), Wakefield languished in an unconscious stupor. But thankfully she soon recovered (as had Barr) and quietly returned to her job as a stenographer and typewriter in an office. Her physician Dr. Martin reassured her widowed mother that "the crisis had been happily passed." Cut to the next day on a streetcar as it entered a tunnel:[32]

> Passengers aboard ... were startled by a sudden burst of laughter, strident shrill, almost uncanny, from a woman's lips, and by the spectacle of a sudden seizing of the conductor in a fervid embrace and the implanting upon his embarrassed lips of half a dozen swift and burning kisses by as charming a girl as one might find in many a long day.

It was Esther Wakefield! She proceeded to make swift work of the car, accosting other male passengers (including a "fat" man "quite old enough to deserve a better fate") and "laughing insanely" until the police were called on the scene and she was forcibly committed to an asylum.[33]

It is important to highlight the context in which this story circulated. It was originally reported in the *Chicago Chronicle*, but various versions appeared in local newspapers as a curiosity item. It would have made the same rounds as many of the "death by laughter" obituaries, such as "Killed by a Joke" and "Last Laugh Was Not Best Laugh."[34] Wakefield perhaps had more in common with fatal cachinnators such as Bertha Pruett and Polly Jackson than with Josef Breuer and Freud's exploited, tongue-clacking conversion hysterics.[35] Unlike Pruett and Jackson, however, Wakefield was not consumed by her laughter; instead, she dissociated from it. "And here is what still puzzles physicians and seems to be giving a black eye to science," according to the *Standard*, "that she is wholly, completely rational on her days of sanity—is utterly, totally irresponsible on her days of hysteria."³⁶ Her revolving door consciousness—swinging from polite decorum to libidinal detonation—lingered in a volatile condition indefinitely (or at least through any surviving record of her escapades).

Miss Esther and Mistress Wakefield: 1899

The trope of an uncanny double or doppelgänger was a subject of intense fascination at the time. It galvanized gothic horror tales of murderous alter egos run amok such as Robert Louis Stevenson's *Strange Case of Dr. Jekyll and Mr. Hyde* and inspired fantastic trick films with titles like *The Triple Lady* (Star-Film, 1898), *The Four Troublesome Heads* (Star-Film, 1898), and *Artistic Creation* (R. W. Paul, 1901), in which an artist's drawing of a woman's head magically comes to life and gives birth to a child.³⁷ This was the mutating media climate in which unrepressed fancies ran roughshod over suggestive bodily appendages.

The problem of divided selves had a very different flavor in early psychoanalysis, where phenomena also drew on "the symptom pool": the "permissible symptoms" of distress and desire that circulate "in a given culture at a given time," as Showalter paraphrases Edward Shorter.³⁸ Hysteria's "symptom pool" interlaced contagious bodily mimicry with obsessive cultural imagery, giving somatic form to deep affective crisis. As soon as "a powerful affect interrupts the normal course of ideas," argued Breuer, it forces its "way into consciousness," where "hallucinations are introduced into the perceptual system and motor acts are [aroused] independently of the conscious will."³⁹ Breuer's patient Anna O. (Bertha Pappenheim) exhibited a "double conscience" that drilled potholes in her personal memories and seized violent control over her waking life. "In Freud's model of unconscious emotions," as Sara Ahmed notes, "the affect itself is not repressed: what is repressed is the idea to which the affect is attached."⁴⁰ Unmoored from its cognitive reality, affect takes on a life of its own, wreaking anxiety, shame, depression, fear, anger, and repulsion—or aggressive libido and hell-raising jubilation (à la Wakefield).

In Ahmed's style, we might think of Wakefield as an "affect alien": a variant of the feminist killjoy, whose disruption of ordinary affect jams the wheels of the grinding feedback loop between domestic reproduction and patriarchal power. Like Wakefield, Anna O. had her world cracked in two after she was repeatedly denied any outlet (other than daydreaming) for her habitual anxiety, boredom, and intellectual frustration. But what if Anna O.'s alienated "second self" could have laughed loudly and obscenely like Wakefield? In Freud's terms, jokes liberate the vast psychic energy required to maintain inhibitions—to keep that rising, alienated alternate self at bay—effectively laughing off the "quota" of "inhibitory cathexis" that is "ready to be discharged through laughter."[41] In contrast, the hysteric's pathologized alter ego was haunted by nervous attacks, delirious hallucinations, somatic anesthesia, and the loss of necessary words. Her jarring actions proceeded from the unavailability of her inner thoughts.

More of an "affect alien" than an alienated doppelgänger, by every available account, it sounds like Wakefield had an extravagantly good time. She enjoyed her symptoms all too much!

DIALECTICS OF DEADLY LAUGHTER AND HYSTERIC DISSOCIATION

When does a thwarted laugh spiral into a hysterical symptom? In the case of jokes, we have an "indefinable feeling" that correlates with an unsettling sense of "absence," suggests Freud, and "then all at once the joke is there," licensing a "sudden release of intellectual tension."[42] Like laughter, hysteric phenomena arise from the eruption of libidinal energy and taboo flights of fancy. But without a satisfying outlet in waking life, those fugitive impulses turn inward, where their explosive affects smolder, becoming altogether inaccessible to consciousness. Hysteric symptoms, unlike joke laughter, take hold once it is already too late for playful language to give voice to sticky feelings.

Anna O. lost her basic motor functions and powers of speech entirely while under the grip of her secondary state. Emmy von N. (Fanny Moser) suffered deep melancholia, contortions of speech (which caused her to emit sharp, uncanny clacking noises with her tongue), and seizures of terror inciting uncontrollable spasms. Cäcilie M. (Anna von Lieben) felt an "icy grip" in the back of her neck, a "painful coldness in all her extremities," an inability to speak, and terrifying delusions that seeped through "the most striking gaps" in her otherwise "well-stocked memory."[43] She was particularly tormented by hallucinatory visions of rats and mice. Even Dora—*the* " 'mistress' of the Signifier," per Cixous—suffered from nervous coughing, total loss of voice, auratic migraines, and tunneling depression.[44] Although these muffled fragments of "passionate voices" have provoked feminists to read Freud's authoritative narratives with the "utmost suspicion," as Toril Moi insists, it cannot be denied: hysteria was utter hell.[45]

The "death by laughter" cases reveal abbreviated alternatives to hysteria's surreal dissociation into multiple selves. How many women would have preferred acute rhapsody in lieu of vanishing into their bodies entirely, unmoored from their official lives? In the instance of death by laughter, there was always a trigger: maybe a dentistry joke, a culinary gaffe, or an out-of-tune musical instrument. But hysteric symptoms arose without warning—unless directly solicited through suggestion or hypnosis—and then recurred long after initially subsiding. When intense feelings adhere to unlocatable memories, they might never fade if punitively denied a satisfying outlet for discharge, let alone vindication.

An injury "repaid, even if only in words, is recollected quite differently than one that has had to be accepted" or swallowed.[46] "The essence of the talking cure," argues Teresa Brennan in *The Transmission of Affect*, consists in "reuniting the repressed with the words that expressed the affect attached to it or which converted the affect from one state to another ... (as when depression is converted to anger)."[47] Freudian "talking," however, discouraged political passions such as anger, instead soliciting the revelation of sexual trauma to mitigate maladaptive pathos. "Your anger is a judgment that something is wrong," preaches Ahmed in the context of sexual harassment. "But in being heard as angry, your speech is read as motivated by anger."[48] In other words, it is a vicious circle between the hystericization of anger and its stone-cold denial. Curative talking thus aimed to placate aberrant affect with biographical rag-picking rather than risk unleashing the tumult of its biosocial protest.

Where do we draw the line, then, between signifier and utterance—or symbolic inscription and Medusan volcano—in the business of reparative talking? Do wayward feelings always have to be articulated in sensemaking language to clarify their source and direction? Or are they equally (if not more) powerful when let loose in their sheer affective capacities?

This has long been a crux of debate among hysteria's feminist theorists: to symbolize or to carnivalize? Laughter opened a field of antiphallic mischief for Cixous's French interlocutors, but it widely missed the mark of hysteric malfeasance. "Isn't laughter the first form of liberation from a sexual repression?" urges Luce Irigaray: "*Isn't the phallic tantamount to the seriousness of meaning? Perhaps woman, and the sexual relation, transcend it 'first' in laughter,*" which precedes and exceeds the "mask" of hysteria.[49] Irigaray locates the latter (hysteria) as a "stigmatized" pit "where fantasies, ghosts, and shadows fester and must be unmasked, interpreted."[50] The primacy of laughter, in contrast, can speak for itself.[51] Julia Kristeva opposes "situationist" laughter that merely "places or displaces abjection" to the apocalyptic, piercing, abject laughs that ignite "the spark of the symbolic" until the "desire to speak explodes."[52] The latter laughter, however, differs sharply from hysteria, which "brings about, ignores, or seduces the symbolic," according to Kristeva, "but does not produce it."[53] Only abjection can be productive of language.

As a hysteric symptom, laughter lingers in the abyss of bodily signs that are "heard but not yet understood."[54] Their latency is precisely what invests hysteria's strange immortality. The laughing female hysteric survived seemingly any degree of violence inflicted upon her. Her hysteric laughter, like any other symptom, represented the word turned into flesh—it did not liberate alienated affect: it tattooed it on one's body in magically erasable pen.

SCIENCE OR SIDESHOW? CLOWNIST CONTORTIONS AND CARNIVAL SOMNAMBULISM

The laughing female hysteric was like a funhouse mirror of the fatal female laugher, whose mental inhibitions persisted to the brink of self-destruction. In contrast, the hysteric could explode in cachinnation and sob for days on end without so much as a trace on her body. The spontaneous appearance and disappearance of symptoms, according to Charcot, is precisely what paved the way toward their possible cure. Their limitless manipulability was viewed as evidence of their psychosomatic impermanence.

Grande Hystérie, Artificial Hypnosis, and Feline Metamorphosis

Every Tuesday, Charcot paraded his star hysterics on-stage for his famous weekly lessons. The lavish rectangular amphithéâtre seated up to four hundred spectators, enticing medical researchers and tourists alike. The room overflowed with "a multicoloured audience drawn from tout Paris," exclaimed Axel Munthe, "authors, journalists, leading actors and actresses, fashionable demi-mondaines, all full of morbid curiosity to witness the startling phenomena of hypnotism almost forgotten since the days of Mesmer and Braid."[55] Charcot was indeed quite the showman. Lecturing from a raised podium, he employed bright footlights, wax molds, graphic illustrations, and a photographic slide projector, while himself imitating his patients' tics and tremors as he described them.[56]

He claimed that an attack of "grande hystérie" proceeded in four stages: (1) epilepsy, mimicking epileptic convulsions; (2) clownism, or grand movements,

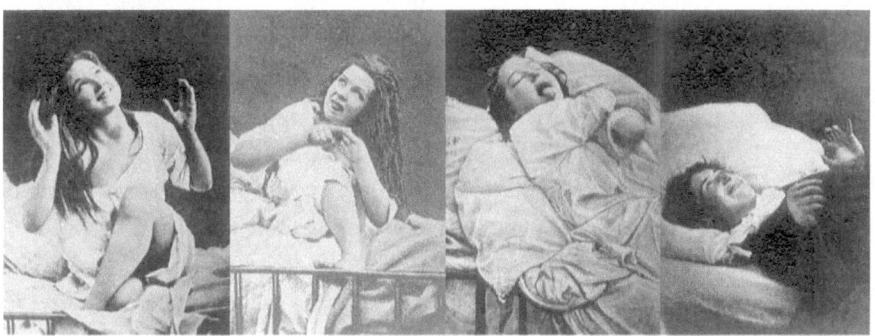

FIGURE 4.2 "Attitudes Passionelles." D. M. Bourneville and P. Régnard, *Iconographie photographique de la salpêtrière (Service de M. Charcot)*, 1876–1877).

resembling a circus performer's acrobatic contortions; (3) passionate poses, displaying intense emotions that ranged from lust to ecstasy to terror; and (4) delirium, inducing vivid hallucinations. When incited by artificial means such as hypnosis, however, the course of the attack could be condensed into three stages: (1) catalepsy, in which the patient's body became "totally anesthetic" and could be "moulded at will like a waxen figure";[57] (2) lethargy, impersonating a "cadaver before rigor mortis had set in," which could enable her to maintain any physical pose for hours or even days;[58] and (3) somnambulism that evacuated her will into a blank slate for carrying out the doctor's multifarious commands. Charcot publicly solicited these artificial attacks—using shining glass balls, revolving mirrors, and dangling pocket watches—so he could exert precise control over every aspect of their trajectory.

His "star hysterics" were international celebrities. Blanche Wittmann—the Salpetrière's headlining hystero-epileptic—was widely hailed as "Queen of the Hysterics." Her grand attacks became iconic, immortalized by André Brouillet in his well-known painting, *Une leçon Clinique à la Salpetrière* (1887), in which Blanche dramatically collapses before an enthralled audience while Charcot drills through a dry lecture on epileptic taxonomy. Wittmann was also fictionalized in novels, caricatured in cartoons, and parodied onstage from the salacious cabaret to the gothic Grand Guignol. Herself an unruly and defiant woman when first committed to the hospital (where she had previously served as a low-wage ward girl), Wittmann became *the* model hysteric of Charcot's whole shebang in what's now understood as an iatrogenic dynamic between patient and doctor. Her symptoms seamlessly fit the mold of Charcot's theories, which likewise were adapted to explain and classify the course of her improvised outbreaks. She gave sensational flesh to Charcot's nosological word.

Augustine Gleizes exemplified "the greatest discovery of the end of the nineteenth century," according to the surrealists Louis Aragon and André Breton.[59] Along with Augustine: Justine Etchevery, Rosalie Lerroux, and Geneviève were among the hospital's many enigmatic icons—their images plastered over the walls of the neurology ward, published in Charcot and Albert Londe's three-volume *Iconographie photographique de la Salpêtrière*, and widely reproduced by the popular press. Even Sarah Bernhardt visited the crowded amphithéâtre to observe a staging of grande hystérie in preparation for her demanding role in *Adrienne Lecouvreur* in 1884.[60]

In his genealogy of "insanity" and its relation to scientific reason, Michel Foucault seizes on hysteria as a missing link between medical knowledge and epistemological truth. "As positivism imposes itself on medicine and psychiatry" in the nineteenth century, the asylum's morality narrative "becomes more and more obscure, the psychiatrist's power more and more miraculous, and the doctor-patient couple sinks deeper into a strange world," writes Foucault.[61] This was also "the period when the predominance of women among the institutionalized insane first bec[a]me a statistically verifiable phenomenon," notes Showalter, who critiques Foucault's inattention to gender.[62] Hysteria encompassed nearly 20 percent of all diagnoses at the Salpêtrière Hospital in 1883 (twenty times its 1 percent rate in 1845).[63] Charcot thus "descended into hell; but he didn't feel so badly there," adds Georges Didi-Huberman, "because the four or five thousand women of hell furnished him with *material*."[64] Indeed they did: some women "smelt with delight a bottle of ammonia when told it was rose water," recounts Munthe; "others would eat a piece of charcoal when presented to them as chocolate ... Another would walk with a top hat in her arms rocking it to and fro and kissing it tenderly when ... told it was her baby," or "flap her arms as if trying to fly when turned into a pigeon."[65] No extremity of psychological exploitation could ever satiate the spectacle machine of female hysteria.

There were, of course, overwhelming concerns about the abuse of hypnotic techniques, even when deployed toward allegedly curative ends. "It is a painful sight to see a number of people being reduced to soulless beings, disinherited of will," cried a New York correspondent, "that logic, reason, soul, will can all be subjugated, nay, temporarily annihilated, by the revolution of a glittering mirror."[66] The practice of animal magnetism (or mesmerism), whereby bodily symptoms could be transferred using magnets through the conduit of invisible animal/vitalist spirits, ran back to the discredited eighteenth-century experiments of Franz Mesmer. It was further feared that neurology would inspire lay hypnotists, abetting criminality, Svengali seduction, charlatanism, and even the tyrannical solicitation of mob violence.

Charcot refuted this moral panic because he viewed susceptibility to hypnosis as a unique trait of hysteria; his archrivals of the Nancy School, in contrast, posited it as a general physiological condition that can be induced in all individuals. One visitor to the Nancy clinic observed a hypnotic subject as "very much of an automaton . . . he at once accepts all ideas imposed upon him whether through word or touch," his mind clinging "to the last suggestion received."[67] Was hypnotism the mark of hysteria or a harbinger of mass psychosis? In one case, Charcot compelled a female somnambulist, a little girl of twelve, to stab him in the chest repeatedly with a dagger; she attempted to do so (against her own efforts at self-restraint) but the doctors had jovially replaced her blade with a piece of parchment.[68] The attempted murder did not even yield a paper cut.

These feats of hypnosis often had the flavor of fraternity hazing: making women imagine themselves naked in front of the audience or ludicrously metamorphose into a pigeon or ostrich. "The paralyzed walked, the deaf heard, and the blind saw," taunts Asti Hustvedt in *Medical Muses*.[69] Cataleptic patients displayed alarming anesthesia of the skin, as one correspondent depicted Charcot's "living subject," a twenty-two-year old former chambermaid: "long needles are run through her arms and legs, and she never feels the slightest pain."[70] Another girl transformed into a cat: "When the fit comes on [she] moves about on her hands and feet with really amazing agility, purring or hissing, as it may happen to be precisely as a cat does."[71] One woman allegedly slept continuously for fifty-four days, continuing to eat and drink, but remained completely unphased by a large gong "beaten violently at her bedside" directly over her head.[72]

Sadistic flourishes such as these—pushing the patient to the very breaking point of her emotional will and physical endurance—were meant to sort the true hysterics from the mere pretenders. While hypnotized, a "true" hysteric could sustain impossible acrobatic contortions, rigid aerobic planks, and biblical crucifixion poses for torturous duration. As Charcot's colleagues Charles Féré and Alfred Binet claimed, it was "impossible for an awake person to imitate even one of the physical phenomena of hypnotism."[73] One patient testified in an interview with Alphonse Baudouin after Charcot's death (upon which all her own symptoms mysteriously, spontaneously disappeared): "Fakery! Do you think it would have been easy to fool Monsieur Charcot?"[74] The autocratic referee of hysterical truth, Charcot harvested symptoms whose paradoxical authenticity rested on their infallible mimesis.

Epileptic Clownism and Carnival Somnambulism

The revolving door between Charcot's clinic and the circus never stopped spinning, as Gilles de la Tourette liked to joke. "No matter how much Charcot tried to distance himself and his hysterics from the carnival hypnotists," adds Hustvedt, "the rest of the world refused to oblige."[75] Many of his former patients found gainful employment as burlesque trance walkers and professional somnambulists after leaving the hospital. "As entertainment somnambulists, hysterics were well paid, received a cut of the night's profits, as well as food and lodging," claims Hustvedt.[76] Likewise, "one didn't have to go to Charenton or the Salpêtrière to witness" grand displays of epileptic clownism: "All of these movements could be seen nightly on the stages of café-concerts and cabarets," Rae Beth Gordon details.[77] There were spastic jugglers, human skeletons who sang in high falsetto, "freak dancers" exploiting their own "deformities" while gamboling through fast-paced can-cans, along with cross-dressing cataleptics, writhing serpentine mimics, and other unlikely figures such as the Homme-Aquarium "who could swallow several liters of water, including the frogs and fish residing therein."[78] But Charcot's neurology ward towered at the epicenter of the nerve-shattering city's busy corporeal traffic between the stage and the hospital.

An avid lover of the circus, Charcot described the second phase of the hysteric's attack as "clownism," characterized by acrobatic contortions and convulsive gestures that resembled the pratfalls and pantomime of a circus buffoon. The essence of clowning, according to Henri Bergson, consists in its "capers and movements," coupled with a posture of thing-like rigidity, which forms "the strictly 'clownish' element of the clown's art . . . Gradually, one lost sight of the fact that they were men of flesh and blood like ourselves" and not "solid wooden dummies."[79] Did Bergson have hysteria in view when formulating his philosophy of the comic in 1900? These "postures and attitudes [were] the oddest imaginable," explained Charcot, "so as to fully legitimize the denomination of *clownism* which I have proposed to designate this part of the second period of the fit."[80] In the throes of "clownism," hysterics attained wooden rigidity in their upper and lower limbs, climaxing in an "arc-en-cercle," where one arched her body in a semicircle—"a seemingly impossible contortion"—with only the head and heels still touching the ground.[81] Clownism saturated the wider iconography of hysteria—popularized by Londe's photography and Paul Richer's figurative portraiture.

Charcot also hosted lavish Bals des Folles (masked "lunatic balls" of "mad mummers"), which became the talk of the town, rivaling even the frog-guzzling

FIGURE 4.3 "Periode de Clownisme." D. M. Bourneville and P. Régnard, *Iconographie photographique de la salpêtrière (Service de M. Charcot)*, 1876–1877).

Aqua Man or the Pétomane, whose sphincter could extinguish a candle from thirty feet away while he whistled "the fart of the mother-in-law."[82] Many joy seekers actively favored the clinic over the circus or cabaret: "Carnival this year was flat and dull enough to have satisfied the most serious here," lamented a foreign correspondent for the *New York Herald* in 1881. "Mardi Gras was a mockery, and Mi-Carême opened in such utter and monotonous sadness that it was a perfect relief to get an invitation to the annual costume ball of the Salpêtrière."[83] He then proceeds to recount in lurid detail his exploits at the masked ball, where he traded battle stories with a woman in a straightjacket, cavorted with a trance-talking fortune teller, and eventually settled into a revue of "Songs Without Sense," principally "brayed" by an "offensive hussy" intoning "some lackadaisical ditty from the music halls."[84]

Like the cross-dressing, frog-eating, and limb-juggling neurasthenic headliners of the cabaret, female hysterics were unquestionably the star attractions of the clinic—equally enthralling but seemingly subservient to the exacting dictates of their hypnotist ringmaster.

HYSTERIA'S WANDERING WOMB

"Think of how hysteria was understood as a 'wandering womb,'" prompts Sara Ahmed in *Willful Subjects*, "a womb that does not stay in place, that does not reproduce... causing that body to become unreproductive."[85] As a "wastebasket" for wayward femininity, hysteria's nineteenth-century triggers comprised "uterine derangement," "political excitement," "laziness," "novel reading," "bad whiskey," "religious enthusiasm," and "excessive masturbation."[86] Simply put, if you could not accurately diagnose it, then hystericize it! Given its changeable form, why has hysteria long persisted as *the* "female" malady rather than opening its field of play to gender fluidity and nonconformity? If there is an "equivalence between femininity and hysteria," it's because hysteria itself "has been feminized: over and over again," argues Juliet Mitchell in *Mad Men and Medusas*.[87] For Charcot, hysteria's sexual division boiled down to the mutability of one's symptoms, which "is without doubt that which seems to constitute the capital difference between the two sexes," he claimed.[88] Female symptoms were viewed as "unstable," "capricious," and "most unexpected," and were thus cured through enforced bed rest and clownist hypnosis.[89] In contrast, male symptoms (also known as "railway spine") were "remarkable" for their "permanence" and "tenacity," eradicated only by vigorous activities such as cattle ranching and game hunting.[90]

"Because hysteria represented a *great fear* for everyone," writes Didi-Huberman, "it was the bête noir of physicians for a very, very long time: for it was aporia made into a symptom. It was the symptom, to put it crudely, *of being a woman*."[91] To paraphrase, aporia is the symptom of being a woman. But hysteria's "corsets are always there," maintains Cixous in a July 2020 phone interview, so its temporality can never quite catch pace with its absolute tense of "not yet."[92] In its subjunctive address, hysteria's aporia further evokes what Rox Samer (in a very different context) calls the " 'couldness' or possibility" of trans phenomenology's "unfinished body."[93] Their object of analysis is none other than a wandering clown: "trans Chaplin," the iconic persona whose "bodily transformations" into "animal, plant, or object" makes "the largely invisible but nevertheless real sensuous process of transitioning perceptible."[94] Samer's investment in snatching the fluidity of transition from the iconography of the archive bears underexplored parallels with the corporeal mutability of female hysteria. The difference is also one of movement: the "unfinished" trans body is always in process, while the corseted hysteric, ever elsewhere, can only dream of lasting inscription.

Queer Potentials: Past and Future

In her 1994 "manifesto for lesbian feminism," Heather Findlay celebrates the hysteric as a "distinctly queer figurehead" for psychoanalytic queer theory.[95] Findlay pits Jacques Lacan's 1951 "Intervention on Transference" against Gayle Rubin's analysis of "the traffic in women" (1975) to articulate a queer methodology for "lesbian, feminist-Lacanian analysis," she adds, "if we can imagine such a creature."[96] (The essay is initially presented as her acceptance of a dare from Judith Butler.) Its key stake, according to Findlay, "would be to come to terms with how *every* identification is based on a misrecognition."[97] Findlay thus stresses the coalition-building potentials of misrecognition as an alternative to identification, whereby the only basis for solidarity is seeing in the other a reflection of one's own struggles and oppression. "Rather, feminists must 'articulate' with the anti-racism movement on the basis of a misrecognition," she suggests, exploring self-critical modes of intersectional commitment.

Despite Findlay's evocative gesture, hysteria has not been a key signifier for queer theory nor has queerness been a paramount concern for feminist theorists of hysteria. There are certainly resonant images of queerness in the archives of hysteria, such as Augustine's iconic escape from the hospital crossdressed as a man—which has recently been fictionalized in the films *Augustine*

(Alice Winocour, 2012), *Charming Augustine* (Zoe Beloff, 2005), and *The Mad Women's Ball* (Mélanie Laurent, 2021). Dora slapped her male seducer Herr K. in the face and pursued greater intimacy with his wife, inspiring Cixous's alignment of écriture feminine with "bisexuality" (as "the nonexclusion of difference or of a sex" and "the presence of both sexes" within oneself).[98] For Cixous, hysteric language and queer desire (like Medusan laughter) go hand in glove. Queer theory's ambivalence about psychoanalysis (the lingua franca of feminist hysteria studies) and queer sexuality's historical experience of being gaslit and hystericized (e.g., negated by "conversion therapy") further shed light on the rift between queer and hysteria-oriented feminisms. Beyond that, queer affect theory favors very different methodological categories to account for the emotional politics of sexuality and language. "Mixed feelings," "ugly feelings," "disaffection," and "killjoy" commitments seek to redeem hysteric affect on its own terms—to convert "personal affective expression" into "public political action"—rather than dwell in its abyss of symptoms, which is ostensibly the gesture of feminist reading at the scene of hysteric conversion.[99]

In her chapter "Beyond Queer," Anne Worthington posits queer theory as the successor to psychoanalysis in that both emerged as responses to the fundamental problem of hysteria. As we know, psychoanalysis was born from the ashes of hysteria in the late nineteenth century; then, "is not queer the logical outcome of hysteria's questions of the century post-psychoanalysis?" asks Worthington.[100] She emphasizes the riddle of gender identity and its relation to sexual object choices (who "can make rational sense of why they like whatever it is they like"), claiming queer as a "site for the articulation and protest of hysteria today."[101] Indeed, queerness is part of the big tent of "hysteria activism," exemplified by coalition groups such as *Hysteria* (London), *HysteriaFemCon* (Calcutta), and *The Association of Hysteric Curators* (Los Angeles) that stake "their claim to hysteria in order to expose the wounds and traumas inflicted by patriarchy," Elke Krasny avows.[102] As the signifier hysteria becomes increasingly de-specified in the crisis-ridden present (enlarged by anxiety about gaslighting, far-right authoritarianism, and simulacral spectacle), the counterpolitics of hysterical feminisms have become radically inclusive in their mission statements, if not also in their activism and membership bodies.

As archival specters, hysteria and queerness have always incurred a certain conflation whereby the hypervisibility of hysteria repeatedly eclipsed and erased the existence of queerness. As Xine Yao notes in *Disaffected*, "to educate a woman is to render her queer," with reference to Edward H. Clarke's *Sex in Education* (1873), which Yao quotes: "the benighted female becomes afflicted by 'the hermaphroditic condition that sometimes accompanies spinsterism' and leads to 'neuralgia, uterine disease, hysteria, and other derangements of the nervous system.'"[103] For Yao, assertions of "unfeeling" and "anti-social affect" (such as frigidity and inscrutability) offer vital alternatives to "dominant ways of being and enable new structures of feeling to arise."[104] If the "hysterical" laughter of feminist joke telling attempts to fill the void of homophobia with proud punch lines (as per the documentary *Hysterical*), queer disaffection lives in that unfilled void. In that sense, it is radically hysterical!

BLACK MADNESS, DOUBLE CONSCIOUSNESS, AND HYSTERICAL MINSTRELSY

The twentieth-century "problem of the color-line" created yet another roadblock for the wandering uterus.[105] Conversion hysteria commuted the womb into a metaphorical entity because one's nomadic organ was obviously not the cause of their choking sensations, phantom paralysis, or cataleptic plank poses (and so forth). Medical metaphor or quack conspiracy, it posed an unresolvable contradiction for white supremacist biopolitics. White women's wombs needed to be solid and literal, not nervous and figurative. Female hysteria thus threatened the whole enterprise of the uterus (i.e., its fertility), in addition to severely disrupting female reproductive labor such as family care and housework.

In "The Race of Hysteria," Laura Briggs unearths "two kinds of radically discontinuous bodies and constitutions" from the archives of American medical psychiatry: "one white, nervous, and plagued by weakness; the other racialized, colonized, and hardy."[106] American nerve specialists regarded hysteria as a benchmark of white civilization, which, according to George Beard, departed from ancient civilization, not least of all due to "the mental activity of women."[107] So wrote Beard in florid prose in his widely read study of *American Nervousness*: "The first signs of ascension, as of declension, in nations are seen in women. As the foliage of delicate plants first show the early warmth of spring . . . so the impressible, susceptive organization of woman appreciates and exhibits far sooner than that of man the manifestations of national progress or decay."[108] And if white women's hotwired nerves were the harbingers of civilized progress, by Beard's logic, their diminished fertility and reproductive incapacity also foreboded its irreversible decline.

Briggs states this bluntly, arguing that hysteria's "narrative shared with racist eugenics a concern about white women's low birth rate and the fertility of non-white women."[109] Endemic panic about racial biopolitics fueled a contradictory desire to segregate and to consume displays of Black hysteria. These performances tapped "into near-undefinable elements of rhythm and gesture" and "conveyed a vitality" white spectators "were eager to appropriate," as Gordon argues.[110] She explores the arrival of the American cakewalk in Paris circa 1903 as a flashpoint for the "unusual concurrence of medical pathologies and of Darwinism in the Parisian music-hall," following the traffic between medical epilepsy images, their frenetic enactment on the popular stage, and colonialist appropriations of African rhythm in France from 1875 to 1910.[111] "The simultaneity of these three spectacular displays of the body in movement—hysteria, epileptic singers, and African dance—could not help but create some degree of amalgam in the popular imagination," suggests Gordon in *Dances with Darwin*.[112] Riotous stage acts such as the Zulu dancers of the Folies Bergère and the Châtelet Théâtre's *La Vénus noire* (1879) inspired wide fascination and white imitation, linking the clownist hysteric's "second self" to primitivist depictions of the African body. At the same time that nervous hysteria ran rampant as a white woman's ailment, Black bodies were essentialized as organically hysteric—like Augustine without an unconscious.

If the French cabaret was haunted by the American minstrel stage (conflating eugenic panic and epidemic epileptics in the French public imagination), a similar collusion took root in the U.S. theater. White spectators looked to Black spectacle to escape the unconscious bogeyman of modern neurosis. By the end of the nineteenth century, the most popular U.S. entertainment traditions—vaudeville, variety theater, burlesque revues, comic extravaganzas—had evolved from the racist antebellum pastime of blackface minstrelsy. (And indeed, popular comediennes—from Fanny Brice to Sophie Tucker—repeatedly donned burnt cork.)

Saidiya Hartman dissects the spectacle of blackface as a site of affective hysteria where displays of Black suffering (in melodrama) and racist caricatures of savage enjoyment (in minstrelsy) aroused conflicting sensations: "pity and fear, desire and revulsion, terror and pleasure," writes Hartman. "Blows caused the virtuous black body of melodrama to be esteemed and humiliated the grotesque black body of minstrelsy."[113] Black flesh was thereby transposed in its "figurative capacities" into a "fungible commodity," affectively available and productively inexhaustible.[114] "Specifically its abstractness and immateriality enabled the black body or blackface mask to serve as a vehicle of white self-exploration, renunciation, and enjoyment," Hartman asserts.[115] In that sense, the carnal spectacle of blackface (consumed rapaciously by white spectators) offered an escape hatch from the automatism of hysteric dissociation. The utter lack of distance between self and mask, in the case of Blackness—as opposed to the revolving-door consciousness of alternating selves—held hysteria's color line.

Double Consciousness Versus Double Conscience

W. E. B. Du Bois's formative metaphor of "double consciousness," as the subjective condition of Blackness in America, bears an uncanny echo with the psychoanalytic notion of "double conscience," or the hysteric's affliction by multiple, alienated selves. "It is a peculiar sensation," writes Du Bois, "this double-consciousness, this sense of always looking at one's self through the eyes of others, of measuring one's soul by the tape of a world that looks on in amused contempt and pity."[116] The second self or internalized onlooker of Black double consciousness fails to disappear into the recesses of the psyche because it is actively policed by the ubiquity of surveillant white gazes that pose immediate physical danger. It thus strays from the hysteric's dissociated double, whose "unmotivated ideas, alien to normal association . . . force their way into consciousness" and spark vivid hallucinations in the thick of "twilight states and states of exhaustion," as Breuer described hysteric "double conscience" in 1895.[117]

Esther Wakefield's laughing excitations unleashed her flamboyant spirit that remained alien to her primary self, cut from the cloth of white bourgeois femininity. "It is true," in contrast, "that a spirit alien to the patient's waking consciousness holds sway," wrote Breuer, "but the spirit is not in fact an alien one, but a part of [her] own."[118] Double consciousness had no time for alienation, demanding grueling simultaneity over delirious alternation. Du Bois's punctuation in his prose further puts pressure on the deadline of double consciousness, which diverges from dissociation also in its temporal dimensions. "One ever feels his twoness,—an American, a Negro; two souls, two thoughts, two unreconciled strivings; two warring ideals in one dark body, whose dogged strength alone keeps it from being torn asunder."[119] It was a distinction between the flickering presence of white shattered nerves versus the iron cage entrapping negated Black selves.

Repressed alter ego or perpetual double? In *Crazy Funny: Popular Black Satire and the Method of Madness*, Lisa Guerrero takes up Du Boisian double consciousness in precisely this vein: as a "split personality disorder" by which Black people were denied the "potential" and "flexibility" to "achieve an integrated ego."[120] Twenty-first-century Black satire, she argues, confronts the "*disintegrated* ego" of Black consciousness, wrought by centuries of slavery and racism, giving cathartic relief to its gaslit abjection. "If the satirical mode" takes its object of ridicule to its logically absurd conclusions, "and if racism and racialization already verge on the inherently absurd," observes Danielle Fuentes Morgan, "the distinction between the reality and the satire may be indistinguishable."[121] The fever dream of double consciousness superimposed the impossibility of suppressed desire over the somatic experience of ordinary racism.

Like Morgan, Guerrero emphasizes the lack of distance between reason and madness (racism and absurdity) that has always haunted the scene of Black cultural production. But "this split [or lack thereof] no longer serves a purpose for satirists and their characters," Guerrero claims, "since the only purpose the split had ever served for black people was to situate them within the logic of a society ruled by white supremacy."[122] In other words, Blackness has long been gaslit as mad and irrational but refused the nuanced discourse of its psychological expression and cultural mediation. It is the role of Black aesthetics to disrupt "the loose rendering of Blackness and madness as analogous to each other," argues Therí Alice Pickens in *Black Madness :: Mad Blackness*.[123] Pickens focuses on Afrofuturist speculative fiction, such as Tananarive Duo's *African Immortals* series (1997–2011), Nalo Hopkinson's *Midnight Robber* (2000), and Octavia Butler's *Fledgling* (2005). In both psychiatric and cultural discourses, Blackness and madness "are examined as extensions of one another," according to Pickens, "too slippery to parse, yet so inseparable that one can elide or replace the other."[124] This doubling has vast material stakes because the denial of resources toward Black mental health care is further predicated on ideologies of Blackness as itself quintessentially mad. But unlike the dissociative depth of "clownist" hysteria, Black madness has been viewed as entirely of the flesh.

Index of an Absent Uterus

Christina Sharpe evocatively raises the specter of "hystera" as a condition of possibility for Black oppositional readings in *Monstrous Intimacies*. Temporarily placing the ailment back inside the womb, Sharpe analyzes Gayl Jones's novel *Corregidora*, which depicts generational traumas of slavery that haunt Ursa, a Black woman in 1940s Jim Crow Kentucky. "The entire narrative of *Corregidora*," Sharpe argues, "comes down to the very thing that is the origin of the word *hysteria* itself."[125] At the novel's narrative spine, Ursa Corregidora is forced to have a hysterectomy after "falling" down a flight of stairs (in truth, she is assaulted by her husband). Sharpe links this event to the family's structural condition of "suppressed hysteria," which "involves also a repression of the structures through which hysteria becomes visible" and is the "very hysteria that Ursa sacrificed her womb to be rid of."[126] As an index of an absent womb, her scar takes the place of those suppressed bodily signs that were never allowed to register even as enigmatic symptoms. It means the end of the line (no future generations to haunt), but it also indicates a dual imperative to remember: the rape, incest, and physical abuse inflicted on them by Corregidora, their Portugese enslaver.

Ursa hears calls from her matrilineal kin in an inner voice (always italicized), carried forth from dead generations:[127]

> *They burned all the documents Ursa. But they didn't burn what they put in their minds . . . Except we got to keep what we need to bear witness. That scar that's left to bear witness. We got to keep it as visible as our blood.*

Her scar represents a "hieroglyphic of the flesh" ("as visible as blood"), to invoke Hortense Spillers's notion of Black flesh: "that zero degree of social conceptualization that does not escape concealment under the brush of discourse."[128] Denied the depth of unconscious hysteria, Ursa's indelible scar "bear[s] witness" to the violence and dehumanization that "they" (white masters) had stashed away "in their minds."[129] As Sharpe notes, the scar is a gesture "to mark herself . . . and reproduce horror on her body and into the next generation" as "a scar of her own. The evidence that she will hold up to bear witness to the horrors of slavery and its prolonged effects is *her* body, evidence she can feel."[130] With the loss of her fetus and removal of her womb ("I can't make generations," she reflects while imagining how her ancestors passed their "days" like "pages of hysteria"), the scar inscribes the dead letter of hysteria on Ursa's flesh.[131]

Laughter is an important motif in the novel, always hovering around the limits of the unsayable. When Ursa prompts Tadpole (the owner of Happy's, where she sings the blues) to touch her scar, adding "it's worse when you touch it than when you look at it," he laughs upon taking his hand away.[132] His laughter is not at her scar but at Ursa's ex-husband (who caused the scar); Mutt Thomas has been spying on Ursa outside the window, and she jokes to Tad: "Tell him that 'can't come in' means 'can't look in' either."[133] In response, Tad laughs. His laughter fills the void between vision and touch, displaced from the tactility of the scar onto the voyeurism of its perpetrator. Mutt created the scar, but it is no longer named for him (unlike the fetus, who would have been), which is made abundantly clear by Ursa's doctor, who mistakenly refers to Mutt as Mr. Corregidora—despite its evocative suffix ("dora"), Ursa's family name was taken from a Portuguese slaveowner who forcibly impregnated Ursa's Gram and Great Gram.

The child of incest, Ursa's mother laughs upon recounting the story of Ursa's conception with Martin, her father, a Black man who left in Ursa's early childhood. Mama "laughed a little, the kind of laugh that's not really a laugh, as if one had to make more effort to get a laugh, and she hadn't made enough effort."[134] Laughter asserts the impossibility of pretending that their lives aren't written by the "pages of hysteria" endured by "how many generations?"[135] In the end, Ursa returns to Mutt, but she never forgives him; instead, she imagines laughing at him: "If I had been anyone else, and the consequences hadn't been what they were, seeing him . . . would have made me laugh."[136] In lieu of her aborted laugh, she performs oral sex and tries to embody its jouissance: "pleasure and excruciating pain at the same time, a moment of broken skin . . . just before sexlessness" that makes her lose sight of whether she's Ursa or her Great Gram and whether Mutt's Mutt or Corregidora.[137] Their bodies shake and they sob with heavy tears, but not of laughter.

BATTLE ROYALE: AUTHORITARIAN GASLIGHTING VERSUS MEDUSAN HYSTERIA

Hysteric symptoms—our pipeline between affective panic and impossible utterance—shape the multifarious crises of the twenty-first century. "What the hysteria over critical race theory is really about," explains Fabiola Cineas, is the suppression of speech in order "to ban anti-racist teachings and trainings in classrooms and workplaces across the country."[138] A nuanced academic framework that reveals how racism is embedded in U.S. institutions has now become a catch-all signifier deployed to gaslight and disempower antiracist discourse—a bogeyman for far-right hysteria. Long eclipsed as a diagnostic category in psychiatric medicine, when one uses the term "hysteria" today, it is typically in the realm of metaphor. As a hostile accusation, it might refer to anything from a ridiculous cultural fad to a dangerous political obsession: "cryptocurrency hysteria," "cancel culture hysteria," "antivaccine hysteria," and on and on. Beyond its cynical weaponization (i.e., hystericizing the other's complaint), it serves as a way of marking incommensurable realities: what feels unbearable to survive and yet impossible to transform—lest we ourselves become hysterics!

Teen Vogue published a viral editorial in December 2016, "Donald Trump Is Gaslighting America," which linked Trump's misogynistic, xenophobic chest-thumping to the antireal effects of his systematic lies to drive Americans to doubt the truth of their own minds.[139] "It was as though America had acquired its own Shroud of Turin, immune to all doubts produced by fiber analysis," observes

Joan Copjec in "Hysteria and Democracy in America."[140] Copjec refers not to Trump (although she does invoke him presciently) but to his ostensible predecessor, Ronald Reagan, who sailed into the Oval Office on a similar wave of prior celebrity, white supremacist pandering, and verifiable untruths. The news industry's "referential failures" to disprove Reagan's abject lies, according to Copjec, exposes the limits of visible evidence to penetrate the "signifying space" where the "letter" of truth "remains unobserved."[141] In other words, the lies we want to believe take cover in plain sight, especially when empirical signs hold less and less sway over the insuppressible symptoms of mass hysteria. Nearly three decades later, it does not take a Lacanian to intuit that false belief will survive its repeated refutation by cold hard evidence, just as irresponsible attachment (to the object *a*: that "unnameable excess, the exorbitant thing that is loved") can never be shamed into renouncement or silenced through the infamy of its public embarrassment.[142]

With the resurgence of hysteria, feminist bodily language—art, activism, multimedia expression, and gestural experimentation—has risen to meet the obscenity of the current predicament. In the twenty-first century, feminist writers and creative makers reclaim the mantle of hysteria. The photographer Cindy Sherman, filmmaker Zoe Beloff, artist Mary Sibande, vocalist Sage Harlow, curator Cindy Rehm, and sculptor Shana Lutker all vividly (in very different ways) conjure the archives and iconography of hysteria's medical bodily poses, "gHosting" them, as Laura González puts it, in order to channel their mimetic qualities and thereby disentangle hysteria's affective dangers from its enduring fascination.[143] How else can feminist practices deploy "historical concepts and ideas on hysteria" to "create new ways of thinking *with* and thinking *through* hysteria?" asks Johanna Braun.[144] Toward that end, she has coordinated a massive, international research project, "The Hysteric As Conceptual Operator," which explores the contemporary resonances of hysteria's medical archives amid the viral COVID-19 pandemic, insanity of authoritarian gaslighting, and flourishing of feminist political activism.[145]

Hysteric symptoms—from the loss of language to the involuntary mimicry of an acrobatic circus clown—flare up when the discharge of anxiety lacks a lifeline into the symbolic: the signs that legitimate shared reality over cynical lies uttered in bad faith. As the gap between reality and simulacrum no longer holds—but dissolves into a vortex of nonstop, unanchored, spectacle-based, and profit-driven signs—is there any room for play remaining between empirical truth and its suggestive distortion? This question has tangible implications for the duality of psychiatric and comedic forms of laughter that we have been chasing throughout this chapter.

It was Cixous's wager all along for feminist hysteric laughter to demolish the symbolic (beyond merely subverting it) and give semiotic flesh to those "carnal, passionate body-words" that would further unleash thunderous poetic signs.[146] No degree of incisive wit or fierce punching up can ever do that work when surreal spectacle runs roughshod over legitimated signs. Hysteria's ghosts might yet chart a Medusan alternative to the hegemony of dystopian gaslighting. They levitate from the abyss of absolute hysterical laughter.

5
Laughter

The Forgotten Symptom

From the madwoman in the attic to the Wicked Witch of the West, demonic laughs curdle in the throats of Medusan female villains. Do these mischief makers always laugh in sadistic delight at the spectacle of another's suffering, like Jane Hudson (Bette Davis) upon serving her paraplegic sister Blanche (Joan Crawford) a dead rat on a silver platter in *Whatever Happened to Baby Jane?* (Robert Aldrich, 1962). Or perhaps her laughter is a message without a code: ambient cacophony to underscore affective calamity. Noncomedic laughter envelops cinematic asylum scenes—from surrealist visions in *A Page of Madness* (Teinosuke Kinugasa, 1926) to acousmatic cachinnation in classic Hollywood's *The Snake Pit* (Anatole Litvak, 1948) and Ryan Murphy's campy/creepy *American Horror Story: Asylum* (FX, 2012–2013). Confusion between ruthless evil and ordinary disaffection is precisely the point.

Diagnoses of "pathological laughter" have been variously exploited for their narrative intrigue and visual spectacle. In its clinical designation, pseudobulbar affect (PBA) refers to the disorder of uncontrollable laughing or crying caused by a disconnection between the prefrontal cortex (which controls emotions) and the cerebellum (where voluntary movements are coordinated). When depicted as a neurological condition (PBA), as opposed to an emotional predisposition (hysteria), paradoxical laughter arises as a masculine affliction in its gendered narrative coding. It bedevils alienated male characters, such as Arthur Fleck in *Joker* (Todd Phillips, 2019), Ki-woo in *Parasite* (Bong Joon-ho, 2019), and Ramon Silva in a television episode of *House* (November 22, 2010). Silva's involuntary laughter is climactically diagnosed as a symptom of his multiple sclerosis. Similarly, Fleck's laughter stems from a neurological impairment, and Ki-woo's is implicitly triggered by a severe head injury and sustained trauma.

FIGURE 5.1 Jane (Bette Davis) laughs demonically after serving her sister a dead rat on a silver platter. Frame enlargement from *Whatever Happened to Baby Jane?* (directed by Robert Aldrich, 1962; Burbank, CA: Warner Bros. Pictures).

In the examples of *Joker* and *Parasite*, pseudobulbar laughter further gives voice to horrific absurdities endemic to late capitalist inequality and its marketized funhouse of escalating human misery.[1] To observe that "it would be funny if it wasn't so [insert placeholder for not funny]" is now a cliché, especially in reference to electoral politics, corporate will to power, and institutional dysfunction.[2]

But the madwoman's laugh opens onto a very different realm of political meaning. One might say that unmotivated female laughter has been insistently hystericized—gaslit, assumed incoherent, but denied the narrative solidity of a concrete diagnosis or symbolic complaint. When the specter of female hysteria rears its Medusan head in twenty-first-century popular culture, it elicits suspicions of borderline personality disorder, histrionic personality disorder, narcissistic personality disorder, or "bipolar-driven promiscuity," exemplified by eroticized depictions of female mental illness in films such as *Fatal Attraction* (Adrian Lyne, 1987), *Single White Female* (Barbet Schroeder, 1992), *The Crush* (Alan Shapiro, 1993), *Mad Love* (Antonia Bird, 1995), *Girl, Interrupted* (James Mangold, 1999), *Thirteen* (Catherine Hardwicke, 2003), *Black Swan* (Darren Aronofsky, 2010), *Benedetta* (Paul Verhoeven, 2021), *Pearl* (Ti West, 2022), and too many others to name.[3]

In effect, the laughing madwoman remains thoroughly hysteric—in both her diagnostic status and her allegorical substance. Just as Jean-Martin Charcot spent years poring over autopsies of deceased epileptic patients in futile hopes of finding evidential lesions in the brain, today the search continues apace. Laughter itself offers a missing link between undiagnosed mental health and pathologized female excess. Decoding the gender politics of these involuntary laughs, I argue, holds the key to their deeper emotional expression and enigmatic cultural value.

RIDDLES OF "RIRE HYSTÉRIQUE"

Hysteria took center stage in the nineteenth-century theater of neurology precisely because its root origins could never be fully mastered or exposed. In certain ways, the will to relocate madness in microscopic abnormalities of the brain harkens back to the female malady's depiction as the consequence of a wandering uterus. The analogy only goes so far, but both assume an objective physical cause for what cannot be discerned by the naked eye rather than linger in the void of unruly bodily signs. (Established treatments for involuntary laughter target bilateral lesions in the corticobulbar tract of the brain, which induce emotional lability and exaggerated changes in mood.) Hysteria's sensational visibility appealed to the empirical riddle of its unsolvable mystery in the nineteenth-century clinic. As I have explained, it designated a condition whereby the word turned into flesh. Its basis was not in the brain but in the affective recesses of the psyche—of buried memory, embodied habits, difficult feelings, and suppressed libido.

Fou rire (colloquial "crazy laughter") only reached that threshold of "emotional pathology," according to the Argentine physician José Ingenieros, when it proceeded from "a trifling cause" in response to a "painful condition," as in the case of a woman whose "rire hystérique" he claimed was genital in origin.[4] Even brief mentions of "rire hystérique," however, remained rare in the context of clinical diagnosis. If women's ordinary laughs were hystericized as excessive or inappropriate (and therefore unreadable), their clinical variants fell by the wayside of psychiatric research, discarded as "probably of value" but "theoretically . . . insufficient" for the purpose of useful investigation.[5] With a few gynecological exceptions, hysteric laughs were at once taken for granted and all but written out of the case studies.

Leading practitioners (Charcot, Sigmund Freud, Josef Breuer, Pierre Janet, Paul Briquet, Alfred Binet, Charles Féré, et al.) gave pride of place to every other symptom than laughter—from fugue states, motor impairments, and double vision to sneezing, yawning, and uncanny tongue clacking. For example, in

Janet's comprehensive account of the major symptoms of hysteria, there is only *one* mention of hysteric laughter (as an involuntary reaction to an illicit abortion), which is briefly sandwiched between incidents of serial hiccupping and medieval epidemics of meowing, whinnying, and barking.[6]

A young woman laughs as jocular medical students tauntingly flush out her uterus: "Thus a girl of bad morals had undergone a little surgical operation" (i.e., an abortion), Janet recounted, "for which she had been half chloroformed" but "young students at the hospital . . . had kept joking her and making her laugh."[7] She soon lost control, allegedly due to the chloroform but no doubt aggravated by the fraternal chorus of tendentious taunts during an invasive medical procedure associated with public shame and social scandal. As a consequence, her laughter "transformed into an independent automatic phenomenon, and persisted as a tic."[8] It became hysteric when severed from any relation to "joking," here clearly incited by the burdens of memory surrounding the scene of her abortion, sexual enjoyment, and their pervasive silencing.

Hysteric affect was foremost characterized by the somatic deflection of distressing cognition. "No affect reaction is permitted," wrote Herman Hoppe, "they are not cast off and forgotten, but they are buried . . . by shame and disgust."[9] In effect, conversion symptoms—from hiccupping to hallucination—transposed visceral suffering into corporeal writing, relegating all other affective sensations (such as joy, anger, or arousal) to the sinkhole of inadmissible memory. But what was repeatedly avoided (and remains widely unthought) is that room for play between festering repression and invigorating redemption. Throughout this book, I have emphasized the unresolved encounters between joy and its opposites, following them to their unstable and allegedly lethal conclusions. As we know, "hysterical laughter" (in the colloquial sense) ensued from mixed feelings and unleashed morbid convulsions throughout the nineteenth century. In the gendered archives of madness and enjoyment, women's laughs were pathologized as hysteric or hysterical if they betrayed any uncertainty of feeling or instability of pleasure.

To laugh madly, for women, implied a lack of proportion between response and its trigger. But there was always a thread, however tenuous, between the spark of comedy and the explosion of laughter. After all, what is laughter if not a sanctioned outlet for gross guttural noise and the abandonment of bodily control?

The cackling madwoman could have been a poster child for the nineteenth-century asylum. Yet her laughter was not allowed to speak, even via the analyst's tongue. Of all the symptoms of hysteria, laughter at once epitomized the ailment and disqualified itself from further interpretation. "All of us always know what the idea is which makes us laugh or cry or blush," claimed Breuer, "even though we have not the slightest understanding of the nervous mechanism of these ideogenic phenomena."[10] Yet "this is not the case with very many or indeed the majority of hysterical symptoms."[11] Caught in the headwinds of repression and enjoyment, hysteric laughter took comedy's gambit of "unknowing" to its disturbing somatic conclusions.

Comical laughs already walked a razor-thin line between forbidden license and symbolic protest. Hysteric laughs too closely resembled their ordinary variants: thunderous convulsions, fragmented insights, wild complicity between ideas and organs. But they were not enough like true symptoms, occupying an uncanny valley of risible affect unmotivated by immediate context. They simply did not unlock that dissociated "second self" whose repressed fancies and unbearable mental yearnings gave vital material to the rising scientific fields of neurology, alienism, and psychoanalysis.

HYSTERIC POSTURES: SPIRITISM, AUTOMATISM, "CLOWNISM"

When did hysteric laughter attain to the neurologist's notepad? In Charcot's clinic, laughter was never a far cry from "clownism": those impossible, acrobatic contortions that patients assumed between epileptic seizures and passionate poses. Julie, a nervous adolescent, was conducting a séance when her piercing laughs escalated into horrified cries and then clownist paroxysms. Charcot recounted this scene vividly in his lecture on "Spiritism and Hysteria," which opens with a warning about the hysteric hazards of having a lively imagination "in persons predisposed thereto."[12]

Julie was in many ways a perfect candidate for hysteria. She lived in a convent near a remote military penitentiary where her father served as an officer. Her everyday routine was extremely tedious and gloomy, thus exciting her "natural disposition" of nervousness, which Charcot described: "From her infancy she has been very nervous. At the convent, as at home, she has been unruly and difficult of management, laughing and crying for the most trifling cause."[13] Again, it was the chaotic instability between laughter and tears that gained either one admission as a hysteric symptom—one without the other did not appear worth detailing. "You see the patient has been taken, during our examination, with convulsive laughter which she cannot moderate," declared Charcot, "and which will soon be followed by a shower of tears."[14] If laughter at jokes parlayed irrational thoughts into a pleasurable escape through one's body, laughter-as-hysteria collapsed the necessary distance between mimetic sensations and difficult words.

FIGURE 5.2 Frame enlargement of scene depicting a séance in *Dr. Mabuse, der Spieler* [*Dr. Mabuse, the Gambler*] (directed by Fritz Lang, 1922; Berlin: Uco-Film GmbH).

Denied the habitual satisfaction of ordinary pleasure, hysteric women retreated into their automatisms, which assumed a range of guises. For example, wives of the prison officers devoted themselves to spiritualism "with passionate interest" to break up the monotony of corporeal discipline with occultist possession, holding séances every other day and devouring literature on paranormal science.[15] Julie was home for the Easter holidays when it was determined by a firm rapping at Friday's table-tipping session that she would play medium at the next séance. She happily obliged but then froze in terror while transcribing a message from an undead spirit with her pencil. The séance was ended, but Julie later agreed to continue at her neighbor's insistence, who wished to communicate with her deceased sister. Upon arrival, the visiting ghost announced itself not as the neighbor's sister but as "Paul Denis," a male stranger, whose words Julie outlined "in such odd characters that the young girl has never since then been able to trace letters like them."[16]

It was in this uncanny context, scrawling funny letters from the incorrect ghost ("the hand-writing was that of a man," insisted Charcot) that Julie broke into gales of shrieking laughter:

Then Julie, with a shrill laugh, rose immediately, and, like one mad, in wild delirium ran back and forth through the house, uttering inarticulate cries, then rolled over and over on the floor, presenting a series of hysterical paroxysms characterized chiefly by contortions (clownism).[17]

In the days that followed, Julie suffered spontaneous fits, involving auratic seizures, clownist contortions ("at times [her head] was almost brought into contact with the pelvis"), and baffling noises.[18] She "uttered moans, had fits of laughter, but did not speak."[19] These attacks lasted for hours on end, and the only way to suppress them, according to Charcot, was to apply direct pressure to her hysterogenic zones, especially her breasts, buttocks, and inner elbow joints.

We cannot help but observe the direct line of dictation from undead male language to illegible female laughter. Julie's possession by the strange writing of the wrong ghost incited her attacks. But even her recurring laughter was still not allowed to speak because Charcot disregarded it as flighty and unimportant. Again, she "had fits of laughter, but did not speak."[20] The ejection of Julie's enjoyment from her volcanic cachinnation—emitted through an alien self, triggered by an undead male spirit—condemned her laughter to the abyss of nonmeaning. Affectively unstable, corporeally impossible, and vividly surreal, Julie's laughter was forsaken by the neurologist's will to sensemaking interpretation. Whatever forbidden pleasures or speculative insights her affective crisis might have disclosed: they were chalked up to mere nervousness.

AUTOMATISM: FROM CIRCUS PRATFALLS TO CLOWNIST HYSTERIA

Can you imprison the spirit of the comic within a definition? Henri Bergson famously defied this proposition in his pithy and widely read essays on *Laughter*: "we shall not aim at imprisoning the comic in a definition."[21] And yet, all the same, he eagerly cast out the comic from the category of the living, ossifying it as an "automatism." Epitomized by hapless pratfalls, automatisms possess "that side of a person which reveals his likeness to a thing, that aspect of human events which, through its peculiar inelasticity, conveys the impression of pure mechanism, of movement without life."[22] Circus clowns need not apply for élan vital—that animate force or creative whimsy separating adaptive life from knee-jerk repetition.

As we know, Charcot modeled his lectures on the circus, fancying himself as something of a lay ringmaster. He trotted out his star epileptic hysterics, classifying their convulsive contortions as clownism. It is no surprise that many of his former patients found gainful employment as carnival somnambulists and trance walkers after escaping the clinic. One woman even graced the cover of the popular French humor magazine, *Le Rire* (not to be confused with Bergson's essay *Le Rire*, which was first published in *Revue de Paris*).[23] Axel Munthe describes this scene at length, placing her anachronistically in Charcot's own neurology ward (Charcot died before the magazine debuted).[24] According to Munthe, "Geneviève was sitting dangling her silk-stockinged legs from the long table in the middle of the ward with a copy of *Le Rire* in her lap with her own portrait on the title-page."[25] Although verifiably apocryphal, this anecdote is no less telling for having been spun entirely out of whole cloth. Female hysterics were the epileptic doppelgängers of circus acrobats.

Automatism was a crucial concept also for theorists of hysteria, although it had very different implications in that field. Janet associated automatism not with one's absence of mind but with the mind's hidden depths: all that lay beyond acceptable consciousness. For Janet, hysteria unleashed a tumult of automatisms, or automatic behaviors that could not be controlled by inhibition or will. "It must be confessed," intimated Janet, "that there is a particular disease which unites in a wonderful manner . . . the preservation of automatism and the diminution of personal synthesis; this is the hysterical state."[26] On a good day, automatisms were like the glue that held together physical gestures, pure sensations, and memory or intellectual cognition. For example, one might associate the physical convulsions of laughter with a certain pleasant feeling provoked by a specific gag that one finds irresistibly funny: "a psychical titillation" that "acts like tickling" and "shows itself in laughter," as Théodule Ribot put it in 1896.[27] (I always think of Léontine smashing dishes over her shoulder in the futile gesture of cleaning them.)

Under the burden of traumatic hysteria, however, those automatisms became delinked among their constitutive actions, impulses, and aims. Janet's example of the woman given chloroform during her abortion springs to mind as she was kidded (or aggressively taunted) by the male medical students; her laughter persisted as an unwilled tic, long after its direct solicitation. In contrast, for Bergson, laughter is precisely what suppresses automatism: corrective mockery at the spectacle of depersonalized gesture.

Their meanings are not quite opposite, but they are sharply divergent. In Janet's terms, nonhysteric automatism demands the nimble coordination of affect with gesture and cognition (to the point that it becomes unconscious or second nature), whereas Bergson's automatism disallows the alertness necessary for performing habitual movements unhindered by conscious meditation.

Do you pause to think before you laugh? Isn't there always an interim, no matter how miniscule, between a comic gag and its punctual hilarity? It is tricky to say for sure. Perhaps this is what makes laughter such a tantalizing litmus test for automatism—for determining whether one's automatic gestures recur as feats of creative agility or as symptoms of feckless submission. No doubt they entail a bit of both because flexibility and resignation are like two sides of the same coin.[28] But on the question of automatism, Janet and Bergson were willing to draw a line in the sand.

Janet counted laughter as a hysteric symptom but was hasty to dismiss it as "probably a phenomenon of derivation of the nervous strength very difficult to account for."[29] In other words, who can say whether hysteric laughs arise from idiosyncratic taste (i.e., the joke that *only you* find funny) or from deeply buried "subconscious" memories? (Subconscious was Janet's key term; Freud distanced himself from it in favor of the unconscious.[30]) Hysteric phenomena, unlike wills and beliefs, "are immediate and irreflective . . . they do not in the same manner involve the whole personality, and do not bear with them, like reflective beliefs, the feeling of reality."[31] Uproarious laughs, in contrast, always hold a glimmer of that secret, off-limits side of oneself, giving it momentary pride of place over the official version. With hysteria, there was no pretense of a "whole personality" for raucous laughter to upend. Likewise, in the case of comic automatism, affect failed to penetrate the unconscious (of either the laugher or the object of mockery) because the latter had already been emptied of their creative presence in the world—not as a hysteric but as something like an inartful clown.

Hysteric automatisms were wellsprings for paradoxical laughs, which intensified in force as their substance became more and more remote. As Janet put it, "the preservation of automatism and the diminution of personal synthesis: this is the hysterical state."[32] To be gaslit by an authoritarian liar is one such fast track to losing "the feeling of reality."[33] First, you second-guess your immediate intuitions; then, you abandon any confidence or energy of personal conviction; finally, the ties that bind memory to emotion to material reality unravel altogether. Sometimes, mad laughter is all that remains, if only because laughs have that special ability to masquerade as insightful abreactions, even when they are really just hopeless, morbid symptoms.

It is hard to believe that Bergson would have been totally unaware of these implications when writing his short book on laughter, which he published a decade after Janet's *Psychological Automatism*.[34] "Nowhere in this essay does Bergson refer to the psychiatric definition of the term [automatism]," Rae Beth Gordon notes. "Yet he uses it to mean unconscious or involuntary acts as well as to underline the automaton-like character of mechanical gesture."[35]

The absentminded oaf who inadvertently walks into a glass door is still a far cry from the automatized hysteric, whose involuntary gestures somaticize her inescapable mental burdens. Soulless distraction or nervous automatism? Again, the word becomes flesh when there no longer remains any manipulable distance between sensation and memory as that relation is habitually negotiated through our movement in the world.

Ribot does invoke hysteric laughter as a limit case of automatism in *The Psychology of Emotions*. He specifies "hysteric laughter alternating with tears" as evidence of laughter's complicated relation to its own criterion of pleasure, as when conflicting emotions find satisfying relief through risible excitation.[36] However, he holds back from theorizing hysteric laughter as such (beyond its traces in the self-violation perpetrated by comic incongruity); instead, he pivots to the problem of "aesthetic sentiment" (and male creative genius) in the field of emotional pathology. Yet again, hysteric laughter is left dangling in the void between comic philosophy and experimental psychiatry.

JOKES AND THEIR RELATION TO FEMALE HYSTERIA

According to Freud, laughter at jokes and hysteric symptoms represented mutually constitutive—and mutually exclusive—formations of the unconscious. An avid auditor at Charcot's *amphithéâtre*, Freud cut his analytic teeth as a medical spectator of Blanche's and Augustine's hypnosis-induced clownism. Indeed, Breuer and Freud's *Studies on Hysteria* laid the groundwork for psychoanalysis: the ambitious apparatus of how all those unspoken and inadmissible sides of oneself ruthlessly dictate every aspect of our waking life and explicit desire. The unconscious yields only glimpses of its grotesque machinations, tantalizing clues that find devious ways to permeate everyday expression. As we know, these remnants assume multifarious guises, such as vivid daydreams, cryptic nightmares, uncanny omens, slips of the tongue (or parapraxis), and sharply disarming jokes. When a playful witticism liberates and gives license to a taboo or unattainable inkling, it cannot help but provoke truly tempestuous laughter.

Freud tried to formulate a universal syntax for jokes that would shed light on the underlying conditions of the human psyche. But we know from his many failed examples (such as his running gags about Hirsch-Hyacinth the corn-extractor[37]), to each funny bone its own tickler. If jokes give voice to the unconscious, they also betray the idiosyncratic individuation of the psyche. This is the driving contradiction of psychoanalysis, which further emphasizes the impossibly slow work of altering (let alone transforming) the collective psychic conditions that shape and constrain individual fantasy and its material possibilities. Jokes are no exceptions to the immovable slowness of radical change: how endemic structures of fantasy and anxiety uphold the material and symbolic order (cis-heteropatriarchy, racism, colonialism, ableism, class hierarchy). In other words, revolution in the streets will not topple the pillars of oppression as long as their libidinal grammar remains fundamentally intact.

This is the most powerful thesis of psychoanalysis, which locates the symbolic authority of libidinal fantasy at the nexus of individual will and inherited obsession. Whose sexed body or identity-based position will have material purchase on the structural formations of the psyche? That bait and switch between universality and exclusion found essential grounding in the gender politics of hysteria and laughter. While Freud (like Charcot) treated male hysterical patients in order to generalize his theory of hysteria, women remained notoriously absent from other, supposedly universal archetypes of the unconscious that he elaborated—most significantly, for our purposes here, laughter at jokes.

Hysteric symptoms (including laughter), unlike comedic jokes, do not bring the unconscious into direct contact with one's waking self because hysterics sleepwalk through their ordinary lives. Jokes, in contrast, conjoin "bewilderment and enlightenment," as Freud put it.[38] They erect autonomous zones where incommensurable affects and contradictory impulses can enjoy their anarchic coalition for just a little while. Jokes unite disparate or unrelated things. Hysteric symptoms could never be entrusted with the slippery diplomacy of joke work. They would decapitate the king (i.e., the head of conscious reason), whereas jokes only temporarily uncrown the king. Simply put, hysteric symptoms do not inhabit waking life—they annihilate it.

FEELING BLUE: SMUTTY JOKE OR SAD SYMPTOM?

Women have pride of place as neither laughers nor joke tellers in Freud's key text, *Jokes and Their Relation to the Unconscious*, which he wrote several years after publishing *The Interpretation of Dreams* (1899). Like dream wishes, jokes sidestep the burden of libidinal censorship. But women's relation to the joke is nebulous, depending on the doubling of their absence and negation. First, Freud tells us that female repression—itself the hallmark of hysteria—makes it

FIGURE 5.3 A fashionable woman gazes through opera glasses at a nude sculpture, to the dismay of conservative onlookers. (Say the title aloud while viewing.) Illustration by L. Métivet. *Le Rire*, May 23, 1896. Image courtesy of Wikimedia Commons.

"impossible for women . . . to enjoy undisguised obscenity."[39] It was common wisdom that ladies "should be thought to leave some touches of the joke undiscovered," as one etiquette guru advised: they "should be assured that there is nothing beyond worth knowing, or that there is nothing in the joke, except its pretension to mystery."[40] In other words, ladies had better be wary of their libidinal unconscious, not least of all as it implicates the temptations of blue or raunchy innuendo.

In addition to absenting their secret urges from the seat of jokes, women themselves are physically banished from the ground zero of laughter: "the obstacle standing in the way is nothing other than women's incapacity to tolerate undisguised sexuality."[41] If salacious jokes give gentlemen compensation (through predatory laughter) for keeping their primal sexual urges at bay, according to Freud, that soft reward can only be indulged in female absentia. This reading has explicit class and regional connotations:

> Among country people or in inns of the humbler sort it will be noticed that it is not until the entrance of the barmaid or the innkeeper's wife that smuttiness starts up. Only at higher social levels is the opposite found, and the presence of a woman brings the smut to an end.[42]

The sexual division of laughter marked a triumph of bourgeois self-repression because female presence discouraged smutty humor "only at higher social levels." Freud viewed it as a feat of personal decorum to pursue sexual enjoyment from a libidinal distance (via jokes). Just as nervousness experts esteemed female hysteria as a hallmark of modern industrial progress (or the occupational hazard of an overtaxed mind), psychoanalysis applauded witty smut as the trophy of a well-governed libido.

Although inessential, the therapeutic value of hysteric laughter became irresistible to Freud from time to time. In a telling example, he goaded his patient Emmy von N. "to laugh heartily" at the vivid mental images that terrified her, stirred up by childhood memories of an ethnological atlas.[43] "My therapy consists in wiping away these pictures, so that she is no longer able to see them before her," boasted Freud.[44] Visual memories of the atlas gave Emmy "a great shock," prompting her to make those awful, compulsive, uncanny "clacking noises" with her tongue.[45] The book contained illustrations of "American Indians dressed up as animals," which filled her with terror: "Only think, if they [the pictures] came to life!"[46]

Freud effectively told Emmy to laugh it off: "I instructed her not to be frightened of the pictures of the Red Indians but to laugh heartily at them . . . And this did in fact happen . . . she looked at the book" and "laughed out loud at the grotesque figures, without a trace of fear and without any strain in her features."[47] He further commented that she "gave evidence of a sense of humour that I should not have expected in such a serious woman."[48] Given this reparative power of raucous laughter, why didn't Freud suggest such a remedy for his other female patients?

For example, why not encourage Cäcilie M. to continue cackling after her sudden, involuntary, loud outbursts at last alleviated the painful headaches that seized her while reminiscing about her frightening grandmother? (Instead, she "swallowed" the insult, as Freud manipulated Cäcilie's gift for somatic "symbolization."[49]) Likewise, he could have emboldened Elisabeth von R. to laugh away her emotional conflicts rather than applying pressure to her head while insisting that she "report to me faithfully whatever appeared before her inner eye."[50] He even chastised Dora (Ida Bauer) for her laughter at the feeble efforts of various medical doctors (including Freud) to rationalize her defiant conversion.

Freud's motivated appeal to hysteric laughter at the iconography of colonialist paranoia bears further interpretation. On a manifest level, the whole scene is extremely racist. Emmy's terror conjures white supremacist ideologies that justified brutal, extractive, profit-driven, routine monstrosity against racial others under the guise of protecting white womanhood from its infamous fragility. Her proximity to patriarchal power in this instance—via the displacement of otherness from woman to native person—licensed her supercilious laughter, an otherwise fraught asset for women in the context of psychoanalysis.

Freud later analogized the sexuality of adult women to a "dark continent" in "The Question of Lay Analysis."[51] As Mary Ann Doane explains, this phrase "transforms female sexuality into an unexplored territory, an enigmatic, unknowable place concealed from the theoretical gaze and hence the epistemological power of the psychoanalyst."[52] In Emmy's case, Freud enlists her as a coconspirator in the mockery of her own "dark continent," invoking a glimmer of that forthcoming metaphor to bring Emmy's hysteric sexuality to the light of day. In other words, Emmy's libido was no longer a "dark continent"—an abyss of fugitive desire interlaced with paranoid colonialist imagery—once Freud granted it the license of tendentious laughter. In the case of "civilized" predatory jokes, female absence made all the difference between satisfying gratification and explicit frustration. ("Blue balls or blue gags?" a feminist comic might inquire.)

But hysteric symptoms, in contrast to erotic laughs, have no grasp on the distance between illusion and reality—they proceed from a tunneling nondifferentiation between these two entities. Here, Emmy's vivid imagination receives temporary symbolic legitimacy via the grotesque, paranoid hallucinations of Austro-Germanic colonialism. If there was any objective proportion (between iconography and reality) to the images in her ethnology atlas, then they would be the last pictures to bridge the gap between hysteric vision and reparative laughter. Well beyond Emmy's neurosis, they would have been Freud's worst nightmare.

PATHOLOGICAL LAUGHTER IN CLINICAL NEUROPSYCHIATRY

The nineteenth-century hysteric symptom of laughter evidently had more in common with joke laughter than its medical observers would have us believe. (In contrast to hysteric symptoms, jokes exist to unite conflicting impulses.) Because hysteria was a ragbag diagnosis for any unexplainable affliction, it would be impossible in retrospect to isolate hysteric laughter's motivated occurrence from its nervous automatism, let alone to delve into the hemispheres of the brain where it is visualized as a cerebral disorder (à la PBA).

In nineteenth-century research on emotional "brain-disease," hysteric laughter melted into uncontrollable tears, which Darwin attributed to the "hemiplegia, brain-wasting, and senile decay" that have a "special tendency to induce weeping."[53] Laughter "becomes a disease only when its character has changed," remarked a medical reporter. "In every asylum there are patients who cry too much and too easily, and there are others whose loud laughter can be heard all through the building."[54] In one case in 1896, a man in Austria was struck by "a nervous disease that manifested itself in paroxysms of laughter."[55] These periodic laughing attacks had tormented him for over three years. In contrast to Esther Wakefield, whose laughing doppelgänger was lavishly editorialized, Herr X's condition received minimal exaggeration, focusing on its physical effects alone: "The attacks set in with a tickling sensation arising from the toes of the left foot . . . The mouth and eyes were closed spasmodically, the eyeballs turned upward . . . At the height of the attack the patient at first smiled and then laughed aloud without any other sign of merriment."[56] These tidbits appeared in a widely circulated curiosity item, "IS LAUGHTER A DISEASE?" that was reprinted in newspapers across Britain, the United States, and India (and presumably elsewhere in the sprawling Anglo empire). It was not addressed to a primarily medical readership but sought to solicit a democratic range of eyeballs, as suggested by its bold headline. It is thus revealing that the author would limit his inquiry to hysteric laughter's physical phenomena.

We might contrast this to the hyperbolic portrayal of Wakefield's laughing attacks, whereby the bite from a "kissing bug" allegedly caused her to emit "a sudden burst of laughter, strident shrill, almost uncanny" and then to assault a streetcar conductor by "implanting upon his embarrassed lips of half a dozen swift and burning kisses by as charming a girl as one might find in many a long day."[57] Did Herr X also exhibit his mirthless laughing convulsions in inappropriate and publicly disruptive situations? One can only imagine because popular accounts of his peculiar illness did not deem these anecdotal events worthy of embellishing.

INAPPROPRIATE HILARITY AT THE CRANIAL TURN

The turn to the brain in neuropsychiatric treatment for affective disorders would have obsessed Charcot, who searched compulsively for cranial lesions. He unconvincingly posited that hysterics suffered from "dynamic lesions" of the nervous system, "a transient and undetectable disruption of brain function," although he was unable to find any evidence in the brain itself.[58] There has been a recent, growing body of research on brain disorders involving pathological laughter, ranging from pseudobulbar palsy to Alzheimer's disease to amyotrophic lateral sclerosis (ALS). "Stroke is probably the most common cause of pathological laughter and crying," according to a *Textbook of Clinical Neuropsychiatry*.[59] A peer-reviewed study on "Involuntary Laughter and Inappropriate Hilarity" published in *The Journal of Neuropsychiatry and Clinical Neurosciences* claims that the most common causes of laughing disorders include bilateral strokes, multiple sclerosis, and severe brain trauma.[60]

Although cranial anatomy and its risible tolls are well beyond the scope of my own expertise, the analysis of laughter pursued by neurological research on brain-based disorders is highly relevant for our purposes. Again, it all boils down to the disconnection between laughter and humor, which becomes visible by studying the topography of the brain. Mario Mendez et al. emphasize the sharp distinction between "disorders of laughter" such as PBA versus what they classify as "disorders of mirth or humor."[61] These latter afflictions are exemplified by *moria* ("pathologic giddiness") and *witzelsucht* ("joking addiction"), whereby the patient makes compulsive (and often offensive) jokes and witticisms but remains "paradoxically insensitive to humor," tending not to laugh much themself.[62] (Think of perfunctory punster Pennywise, the homicidal clown who terrifies humorless children in Stephen King's *It*.[63]) Witzelsucht affects an entirely different region of the brain than involuntary laughter, targeting the right orbitofrontal lobe, whereas pseudobulbar laughter originates from the lower brainstem: the seat of cerebral control over the laughing explosion.

After all, we always possess some degree of will to inhibit our most uproarious outbursts—no matter how irresistible their comedic trigger.[64] Laughter only becomes hysteric when the will has been completely overpowered, opening the door to inappropriate disturbance, immoderate amplification, and the instability between laughter and tears (because losing control over one's inhibition can be a cause for suffering and madness in itself). "Laughter and crying are considered pathologic when contextually inappropriate, sudden, uncontrollable, and continuous," note several neurologists in a 2016 study of the causes of pathological laughter.[65] In the absence of sophisticated brain-imaging mechanisms, the dissociation of affect from the abyss of unconscious memory offered nineteenth-century doctors a tangible explanation for how laughter could signify in its nonrelation to humor.

Whether a bulbar symptom of what would later be diagnosed as palsy or the social consequence of an exhausted will and frustrated libido, the laughing germ alone sufficed as grounds for a woman's institutionalization. It offended all that was expected and idealized by the nineteenth-century "cult of domesticity" and mythos of "true womanhood."[66] A widely read *Handbook of Uterine Therapeutics* even advised on the feminine modulation of hysteric laughter, comparing it to the tuning of an acoustical instrument.[67] In cases of womb inflammation, "the slightest pressure on either of the ovaries causes hysterical laughter . . . as easily as sound is produced by striking the keys of a piano."[68] That is how hysteric laughter could amplify as a cultural trope (irrefutable evidence of madness) while remaining muzzled as a talking symptom: a gateway to the unconscious (or subconscious) playground for those secret, multiple, unwieldy sides of oneself.

THE EIGHTEENTH BRUMAIRE OF HYSTERIC LAUGHTER

When does hysteric laughter take on allegorical dimensions as a hallmark of collective madness? Instability between laughter and tears is a perfectly sensible response to the onslaught of indigestible shock and political crisis, which find aesthetic grounding in the dissolution between tragedy and farce. Karl Marx famously invoked their collapse (of tragedy into farce) upon the unlikely rise of a buffoonish dictator, Louis-Napoléon Bonaparte, who was democratically elected as France's first president in the wake of its failed 1848 revolutions. Several years later, Bonaparte seized power by force and proclaimed himself emperor, in the mold of a certain uncle to whom he bore a passing family resemblance. What Marx meant by his cheeky addendum to Hegel—that "all great world-historic facts and personages appear twice . . . the first time as tragedy, the second time as farce"—he immediately clarified: when past traditions lose their symbolic legitimacy but continue to monopolize the realm of material possibility, they inevitably become farcical, further fostering the ascendance of ludicrous nephew-tyrants such as Napoléon III.[69]

For Marx, tragedy and farce are not mutually exclusive as aesthetic experiences of capitalist crisis but are hopelessly entangled. Because "the bourgeois gladiators" needed to "conceal from themselves the bourgeois-limited content of their struggles and to keep their passion on the high plane of great historic tragedy," Marx wrote, they adorn their "self-deceptions" in "the ideals and the art forms" of past idols.[70] And the persistence of these dead forms over the zombie-like embrace of capitalist productive power translates any of its "mother tongue[s]" into capital's own derivative language of "rotten farce."[71] Under such historical conditions, hysteric laughter ceases to appear as an isolated symptom and seizes hold as a collective phenomenon.[72] Its farcical politics "weigh like a nightmare on the brains of the living," whose bodies are eaten alive by the surplus wage theft of breakneck capitalism.[73]

Is it a symptom of collective neurosis to laugh at the recurrence of farce when its consequences are the farthest thing from funny? For example, imagine the U.S. president's personal lawyer confusing a luxury hotel brand with a landscaping company that specializes in lawn mulching and, as a result, hosting a highly public press conference against a brick wall at the nexus of a crematorium, a jail, and a dildo shop.[74] Indeed, the Four Seasons Total Landscaping fiasco provoked resounding mockery and enjoyment across the internet, but it also prefaced the violent attacks on the U.S. Capitol, led by armed white supremacists on January 6, 2021.[75]

Then what work, if any, did that laughter actually do? The uncanny archives of laughing female hysteria, I wager, shed light on the problem of tragic laughter at the sovereign crisis of farcical politics. As a symptom—unlike hallucinations or somnambulism—laughter was never allowed to speak; it conveyed a message without a code and was therefore not sufficiently "enigmatic" to require further analysis or interpretation.[76] Meanwhile, as we know, ordinary female laughter was subjected to rigorous suppression by everything from whalebone corsets and etiquette manuals to "death by laughter" obituaries. Neither a symptom of dissociated affect nor an emblem of anarchic jubilation, hysteric laughter echoed from the halls of mental asylums and gothic Victorian attics. It gave voice to powerful feelings unanchored from disturbing memories and their corresponding embodied emotions. But in the absence of cranial evidence to prove otherwise, we have to assume that a few of those laughs were willfully defiant, maybe even enjoyable. As speculative fodder for antiauthoritarian politics, we will now ask: what happens if those laughs become contagious?

6

Mass Hysteria, Collective Laughter, and Affective Contagion

What is the line between anxiety and enjoyment when it comes to the spectacle of hysterical bodily contagion? In one irresistible example, hilarity spreads like wildfire to German subway riders in "Lachen in der U-bahn": a cell phone video that quickly went viral in 2011 after capturing an outbreak of cachinnation among total strangers. A woman appears to laugh at some funny thing on her phone in private amusement, but the sight gag of her silliness provokes her fellow passengers to join in the chorus, overpowering almost everyone in the train car.[1] "How often has it been said that the fuller the theatre," wrote Henri Bergson, "the more uncontrolled the laughter of the audience!"[2] It is tantalizing to watch the suggestible transmission of a laugh seize hold in a crowded public space, temporarily uniting a heterogeneous social body. The soundscape of the video layers idiosyncratic individual voices over the rising cacophony. We hear strange snippets of nasal wheezing, throaty cackling, and melodic giggling as the revelry amplifies. But it is impossible to assign the sound of a laugh to a visible body, let alone to the unseen laughs that anarchically echo from off-screen.

The problem of filming affective contagion in the thick of the burst shapes the dynamic format of this short documentary. Its impromptu cinematographer pans and zooms around the moving car, which gyrates in harmony with its uproariously laughing bodies. A woman with blue-and-magenta dyed hair, a young man reading a book, and a blond ponytailed lady who repeatedly bobs her head in front of the frame: they are among the U-bahn's ecstatic fellow travelers.

FIGURE 6.1 "Lachen in der U-bahn"—official. YouTube video posted by Angela Mecking on December 7, 2011.

What emerges is a noticeable sexual division of laughter and annoyance. The women mostly chime in, while several men (including a teenager with a faux-hawk) look alternately puzzled and perturbed. "It may, perchance, have happened to you," warned Bergson, "when seated in a railway carriage . . . to hear travellers . . . [as] they laughed heartily. Had you been one of their company, you would have laughed like them; but, as you were not, you had no desire whatever to do so."[3] The louder the laugh, the angrier its holdouts.

Like a virus, contagious laughter can survive only by infecting fresh bodies. "Lachen in der U-bahn" continues to reverberate in its digital afterlives, garnering over 7.5 million YouTube views and thousands of hyperbolic comments: "the legend is, they're still laughing," "every human laugh in the same language:)," and "Laughter is a virus lol my cheeks hurt."[4] But until it reaches herd immunity, there will always be asymptomatic bystanders, such as YouTube user "King Sisyphus" who commented in 2016: " 4 years passed and I'm still curious why they;re laughing:))"[5] although perhaps he made that remark only in jest. "Lachen in der U-bahn" reveals a utopian scene of hysterically contagious laughter, unhinged from its comic impetus and overwhelmingly transmissible within an enclosed space.

THE MOST REVOLUTIONARY AFFECT OF THE MASSES

The German laughers on the U-bahn carry the torch for what Walter Benjamin once unhyperbolically described as "the most international and most revolutionary affect of the masses": their laughter.[6] Benjamin viewed collective laughter as an escape hatch from mass hysteria, as he put it: "a psychic immunization" against the eruption of "mass psychoses" that industrial technologies "have engendered in the masses at large."[7] In contrast to invigorating affects, exemplified by the therapeutic powers of collective laughter, when feelings spread uncontrollably through a crowd, their deluge can escalate into mob hysteria.

Gustave Le Bon thus controversially declared: "Crowds are only powerful for destruction."[8] In *The Crowd: A Study of the Popular Mind*, Le Bon compares members of a crowd to victims of hypnotic contagion whose "power acts like those of microbes [and] hastens the dissolution of enfeebled or dead bodies."[9] Self-possessed individuals succumb to the crowd's emotional fervor—whether positive (openly joyful) or negative (sadistically vengeful)—and become "barbarian[s]—that is, . . . creature[s] acting by instinct."[10] Crowds strip people of their capacity to reason, unleashing their most violent emotions and reducing all participants to mesmerized sleepwalkers. Le Bon conservatively associated the dangers of mass psychology with progressive demands for universal suffrage and the abolition of class exploitation. Any crowd in his account, whether revolutionary or reactionary, represented a destructive threat to orderly society.

The tensions between democratic politics and unruly mob psychology that Le Bon and Benjamin both analyze—with very different conclusions—converge on the cusp of mass hysteria. At what point does collectivizing affect (such as radical laughter) spill over and eradicate one's will in the very process of emboldening the people? Though indomitably festive, the U-bahn revelers betray no indication of mindless credulity or violent intolerance. They are a crowd spontaneously having a good time. But the crowd "cannot tolerate any delay between its desire and the fulfillment of what it desires," warned Sigmund Freud in his engagement with Le Bon, further comparing it to "an obedient herd, which could never live without a master . . . They demand illusions, and cannot do without them."[11] Freud thus hystericizes the crowd as a social formation: prone to hypnosis, dominated by unrepressed desires, and bewitched by the word of a powerful authority—like Blanche Wittmann writ large.

Crowds give people temporary permission to misbehave but without engaging their capacity for mental play, effectively turning all its members into temporary hysterics. At the crossroads of enjoyment and madness, crowds basically represent the worst of both worlds. As we know, early psychoanalysis emphasized the rigorous separation between laughing affects and hysteric symptoms as discrete emanations for unconscious expression. Joke laughter spontaneously aligns taboo urges with permissible impulses, whereas hysteric symptoms proceed from the fatal severing between these entities.

Laughter has long been described in suspiciously hysterical terms. The euphemism first took hold in the late nineteenth century when the notion of laughter as "hysterical" shifted in meaning from nervous breakdown to satisfying amusement. Prior to that time, hysterical laughter was the last thing you would ever want to experience with your body. It entailed intense individual suffering, usually triggered by impossibly mixed feelings. Affectively self-isolating, hysterical laughter only caught the germ of contagion once its heavy pathos had surrendered to suggestive enjoyment.

But that sense of excruciating inner turmoil never went away. I repeat, the nervous pathos of hysterical laughter was not widely contagious until it could parlay painful ambivalence into invigorating catharsis. At the same time, the notion of emotional contagion acquired an increasingly sinister dimension in the context of modern crowd psychology. Out with Lady Audley, in with epidemic laughter!

CONTAGIOUS LAUGHTER AND ITS HYSTERICAL LIMITS

It is a slippery slope from the joyful feast of collective feeling to the anxious transmission of regressive mass hysteria. Broadly defined, mass hysteria (or "mass psychogenic illness") refers to the spread of "collective illusions of threats, whether real or imaginary, through a population and society as a result of rumors and fear."[12] For example, an outbreak of hysterical coulrophobia (fear of clowns) caught fire amid the global political upheavals of 2016, stoking endemic paranoia, numerous false reports, and unjust arrests of people who were accused of dressing in clown suits, lurking in the woods, and preying on small children.[13] The Great Clown Panic of 2016 exemplified mass hysteria in its peculiar solicitation of mysterious (and often truly bizarre) symptoms that lay bare looming collective anxieties. Hysterical panics prolong the crowd's temporary delirium through networks of gossip and rumor, transmitting delusional beliefs unaccountably among already like-minded groups.

The Great Clown Panic of 2016 is further illustrative, for our purposes, because it transmutes a figure of happy laughter and easy joy into anxious hysteria and mass paranoia. We laugh at clowns, as many comic philosophers have observed, from a dual position of unconscious imitation and emotional indifference. The clown's spastic disaster inhabits our body on the level of imagined mimesis, pulling back from the brink of physical enactment. As Paul Bouissac further notes in *The Semiotics of Clowns and Clowning*, "Young children are usually frightened at first when they are exposed to real clowns," whose "altered faces" he describes as "verg[ing] on the alien and uncanny."[14] But that initial discomfort only fuels the ultimate satisfaction of laughter as a release of excitable tension.

More than any other tic or gesture (such as sneezing, yawning, hiccupping, crying, or coughing), laughter is overwhelmingly contagious. This is both the site of its danger and the source of its power: "laughter is infectious or contagious, with uneasy suggestions of disease," observes Kathleen Rowe Karlyn in her playful foreword to the feminist anthology, *Hysterical!*[15] She further compares collective hilarity to "something we can 'catch' as easily as the common cold when our defenses are down and the right bug strikes."[16] For feminist comedy scholars, the devil of contagion is well worth the gamble because it advances shared political investments through jokes that "punch up" against patriarchal power and white supremacist domination. Cynthia Willett and Julie Willett invoke contagious feminist laughter as a vehicle for "biosocial catharsis" in *Uproarious*, arguing that it "does not stem from feelings of superiority or in-group/out-group hierarchies" but instead "prompts ... community from a loosely defined sense of mutual belonging."[17]

In contrast, humor behaviorists have chased after the naked germ of contagion native to laughter—its raw affective appeals that transcend shared jokes or social alliance. Neuroscientist Robert Provine has even tried to extract the core element of contagion from contexts as disparate as television laugh tracks, religious holy laughter rituals, and epidemics of mass laughing hysteria.[18] (I will describe these references in detail later in the chapter.) "The efficacy of laughter to elicit laughter," he argues, "suggests that humans may have a feature 'detector' for laughter, a neural circuit that responds exclusively to this vocalization [of "ha-ha"] and triggers the motor pattern of laughter in listeners."[19] Indeed, Provine owned over one thousand laughing boxes (simple machines for playing prerecorded laughs) and frequently enlisted his students as human subjects in his contagious laughing experiments.

Although the laugh detector has never been precisely located or visualized in the brain, it arises from laughter's activation of the prefrontal cortex, its involvement of the limbic system (via the amygdala and hippocampus), and release of endorphins that foster euphoric bodily pleasure. But in Provine's account, the acoustic and rhythmic properties of laughter alone are enough to lubricate its frisky circulation of that archetypal ha-ha. Shared values or social connection need not adhere to its raw physiological transmission.

COLLECTIVE LAUGHTER IN THE BELLY OF THE BEAST

Laughter's collectivizing power is both the locus of its utopian possibilities and the germ of its mob-fomenting monstrosity. Lynch mobs laugh. Anti-immigrant crowds laugh at xenophobic insult jokes spewed at far-right political rallies. Ecstatic congregants speak in tongues and break into holy laughs as embodied pathways to divine transcendence at religious revivals. Television laugh tracks laugh for us when we are too alienated or exhausted to seek out embodied spaces in which to make laughter for ourselves. International laughing clubs have proliferated toward that end, enticing participants eager to take leaps of faith into laughter without any humorous cause: the physiological explosion of pleasurable convulsion expanded to its contagious extremes. Uninformed observers have even mistaken practices of laughter yoga for outbreaks of mass psychogenic illness, which have likewise implicated laughter. For example, the 1962 Tanganyika laughter epidemic, which I will discuss, has become hypervisible due to its laughing dimensions alone, often to the exclusion of confronting its colonialist contexts and other relevant motor symptoms at play.

Most obviously, audiences laugh—at comedies, at horror films, at moments of bad irony in otherwise serious and nonhumorous works. Their rallying point around a common cultural text (whether laughing on cue or off-kilter) is exactly what gives hysterical laughter its safely containable license to collectivity, without fear of destructive escalation. Julian Hanich theorizes this phenomenon as "the audience effect" in the context of film spectatorship, prizing laughter as "notoriously contagious" because it "has a specific livedbody dynamic . . . when viewers are affected—and infected—by the laughter of others."[20] In cracking up or "flooding out," as Jacob Smith has it, the sound alone "stimulates" listeners, epitomized by an unknown woman's "unsettling and infectious laughter" that also cracks up the performer on a vinyl record.[21] This is why "movie theaters will continue to thrive as places of public gathering," affirms Doron Galili, who quotes William Paley: "Laughs engender laughs, thrills sweep like currents through multitudes."[22] At its most extreme, contagious laughter has even been deployed as a homeopathic antidote to deadly viral disease.[23]

During the 1918 flu pandemic (which infected one-third of the world's population), movie exhibitors solicited customers by advertising "the laugh cure" as "thousands of times more contagious than the influenza" and "the best epidemic for the world."[24] In the hellmouth of airborne plague, theater managers were encouraged to play comedies and then turn up the house lights: "Get as much light as you can without hurting your screen values," advised *Motion Picture News* in 1918. "Immediately everyone will be able to see others and nearby laughers will no longer keep laughs exclusively to themselves."[25] Evangelists doubled down on the physical contagions of laughter to override fears of lethal exposure—collective enjoyment only came at the cost of a ticket, unless you caught more than the laughing bug.

Humor philosophers, in contrast, explore the friction between comic meaning and affective contagion in their hot pursuit of laughter's collectivizing potentials. This wager goes well beyond the spread of enjoyment: it mobilizes the uproarious crowd as a radical counterforce to the conformist mob. Alenka Zupančič thus declares laughter to be "decidedly a *collective*-forming affect, more so than any other," and a vital resource for fighting the rise of resurgent authoritarianism and white supremacy.[26] Wild laughter's "decentralizing thrust" invests its "political value," claims Amelia Groom, disrupting language that "operates in a closed system" that can "only reproduce its own terms."[27] (Groom focuses on collective laughter's Medusan imperative for feminist cinema.) "Its uncontrolled noise is precisely the point," causing a "total breakdown" in the circular logic of hollow words and self-isolating thoughts.[28]

For Zupančič, the tipping point from raw contagion to political collectivity is breached by laughter's special capacity to break something, which she associates not just with its affective disruption but with its risky, confrontational truth telling. "It is rather obvious," Zupančič observes, "that this turn to feelings, affects, sensibility, and their consideration/protection (as opposed to being equipped to fight, retort, and deal with things) is a very unfriendly environment for comedy (and jokes)."[29] She further suggests that ethical reticence about insensitive comedy has enabled the far right to monopolize edgy humor and weaponize it against liberal democracy, fueled by the crowd's craving for transgressive laughs that obscenely violate congealed behavioral norms.[30]

Protective laughs that seek to shelter precarity and affirm established consensus do not have the nimble energy to create heterogeneous social collectives, mobilized by the wild contagions of laughter. As the Willetts proclaim, "Humor can transform a politics of anger and resentment into a politics of joy."[31] While they aim to bridge the gap between ethical solidarity and shape-shifting collectivity, Zupančič is happy to draw a line in the sand in her call to arms for unapologetic laughter. Only by violating the laugher's fragile orientation toward an (increasingly catastrophic) present can laughter itself help repel the rise of conspiracy theories, delusional rumors, and revamped mass hysteria that has run roughshod over democratic institutions under postindustrial late capitalism.

It was in a similar spirit that Benjamin famously declared laughter to be "the most international and the most revolutionary affect of the masses."[32] He penned these words in a brief film review of Charlie Chaplin's *The Circus* (1928), published in 1929 between the horrors of World War I and the consolidation of Nazi power. His conviction hinged on the emotional hybridity of Chaplin's work and its resonance to evoke nuanced aesthetic reactions, depending on the cultural context of its reception. Chaplin elicited pathos in Russia, intellectual meditation in Germany, and sheer delight in England, according to Benjamin. But beyond that versatility, given film's supreme power over the masses—its "immense significance" and authoritative "precedence over the public"—laughter itself held the key to the medium's visual capacities to avert the catastrophes of fascistic mass hysteria.[33]

To that end, Benjamin upped the ante on his own affective wager, invoking collective laughter as "one such preemptive and healing outbreak of mass psychosis."[34] It was not ego-affirming escapism but violent slapstick comedies and grotesque metamorphic cartoons that provoked reparative laughter. These innervating images offered alternative lines of flight from "the dangerous tensions which technology and its consequences have engendered in the masses at large," observed Benjamin, "tendencies which at critical stages take on a psychotic character."[35] But by then, it was already too late, in the aftermath of the 1933 Reichstag Fire, when Nazis seized control of government, and amid their speedy remilitarization of the Rhineland, which entrenched their strategic position on the continent.[36] What good was detonative utopian laughter?

Cartoon destruction had missed the boat of diverting unimaginable catastrophe. It was at best an emotional palliative. As Zupančič aptly notes, "Comedy cannot change the political and economic circumstances, but it can help us see that sticking to our world doesn't help in the present."[37] At the very least, collective laughter empowers the crowd to resist feckless escapism or cowardly nihilism.

But how to extract contagious laughter's collectivizing germ from its thoughtless conformity? It is time to return to the belly of the beast: the late nineteenth century, when the "hysterics" of women's unstable emotions were gleefully unleashed upon the masses at large. In the rest of this chapter, I will pursue the dialectic between *conversion hysteria* and *crowd psychology* across a variety of suggestive examples: laughing mobs; contagious kick dancers; viral conspiracies; expectant anxieties; apocalyptic panics; and, of course, speculative utopian collectives.

MASS HYSTERIA, CONTAGIOUS CROWDS, AND IMITATIVE CONVULSIONS

The euphemistic embrace of "hysterical" collective laughter intersected with the rise of pathological crowd psychology in the late nineteenth century. Like impulsive prejudices, conversion symptoms held strong mimetic powers. "In a town in southern Illinois, epidemic hysteria in the form of exhausting laughter, had made its appearance," reported the *Evening Press* (Grand Rapids, MI) in 1903, comparing the spread of mirthless giggling to medieval outbreaks of dancing, meowing, biting, and barking.[38] "Epidemic hysteria is a boarding school specialty," opined the *Savannah Morning News*: "one invertebrate girl with a letter from home" could "bowl over a whole school, collapsed in hystification and despair" from "imitative hiccoughing" if she "happen[s] to be in a receptive mood."[39] But "hysteria is no mere women's ailment," added the *Salt Lake Tribune* in 1911. "Hysteria, simple, unattractive hysteria, is the fountain of all."[40] The basis for their universality thesis was a scandalous book by the German nerve specialist, Hermann Aub, which chalked up post-Impressionist art and nihilist philosophy to *Hysteria in Men*, citing Vincent van Gogh, Friedrich Nietzsche, and Arthur Schopenhauer as "degenerate" "victims."[41]

If the blazing contagions of nervous hysteria threatened traditional ideals of stolid masculinity, the modern hysterical crowd was implicitly (if not overtly) feminized. "Crowds are distinguished everywhere by feminine characteristics," claimed Le Bon, who associated gendered stereotypes of moody dyspepsia with the crowd's vulnerability to fall prey to fanatical sentiment.[42] Adolph Moses thus warned in 1896 of the "popular insanity" and "irrational obsession" driving the "Jew-baiting movement in Europe," comparing fin de siècle anti-Semitism to medieval witch hunts, Holy War Crusades, and American plantation slavery.[43] Communal insanity "consists in the inability of large masses of men to think," pleaded Moses, especially when "a fixed idea can sustain itself against facts" and reproduce itself by way of "collective hysteria."[44]

But emotional contagion and ideational suggestion are not so easily separable. Their entanglement further implicates the wager of collective laughter. Even joyful group laughter can enable spontaneous vigilante violence, inflamed by the vivid resurgence of paranoid and fear-based delusions. Exhibit A: The Laughing Mob. If outbreaks in girls' schools were disruptive for their vocal mayhem and unwieldy duration, laughing mobs possessed a frantic intentionality that was both impulsive and calculated. *The Crisis* newspaper (founded by W. E. B. Du Bois in 1910) recited an "Old Story" about a Black man unjustly accused of murdering a little white girl.[45] "Immediately a frenzied, hysterical mob gathers and attempts to lynch the poor wretch," either goaded to completion through euphoric contagion or deferred in their bloodlust by the coercive extraction of a false confession.[46] "American civilization is not yet out of the jungle when it permits mob laughter," noted a respondent to the 1936 NAACP report on America's barbaric lynching record in 1930.[47]

What are the affective differences between white supremacist mobs and progressive political crowds? Dissonance within the crowd can foster its social diversity, Claudia Breger suggests, whereas supremacist mobs exact feverish uniformity.[48] "There is something about the contagious hysteria of a mob that makes its members for the time being forget their common sense and self-respect," urged the Illinois Black press in 1917.[49] The author invokes laughter as "blind, cruel, and unreasonable"—a "hysterical brutality" conjured to divide and conquer.[50] (Black workers migrated north and wealthy industrialists manipulated mob fury to prevent interracial class comradery.) Contagious laughter reverts to mob hysteria in the absence of political solidarity. Given the spontaneity and improvisation at play in collective laughter, where to draw the line between progressive disobedience and supremacist enclosure? We look now to the devil of raw contagion.

Crowd laughter greased the wheels of homicidal bloodlust but was not pestilent itself as a conversion symptom. To give a counterexample, Exhibit B: Religious Revivalism. Late nineteenth-century reports of Baptist and Methodist revival movements in the U.S. South frequently compared ritual practices of holy laughter, trance talking, and spiritual catalepsy to conversion hysteria. The cultivation of "strong religious emotion" found relief in "floods of tears" in one congregant, "in another in hysterical laughter, in a third by unconsciousness . . . in yet another complete catalepsy may be produced, every muscle becoming rigid and so remaining for hours," according to J. M. Buckley's 1896 "History of Methodists."[51] (It was not a far cry from the plank poses or acrobatic clownism on display in Jean-Martin Charcot's neurology clinic.) Buckley associated these phenomena with the feminization of religious ministry to exploit the revivals as hysterical evidence against women's demands for political enfranchisement and universal suffrage.

Participants would acquire "the gift of tongues" and "fall in trances to lie for hours in a nervous rigor . . . [some] lay as dead for hours. Others apparently unconscious of all about them, lay and screamed, often unintelligibly. Some danced and leaped and laughed and sung about thru the congregation," according to a 1907 report on the "outbreak of old-time ignorance," which was directly juxtaposed to a damning editorial on the consequences of "Women as Wage Earners."[52]

Maternal negligence, rapid depopulation, and the loss of male wages would surely ensue should hysterical women continue to infiltrate the workforce.[53]

No degree of fear mongering was too extreme to prevent those suffragists, immigrants, and people of color from "getting the power." Meanwhile, Black women preachers occupied the pulpit (beyond the "bushes"—in churches, urban centers, and traveling shows) to spread the gospel about voting enfranchisement and the abolition of Jim Crow.[54] For example, Florence Spearing Randolph decried racism and sexism in her fiery oration for women's suffrage and Black civil rights.[55] The *Trenton Evening Times* noted: "She is generally recognized as a powerful and emotional speaker" who "is a strong advocate of rights for the negroes and frequently speaks along this line."[56] Hystericization of antiracist, feminist ministry was used as a bludgeon to disarm its political appeals to emotional contagion.

Reports on religious revivalism savvily exploited physical similarities between progressive gospel and neurotic phenomena to insinuate sweeping generalizations about the hazards of democratized power. It would be hard to imagine a less subtle example than: "Raids by Suffragettes Epidemic of Hysteria: Excitable Women Join Violence Movement as Sort of Holy Crusade."[57] The article further depicts suffragette leaders as "cool headed" hypnotists, preying on "a multitude of excitable females who regard window smashing as a species of holy crusade" and imprisonment as the "acme of martyrdom."[58] The meaning of this broader rhetoric was clear: any buffer between the democratic crowd and the myth-mongering masses would be bulldozed by the liberation of women and oppressed racial minorities.

THE CONTAGIOUS WORD: TABOO, ANXIETY, CONVERSION

The contagious threat of female hysteria was a potent foil for dictating which crowds were on the side of extralegal social order and which threatened to tear down the whole circus. For example, the conservative *Times-Republican* (1920) decried a labor strike by mortar mixers in Sioux City, Iowa, as an outbreak of "contagious hysteria," comparing the protesting workers to tarantist dancers for demanding wage increases, overtime pay, and nine-hour workdays.[59] (Tarantism—or the irresistible impulse to dance—had menaced mainland Europe since the medieval dancing plagues of Saxony, Apulia, and Strasbourg.[60]) But the *Times-Republican*'s confusion of contagious conversion with mass demonstration (let alone the labor union with the mad crowd) bears further elaboration.

FIGURE 6.2 "Dance at Molenbeek. A depiction of dancing mania, on the pilgrimage of epileptics to the church at Molenbeek." Painting by Pieter Bruegel the Younger (1600?). Image courtesy of Wikimedia Commons.

There is a precise difference between anxiety hysteria and conversion hysteria, although these differences have been less carefully theorized on the level of mass contagion. Freud coined the term "anxiety-hysteria" in 1908, as Ernest Jones outlines in "The Relation Between the Anxiety Neurosis and Anxiety-Hysteria," to designate certain phobias whose structure strongly resembles those of ordinary hysterical symptoms. Anxiety neurosis gives way to full-fledged anxiety hysteria when the elicitation of anxiety—as "the combination of undue physical excitation and insufficient efferent discharge"—acquires an autonomous power that demands extreme phobic avoidance.[61] But phobic anxiety does not necessarily involve physical conversion. As Juliet Mitchell explains, "In conversion hysteria, the [illicit] idea is converted into bodily expression; in anxiety hysteria the anxiety is so extreme that the subject takes avoidance action."[62] For example, anxiety about the unruliness of crowds could escalate into an agoraphobic avoidance of all public spaces or exposed locations. But if that phobic individual were confronted by an actual crowd and responded in kind to this impossible encounter with a hysterical attack (mirthless laughter, screaming, seizures, hallucinations, etc.), then rigorous aversion would reach the threshold of psychosomatic conversion.

This distinction between anxiety hysteria and conversion disorder does not map neatly onto its contagious dimensions. Freud, for example, associated any prohibition of a shared unconscious taboo with the fear of contagion, emphasizing how contagion spreads between people through intermediary objects.

"The magical power that is attributed to taboo," he writes in *Totem and Taboo* (1913), "is based on the capacity for arousing temptation; and it acts like a contagion because examples are contagious and because the prohibited desire in the unconscious shifts from one thing to another."[63] In other words, collective desires to violate social taboos are multiply contagious, both in their imitative temptation upon witnessing an act of transgression, and in the way their displacement shifts from the thing itself to irresistible substitutes. Objects can become contagious when they provide a temporary fix for an unresolvable psychic conflict.

Judith Butler gives the example of queer utterance and its threat of transference (to antigay interlocutors: "If I say, 'I am a homosexual' in front of you, then you become implicated . . .") to illustrate how the situated taboo of queer self-naming turns contagious in language.[64] "Indeed, it is the incessant transferability of this desire that is instituted by the taboo," argues Butler in *Excitable Speech*, "and that informs the logic of contagion."[65] They invoke this form of taboo-breaking utterance as "the contagious word."[66] Concisely, it is the threat to others of renounced identification that makes queer self-interpellation particularly contagious.

Although Butler's examples of contagious words do not center on humor or laughter, they shed light on the contagious dynamics of all funny utterances. Jokes themselves are inherently charged with bridging the gap between taboo and transgression. If the laughter they provoke becomes socially contagious, however, that contagion can always take cover in the exception of the joke's form. In other words, its implications are easily bracketed, disavowed, and again repressed. A simple example relevant to Butler's analysis would be the predominance of homophobic jokes as defense mechanisms against the contagion of queer signifiers. More generally, the infectious laughter sparked by affirmative queer jokes often works to defuse the threatening or unthought implications posed by their meanings.

For example, transgender comic Jaye McBride incisively parlays the embattled contagion of queer recognition into empowering punch lines that thematize culture war transphobia and trans civil rights. She recalls in one of her stand-up sets: "My brother disowned me when he found out I was trans, but I try and take the high road. When I heard that he and his wife had a child, I sent them the nicest greeting card. It said 'Congratulations! It's a boy! For now!' "[67] McBride's joke temporarily aligns irreconcilable cultural views: the transphobic complaint that queerness requires repression and "conversion" versus the antinormative rallying cry that to enforce one's assigned gender at birth is both cruel and ridiculous. The joke thereby weaponizes the feared linguistic contagion of queer and trans personhood against the temporal straitjacket of developmental gender norms. But the promise "For now!" projects that contagion into the future—as a looming potentiality with radical implications for social change, though one that, for the time being, remains bracketed within the punch line of the joke.

In theory, Freud's and Butler's concepts of contagion both stick squarely to the realm of symbolic language and its unconscious dimensions. The social collectivity of taboo-breaking commitment cannot be realized through the vehicle of contagion because political solidarity among heterogeneous social bodies is too easily fragmented by particular attachments to words and things (unrealized alignments that get stuck on unsatisfying objects). Contagion makes for fickle friends . . . or foes! This has bearing on the implications of linguistic contagion toward understanding the mass dimensions of conversion hysteria. It is no accident that homophobic "conversion"—i.e., the hateful practice of forcing lesbian, gay, bisexual, transgender, queer/questioning, intersex, asexual (LGBTQIA+) people to live in the closet—adopts the same signifier as "conversion hysteria," which inflicts disallowed recognition onto the fraught expressivity of the body. Just as linguistic contagion cannot do the work of mass social movements (it's a spark but not a conflagration), it also falls short of hysterical conversion, whereby symbolic articulation and somatic rebellion become one and the same, and therefore dually incomprehensible. To repeat my earlier point, the distinction between phobic anxiety and hysterical conversion does not map neatly onto their contagious dimensions.

CONTAGIOUS ANXIETY: TO GYNOCIDAL MURDER FROM FADDISH TICKLING FEATHERS

What makes hysteria contagious beyond its colloquial usage as emotional excess or collective disturbance? In "Mass Hysteria: Two Syndromes?," British psychologist Simon Wessely argues that "the boundaries of collective behavior and mass hysteria have yet to be drawn," which he begins to resolve by elaborating the distinction between mass anxiety hysteria and mass motor hysteria.[68] Is all normal behavior essentially hysterical? In a repressive society, there can be no doubt. But in contrast to mass anxiety hysteria, which is typically shorter in duration and contained to the exaggeration of an imminent threat or excitation, mass motor hysteria unleashes symptoms that can last for months or even years on end, consuming the entire body. These symptoms run the gamut from twitching, yawning, dancing, laughing, and sneezing to kicking, screaming, convulsing, aphonia, somnambulism, and vivid hallucinations. In other words, mass motor hysteria projects the contagious transmission of somatic conversion symptoms onto the population at large. Its outbreak goes well beyond any analogy to the volatile crowd; its spread arises not from the immediacy of passionate feelings but from collective, deeply repressed environmental stressors that lack any cohesive outlet in symbolic representation or social expression.

Examples are always helpful; let us start with anxiety. In their eye-popping *Encyclopedia of Extraordinary Social Behavior*, Hilary Evans and Robert Bartholomew offer the following outbreaks as instances of mass anxiety hysteria: the Brooklyn Bridge Panic (1883), Russian Poland Balloon Scare (1892), Winnipeg Balloon Mania (1896), Massachusetts Feather Tickling Fad (early 1900s), BBC Radio Hoax (1923), French Phantom Hat Pin Stabber (1923), Argentine Mars Earthquake Panic (1939), and California Zoot Suit Riots (1942–1943). (For a much longer list with extended time line and brief descriptions, see the additional examples at the end of this chapter.) Many of these incidents resemble the Great Clown Panic of 2016; the Phantom Hat Pin Stabber also involved numerous false reports of an imaginary assailant wreaking havoc in 1920s Paris with a long, sharp hat pin. Even fads and trends breach the threshold of mass anxiety hysteria when they incite moral panic, such as the early 1900s New England fad of purchasing long-handled feather dusters for erotic tickling. ("Tickle-for-a-nickel," anyone?[69])

Feather dusters, hat pins, and clown masks galore: emotional contagion between people is mediated by the sticky proliferation of commodity fetishes. To invoke Freud, perverse commodities are mere substitutes for the lack of adequate objects to satisfy taboo desires. Like their temporary outlets, episodes of anxiety hysteria are typically contained to a particular context or location, such as a deviant trend or strange workplace smell or alarmist radio broadcast. We all know about the mass hysteria incited by Orson Welles's 1938 *War of the Worlds* radio broadcast in New York, but similar panics arose from fictionalized Martian telephony in Argentina (1939), Chile (1944), and Ecuador (1949).[70]

According to Evans and Bartholomew, the "characteristic features of anxious hysterical contagion include (1) symptoms with no plausible organic basis, (2) that are transient and benign, (3) have rapid onset and recovery, (4) and occur in a segregated group (5) in the presence of extraordinary anxiety."[71] As Wessely claims, "What is communicated in mass anxiety hysteria is not any single behavior, or a 'fantasy idea' . . . , but a collective feeling: anxiety."[72] To paraphrase Silvan Tomkins, an architect of affect theory, contagion is hardwired into the affect system, enabling affects to circulate forcefully by way of corporeal and visual suggestion. As he puts it, "without [the affect system's] amplification, nothing else matters—and with its amplification, anything can matter."[73] Anxiety proceeds from the intensification of affective uncertainty or symbolic contestation over *what matters*. It can spread invisibly or by way of very common symptoms: chest pains, shortness of breath, dizziness, headaches, and nausea.

But what *is* anxiety? Unlike fear, which has a concrete referent, anxiety is fundamentally anticipatory: a way of preparing the subject for the likelihood of future upheaval or danger. In her compendium of minor negative affects, *Ugly Feelings*, Sianne Ngai suggests that all anxiety is doubly projective; in addition to being "projective" in the sense of a deferral that is future-oriented, "anxiety has a spatial definition as well," observes Ngai. It "is invoked not only as an affective response to an anticipated or projected event, but also as something 'projected' onto others in the sense of an outward propulsion or displacement—that is, as a quality or feeling the subject refuses to recognize in himself."[74] Unfilled anxiety is therefore defensively contagious, as with Butler's example of the homophobic spurning of queer identifications. Carol Becker defines anxiety broadly "as a representation of the tension between what is and what could be," emphasizing its affective adherence to missed political opportunities (especially in the interregnum between popular "waves" of feminist activism).[75] Anxiety-without-discharge, as we've discussed, can mean the very difference between laughing at a joke (or laughing contagiously) versus internalizing its impossibility, whereby the disconnection of affect from memory might give rise to inscrutable, agonizing symptoms.

Conversion hysteria, I repeat, puts impossible words and inadmissible thoughts into the body. But contagious anxiety, in contrast, projects those impulses outward, concretized by shape-shifting rumors and hyperbolic panics. That is also what qualifies contagious anxiety as "mass hysteria": the enlargement of unsubstantiated inner thoughts into the collective realm of symbolic belief. Once in orbit, those contagions balloon into the most incredible delusions: Martian invasion, predatory hat stabbers, covert windshield snipers, weaponized skunk oil bombers, terrorist aerial ballooners, lethally dangerous television characters, and child-eating Satan worshippers. Evans and Bartholomew capaciously catalog the sheer expanse of anxiety-based phenomena from silly fads, bizarre trends, and shadowy rumors to violent panics, mob riots, xenophobic witch hunts, and ethnic massacres.

There is an intangible but important structure of relation between mass motor hysteria and mass anxiety hysteria, which are at once very distinct and like two sides of the same coin. Let us briefly revisit the notorious Salem Witch Trials (1692–1693), which have come to epitomize the abuse of power on the altar of mass delusion. What began as a contained outbreak of conversion hysteria (wild, convulsive dancing among little girls in a highly repressive Puritanical environment) rapidly intensified into a gynocidal campaign against female demonic possession. In the form of mass anxiety hysteria, the groundless trials proceeded from somatic evidence that Satan had commandeered the bodies of the town patriarchs' wives, daughters, neighbors, servants, and slaves. In a nightmarish world, murderous exorcism is one such avenue to the purgation of endemic anxiety upon the corporeal spread of unexplainable conversion symptoms.

ALL OUR HYSTORIES: LAUGHING EPIDEMICS, DANCING PLAGUES, ALIEN ABDUCTIONS

From medieval dancing plagues to modern epidemics of industrial fainting spells, contagious suggestion erupts from what is broken within a particular social order where its disastrous germ seizes hold. Above all, hysteria was/is a mimetic disorder, shaped by the pool of "legitimate symptoms in a given culture at a given time," as Elaine Showalter outlines—a channel for embodying "culturally permissible symptoms of distress."[76]

For example, at a silk mill in Wilkes-Barre, Pennsylvania in 1888, a young woman worker suffered an epileptic fit, which, according to the sensationalist press, "naturally" excited her coworkers, who "without any warning [gave] indications of the affection": piercing screams and convulsive seizures "of the most violent form ... until no less than sixteen had either fallen to the floor or reeled about in a frenzy of hysterical madness."[77] The first recorded incident of mass motor hysteria in an industrialized workplace, claim Evans and Bartholomew, occurred in 1787 at an English cotton mill in Lancashire, shortly after the invention of the mechanized power loom.[78] Poor and dehumanizing labor conditions sowed the seeds for violent fits, fainting, and convulsions (allegedly incited by a woman who had been scared by a mouse), but suggestively spread to other workers in the mill. If female hysteria was a "protolanguage" for an emergent feminist politics, epileptic fits slowed down the grueling hustle of factory mass production in the aftermath of industrial revolution.

As with contagious anxiety hysteria, the range of examples classified as mass motor hysteria is extremely varied and would require social and cultural contextualization that goes well beyond the scope of this book. But to widen the spectrum briefly, the following afflictions have been specified as instances of mass motor hysteria: the Cambrai Convent Outbreak (1491), Strasbourg Dancing Plague (1518), Hoorn Orphanage Possession (1673), Swedish Preaching Epidemic (1841), Klikuchestvo Shouting Mania (1861), Louisiana Twitching Epidemic (1939), British Military Fainting Epidemics (1951), Tanganyika Laughter Epidemic (1962), Italian Fatigue Outbreak (1978), Philippine Devil Hysteria

(1994), and Orissa Cat Calls (2004). (See the end of this chapter for a longer list with brief descriptions.)

Crucially, these occurrences were all precipitated by severe environmental stressors. Unlike mass anxiety hysteria, which spreads initially through affect but is contained to the scene of the outbreak, mass motor hysteria takes root in the collective conversion of taboo impulses into strange bodily expressions, which can then last for months or even years on end. For example, the Morzine Outbreaks in France recurred for seven years (1857–1864) in surges of hallucination, trances, convulsions, glossolalia, running, and barking. The epidemic was allegedly triggered by the cyclical migration of Morzine's male labor force and the rise of occultist gossip among its remaining female inhabitants. Detonating from pervasive repression and punitive isolation, surreal attacks attain somatic conformity by way of imitation and suggestion.

Tanganyika Laughter Epidemic of 1962

Toward the question of laughter and its relation to mass motor hysteria, there is no example of greater relevance than the Tanganyika Laughter Epidemic. (Its historical and geographical contexts go well beyond the purview of this book.) Serial laughing epidemics notoriously afflicted schoolchildren in East Africa in the 1960s in the immediate aftermath of hellish colonization and rapid decolonization across the region. A germinal outbreak took place in Kashasha on January 30, 1962, just a month after the Tanganyika African National Union (TANU), led by Julius Nyerere, established independence and formed an autonomous government on December 9, 1961. The patients zero were three teenage girls attending a strict missionary school, where they started to laugh inappropriately. Their laughter persisted long past the point of enjoyment or pleasure, enduring for hours, infecting their classmates, and mutating into other painful symptoms such as hyperventilation, nausea, choking, kicking, and vomiting.

By March 18, the laughing attacks had seized ninety-five of the 159 girls in the Kashasha school, with symptoms lasting for seven days on average (and for up to sixteen days), eventually forcing the school's temporary closure. The outbreak recurred in waves, spreading further throughout the region, and shuttering nearby institutions such as Ramashenye girls' middle school, where forty-eight of 154 pupils were vexed in a similar manner in June 1962. The epidemic did not subside until June 1964, after causing fourteen schools to close temporarily and "afflicting about 1,000 people in tribes bordering Lake Victoria in Tanganyika and Uganda."[79] Other incidents of laughing epidemics arose in Musoma (northern Tanzania) in May 1966; in Ankhole, Uganda, in July 1971; and in Mwinilunga, Zambia, in May 1976, where "the recent strict disciplinary measures taken by the new administration, such as rigid separation of boys and girls, may have prepared the emotionally charged background," according to an ethnographic study published in *The British Journal of Psychiatry*.[80]

Cases of "Laughing Mania are most evident In Central and East Africa and typically occur to pupils in missionary schools," assert Evans and Bartholomew.[81] (They further compare the East African postcolonial laughing epidemics to the Holy Laugh Movement that emerged in the Toronto Airport Church in 1992, catalyzed by the mesmeric revivalist pastor, Rodney Howard-Browne of the Toronto Blessing.[82]) There have been many rationalizations for why laughter in particular predominated as a symptom. First, it was in the "symptom pool," available for mimetic suggestion and contagious transmission. Second, the nervous laughter of teenage girls, germinal to each of these outbreaks, betrayed the physically repressive conditions of African seminary education where Westernized institutional norms harshly conflicted with ingrained community values in the wake of uneven decolonization.

Last but not least, there were massive instabilities in the region wrought by decades of extractive invasion since the 1880s (by the Germans and then the British). Prior to independence in 1961, Tanganyika had been devastated by drought, famine, poverty, tsetse fly infestations, and failed attempts at compressed modernization administered by the colonial occupiers (such as the disastrous "groundnut scheme" of 1946–1951).[83] Shortly after independence, TANU swiftly abolished racial divisions in all schools as of January 1, 1962. Interlocking factors of prolonged colonialism, breakneck decolonization, and repressive school environments preyed on the communal sensorium and found cryptic relief in the girls' mirthless contagious laughter.

Mass Hysteria and Its Nonrelation to Laughter

Humor scholars and critics have fixated on the isolated symptom of laughter, exploiting the uncanniness of its morbid expression (like the "death by laughter" obituarists of yore).[84] For example, Robert Holden, self-proclaimed happiness guru, describes the Tanganyika outbreak as follows: "The giggling gathered pace and soon the whole class was merry. Teachers were tickled by this spontaneous, joyful outburst and joined in. Soon the whole school was swimming in a tide of laughter."[85] Clearly this is offensive and inaccurate on many levels, including its historical decontextualization and its characterization of "mass psychogenic illness" as in any way "merry" or "joyful."

Robert Provine, although cautious to avoid exploiting the outbreak as an "exotic quirk of an alien culture," as he puts it, hastily analogizes the Tanganyika Laughing Epidemic to "laughing jags" that would be more familiar to his Western readers.[86] His examples include television newscasters who suffer "laughing attacks" during network broadcasts; the "social biology" of catching someone else's laughter (as in the German U-bahn video); laughter yoga (or the exercise of creating laughter "from nothing"); and canned laugh tracks, which he confusingly describes as "mini-epidemics in the name of entertainment."[87] Again, Provine is mainly interested in this African outbreak as empirical proof of laughter's contagious universality in its "naked" form, divorced from any comedic impetus. Unlike Holden, who imputes enjoyment to laughter, Provine emphasizes the absence of pleasure or fun as tangible evidence of laughter's contagious universalism, effectively negating all other motivations at play (e.g., social repression, gender hierarchy, and geopolitical trauma).

Christian Hempelmann takes a hard line against assigning any relevance to the symptom of laughter whatsoever, claiming that contagious laughter "on an epidemic scale is physiologically impossible."[88] He thus categorizes the Tanganyika Laughing Outbreak as a motor-variant form of mass psychogenic illness (MPI). Like medieval dancing plagues or industrial twitching epidemics, these go beyond the spread of anxiety and panic, involving full-body convulsions, seizures, running, kicking, and indeed laughter. Although similar incidents recurred in the 1960s—also amid struggles for African liberation—in neighboring countries of Uganda, Kenya, Rwanda, Burundi, and Zambia, they received less cultural attention, according to Hempelmann, because they did not centrally implicate laughter. There is something about the symptom of laughter. One could make the argument that MPIs have aroused popular visibility (and discursive engagement) in almost direct proportion to the uncanny weirdness of their symptoms. When unwilled actions become grotesquely severed from their associated affects, laughing, dancing, and clown hallucinations assume pride of place.

But in the case of hysterical laughter, psychiatric interest uniquely adheres to the context of contagion. As we know from chapter 5, laughter was excluded as a noteworthy symptom across case studies of hysteric patients. For this reason, I am less willing than Hempelmann to discard laughter altogether. The thesis of this book is that laughter never means what you think it does, least of all in connection to gender and madness.

Death of a Protolanguage; or, Death Threat to the Author?

It is a risky proposition to uproot hysteria from the archive and locate its contagious afterlives in the precarious present. Elaine Showalter, in her controversial gesture to do just that, defined such epidemics as *hystories*: "cultural narratives of hysteria" that "multiply rapidly and uncontrollably in the era of mass media, telecommunications, and email."[89] In the wake of the diagnostic death of "hysteria" (as a medical condition), Showalter argued that conversion hysteria had become even more contagious, "amplified by modern communications and fin de siècle anxiety."[90] To paraphrase her key claims: the more unstable and alienated the society (in times of economic privatization and media hyperconnectivity), the further transmissive one's conversion symptoms threaten to become.

I repeat, *Hystories* was extremely controversial in the late 1990s, and Showalter has since expressed regret in having written it (because of the scandal it caused, if not also the ethics of some of the book's specific examples).[91] She received hate mail and death threats, and the venues that hosted her book talks had to hire private security details. "I got used to having photographers from the local press pools show up at the bookstores to get the picture in case I got shot," she half-jokes, adding: "Writing *Hystories* taught me that it is much safer and calmer to write about hysteria in Charcot, Freud, and [Henrik] Ibsen."[92] The book indeed paints with a broad brush in its concept of hysterical epidemics. It compares Victorian female hysteria to recent phenomena as various as chronic fatigue syndrome, multiple personality disorder, and Gulf War syndrome, and as conspiratorial as alien abduction, recovered memory, and satanic ritual abuse confession narratives.

The book's assessment of contemporary mass hysteria also departs from *Female Malady*'s reparative historiography (see chapter 4). Whatever feisty protolanguage of literary protest Blanche's and Augustine's acrobatic postures may have anticipated, Showalter pathologizes their mass dimensions in the age of late capitalist telecommunications as purely dystopian. But where does collective laughter (and other hopeful, contagious symptoms) fit amid these "hystories," or self-historicizing outbreaks of mass hysteria?

In the final section of this chapter, I will turn my gaze toward the revamped media metaphors of mass hysteria in the twenty-first century, which run the gamut from rebellious feminist performances to far-right, viral conspiracy theories. My point is not to analogize outmoded medical diagnoses to amorphous digital phenomena but to extract their dialectical potentials toward envisioning a break from the psychosocial swamp pits of the catastrophic present. It is my final wager that any collective outbreak of imaginative political resistance will have a foothold in the affective contagions of their most destructive alternatives.

RECLAIMING HYSTERIA?: #MASSHYSTERIA, VIRAL AFFECT, AND COMEDIC METAPHOR IN THE (ALREADY VERY LONG) TWENTY-FIRST CENTURY

Once again, *hysteria is back*. Since 2016 (the leap year of Brexit, Donald Trump's election, and the Brazilian coup—among other things), book volumes, journal issues, academic symposia, and art exhibitions have proliferated on the topic of hysteria. "Hysteria has returned. We are witnessing a hysterical turn in the twenty-first century," announces Elke Krasny.[93] But the hysteric is now "diagnosed as performer, and has moved beyond the limits of medical discourse," claims Johanna Braun.[94] The dominant gesture of this evocative resurrection is to come to terms with the present, in its declining powers of reason, apocalyptic environments, and weaponized culture war politics. Solving the mystery of hysteria acts as a Rosetta stone for decoding the precession of simulacra.[95] Its enigmatic complaint—which traverses inorganic illness and multimedia performance, and which seeks to put into language unknown desires that take demonic possession of the body—has become again, to say the least, rather compelling.

Krasny offers the term "hysteria activism" to encompass a new wave of feminist collectives that seek to appropriate an old signifier against its largely pejorative usage in the twenty-first century. (Hysteria's negative context transcends ideological partisanship as both liberal and conservative commentators frequently accuse the other side of "mass hysteria."[96]) For Krasny, the activist return of hysteria stems from both its necessary appeal to emotion in an era of "post-truth" and its reclamatory gesture of defiance (in fierce company with "nasty women," sex-positive "witches," "feminist killjoys" galore).

"Hysteria is feminist activism," Krasny argues, quoting the mission statement of Hysteria, a London-based feminist collective that "pleasurably challenges capitalism" with "hysterical solidarity."[97] Likewise, HysteriaFemCon (Calcutta), the Association of Hysteric Curators (Los Angeles), and Akademische Burschenschaft Hysteria (Vienna) all embrace the psychosomatic unruliness of hysteria as a collectivist rallying cry against patriarchal abuse. Although inflected by earlier hysteria-affirming feminisms, Krasny observes, "today's hysteria activism is much less a reinterpretation or a rediscovery of [prior] feminisms' interest" in the topic than "a reaction to hysteria and hysterical being used as pejorative keywords for the twenty-first century."[98] That said, hysteria is perhaps the most overdetermined word in the English language; its archives and histories have a way of haunting all future instantiations. As Braun notes in her introduction to *Performing Hysteria: Images and Imaginations of Hysteria*, "the current manifestations surrounding hysteria" are broadly shaped by "historical performance practices" and visual culture.[99] The essays in Braun's volume thus mine the archives of formative hysteria-oriented feminisms to explore recent genres ranging from Me-Too-era horror films to postmodern novels and cyborg-themed television series.

To name someone or something as "hysteric," in misogynist terms, is to negate their claim to subjectivity or epistemological truth. Feminist hysteria collectives wage battle royale against all shame-mongering profanations of the ailment. They operate overwhelmingly through a weaponization of the signifier. That is also their main point of departure, I would argue, from earlier hysteria-positive feminisms—beyond their more divergent or diverse cultural iconographies. These movements do not seek to linger in the gap between reality and desire (per analytic feminist theory) but to demand change by exploding into being a new order of experience altogether. For example, *Hysterical Feminisms* proclaim in their mission statement: "HYSTERIA believes in repudiating every instance

Mission

HYSTERIA strives for radical openness by engaging in fluid critical dialogues that shake the guise of normalcy, which disables structures of oppression operating and thriving.

HYSTERIA is a collective borne from juxtaposing and interlacing multiplicities of feminisms that react to histories of subjugation.

HYSTERIA believes in repudiating every instance of domination in all its manifestations, seeking to incorporate all struggles of the oppressed into our activism.

HYSTERIA aims to combat language that alienates marginalised peoples with whom we stand in solidarity. HYSTERIA places these voices on centre stage supporting a spectrum of expression emphasising those speaking in the first person.

HYSTERIA strives to expose power relations and the realities of exploitation, insisting on the equality of all through a continuous discussion on what equality entails. We refuse to settle on any rigid definitions.

HYSTERIA is critical towards the creation of illusionary binaries such as 'safe'/'dangerous', 'private'/'public' that take the emphasis away from the oppressive structures which HYSTERIA strives to expose.

HYSTERIA knows that feminisms are for everyone, and not reserved for the privileged few. Feminisms should transcend and agitate all colonially-imposed boundaries and borders.

HYSTERIA pleasurably challenges capitalism by documenting critical feminisms.

Without hysterical solidarity we are deluded by the composure of patriarchy

FIGURE 6.3 "Hysterical Feminisms" mission statement. Screen grab by author on July 16, 2022. https://hystericalfeminisms.com/about/.

of domination in all its manifestations, seeking to incorporate all struggles of the oppressed into our activism."[100]

This is a righteous and energizing call to arms, but one whose specificity of critique is potentially drowned out by its urgency of collective plenitude. The antagonisms internal to twenty-first-century feminisms, which earlier waves problematically universalized, are more often now blanketly collectivized in exigent appeals toward something alternatively better. But who withers away within that collective? And how to theorize the relation between inclusive collectivity (through mutual opposition against white heteropatriarchy) versus its differential expedience for various groups and peoples within the collective? For example, disability scholars and activists are by no means uniformly on board with the rhetorical appropriation of debunked mental health diagnoses.[101] The metaphors of mass hysteria and collective madness hold very different stakes for the fight against disability discrimination and injustice, as opposed to their reclamation by neurotypical feminists who feel "driven out of their minds" by a violently sexist and glibly manipulative political media environment.

Against this diffuse generality, Anouchka Grose places hysteria back in the twenty-first-century clinic in her 2016 collection, *Hysteria Today*. She emphasizes the diagnostic holdovers through which old-school hysteria still hides in plain sight, ranging from dissociative identity disorder to anorexia nervosa. But this is more than a feat of diagnostic rag-picking through mutating psychiatric criteria. As she writes in her introduction, "Reclaiming Hysteria," hysterics "use their dissatisfactions and discomforts as a means to interrogate the Other, to make it say something back, to attempt to unsettle it."[102] In tension with the methods of hysteria activists, who lambaste the other in order to seal the cracks within a very broad-based collective, analytic hysterias live in those cracks—not necessarily on the level of identity-based difference but within the constitutive self-difference that forms the groundwork for identity. As Grose puts it, "Beyond their wish to make sense of something lies the realisation that sense can't cover everything, or that one's existence can't be sewn up with words."[103] Hysteria thus resurfaces to name the impossibility of its own reparative signification.

Mental Illness as Comic Metaphor

Where does laughter fit in this weaponized climate of feminist "hysteria activism"? As we know, the language of mental disability has long infused the metaphors of uproarious comedy—from late nineteenth-century imaginations of collective enjoyment as "hysterical" to the persistence of problematic qualifiers for comedy in the present day. (Examples include "crazy funny," "laughing mad," "insanely hilarious," as well as ingrained comic archetypes such as the "screwball," "nut," "lunatic," "lame-brain," "idiot," "cuckoo," and so forth.) I have elaborated some of these intersections between comic metaphor and mental health epithet already in chapters 4 and 5, so I will gloss over any ground that has already been covered.

First, hysteria-positive metaphor offers a redemptive framework for the libidinal unruliness of feminist comedy. This approach is exemplified by *Hysterical!* and *Uproarious*, as well as by *Who's Laughing Now? Feminist Tactics in Social Media*, which explores the virality of subversive feminist laughter within the digital realm.[104] These books inherit long-standing optimistic impulses in feminist comedy studies, forged by Kathleen Karlyn's *Unruly Woman*, Mary Russo's *Female Grotesque*, Bambi Haggins's *Laughing Mad*, and Glenda Carpio's *Laughing Fit to Kill*—among many other key texts.[105] They further foreground the cathartic transposition of sexual repression into collective agency through the furious conduit of contagious, convulsive laughter.

Second, laughter itself is viewed as a trace of dissociative inner consciousness, which finds some relief in its symbolic expression through irrational absurdity and

FIGURE 6.4 Women laugh hysterically at the patriarchal Dutch judicial system during a murder trial. Frame enlargement from *A Question of Silence* (directed by Marleen Gorris, 1982; Netherlands: Sigma Film Productions).

social satire. Among the most compelling uses of this approach engage centrally with crises of anti-Black racism.[106] Lisa Guerrero's *Crazy/Funny: Popular Black Satire and the Method of Madness*, for example, analyzes twenty-first-century Black satire—from the television sketch series *Key & Peele* (2012–2015) to Paul Beatty's novel *The Sellout* (2015)—through a psychosocial lens in order to "reframe how madness may be understood differently from the perspective of the black subject."[107] Guerrero views madness as a form of "black embodied knowledge" that resonates through satire, which offers a vital discourse of Black satiric epistemology.[108] In her account, satire further reveals the Black exception of mental illness, consisting both of the denial of subjectivity to stereotyped Black madness and the "dissociated consciousness" or "disintegrated ego" wrought by centuries of slavery and systemic anti-Black racism.[109] Imaginative extremities of satire create zones of anarchic indistinction between white reason and its pathologized others.

Exploring similar comedic media, Danielle Fuentes Morgan poses antiracist satire as an ontological lifeline in *Laughing to Keep from Dying: African American Satire in the Twenty-First Century*. Her key term in this book is "kaleidoscopic Blackness," which she defines as "the multiple autonomous ways of being Black" that "prevent psychic social death."[110] Satire can give truth to the negation of "kaleidoscopic Blackness," epitomized by the Fanonian-cum-absurdist "sunken place" in Jordan Peele's horror satire *Get Out* (2018), and by speculative tropes of Black simulacral visibility depicted on satiric shows such as *Insecure* (2016–2021), *Atlanta* (2016–), and *Key & Peele*.[111] But the interiority of Black kaleidoscopic thought is utterly singular to Black identity, as she writes: "the hidden, private realm of Black thought and feeling beyond any expected performance of Blackness."[112] To signify kaleidoscopic Blackness as exchangeable for intersectional community building would irreversibly deliver it into the realm of racial performativity and communicative capitalism.

One last crucial example of this second category, antiracist mad satire, finds expansive formulation in La Marr Jurelle Bruce's *How to Go Mad Without Losing Your Mind: Madness and Black Radical Creativity*. Bruce does not limit his inquiry to comedy, although he engages with the stand-up of Richard Pryor and Dave Chappelle. The feminist impulse of his liberation of madness hovers around Black female writing and song, particularly works by Ntozake Shange, Suzan-Lori Parks, Nina Simone, Gayl Jones, and Lauryn Hill. He offers four intersecting categories of madness, which traverse the phenomenological, medical, affective, and biosocial. Bruce enumerates them as: (1) *phenomenal madness*, "an intense unruliness of mind"; (2) *medicalized madness*, which he deontologizes as constructs of the "psy-sciences"; (3) *rage*, "an affective state of intense and aggressive displeasure"; and (4) *psychosocial madness*, "radical deviation from the *normal* within a given psychosocial milieu."[113] For our purposes, Bruce's pursuit of "mad methodology" calls for "radical compassion" toward "madpersons, queer personae, ghosts, freaks, weirdos, imaginary friends, disembodied voices, unvoiced bodies, and unReasonable others."[114] Rather than displace abject madness onto feckless patriarchal enemies, which is often the gesture of hysteria-positive feminist comedy, Bruce extends the redemption of hysterical unreason deep within the collective.

Third, and I will be brief with this last category: in stark contrast to hysteria-positive feminist laughter or antiracist dissociative satire, alt-right insult comedy and trolling have posed increasingly provocative objects of study for liberal and leftist comedy scholars. "The Right-Wing Comedy Complex" (as it was initially titled), renamed *That's Not Funny: How the Right Makes Comedy Work for Them* and cowritten by Nick Marx and Matt Sienkiewicz, represents perhaps the most comprehensive foray into this disturbing realm.[115] As the pun "complex" implies, partisan comedy itself is pathologized as a collective neurotic condition, cultivated by another complex: the far-right corporate news industry. Many recent articles, such as Viveca Greene's "'Deplorable' Satire: Alt-Right Memes, White Genocide Tweets, and Redpilling Normies" and Julia Rose DeCook's "Trust Me I'm Trolling: Irony and the Alt-Right's Political Aesthetic," similarly deploy mental health metaphors to symptomatize alt-right comic obscenity.[116]

I'd further argue that this recent turn to far-right humor arises from the shattered belief that satire itself somehow harbors a left-wing bias (see "Why There's No Conservative Jon Stewart" and "Where Are All the Right-Wing Comedians?"[117]). The perceived lack of threatening laughter on the right shored up long-standing liberal convictions that media satire alone would expose right-wing hypocrisy, weed out corruption, and foster democratic citizenship.[118] As with the grotesque slapstick cartoons that inspired Walter Benjamin's utopian faith in collective laughter circa 1935, liberal satirical comedy woefully fell short of its political task to avert "mass psychosis," or even resurgent Nazism.

COLLECTIVE CLOSURES, LAUGHING AFFECTS, AND HYSTERIC OPENINGS

What, if anything, remains of "the most revolutionary affect of the masses" in its crucial potential to defuse apocalyptic catastrophe? Part and parcel of the return of mass hysteria, the ratification of crowd psychology for the twenty-first century has again sparked debates about "affective openings" versus "collective closures." As Claudia Breger argues in *Making Worlds: Affect and Collectivity in Contemporary European Cinema*, "the negative intensities haunting contemporary public spheres will not be conquered by appeals to reason alone. Instead, the messy entanglements of affect and collectivity need to be addressed—and worked through—as such."[119] She cites the example of the 2016 Clausnitz incident, juxtaposing a xenophobic crowd protesting the arrival of migrant refugees in East Germany to cinema's world-building capacity to "break apart hate and imagine political change."[120] For Breger, cinema retains a special power to arouse incommensurable affects that do not congeal around the borders of defensive in-group identities. That affective hybridity—melding joy and solidarity with anger, mourning, and existential despair—is precisely what distinguishes open, heterogeneous collectivity from violent crowd contagion.

In Le Bon's and Freud's accounts, as we know, emotional contagion is the conduit for thoughtless conformity. In contrast, affect theorists of twenty-first-century crowds have pursued the concept of contagion in its unruly ambivalence. Radical contagion springs from the ambiguity of affect and instability of its signification. "Wherever you are, there is still potential, there are openings, and the openings are in the grey areas, in the blur where you're susceptible to affective contagion, or capable of spreading it," muses Brian Massumi. But "it's a creative conversion," he clarifies, "not some utopian escape."[121] Massumi draws on Gilles Deleuze's Spinozist understanding of affect as a precognitive force (as opposed to conscious feelings or biographical emotions) that molds receptive bodies toward new horizons of becoming. Sara Ahmed, however, rejects the notion of affective contagion altogether, stressing the interruption of unconscious intensities that cause even positive affects to "move sideways (through sticky associations between words, things, and feelings)," leaving a "rippling effect of emotions" many of which cannot "be admitted in the present."[122] Affects do not merely leap between bodies, in Ahmed's version, because of the delay, repression, and "sticky" attachment that mediate their migration.

This indirection of emotion is precisely the source of contagion's expectant possibilities. In her article on "Contagious Feelings," Anna Gibbs builds on Silvan Tomkins's notion of "redintegrative contagion," which is "less organised, less stable, less predictable," finding a "hospitable milieu" in televisual modes of distraction that give rise to "subjectivities characterised by disequilibrium."[123] (Redintegration in cognitive psychology designates the revival of the whole of a previous mental state from the brief sensation of its fragment or part.)

Although "bodies can catch feelings as easily as catch fire," according to Gibbs, that incendiary immediacy is irreversibly fractured by the simulacral intensity of twenty-first-century crowds.[124] In other words, "redintegrative contagion" finds both an apt medium and hazard of further dispersal in the digitized networks of the crowd.

At their most dangerous, these destabilized subjectivities—unmoored from truth, certainty, or hopeful solidity—have triggered the return of old-school contagion: mob panic, myth-mongering conspiracy, and regressive mass hysteria. But they also present revolutionary openings for political assembly when shattered egos resist taking refuge in shallow, neoliberal, anticollective subject positions.

It is the crowd's very outbreak of deindividualization that's given Marxist scholar-activists faith in contagion as a potential lightning rod for social movement politics. "The celebration of autonomous individuality prevents us from foregrounding our commonality and organizing ourselves politically," urges Jodi Dean in *Crowds and Party*, which begins with an anecdote about how the collective strength of the Occupy movement "devolved into the problem of [mere] individuals."[125] Likewise, Jackie Wang turns to psychoanalytic theories of "oceanic feeling" (coined by Romain Rolland in a 1927 letter to Freud) to elaborate her project of "communist affect," emphasizing how "the disintegration of the ego alters one's orientation to the world and others."[126] For Wang, the spread of self-effacing affect paves the way for communist collectives to live out their radical, experimental politics.

It is a seductive but rather obscene leap of faith to hitch one's hopes to the contagious transmission of communist or even reparative affect. "Hope, often a fracturing, even a traumatic thing to experience," Eve Sedgwick famously observed, "is among the energies by which the reparatively positioned reader tries to organize the fragments and part-objects she encounters."[127] For Sedgwick, reparative hope is not contagious (unlike paranoia, with which she diagnoses the critical humanities), but affectively singular and generously empathetic. In other words, the future of open collectivity also depends on the ability of readers and thinkers to resist the paranoid contagions of the academic crowd.

At the same time, to invoke Zupančič's urgent call for detonative comedy: any affect—whether contagiously self-isolating or riskily ego-destroying—must withstand sticking to a world on the brink of barbaric implosion. The crises of the present (class misery, climate chaos, racist misogyny) that have rekindled the contagions of collective hysteria will be unmoved by reorientations of affect alone. At most, affect provides the spark; at worst, it lights the match.

THE TRAIN IS LEAVING THE STATION

To bring this chapter full circle, let us once again return to the scene of the Berlin U-bahn, where contagious hysterical laughter steamrolled a car of unsuspecting German passengers. Upon further sleuthing, however, it appears that this outbreak of contagious laughter was no accident at all, but a cunning social experiment. In fact, the camera operator (Matt Grau) and patient zero laugher (Angela Mecking) were both members of the same Berlin laughing club (Haupstadt Lacht), which is an active chapter of the International Laughter Yoga University.[128] Their entire team had decided to cancel their usual studio session and conduct an impromptu exercise on the Berlin underground, as Mecking put it, "just to have fun and see how people reacted!"[129] In her blog report, Mecking further claims that the success of the experiment—both in its immediate embodied dimensions and digital afterlives—proves definitively that "laughter is contagious."[130] As she declares, "The overwhelming reaction shows that people worldwide are longing for something—for joy, for connection, for love in every aspect of their life. It is also an indicator for the change of mind which is already happening all over the world. So let's laugh and love!"[131]

It feels tempting to counter the spread of xenophobic hate with the contagious endorphins of love, but we know better. The U-bahn riders may have imagined their laughter as hysterical. Its joyful solicitation, however, carried only a glimmer of that world-cracking fusion between comedic pleasure and conversion hysteria. When forbidden thoughts find a narrow window of possibility through socially permissible jokes, laughter is rightly esteemed as therapeutic, if not transformative. But it is only the laughs that can access and liberate words already turned into flesh—collective conversion symptoms—that might yet create revolutionary affective openings toward a less alienating, hostile, and exploitative world.

ADDITIONAL EXAMPLES

The following lists are not based on my own primary research. They integrate secondary documentation with pithy summary. I include them to convey the variety of symptoms and examples at play (in their historical, geographical, and material scope) as well as the occupational hazard of credulous exaggeration when writing about topics of mass hysteria, contagious anxiety, and collective conversion symptoms. The chronology, language, and regionality of these cases go well beyond my own expertise or capacity to contextualize.[132]

Mass Anxiety Hysteria[133]

Andree Balloon Mania (1896, Winnipeg): Numerous false accounts of phantom balloon sightings were reported in anticipation of a delayed aerial expedition.

Aurora End-of-the-World Panic (1938, Europe): A vivid aurora borealis was widely mistaken for an omen of imminent apocalypse.

BBC Radio Hoax (1926, England/Ireland): Radio host Ronald Knox fomented mass panic with false reports about mob riots and labor uprisings in London during his evening program.

Bird Flu Pandemic Scare (2005, global): The global outbreak of bird flu (with over 100 cases reported from 2003–2005) stoked anti-Asian xenophobia in the United States, where hundreds of people started poisoning domestic birds along their migration routes.

Brigand Great Fear (1789, France): After the storming of the Bastille, false reports spread that antirevolutionary brigands commissioned by the dethroned aristocracy were terrorizing the countryside.

Brooklyn Bridge Panic (1883): Shortly after the bridge opened for public use, an outbreak of panic that it was about to collapse led to the death of twelve pedestrians, who were trampled by a frantic mob.

California Telephone Illness (1984): An outbreak of intensified anxiety symptoms became contagious among 153 telephone factory workers—a dozen of whom were hospitalized—after initial reports of a toxic smell, which was likely caused by cleaning fluids.

Child-Eating Scare (Middle Ages, Germany): Endemic delusions that Satan worshippers were feasting on the flesh of children led to the torture and murder of innocent women accused of witchcraft.

Chinese Needle Scare (2001–2002, China): Numerous false reports were filed by people claiming to have been pricked by "AIDS-infected needles."

Coca-Cola Scare (1999, Belgium): Thirty-three schoolchildren were hospitalized after drinking Coca-Cola and suffering acute respiratory symptoms. No evidence of soda contamination could be found, although the product was recalled after several copycat scares occurred in Belgium and France.

Cyber Ghost Scare (2003, India): School attendance dropped precipitously in the southern state of Tamil Nadu after rumors spread that an internet ghost was terrorizing teenagers.

Ecuador Martian Panic (1949): Twenty people were killed in a fire after an angry mob in Quito torched the building of a radio station that had broadcast an adaptation of H. G. Wells's *War of the Worlds*, causing mass panic about Martian invasion.

Feather Tickling Fad (early 1900s, Massachusetts): This is an example of a fad that was pathologized as epidemic hysteria. The commercial sale of long-handled feather dusters used for tickling ("tickle-for-a-nickel") incited moral panic about contagious sexual deviance.

Frankie Avalon Mania (1959, Wisconsin): Teenage girls reportedly "fainted at a rate of one a minute" and assaulted several police officers at a Frankie Avalon concert in Milwaukee.

Goldfish Swallowing Fad (1939, United States): Reports that a Harvard University freshman had swallowed a goldfish on a dare inspired the short-lived but widespread American fad of competitive goldfish swallowing.

Greek Telephone Panic Attacks (1975): Fainting spells and hyperventilation afflicted 250 of 990 workers at the Athens Telephone Center. Psychiatrists attributed these episodes to transient anxiety attacks, caused by workplace stressors such as noise, heat, exhaustion, and boredom.

Hula-Hoop Fad (1958, global): The popularity of Hula-Hoop toys incited pervasive moral panic about sexual obscenity suggested by repetitive hip gyration.

Illinois Bus Bedlam (2000): Phantom asthma attacks spread contagiously on a school bus after two students with asthma left their inhalers at home and experienced respiratory symptoms.

Irradiated Mail Scare (1992, United States): The U.S. Postal Service began "irradiating" mail after a wave of anthrax attacks; numerous employees reported irritation and anxiety symptoms after handling irradiated mail, which allegedly emitted a particular but undetectable odor.

Mars Earthquake Panic (1939, Argentina): Minor tremors caused mass panic that the world was ending, provoking residents to flee their homes, scream, and fire guns.

Nuclear Disaster Hoax (1982, Illinois): A radio drama about nuclear disaster fallout was cancelled due to mass paranoia about a defunct power plant northeast of Springfield, Illinois.

Phantom Hat Pin Stabber (1923, France): False reports of an alleged assailant wreaking havoc with a long, sharp hat pin led to numerous unjust arrests.

Pigsty Hysteria (1972, England): The odor emitted from a pigsty in Hazlerigg caused 130 children and several adults to become ill with common anxiety symptoms.

Pokémon Illness (1997, Japan): Over twelve thousand Japanese children became severely ill after watching a suggestive episode of *Pokémon*, snowballing from the alarmist media coverage of several initial cases.

Russian Poland Balloon Scare (1892): Phantom military balloon sightings in Russian-occupied Poland led to paranoia and panic that the German military had deployed covert espionage vessels.

Skunked Workers (Ohio, 1948): Nine female workers were sprayed with skunk oil after crossing a picket line; the strikebreakers (aka, scabs) were hospitalized, initially believing the spray to contain toxic chemicals.

Strawberries with Sugar Virus (2006, Portugal): Several hundred schoolchildren developed mysterious symptoms during their stressful final exam season; their symptoms closely mirrored those of teen characters on a popular television program, *Strawberries with Sugar*.

Tulip Mania (Holland, 1634–1637): A gouge in the tulip market fueled widespread desperation to purchase tulips, despite heavily inflated prices.

Windshield Pitting Scare (1954, Washington): Thousands of false reports of a phantom automobile sniper proliferated when residents suddenly noticed strange pit marks in their windshields. Conspiracy theories escalated from gang vandalism to radioactive fallout.

Zoot Suit Riots (1942–1943, California): White Americans repeatedly attacked Latino men wearing zoot suits after xenophobic panic erupted during the trial of nine Mexican American teenagers.

Mass Motor Hysteria[134]

British Military Fainting Epidemics (1951): A series of mass fainting epidemics afflicted British military soldiers while they were standing in formation.

Cambrai Convent Outbreak (1491, France): Perhaps the first instance of "convent hysteria" that was documented in detail, nuns exhibited contagious symptoms of trans-species metamorphosis: climbing trees like cats, sprinting across a field like dogs, and emitting uncanny noises in imitation of various birds.

Contagious Glossolalia: Endemic to religious revivals and camp meetings, the "spontaneous utterance of sounds in a language the speaker has never learned and does not even understand" literally translates to "tongue speaking," also known as "speaking in tongues."

Dancing Manias (1100s–1600s, Europe): Also known as St. Vitus Dance, participants broke into contagious, frenzied, uncontrollable dancing for hours—days, even weeks on end—sometimes naked, and allegedly to the point of death. Other symptoms included screaming, hallucination, fornication, and painful convulsions.

Fainting Vietnamese Schoolgirls (2004): On October 18, fifty-seven high school girls were hospitalized after mysteriously fainting. They recovered quickly, but 143 girls experienced similar symptoms the next day, and twenty were hospitalized for multiple days. The fainting episodes struck another school in the area the next month, afflicting fifty students, who were allegedly instructed to "dress warmly" and not to skip breakfast.

False Memory Syndrome: This is a controversial, global, and transhistorical diagnosis that can implicate anything from false memories of incest and sexual abuse to alien abduction and satanic demonic possession.

Genital Shrinking Scares: *Koro* (the Malay word for perceived genital shrinkage) has recurred across Malaysia, Indonesia, China, Thailand, and India over the past two centuries, designating the vivid perception that one's genitals are shrinking. Although often an isolated symptom, epidemic outbreaks of koro have been recorded in Guandong (1984), northeast Thailand (1976), Bengal (1982), and Singapore (1967).

Hoorn Orphanage Possession (1673, Netherlands): An unnamed evil bedeviled children in a Dutch orphanage, provoking them to yell, howl, flail their limbs, bark like dogs, and tear at their skin and clothing. Uninfected children tried to flee the scene, but many were gripped by the contagion before they could escape.

Hysterical Boredom (1972, Canada): Cree and Ojibway tribes dwelling in a poor, remote village under strict Christian rule experienced outbreaks of lucid nightmares that prefaced convulsive fits, in which inhabitants ran into the woods seizing and screaming. These episodes were attributed to poverty, repression, and creative deprivation.

Italian Fatigue Outbreak (1978): Epidemics of malaise, fatigue, itchiness, dry mouth, and eye irritation spread through an electrochemical plant, afflicting about 427 of five thousand workers. No organic or physical cause could be determined, other than alienation and confinement.

Klikuschestvo Shouting Mania (Russia, 1861): People on a farm in Boukreiewski were convulsed by seizures, and began crying, hiccupping, laughing, screaming, and imitating farm animals until they were exorcised of their demons by the church and doused in holy water.

Koln Outbreak of Erotic Convulsions (1564, Germany): Nuns in a convent were seized with contagious erotic convulsions, which infected others in the community.

Laughing Epidemics (1960s–1970s, East Africa): Serial laughing epidemics notoriously afflicted schoolchildren in East Africa in the 1960s in the immediate aftermath of hellish colonization and rapid decolonization across the region. See more in the chapter description.

Loudun Outbreak of Possessed Nuns (1632–1638, France): Ursuline nuns were possessed by the devil, who compelled them to wander from their beds; climb onto the roof; run through the fields; and, of course, shout religious blasphemies while embodying contortionist and convulsive limb postures.

Louisiana Twitching Epidemic (1939): Contagious twitching spread uncontrollably among teenage girls at a high school, who were allegedly anxious about schoolwork and physically overstimulated by various dance festivals.

Orissa Cat Calls (2004, India): Dozens of schoolgirls suffered fainting spells and, upon regaining consciousness, would meow, walk on all fours, claw at people, and behave like cats.

Philippine Devil Hysteria (1994, Manila): An elementary school was temporarily closed after two dozen students fainted and hallucinated, claiming that they had seen the devil, who appeared in the guise of a gigantic man with horns and a tail.

Qawa Hysterical Schoolgirls (1968, Fiji): An epidemic of twitching, hyperventilation, and musical wheezing afflicted seventeen girls during exam season.

Saint-Médard Convulsionnairies (France, 1730s): "Convulsionnaires" experienced miraculous cures at the grave of Saint-Médard. Their affliction consisted of acrobatic convulsions that became widely contagious to the population at large.

School Writing Tremors (1880s–1910s, Europe): Outbreaks of contagious tremors, shaking, twitching, and other unruly motor afflictions pervaded girls' boarding schools across Europe, particularly institutions that cultivated rigid physical discipline and often assigned tedious, repetitive handwriting exercises.

Singapore Factory Hysteria (1970s): Contagious fits spread among women workers in industrial factories. The first episode occurred in 1973 at a television assembly plant when a woman began screaming; the plant closed temporarily after many coworkers followed suit. Similar outbreaks afflicted mostly women at other nearby factories in the subsequent months.

Swedish Preaching Epidemic (1841): A contagious outbreak of trances, convulsive fits, and spiritual hallucinations were so named because they involved the irresistible incitement to preach.

Ugandan Running Sickness (2002): Contagious running, fears of demonic possession, and hallucinatory visions affected thirty (mostly) female residents of Kayayimba in July. Multiple people reported seeing visions of snakes and then fire.

Unterzell Outbreak (1738, Germany): Convent hysteria amid the last throes of antiwitch mania.

Zimbabwe Zombie School (2002): Outbreaks of shaking and sleepwalking at Methodist Christian schools in rural Zimbabwe transmitted contagious symptoms among students that evoked popular zombie lore.

PART III
Early Cinema

7
Laughter Unleashed

Hysterical Women at the Movies

Women laughed their heads off at the movies. "Laugh? Why, you'll have to tie them to the seats so that they won't roll all over the house in fits of convulsive laughter," declared *The Moving Picture World* in 1912.[1] Hysterically laughing women were widely embraced as "the makers or breakers of any attraction, whether of the screen or stage."[2] As Broadway star Taylor Holmes confessed, if the "women laugh, or are pleased, I don't care what the men do. I go ahead and prepare for a long run," but if they "don't like the show—turn off the pipe organ, Tessie; there's nobody behind you but the ushers, and they're all asleep."[3] Even Charcot's hypnotized somnambulists would have been roused by the commotion of women laughing "themselves into fits, and misfits," which allegedly caused their "corset strings to snap with smothered thud like firecrackers under the bed."[4] The rabid monetization of female enjoyment brought about quite a sea change. As we know, women's laughs were ruthlessly suppressed, muffled, corseted, defanged, gaslit, and hystericized throughout the nineteenth century.

To laugh hysterically, to refresh our memories, meant to suffer extravagantly from sharply mixed feelings—a crisis of affect that predominantly afflicted nervous women who were consumed by their sentiment, often to the detriment of their amusement. With the furious rise of twentieth-century mass entertainment culture, female revelers were caught between a rock and a hard place, solicited for fun but condemned for enjoying it all too much. How many laughing spectators felt like stage actress Marie Nordstrom, who "lost her composure entirely at the hysterical laughing of several women in the audience, joining in the laughter, despite the fact that she bit her lip until it nearly bled to try and check herself"?[5] Incidentally, the show in question was called *Bought and Paid For*: that is precisely the point, female enjoyment was mined as a source of affective capital, conjuring transgressive fun as an exploitable compulsion. After all, "the sound of laughter coming from the open doors is one of the best drawing cards to attract the passer-by that the management has," opined a wise movie exhibitor in 1908.[6] In the same breath that women were admonished not to laugh (because it might kill them!), they were shamelessly implored to do so by a ballooning cabal of entertainment industry impresarios.

EXPLODING INTO MODERNITY

This chapter explores the raucous potentials and capitalist incentives for women's hysterical explosion into laughing modernity. It is a well-established argument that the rise of cinema and other adjoining amusements around the turn of the last century liberated women, unleashing their convulsive mirth onto a rapidly changing world. Variety shows, moving pictures, phonograph parlors, pleasure parks, department stores, dance halls, wax museums, electricity displays, even public morgues numbered among the many uproarious spaces where women could at last savor their participation in "mass culture and a new urban crowd," as Vanessa Schwartz details, becoming members of "a society of spectators."[7] Feminist scholars (including myself) have energetically participated in writing this history of female fun in the mutating madhouse of modern mass culture.

Formative texts such as Miriam Hansen's *Babel and Babylon* (1991), Kathy Peiss's *Cheap Amusements* (1986), Lauren Rabinovitz's *For the Love of Pleasure* (1998), and Jacqueline Najuma Stewart's *Migrating to the Movies* (2005) explore the emergence of cinema as an evocative aesthetic sphere and transformative social space for women and other marginalized pleasure seekers. Drawing on Alexander Kluge and Oskar Negt's *Public Sphere and Experience* (1972), Hansen characterizes early film spectatorship as a "potential autonomous, alternative horizon of experience for particular social groups, such as immigrant working-class audiences and women across class and generational boundaries."[8] Stewart follows film spectatorship as a vehicle for racial migration, emphasizing "the ways Black people were seen, and saw themselves, during a transformative period in American cultural life" as cinema registered "both anxiety and optimism

FIGURE 7.1 "Mae Gordon's Original Insane Moving Pedestal." Photograph from 1907. Image courtesy of The Library of Congress.

about the roles African Americans could play" while pursuing their "legal rights, economic power, and access to politically and commercially grounded public spheres."[9] Moving pictures shaped the popular imagination of modernity's body politic, and theaters themselves offered tantalizing spaces for spectatorial experience and social experimentation.

METHOD WARS: FEMINIST THEORY AND ITS RELATION TO OPTIMISM

Early cinema is a treasure trove for retroactive hope. To that point, I am struck by the diverging prognoses for social optimism posited by feminist historiographies of early cinema versus recent scholarship on the pleasure politics of neoliberal enjoyment. The critique of capitalism and rise of leisure-based consumerism has always been core to the discourse on early cinema, which is broadly animated by a regenerative spirit of optimism—that cinema created alternative life worlds, even if those worlds were simultaneously shot through with exploitation and alienation. The escalation of shock, stimuli, and new sensations "inflect our conception of a public sphere that catered to—and constructed—female spectators in alternative, often antagonistic ways," muses Jennifer Bean.[10] But to what extent does that recuperative ethos still resonate today? Indeed, the desire to unleash forgotten film archives onto the dystopian present often guides the feminist historian's optimistic gaze at the transformative spheres of carnivalesque modernity.

In contrast, feminist affect theorists such as Lauren Berlant and Sianne Ngai have looked askance at the nightmare of "permanent carnival" and diminishing returns of compulsory enjoyment. In their introduction to a special issue of *Critical Inquiry* on comedy, aptly titled "Comedy Has Issues," Berlant and Ngai associate the futility of optimism with a pervasive injunction to enjoy, whereby the "freedom-to-enjoy," as Slavoj Zizek has put it, "is reversed into *obligation* to enjoy—which, one must add, is the most effective way to block access to enjoyment."[11] In other words, the ruthless taskmaster of the superego has become a capitalist carnival barker in the aftermath of financialized, deregulated capitalism in the twenty-first century. Permanent carnival arises when there no longer remains any distance between alienating work and perfunctory fun, as both are devoured by the voracious productivity of an economic system that harvests human joy as a boundless reserve for surplus value and "immaterial" labor.

These extractive theatrics of coercive enjoyment are exemplified by corporate solicitations to "flexible" gig workers (i.e., unsalaried and uninsured): "Be Your Own Boss" and forego your labor rights to "join a community of awesome, friendly people—passengers and drivers alike."[12] TikTok video star by day and Uber/Lyft driver by night, the gig worker is commanded to enjoy "any time," around the clock, fueling a clickbait attention economy in which we're all "supposed to be funny all the time."[13] If comedy—let alone carnival—once signaled a special, optimistic form in which norms could be violated and laws temporarily upended, that raucous exception has now been hollowed out into yet another tactic of biopolitical domination. Berlant thus associates permanent carnival with the hellscape of "cruel optimism," whereby the thing that you want most is episodically the very thing that prevents you from thriving. (Instead, they pose "humorlessness," or the withholding of affective flexibility altogether, as the inevitable fallout of permanent carnival.[14])

Noncruel attachments to optimistic enjoyment remain within reach, however, but they call for the rejection of enjoyment tout court. This spirited abomination of joy is epitomized by Sara Ahmed's playful polemic of the "feminist killjoy." An antagonist to both mandatory fun and predatory humor, against all odds, the feminist killjoy herself has a devilishly good time steamrolling the bad faith of false hope. "Our feminist ghosts are not only miserable," avows Ahmed, "they might even giggle at the wrong moments. They might even laugh hysterically in a totally inappropriate manner. After all, it can be rebellious to be happy when you are not supposed to be happy."[15] Ahmed thus hystericizes enjoyment as an alternative to passive complicity, leveling her critique at the lazy, misogynistic, racist, and colonialist impulses that undergird capitalism's rapacious engorgement of leisure and pleasure as the new horizons of (unpaid/underpaid) work. In other words, the ubiquity of commoditized fun will not set you free, especially when alienating work masquerades as joyful leisure to perpetuate the all-consuming exploitation of unprotected labor.

In this chapter, I revisit the feminist spectatorship debates of the 1990s and early 2000s. I focus on early cinema's commodification of female laughter and unavoidable appeals to those Medusan proto-killjoys who refused to be dominated by way of their funny bone. "Say, girls, I was in the bunch at the Scenic, and—well, I never laughed so hard in all my life. Why listen! I thought my back hair was coming down any minute."[16] Mildred Irving recounts her visit to the ladies' variety matinee in Rhode Island in 1907. Was Irving a laughing stooge of early cinema's entrée into permanent carnival or a wayward hysteric? And how might we cultivate her unruly pleasures today against the multiplying mandates to sad, empty, and cruel forms of enjoyment (such as Uber's interpellation of cash-strapped workers as flexible fun seekers)? Let us investigate!

The desire to linger in one's whimsies and exhibit them performatively bear contradictory potentials in the present. On the one hand, laughing spectatorship energetically fosters rabble-rousing prankster comedy, à la feminist guerilla satires from the riot grrrls of *Vulveeta* (Maria Breaux, 2022) to Amber Rose's SlutWalk. (In that spirit, Australian feminist performance artist Barbara Cleveland laughs continuously into the camera for one hour in *The One Hour Laugh*.[17]) On the other hand, it's an occupational hazard of "communicative capitalism" whereby any inkling of authentic affect is levied into a form of cynical currency at the behest of a rapacious economic system. As Karl Ritter forebodingly described the masses at the cinema in 1929, they "are a glassy-skinned giant monster, transparent to the very circulation of their blood, to their brains and their hearts."[18] But they were also revitalized by holding their laughter and hysteria in tension, for example, roused by the female mimic Madame Lydia Yeamans-Titus who "kept the house in roars of laughter" with her uncanny vocal imitations, which were repeatedly "drowned out" by "the uncontrollable laughter of the audience."[19] (As I will explain later in this chapter, I view cinema as both somatically exceptional but culturally contiguous with vaudeville, the amusement park, and other pleasure centers of silent film's heyday.)

By inheriting cinema's early ghosts of surplus enjoyment, while focusing on the ever-fraught relation between laughter and hysteria, I hope to incite leaps of faith into the throat of unruly hilarity in the apocalypse-mongering present. At once commercial gimmicks and springboards to emancipatory social conflict, cinema's hysterical fever dreams yield vivid object lessons for our own catastrophic times. They demand noncruel forms of optimism that defy the gridlocks of alienated enjoyment and politicized madness today, as we will explore.

HYSTERICAL LAUGHTER IN THE THROAT OF CINEMATIC MODERNITY

Hysterically laughing women and *laughing female hysterics*—once arch doppelgängers—assumed the same convulsive body amid the carnivalesque spaces of cinematic modernity. As I have argued, women's everyday laughter was ruthlessly suppressed and gaslit throughout the nineteenth century; in contrast, hysteric laughter (an unremarkable symptom of medical hysteria) remained widely overlooked and ignored by all the medical experts.

In this chapter, I pursue the head-on collision between laughter and hysteria—enjoyment and madness—through solicitous appeals to female laughing spectators, which fueled the spread of capitalist mass culture, traversing a host of venues from streetcars and department stores to pleasure parks and burlesque shows. "The audience receded from one convulsion of laughter but to be thrown into one more violent," trumpeted a stage revue that played to "crowded houses" at the Alcazar in 1899.[20] Women in the audience "were semi-hysterical from laughter" at Bert Melrose's act, which "was a riot."[21] But have you caught wind of *The Hobble Skirt* (IMP, 1910)?[22] "This picture will make *you* laugh your very back teeth loose . . . For the love of fun and profits, get this hobble skirt thing if you have to scrap for it."[23] Meanwhile, Gus Hill's already "corpulent bank roll" was "steadily fattening" if the "shrieks and outbursts" of the "great many women in the audience" that "laughed itself tired ... can be taken as a criterion," boasted *Variety* in 1910.[24] And so the laughs resounded, loosening the corset and bloating the billfold.

Soundscapes of Mirth (Observations on Throat/Eye Coordination)

If nineteenth-century hysterics lacked an outlet for their outbursts, movies offered sanctioned spaces and evocative imagery for their malaise, if not tangible gateways to thundering activism. They also "made it possible for immigrants and migrants," argues Rabinovitz, "as well as rural and urban Americans conscious of their rapidly changing society ... to participate" more extensively in shaping American culture.[25] Like Rabinovitz, who focuses on American cinema's contemporaneity with amusement parks, Lynne Kirby follows the railroad in *Parallel Tracks* (1997); Anne Friedberg sets her sights on recreational vision in *Window Shopping* (1993); and, more recently, Asli Ozgen-Tuncer has highlighted the material importance of women's shoes in what she calls silent "pedestrian cinema."[26] The long-standing consensus is that movies opened pivotal venues and imaginative horizons for liberating women from their domestic drudgery while giving them new symbolic language to unleash their gaslit hysteria onto the mass politics of everyday life.

At the same time, their radical voices were commoditized as never before. Laughing singers, spielers, barkers, hee-haw girls, professional criers, screamers, animal mimics, and ventriloquists formed the aural soundscapes of raucous modernity. Such blaring noises were sources of endemic unease and municipal regulation. In 1907, the city of Philadelphia issued a public noise ordinance against the use of phonograph machines outside movie theaters to lure patrons, while also attempting (and failing) to censor the "horrid din" of professional spielers and barkers.[27] In Chicago, the police actively prohibited spielers from vocal solicitation, citing an incident in Sans Souci Park in which a woman addressed bystanders with a loud megaphone about her "350 pounds" "wiggling" Salome dancer who is "four feet in height."[28]

In their unruly contingency, female voices erred on the side of mobility and disruption. For example, two women, Belle Smith and Kate Walker, were arraigned in Chicago in 1899 for their disorderly public laughter at a new joke about the "kissing bug."[29] Yet when snatched from the body and mastered by phonographic technology, the deviations of the voice could echo any which way. Their infectious recording spawned instant hits such as "Laughing Song" (1897), "Laugh and the World Laughs with You" (1897), and "The Laughing Spectator" (1908), "a revelation for those who have only heard the phonographs in the ferry houses and saloons."[30] The aural spectacle of female silliness infiltrated popular phonography, epitomized by the "Hee-Haw Girl" Ida May Chadwick and "Laughing Girl" Sallie Strembler, whose cylinder rendition of "Ev'rything's Funny to Me" was "one of the most infectious laughing songs ever written," according to the *Edison Phonograph Monthly*.[31]

Strembler intermingles gleeful declarations of her own risqué sense of humor, crooned in high falsetto, with Medusan outbursts of cacophonous laughter. "That sense of the ridiculous is very strong in me; I burst in fits of laughter at everything I see," which she then demonstrates: "HAHAHAHA-HEHEHEHEH-HOHOHOHO!!!!"[32] And so the song continues. Simply put, the genie was out of the bottle, from the female throat to "the gold mould process" whereby a "laugh is sent echoing all over the world."[33] In a similar vein, commercial film advertisements stripped the implied laugh from the convulsive body, claiming cachinnation as a property of the filmic commodity. It would be hard to think of a more relevant example than *Sandy McPherson's Quiet Fishing Trip* (Edison, 1908), an aptly titled comedy that *The Film Index* celebrated as "425 feet of laughter."[34] Similarly, *He Who Laughs Last Laughs Best* (Essanay, 1908) "condensed" at least as many laughs into "500 feet" of film, while *Moving by Electricity* (?, 1908) promised to "keep anyone in a convulsion of laughter the entire time this film is being shown."[35] Film titles might as well have been priced by the mirthful spasm instead of by the length of the reel.

While raucous joy bombarded the polis, the feverish expansion of pleasure-based, commercial markets gobbled up every sensory facet of ordinary life. "Does your wife get melancholy?—Buy a phonograph. And some records . . . that will make her laugh," advised *Edison Phonograph Monthly*.[36] What else of that hysterical excess refused to congeal into pleasure-pedaling surplus value? It would be hard to imagine a more direct line from physical unruliness to feckless commercialism than Bob and Alf Taylor's comedy act, which allegedly sparked "A Boom in Prices" at local corset stringeries in 1895. It was reportedly so funny that women in the audience broke their corset staves in the throes of convulsive laughter.[37] But "it is a vile calumny," as one newspaper reassured its readers, that Bob and Alf were receiving "secret pay" from the "corset stringeries," who found "it necessary to increase their price lists whenever the great fun makers" were in town.[38] Why banish corsets when you could continue to exploit the gimmick of their inutility?

In a similar spirit, a male comedian recounted an anecdote about how a woman "got up and left in the middle of [his] act," according to the maid in the woman's dressing room, who "told me she had laughed so much she broke a corset-stave."[39] He further boasted, "straws may show the way the wind blows, but give me a corset-stave in the show business."[40] Simply put, the promise of corset-busting laughs—loud, toothy, detonative, cantankerous—was an unfailing rainmaker. Meanwhile, the revolving door between hell-raising mischief and profit-seeking avarice widely converged on women's ear-splitting throats.

EARLY CINEMA'S CIRCUITS OF HYSTERICAL SENSATION

What did it feel like to be a laughing spectator of early cinema? Corset busting, sidesplitting, and throat hoarsening do not begin to describe it. In the earliest films, comedy predominated. Housemaids combust (*How Bridget Made the Fire*, AM&B, 1900), women evaporate (*The Vanishing Lady*, R. W. Paul, 1897), elephants go on carnival rides (*Shooting the Chutes*, Edison, 1896), dancing billboards spring to life (*The Poster Girls and the Hypnotist*, AM&B, 1899), and X-ray devices exaggerate the absurd consequences of erotic looks (*The X-Ray Fiend*, G. A. Smith, 1897). There was nothing more uproarious than watching the whole world explode, with human limbs and machine parts raining down from the sky, exemplified by *Explosion of a Motor Car* (Hepworth, 1900) and *Mary Jane's Mishap* (G. A. Smith, 1903), in which an English maid spontaneously combusts through the chimney. But like the performer's head that's bloodlessly decapitated in *The Four Troublesome Heads* (Star-Film, 1898) and *The Maniac Barber* (AM&B, 1899), or the kitchen maid's hands that self-detach to streamline her domestic labor in *The Kitchen Maid's Dream* (Vitagraph, 1907), all upheaval was strictly impermanent.

Cinema invaded every recreational venue; it is thus fitting that so many early film subjects were ripped straight from the circus, the cabaret, and the variety stage: stripteasing pigs, muscle-flexing strongmen, sharpshooting cowgirls, smooching paramours, serpentine-wriggling contortionists, and Indigenous ghost dancers. So-called silent movies were never enjoyed without sound, which ranged from the lone organist or pedagogic narrator to full bands with howling vocalists, and, of course, feisty audience members, who often asserted their own soundscapes entirely. At the Empire in 1911, "nearly a third of the 'audience' were women and one laughed so hard she scared her infant in arms until it cried."[41] The "auditory nerves and the optic nerves" likewise chewed up the scenery.[42] "One almost hears the organ that goes with every merry-go-round, grinding out its ear-splitting tunes," wrote an American writer upon watching moving pictures of a German picnic ground in 1898.[43]

Uncontained by the theater, on a warm day, "when the hazy evenings descend over Broadway," crowds would gather in the streets to marvel at the "large canvas screens unfold[ing] in every place where passers-by can obtain a good view."[44] The spectacle of cinema was endemic to the frenetic hullabaloo of city life, as unavoidable as the ubiquitous tiny screens and towering jumbotrons that engulf Times Square today. Fake pictures of imperialist war in Cuba and the Philippines, public executions of anarchists and elephants, intimate private glimpses of state monarchs at the breakfast table—whatever the masses desired in their hunger "to bring 'things' closer spatially and humanly," to invoke Walter Benjamin.[45] The magical reversibility of traumatic bodily catastrophe, from nervous hysteria to murderous atrocity, channeled the novel powers of cinema and proved irresistible for the anxious, pleasure-seeking masses to feast their eyes on.

In this vein, Hansen headlines *Babel and Babylon* with the fiery scene of female crowds in Chicago flocking to witness the *Corbett-Fitzsimmons Fight* in 1897, a filmed heavyweight match that offered an enticing substitute for the male homosocial space of the boxing ring. "Life-like" and "thrilling," working "the big audience" up to a "high pitch of excitement," according to the *San Francisco Dramatic Review*, such somatic views promised to bring disenfranchised spectators to the remote or off-limits spaces from which they were otherwise excluded.[46] In Hansen's account, the Veriscope boxing match "afforded women the forbidden sight of male bodies in seminudity, engaged in intimate and intense physical action," but at a multisensory distance—deprived of the smell, taste, and noise of the arena, or rather, replaced by a different affective environment entirely.[47] Women screamed, laughed, and roared with applause: "One would imagine himself at a presentation of howling melodrama," observed a male reporter in Boston, "rather than viewing a series of inanimate pictures thrown upon a canvas."[48] The sensory joys of cinema's visual thrills were inextricable from the contexts of its public exhibition.

"It was paid hysteria. Some were paid to hoot. Some to cry. Some to laugh."[49] *The Phonoscope* vividly recounted Vitascope's filmed hanging of William Carr in Kansas City, Missouri, in 1897. "It was revolting—four hundred persons crying and shrieking and laughing, surging under the very gallows, shouting against the horrible, swinging body."[50] A white man, Carr had been convicted of murdering his three-year old daughter; eight hundred spectators attended his lynching, which was captured on one thousand feet of film and viewed throughout the world. Allegedly, the mob had been solicited to laughing hysterics so that their "hideous, grewsome" conduct "might be photographed, disgraced and shown to the world disgraced."[51] Ginned up to bloodthirsty mania for the purpose of being filmed, the mob explicitly diverged from those wild audiences of early cinema, which were already a far cry from the *Psychologie des foules*, to invoke Gustave Le Bon (see chapter 6). But "the crowd, and the experience of belonging to an urban collectivity more generally, did not disappear," argues Schwartz, "rather, their collective violence did."[52] In other words, cinema triggered the mob's bloodlust and then melted it away.

Where did that violent barbarity go? Why, into the "exciting and amusing magical moving pictures," where people "apparently behead and shoot one another" and then "immediately restore them to life again or make them appear in two places at once!"[53] *The Phonoscope*'s 1899 report on "varied uses of the kinetoscope" emphasizes its lighthearted savagery, which both appealed to the hysterical body and liberated it into the realm of the flickering image.

To share a revealing example, when a hailstorm struck outside the Electric Theatre in New Jersey in 1906, 350 women and children were allegedly on the brink of "hysterical" madness. But the manager swiftly gave orders to put the funniest picture on the screen," according to the *Trenton Evening Times*, and soon enough "everything was all right."[54] Though hyperbolic and rather sexist, this account is no less instructive; it imagines cinema as a hypnotic escape hatch from the mortal exigencies of time and space (and even weather), in addition to posing filmic laughter as a therapeutic antidote to hysterical mob panic.

Cinema's overwhelming remedial power is core to my own commitment to its "earliness," in its jarring spontaneity that provided a visual salve for the nervous exhaustion of capitalist productivity and frenzied urban experience. As a category of historical periodization, "early cinema" typically refers to the prenarrative years from 1894 to about 1907, at which point films became increasingly concerned with storytelling and character development. But I approach "earliness," riffing on Tom Gunning's crucial notion of "attractions" (adapted from Soviet montage theory[55]), as an aesthetic based primarily in its hasty, exhilarating temporality—the sheer enthrallment with unforeseen free play of wild, shape-shifting figures.

Cinema's therapeutic effects were undeniable. Its "greatest advantage was its direct emotional appeal and the freedom of the spectators to surrender their feelings," claims Corinna Müller. "In contrast to the theater, which demanded decorum, concentration and emotional control, the cinema allowed movie-goers not only to chat and laugh freely, but also to cry, a benefit that even men appreciated."[56] Although Müller focuses on German audiences, her observations hold strong explanatory power for the visceral appeals of the medium as such. An emblem of modern life, cinema fed the hunger for "a broader cultural climate that demanded 'the real' as a spectacle," offers Schwartz, emphasizing its enticements to a new "audience of and for urban spectacularity" in fin de siècle Paris.[57] But that simulacral vortex haunted cinema's global "transformation of the public sphere, in particular the gendered itineraries of everyday life and leisure," notes Hansen.[58] It was a deal with the devil: cathartic invigoration in exchange for the very commodification of sensory experience, not least of all hysterical laughter.

The Emergence of a Hysterical Medium

The revolving door between radical democratization and all-consuming commodification was only part of the picture. Lucrative hilarity repeatedly butted heads with the comic exploitation of neuropathology. The popularity of cinema itself was "greatly indebted to the body language of hysteria," claims Rae Beth Gordon.[59] In *Why the French Love Jerry Lewis*, Gordon focuses on the French public's fascination with urban spectacle and psychiatric medical culture. In particular, cabaret and café-concert audiences were obsessed with hysteria, which shaped depictions of somnambulism and hypnosis in early French cinema, inspiring British and American titles such as *The Somnambulist* (Gaumont British, 1903), *A Quick Change Mesmerist* (Charles Urban, 1908), and *Hypnotizing the Hypnotist* (Vitagraph, 1911). Gordon emphasizes cinema's appeals to popular neuropathology, which, she suggests, gave rise to a new, destructive-utopian politics.

Escapist pastime or alternate life world? Zoe Beloff poses the question innovatively in her experimental film, *Charming Augustine* (2005), which imagines a counterhistory of hysteria if cinema had been invented one decade earlier.[60] Beloff uses stereoscopic cinematography and three-dimensional effects to render the multisensory delusions of Charcot's female patients as protocinematic revelations. How differently would the late nineteenth-century history and theory of hysteria have unfolded if Charcot's "epileptic divas" (such as Augustine Gleizes) gained early access to cinema instead of being bombarded by Albert Londe's still photography? By animating surrogate figures, movies inspired belief that their lifelike nonreality could somehow transcend the material limitations of their exhibition. Laughter, as we will see, became a privileged signal and pivotal expression of that hysterical projection. Once two ships in the night, laughter and hysteria crash-landed into the nervous body of the uproarious film spectator.

FIGURE 7.2 Frame enlargement from *Charming Augustine* (Zoe Beloff, stereoscopic 16mm film, 2005). http://www.zoebeloff.com/pages/augustine.html.

HYSTERICAL MOVIES AND THE CARNIVAL OF LAUGHTER

It is difficult to characterize and impossible to generalize the sensations that seized early film viewers' bodies in the grips of the somatic spectacle. The Italian journalist Matilde Serao declared herself a movie "spectatrix [*spettatrice*]" in 1916, observing "the curious, even anxious crowds created by the cinema," which were "full to bursting, more than ever."[61] As she recounted, "when the lady sitting in front of me laughed, I laughed too because in the dark everybody was laughing."[62] According to Serao, sensations of mass affective contagion—suspending class, gender, and corporeal hierarchies—were radically unique to the medium. "For one of the most bizarre miracles occurring inside a movie theatre is that everybody becomes part of one single spirit."[63] Nervous outbursts that would spark crisis in ordinary situations took on entrancing collective proportions against the hallucinatory backdrop of motion picture experience.

"Who Goes to the Moving Pictures?"[64] In 1908, *Moving Picture World* (*MPW*) writer W. Stephen Bush surveyed female moviegoers with this query. According to an unnamed woman, the answer is: "'Everyone!' Young and old, rich and poor, intelligent and ignorant," as Bush vaguely embellishes her response. "Rearing children in poverty and yet teaching them to hope, ever busy, ever patient, ever gentle," Bush continues, "these women have found in the moving picture a happy source of enjoyment."⁶⁵ Although condescending and saccharine, Bush's hyperbole belies growing anxiety about the end points of cinematic fantasy for its swelling, unruly audiences. By 1909, it was "estimated that in the United States 750,000 people attend daily the regular theatres, while two and a quarter million attend the motion picture shows," as the social reformist Louise De Koven Bowen reported.⁶⁶ With the rise of cheap nickelodeon and storefront theaters from 1905 to 1907, cinema's overwhelming mass enticements had become firmly entrenched.

The rapid ascent of the medium held decisive implications for both raucous laughter and nervous hysteria. On the one hand, cinema was a palliative for all the above. Female spectatrixes enjoyed a license to laugh as never before, epitomized by the ad line: "Don't you know one of the first missions of the motion picture is to GET YOU TO LAUGH? Then help the picture's mission!" So preached a review of *The Mummy* (Thanhouser, 1911), a comedy about an undead female mummy who falls in love with a modern Egyptologist.⁶⁷ Similarly, nervous women whose stifled ambitions might otherwise curdle into that notorious ailment (hysteria) found an outlet for their malaise in the shadow play.

Mary Heaton Vorse, an American suffragette and novelist, observed Jewish movie audiences on the Lower East Side who "keep body and soul together" after a "long and terrible workday" by going to the shows.⁶⁸ One little girl of ten appeared "so rapt . . . so spellbound, that she couldn't [even] laugh . . . She was in a state of emotion beyond any outward manifestation of it."⁶⁹ Cinema was widely celebrated and variously theorized as a salve for the human sensorium; it could "satisfy the hunger for nervous stimulation more easily than the theater, the variety show, and the circus" with "its quick, distracting tempo that "corresponds to the nervousness of our lives," wrote Carl Forch.⁷⁰ Jane Addams described the nickelodeon as a "veritable house of dreams" for working-class girls, which becomes "infinitely more real [to them] than the noisy streets and the crowded factories."⁷¹ But it was equally available to married women and harried mothers, a place to unwind from the often thankless toils of their grueling domestic labor. As Kathy Peiss notes in *Cheap Amusements*, unlike the dance halls and amusement parks that catered to young singletons, women's intergenerational patronage of cinema was both "profitable and encouraged."⁷² Its assorted delights transcended social and moral hierarchies, often actively upending them.

On the other hand, it was a fine line between the catharsis of hysterical affect and the agitation of screen-addled mania. The so-called movie craze provoked mass moral panic that the medium—with its "surrogates and counterfeits when the genuine item is lacking"—would stupefy its hungry publics into sleepwalkers and reality escape artists.[73] "The stringing together of details at lightning speed, the addiction to images, that mad hopping, chasing, falling over oneself in the race forward—in short, the cinematic . . . casts its spell, takes people's breath away, whips the nerves," wrote Aurel Wolfram, who further diagnosed cinema as "a sign of our spiritual bankruptcy" and "our utter metaphysical rootlessness."[74] In concrete terms, seedy new venues proliferated to accommodate the explosion of desire for cinema, holding anywhere from a couple dozen to several hundred bodies per theater. Notorious dens of vice, they were riddled with insanitation, fire safety hazards, libidinous hanky-panky, and threatening displays of unrestrained emotion. If nickelodeons arrived to supply the audience's overwhelming demands, tastes cultivated in these unruly spaces dictated the products that filmmakers would then devise and prioritize.

The impulses of early cinema ruled the day, channeling the medium's formative fascination with grotesque horseplay, bodily insanity, and revelatory metamorphosis.[75] With titles such as *The Leaking Glue Pot* (Pathé, 1908), *The Results of Eating Horse Flesh* (Pathé, 1908), *The Mock Baroness* (Charles Urban, 1908), and *An Obstinate Tooth* (Essanay, 1908), travesties of class decorum and human anatomy drew the uneasy gazes of moral stewards and killjoy reformists. "Unfailingly popular are the pictured disputes between an impossible mistress and an unnatural servant, in which the maid tumultuously triumphs," lamented Olivia Howard Dunbar, who further opined: "In the world of amusement, no line of less resistance than this has surely yet been offered . . . a harsh, unlovely, shadow-land, repellent, one would suppose, to intelligence and sanity."[76] Perhaps she had in mind *Everything Sticks but Glue* (Pathé, 1908), in which a maid accidentally affixes her appendages to a stovepipe. But the trade press could not resist recommending this film, despite its "grossest kind of horseplay," because it is "funny enough to raise a laugh in any audience."[77] Similarly, *The Results of Eating Horse Flesh*, despite its "unnatural" premise, could unfailingly "bring out the laughter of the audience." At the climax of the film, a surgeon amputates a wooden horsey from a man's stomach, "open[ing] the man as we would a fish," upon which his daughter then ludicrously gallops away.[78]

If idle hands were once the devil's playthings, hysterical laughs became the ad writer's whip hand: "This film will make a horse laugh," promised *The Tramp and the Mattress Makers* (Star-Film, 1906).[79] Even the ghost of William Shakespeare did not rest unscathed by the obscenity of early film farce. (Short-form adaptations of his plays such as *The Tempest* and *Macbeth*, at the same time, provided cultural capital for the industry's artistic legitimation.) In *The Suicidal*

Poet (Lubin, 1908), Shakespeare tries and fails "twelve new ways to commit suicide" until "at last, he eats himself."[80] Tragically now lost, the film was praised as a real "screamer" and "side-splitter."[81] The film industry found itself in a bind, often soliciting laughter at cross-purposes. Vulgar laughter was both a growing moral scandal and the golden goose propping up the whole enterprise. In the wake of threatened boycotts and reformist campaigns, exhibitors and trade press writers made half-hearted attempts to elevate comedies that offered "laughter of the right sort" and to excoriate films that merely pandered to the public's inclination "to laugh too much."[82] And if you "laugh at a thing all the time, you begin to despise it, or at least hold it in light esteem," warned Bush in *MPW*.[83]

Female laughers were foils for the industry's self-contradictory drive to pack "roars of laughter" into every reel while exonerating those laughs as "clean," "natural," "genuinely clever," "original," "well-conceived" to anyone who would listen. (As if they could hear such aesthetic valuations over "the screams of laughter" and "spasms of mirth" that erupted at every scene!) By luring a middle-class, white, decorum-preaching female clientele, the industry hoped to sanitize its reputation and avoid "low comedy" that might encourage "more hysterical laughter and guffaws."[84] As the *Nickelodeon* preached to the chorus, "PLAY TO THE LADIES ... When the exhibitor has enlightened himself as to where his money is coming from it is time for the next lesson. And that is to give some thought as to what women really enjoy."[85] In effect, women's voluble, corset-busting laughs were aggressively solicited and often anxiously bracketed.

To give a revealing example, *The Soul Kiss* (Essanay, 1908) was ostentatiously praised as a "convulsing comedy ... free from the slightest trace of suggestiveness, although it does depend on the slap comedy effects for its hundred laughs."[86] A loose adaptation of Florence Ziegfield's popular stage revue starring Adelade Genee, about a "statue model who makes a million dollar bet with the devil, that her sculpture artist boyfriend will not cheat on her for a year," the film version is a meta-satire about a male theater patron who becomes so enticed by the live show that he goes on a kissing rampage.[87] He serially assaults everyone in his path: "A negress, an Irish woman, then his stenographer and others" until he ends up in jail where he somehow manages to molest the female model on a poster hanging in his cell.[88] Essanay raved that *The Soul Kiss* "created more laughter and innocent fun than any humorous picture produced," presumably because the man is disciplined in the end for his libidinous spree.[89] Or perhaps because slapstick travesties of male sexual predation could be deemed perfectly "innocent," while gendered class revenge comedies about rebellious housemaids and hell-raising tomboys were condemned as having "no real merit beyond a species of horseplay, which should be banished from motion pictures."[90]

The latter quotation refers to a hilarious French film in which a destructive teenage girl roller-skates through the woods and then destroys her house: "chairs are broken, tables are overthrown, and glasses are smashed."[91] Censors took aim at "coarse" or "undignified" comedy, presuming a direct line from feminine audience reception to film's genteel aspiration. Because when it came to laughing spectatorship, the louder the better! "My walls and ceiling fairly trembled from the hysterical screams of my patrons," kvelled a theater manager in Brooklyn in an unsolicited letter to the comedy division of Universal Film Company.[92] Similarly, an exhibitor in Butte, Montana, enthused that *Alkili Ike's Auto* (Essanay, 1911) made the "audience laugh so much that they shook the bolts and nuts off the seat."[93] In the realm of the nickelodeon—and vaudeville house, pleasure center, amusement park, dance hall—wild co-ed cachinnation could not have been more welcome. "If a theatrical performance doesn't make a woman laugh or cry, she thinks she isn't getting her money's worth," claimed the *Augusta Chronicle*.[94] Monetized hysterics were emptied of their vital social contexts in gimmicky reports, extracted from obstreperous bodies who encountered their flickering "surrogates" in cinema's "paroxysm of the spectacle."[95]

As *Motion Picture News* raved, "Slapstick comedy continues to maintain its hold on the amusement-loving public, especially the women and children. Refined slapstick will always be a seller, but the refinement must be in it."[96] Where was the "refinement" in *The Soul Kiss*? The truth is: it didn't matter. Lady laughers were interpellated to ventriloquize the predatory whimsies of an explicitly male gaze (exemplified by *The Soul Kiss*), while so-called "hysterical Bridgets" offered scapegoats to distance the industry's reputation from those if its bread-and-butter laughing audiences.

When specified anecdotally, women's comedic tastes were rendered ordinary and unthreatening; for example, "Women laughed at the pictures of the man getting his own dinner" in *The Trading Stamp Mania* (Pathé, 1911), a comedy of manners about stamp hoarding.[97] At a screening of an educational film on natal anesthetics, *Twilight Sleep* (Motherhood Educational Society, 1915), "the only laugh in the exhibition came when after the 'birth,' the husband was flashed in seated at a desk in his office. Why the women laughed at the husband no one could tell, probably just because he was a husband."[98] Similarly, the satire *Dear, Kind Hubby* (Selig, 1911) had all the women "in hysterics" at the scene in which "hubby" unsuccessfully attempts to cook dinner.[99] One woman in Quincy, Illinois reportedly laughed so hard at a film comedy about public noise disturbance, *His Musical Soul* (Solax, 1912), that she had to get up and leave the theater.[100]

HYSTERICAL SPECTATORSHIP AND HALLUCINATORY FASCINATION

Women's hypnotic fascination with the hallucinatory new medium provoked gleeful solicitation and anxious moral panic. Movies became hysterical when they were feared to mean too much, acquiring a destructive impression that could threaten the reality of other spheres of life. "The suggestive power of the cinematographic projection—its power to simulate real life," warned Karl Ritter, "is so strong that we momentarily experience the compulsion to . . . [forget] that the figures before us are not flesh-and-blood people but merely a representation."[101] Female spectators were test pilots for cinema's excessive impression of reality. Indeed, many of the sexist psychological suppositions that legitimated the science of female hysteria through the nineteenth century further shaped early theories of what Leo Witlin called "the Psychomechanics of the Spectator," whereby "a psychic process is thus converted into mechanical movement."[102] Witlin analogized filmic projection to a hysterical attack.

The specter of madness loomed large amid the ghost play and doppelgänger funhouse of early trick cinematography, with its self-multiplying bodies and absurd object transformations. "What *does* create anxiety in the spectator," argues Gordon, "are the implications attached to experiencing the same dislocations and convulsive agitation, perceptual disturbances (optical illusions, intense afterimages, hallucinations) as an hysteric."[103] Gordon traces the obsession with madness that haunted popular discourses about early French cinema, whose carnal obscenity carried over from the cabaret and carnival. "This is why," remarked the impressionist filmmaker Jean Epstein, "gestures that work best on screen are nervous gestures," an insight epitomized by one of the earliest films in which a man simply sneezes directly into the camera.[104]

Apt hysterics and spirit mediums, women made equally hospitable hosts for bodily possession by film's uncanny afterimages, which fueled conspiracies that they were all afflicted by "the movie craze."[105] Max Grempe defends this assumption in a dubiously titled essay, "Against a Cinema That Makes Women Stupid," recently translated and republished in *The Promise of Cinema*, an essential sourcebook on early German film theory. "But in light of women's greater mental excitability and the preponderance of emotions in their lives," Grempe insists, "living pictures must have a more powerful effect on them than on men."[106] Or as *Moving Picture World* cheekily put it in a review of the two-reel "scream," *Crooked to the End* (Keystone, 1915), it's "bound to make some excitable members of any mixed audience hysterical."[107] Comedy ads widely parroted and parodied the hysteria trigger warnings that peppered reviews of sensational melodramas. For example, *Jerry's Uncle's Namesake* (Vitagraph, 1914), a silly burlesque on temporary baby adoption services, cautioned: "One of those wild comedies that are dangerous for hysterical persons to watch."[108] Although free of surreal effects, the film manufactures an endless influx of rented babies that overwhelm the childless couple, who need a fake namesake to claim their uncle's inheritance.

The disappearance and reappearance of women and babies were among the oldest film tricks in the book, from Alice Guy-Blaché's *The Cabbage Fairy* (Gaumont, 1896?[109]) and *Disappearing Act* (Gaumont, 1898) to *Madame's Cravings* (Gaumont, 1906) and *In the Year 2000* (Solax, 1912), a "serio-comic prognostication" in which "women shall rule the earth."[110] Reproductive trickery inflamed gendered fantasies of taking flight from domestic labor. For working-class wives and mothers, cinema offered a "stopgap" between hope and alienation, remarked the German sociologist Emilie Altenloh: "At the cinema, they live in another world."[111] With its visions of nursemaids who launch general strikes (while cow udders are enlisted as scab labor), kitchen maids who break all the dishes in nervous rampages, and housemaids afflicted by hysterical sleeping sickness, that "other world" often collided comically with the grueling exhaustion of domestic reality.[112] Through moving pictures "alone, new dreams have radiated from that crowd of semi-hysterical women," observed Edoardo Coli, who "pass half the day tucked away in darkened cinema halls, more focused and alert than they've ever been in church."[113] Giuseppe d'Abundo similarly describes the "hypnagogic hallucinations" of a young woman tormented by recurring visions of "gigantic evanescent hands" after watching a movie in which disembodied limbs uncannily disappear into space.[114]

What convulsed on the screen then rebounded onto the spectator, at once liberating nervous impulses through mutating body doubles but threatening to linger and penetrate ordinary waking life. A woman in New Jersey named Jennie Postal allegedly "went postal" in 1910 after a piece of plaster fell from the ceiling and hit her head during a movie.[115] At that exact "moment the film on view displayed a picture of a man throwing a plate at his wife."[116] *Variety* did not specify which film Postal was watching; circa 1910, there were too many probable candidates. Perhaps it was *The Suffragette's Dream* (Pathé, 1909), in which a battered housewife envisions overthrowing the patriarchy, only to be stirred from her reverie by her abusive husband's impatient demands for his dinner. Or perhaps it was *Tale of a Leg* (Pathé, 1910), a "far-fetched comic" about a man who runs amok with his severed leg after it's cut off in an auto accident (which was advertised next to the story about Jennie Postal).[117] "Miss Postal became hysterical and has since been in a delirious condition," *Variety* added, "imagining that someone is throwing plates at her."[118] Then again, maybe "someone" really was throwing plates at her.

MADAME MEDUSA AT THE MOVING PICTURE SHOW

By around 1915, according to established periodizations of silent cinema, the medium was no longer "early," but already culturally entrenched and narratively sophisticated. The ethos of "earliness," to revel in the potentialities of a medium on the cusp of its own transparent language, lived on in the avant-garde, slapstick comedy, animation, and other wayward genres.[119] But it also continued to possess and inhabit spectator bodies well into the so-called classical era.[120] Holding tension between "hysterical laughter and gasping amazement, I have never seen an audience more thoroughly entertained," boasted an American film critic in 1918 upon attending a screening of *Roaring Lions and Wedding-Bells* (Fox, 1917), in which several male suitors compete for a woman by impersonating jungle cats.[121]

In that spirit, I present to you: *Madame Medusa*, an allegorical feminist early film reveler. Who was Madame Medusa? She embodied a spectator position always at risk of overwhelming its own solicitation to uncontrollable laughter and convulsive hysteria. Madame Medusa laughed obstreperously, kibbitzed volubly, writhed convulsively, adorned her chapeau with screen-blocking fruit baskets, but the industry kowtowed to her whimsies all the same. She was not entirely welcome at the live theater—invited to the party but often cast out as disruptive and uncouth. For example, she was the "girl in front of me" at the Julius Tannen act "who laughed so loud everyone looked around at her."[122] Or the female spectator at Tim McMahon and Edythe Chappelle's *Pullman Maids* who "laughed so heartily" that she had to get up and leave her seat during the scenes depicting the wife's "feeding" and various "matrimonial squabbles."[123] Or the women whose laughter "bordered close on the 'hysterical' " at Kate Elinore's "grotesque make-up and costumes" in her stage farce, *My Aunt from Utah*.[124] Louis Reeves Harrington denigrated such laughter as the "hysterical giggle of a Bridget," invoking an Irish stock caricature who might occupy "an orchestra seat of a rainy evening when her master did not care to use the tickets purchased for the occasion."[125] But at the movies, Madame Medusa ruled the roost.

Often enough, she herself stole the show. Her worst offense was not uncouth laughter but extravagant millinery, the absurd dimensions of which obstructed the visibility of the screen. As the mayor of Macon, Georgia ranted in 1912, in his futile efforts to pass an ordinance banning ladies' hats from film theaters, "many a man goes to the moving picture show, pays his dime and for it sees a beautiful hat but no picture."[126] *Motion Picture Story Magazine*'s "Photoplay Philosopher" opined: women's hats "create more disturbances than do the babies, because eyes are to be considered more than ears."[127] As we know, snaky tresses far exceed voluble laughter in their threatened disruption to filmic enjoyment. While exhibitors even advised turning up the house lights during comedies so "nearby laughers will no longer keep laughs exclusively to themselves," aggrieved patrons lobbied their municipalities to pass ordinances banning women from wearing colossal headgear at the movies.[128]

Madame Medusa assumed a variety of shapes and forms. Sometimes she was simply a body among the "hysterical hilarity" of the "whirling masses," convulsed into "one continuous round of laughter."[129] She contracted suggestive symptoms watching films like *A Sure Cure* (Gaumont, 1909), a short lark about the plight of people afflicted with uncontrollable hiccups. She was exhorted to "screams of laughter" by *The Human Squib* (Gaumont, 1909), in which a drunk man wreaks havoc with a burning lamppost, which amplified to "shouts of laughter" at *In the Consommé* (Gaumont, 1909), in which an agonized husband soaks up improbable quantities of liquid after accidentally swallowing a dish sponge. That was the wheelhouse of early cinema, whose celebration of impossible bodies and improbable contortions enthroned the turbulent fancies of Madame Medusa.

Far from ejecting her out of the room, everyone wanted to be within contagious proximity of her self-abandon. Margaret I. MacDonald, a writer for *Moving Picture News*, once spotted her at the Fourteenth Street Theater in Manhattan at a comedy about a motorized armchair that goes haywire: "I found myself laughing so hard at her enjoyment of the thing that the tears actually trickled down my face."[130] Her milieu was the moving pictures, but she would no doubt have enjoyed the vaudeville novelty act of a comedian who zapped his body with currents of electricity like a human "rheostat," molding the "vast audience" into "one solid fit of hysterical laughter."[131] Even the great stage performer Sarah Bernhardt had a Madame Medusa moment, "almost hysterical with excitement," while watching her own flickering effigy onscreen in her filmed performance of *Camille* (Pathé, 1912).[132]

But where is Madame Medusa in the annals of film spectator historiography? When it comes to allegorical bad spectatorship, Uncle Josh has sucked up all the oxygen. A notorious "country rube" and gullible fool, Josh recurs as the butt of the joke in films such as *Uncle Josh in a Spooky Hotel* (Edison, 1900), *Uncle Josh's Nightmare* (Edison, 1900), and *Uncle Josh at the Moving Picture Show* (Edison, 1902), in which he disastrously mistakes moving images for the real thing, tears down the screen, and gets into fisticuffs with the rear projectionist. Uncle Josh was not ready for cinema. His negative example modeled the oafish behavior that ordinary spectators should be careful to avoid. If Uncle Josh embodied the dangers of confusing reality and illusion, Madame Medusa overcommitted to her hysterical misrecognition of the image. She flaunted her corporeality in excess of the screen barrier and its luminous phantoms, her "auditory nerves" and "optic nerves vibrat[ing]" in glorious acrimony.[133]

We find traces of her excessive attachment to the sensory powers of cinema in many early film comedies. For example, Lili Ziedner permeates both sides of the film screen in Mauritz Stiller's *The Mannequin* (Svenska Bio, 1913), in which she fantastically knocks out a movie boxer (played by André Deed) and then tramples her fellow spectators on the way back to her seat; as well as by the tomboy Léontine's exploits in a film theater with a decapitated wolf's head in a lost French comedy from 1911.[134] Whereas Uncle Josh is confused by the difference between cinematic perception and corporeal sensation, Madame Medusa thrives in that gap. If anything, she wants the world of the audience to become more like the realm of the spectacle.

She thus spits in the eye of simulacrum alarmists, who misrecognize the "unrealism of the real society," to invoke Guy Debord, for the commodity spectacle's

FIGURE 7.3 Lili (Lili Ziedner) punches out a movie boxer (André Deed) and then exits the screen. Frame enlargement from *Mannekängen* (Mauritz Stiller, 1913). Image courtesy of the Swedish Film Institute.

wholesale "monopoly of appearance."[135] To paraphrase Debord (and Baudrillard et al.), it is a slippery slope from the celebration of freewheeling pageantry to the utter betrayal of materialist class analysis. But Madame Medusa weaponizes the floodlights against the dominant social order, if for no other reason than doing so marks a significant improvement over her prior embodied situation.

Indeed, feminist cultural historians have long understood the ascent of reality's displacement by spectacle as inevitable whiplash of an economy that only grants tentative power and partial agency to disenfranchised citizens through the enjoyment of commodities.[136] We might align Madame Medusa's position with what Anne Friedberg elaborates as a "mobile virtual gaze," by which cinematic modernity "endowed visuality with its ultimately dominant power," paving the way from window-gazing shopgirls to the fever dream of postmodernity's permanent carnival.[137] But even that would be a partial misrecognition of Madame Medusa's own position; above all, the lucid play of film's corporeal enticements gave tangible reality to her gaslit thoughts and dreams.

Otherwise, what might have become of her? "You see," she "has been taken, during our examination, with convulsive laughter which she cannot moderate, and which will soon be followed by a shower of tears."[138] With this judgment, Charcot condemned Mademoiselle V. to the virtual half-life of abject medical sideshow. Such rapid alteration between uncontrollable laughter and inconsolable tears often bookended women's epileptic attacks, which escalated into those acrobatic outbursts that Charcot classified as "clownism." But cinema's magic body language—cutting off heads, dismembering limbs, triggering epidemic hiccups, and all in good fun—gave free rein to the catastrophic instability of Medusan emotions.

When Maggie raved about town with a blunt-edged knife (because she was chasing after the knife grinder!), everyone "supposes her to be a lunatic and they flee" at the sight of her. So *The Dull Knife* (Vitagraph, 1909) hoisted "the spectator along on a gale of laughter."[139] Madame Medusa wields a garden hose against a "turmoiled crowd, which rapidly disperses," causing her "to laugh so hysterically that she accidentally turns the hose on herself" in *An International Heart-Breaker* (Edison, 1911).[140] Reincarnated as Rosalie and Léontine, she is then ejected from a stage show after hysterically laughing and projectile weeping onto the shiny bald heads of the gentlemen seated in front of her.[141] But she had other tricks up her sleeves, not least of all sneezing: "Everyone was deeply interested in the picture," absorbed in watching a passionate scene of two young lovers locking lips, when Madame Medusa (let's call her) "exploded with a gigantic sneeze" and "the whole house blew up with spontaneous hilarious laughter."[142] Still a better fate than the man who actually explodes from sneezing—canting the frame with his convulsive congestion—in *That Fatal Sneeze* (Hepworth, 1907): a comedy about nasal catastrophe.

The theater was swarming with Medusas at a screening of *Alkili Ike's Pants* (Essanay, 1912) in Chicago, which over 3,200 people attended. The film depicts the plight of a cowboy nicknamed "Alkili," who somehow loses his undergarments just as his girlfriend Sophie gallops away on a wild bronco. (Unlike in *Results of Eating Horse Flesh*, the bronco had not been previously amputated from Alkili's stomach.) But "one old lady who could not control her laughter went home, still giving voice to her merriment at the farcical scenes."[143] Meanwhile, Ethel M. Strouse successfully sued her husband Ernest for divorce on the grounds of "extreme cruelty and non-support," citing as key evidence that "he wouldn't let her laugh at movies." Strouse testified to Judge Welmer: "If I laughed aloud at a moving picture show I was considered rude."[144] I repeat: "Don't you know one of the first missions of the motion picture is to GET YOU TO LAUGH? Then help the picture's mission!"[145] Madame Medusa was more than happy to oblige.

DEATH BY LAUGHTER INSURANCE
(AND OTHER HYSTERICAL GIMMICKS)

Madame Medusas notwithstanding, at the same time, hysterical laughter was widely rebranded as an empty commercial gimmick. "You are compelled to laugh, you cannot control yourself, you cannot resist the contagion," commanded a review of *The Police Band* (Gaumont British, 1908), a caper about the exploitation of frisky music by repressive law enforcement. "And if the film was 200 feet longer, the folks would fairly roll under their seats."[146] So ludicrous police characters were enlisted to interpellate raucously laughing spectators. Theater managers experimented with a variety of morbid stunts to lure in patrons. As if ripped from the obituary columns, Ace Berry of the Circle Theatre in Indianapolis offered to insure viewers for "laughing hysteria" during screenings of the feature comedy, *Charley's Aunt* (Christie, 1925). "Someone suggested by way of a joke that he insure his patrons against laughing themselves to death, but Manager Berry turned this 'joke' into a practical idea and every patron was actually insured under a policy issued by the Central West Casualty Company of Detroit, against becoming hysterical by the laughter" the film incited.[147] According to the *Exhibitors Herald*, it was the first policy ever issued for hysteria; it cost the theater $100, on top of $13 for the large framed certificate that hung in the lobby. If this was indeed the first such policy against hysteria, the idea was not exactly novel.

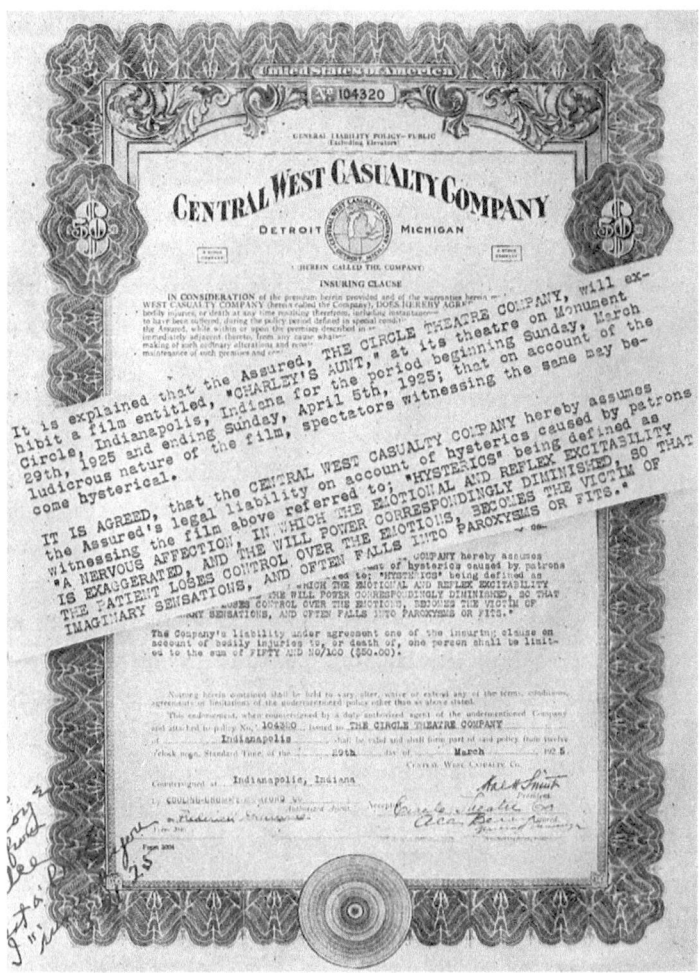

FIGURE 7.4 "Hysterical insurance policy" issued by the Central West Casualty Company to all laughing spectators who see the film comedy *Charley's Aunt* (Scott Sidney, 1925) at The Circle Theatre in Indianapolis in April 1925. Image courtesy of Lantern (Media History Digital Library).

The Madison Theatre in Peoria, Illinois devised a "new angle" in the exploitation of unnecessary indemnity, upping the ante to "death by hysterical laughter" at the horse-themed comedy, *The Hottentot* (Ince, 1922)—in which a man who resembles a jockey is forced to race a feral stallion named Hottentot. The theater issued a formal policy, offering $50 compensation for any death from apoplexy or heart disease triggered by the film's extreme hilarity, according to *Motion Picture News*.¹⁴⁸ While Mary Trelkald's friends were still mourning her alleged death by laughter after playing the winning trick in a bridge game, a theater manager in Milwaukee, Wisconsin loaded fifty fully dressed automatons into a truck with the sign: "They laughed themselves to death seeing Bert Baker and the 'The Bon Ton Girls' at the Gayety Theater," as per *Variety*.¹⁴⁹ The stunt reportedly attracted great crowds and boosted ticket sales immensely for the show. Perhaps he got the idea from the singing comedian, Jack Norworth, who loved to tell the old joke about taking his mother-in-law to the variety theater because she had nearly laughed herself to death at a burlesque act.¹⁵⁰

As Sianne Ngai details in *Theory of the Gimmick*, life insurance and other financialized risk policies proliferated in the wake of the tontine, an investment plan or "mortality lottery" that scammed subscribers into sharing the financial risk of old age. It was effectively outlawed in the United States after a series of embezzlement scandals, but over 9 million tontines were sold in the four decades prior to their prohibition in 1906.¹⁵¹ These predatory policies raised capital by raffling off the dividends of prolonged life expectancy: members contribute to the pool and then reap its rewards as their cohort slowly dies off. While tontines incentivize competitive longevity, laughter insurance gimmicks exploit the thrill of imminent fatality. They were a key part of the publicity campaign for *Safety Last!* (Hal Roach, 1923), iconized by the perilous image of Harold Lloyd hanging from the hands of a large clock on the side of a skyscraper.

A farcical victim of "homogenous empty time" (the fungible measurement of secular time by calendars and clocks), Lloyd's exploits in *Safety Last!* perfectly encapsulate the mortality lottery's cinematic double: immortality spectacle. For example, the Howard Theater in Atlanta, Georgia shamelessly hosted a lavish "exploitation ball," installing phonographs in the lobby to play the "Okeh laughing record" on repeat and offered $500 to the estate of "all who died of laughter at the performance."¹⁵² The managers even wrangled local newspapers to print fake stories about women fainting from laughter at sneak previews of the film. Then again, a ghoulish movie ticket was much cheaper than membership in a tontine. Worst-case scenario, the viewer is out about 27 cents (circa 1923) in exchange for getting to "murmur nervous expletives" amid gales of "hysterical laughter."¹⁵³ Best-case scenario: they give up the ghost and die rich from laughing too hard?

Convalescent Laughter and Epidemic Hilarity

Although very few theaters actually purchased such insurance, the popularity of these gimmicks provoked laughing spectators to experience the risk of their enjoyment in crudely financialized terms. The Biograph Company did not take out a formal policy but cheekily publicized laughter insurance to hysterical movie spectators, "underwritten by Mack Sennett, Mabel Normand, Charles Murray, etc."[154] (At that point, Keystone was an entity of Biograph, brokered through the Triangle Film Corporation.[155]) Similarly, "clinical humor played an important part in the exploitation" of *A Connecticut Yankee* (Fox, 1922) when the Rialto Theatre in Oklahoma City hired a municipal ambulance to blare its sirens around town, waving the sign: "Prompt Service for Those Who Laugh Themselves Sick."[156]

Convalescent humor rhetorically intervened in a copyright lawsuit against the playwright Abraham Goldknopf, who was accused of plagiarizing William C. deMille's *The Woman* with his farcical travesty *Tainted Philanthropy* in 1912. The presiding judge attended a double bill of both shows while deciding the suit, giving comment to the *New York Times*: "*The Woman* is a well-constructed, intelligently written, and highly interesting play. *Tainted Philanthropy*, on the other hand, is written without a suggestion of the knowledge of stagecraft, with dialogue that is frequently ungrammatical . . . [and] a succession of supposedly serious incidents that kept the audience in a state of helpless laughter."[157] *Variety* had a more favorable take than Judge Holt, boasting that the "invited guests laughed themselves sick."[158] In the end, the judge decided in favor of Goldknopf, exonerated by the grotesque infirmities of *Tainted Philanthropy*'s ghoulish burlesque.

The evidential status of audience laughter here reveals the larger stakes of hysterical enjoyment in political and economic spheres, where its monetary value eclipsed the mere sale of tickets or amplified publicity. Snatched from the throat and cajoled from the body, hysterical laughter assumed an increasingly abstract utility—a hollowed-out sign that could be deployed any which way, from risk-based insurance to exculpatory evidence.

As a biopolitical weapon, laughter increased its morbid appeals amid the public health crises of the 1918 influenza pandemic, which caused mass theater closures and threatened the essential livelihood of the film industry. It was barely hyperbole, for example, when *Variety* prescribed hysterical laughter as "the most contagious thing in the world, thousands of times more contagious than the influenza."[159] Women's laughs and smiles were particularly profitable in these terms. From the female throat to the convulsing diaphragm, Vivian Martin's smiles in *Mirandy Smiles* (Famous Players-Lasky, 1918) became "as contagious as the influenza," taunted *Motion Picture News*. (It is estimated that 50 million people worldwide, and at least 675,000 Americans, died from the flu; by contrast, 117,000 American soldiers were killed in World War I.) Epidemic enjoyment repeatedly contended with dangerous disease in a zero-sum game of affective capitalism versus killjoy health regulation.

The gimmick of nonlaughter (i.e., contagion immunity) proved equally entrancing. In 1918, Mary Veillette reportedly won a $10 prize by sitting through an entire screening of Charlie Chaplin's *Shoulder Arms* (First National, 1918)—a slapstick comedy about the traumas of trench warfare—without "anything suggesting a smile." But she claimed that she'd been scammed: "Twice I saw the Chaplin films," she protested, "twenty dollars I should have as prizes because twice I did not do so much as laughing."[160] Like "Sober Sue," the Hammerstein-headlining Black woman whose traumas had allegedly anesthetized her to vaudeville (see chapter 2), Veillette mourned her own immunity to enjoyment: "Iss sadt, with troubles so much I should die to have" found him "fonny," quoted *MPW*.[161]

To die laughing or to survive in want of doing so? The death drive toward enjoyment has taken on various concepts and guises in feminist theories of unpaid and underpaid, invisible domestic labor. Whereas so-called women's work (child-rearing, cooking, menial chores) is necessary to maintain and reproduce life, the destructive obligation to enjoy has increasingly permeated the life-sustaining domestic sphere. If early cinema offered an alternative realm—an escape from the endless toils of housework—spectacle-based media now bombard the home, further threatening any tenuous distinction between labor and leisure. When the rhythms of gendered housework collapse into the marketized pressures of permanent carnival, the ravages of enjoyment become an explicitly feminist problem: a new frontier of "wages for housework."[162]

As Nancy Fraser argues in *Fortunes of Feminism*, capitalist crisis consists "less [in] economic breakdown in the narrow sense than [in] disintegrated communities, ruptured solidarities, and despoiled nature."[163] A feminist theory of labor value would thus highlight "the assault on social reproduction now being waged by finance capital" (i.e., its dismantling of the social safety net), which treats the "fundamental bases of social life as if they were ordinary commodities and subject[s] them to market exchange."[164] In the context of enjoyment, which turns off-the-clock recreation into a relentless venture in market speculation, the crisis necessitates an all-consuming imperative to enjoy: *you must enjoy*! Enjoyment is the secret justification for gobbling up ordinary life as a value-laden commodity.

It would be hard to divine a more apt example than *The Installment Collector* (Essanay, 1908). Although a fairly conventional slapstick chase film, its themes are highly resonant for our purposes. It depicts the plight of a man who gambles his future on a series of episodic decisions between immediate enjoyment and debt-based obligation. He purchases an encyclopedia on an installment plan and then consecutively misses each payment while cavorting around town with various women (in a café, at the theater, on a rowboat, inside a train). Finally, he is jilted by his fiancée at the altar as she explodes in wild rage when the debt collector interrupts their wedding ceremony. The film "is excruciatingly funny," raved *MPW*, "one continual roar of laughter" in "every scene."[165] The film's abstraction of piecemeal enjoyment (each exploit undersigning a future unpayable debt) goads the prolongment of the audience's "spasmodic," "unending" laughter. (It is always safer to enjoy the other's irresponsible enjoyment than to partake directly oneself.)

And where was Madame Medusa amid these speculative risk economies of hysterical mass spectatorship? Watching the *Installment Collector*, perhaps she would have found greater solace hitching her hotwired nerves to the tantrums of the wronged fiancée, who storms off in a huff rather than become maritally and legally entangled in her paramour's reckless whimsies. That is the point of cathartic hysteria: it owes no debt to the future, lest that future drop dead on arrival.

HYSTERIA-HISTORIOGRAPHY AND THE IMPULSE TO WRITE

The Medusan spectator occupied a position whose liveliness is negated by anything short of dazzling rupture. In that spirit, I approach early cinema as a somatic language and a proxy reality for spectators on the cusp of having their own symbolic voice in the world. Just as feminist theorists have taken up conversion hysteria as an unruly alternative to the ruthless strictures of patriarchal language, feminist film historians have looked to the fragments, erasures, inconsistencies, and wayward fantasies left behind by the early film archive. The remains of early cinema, I argue, offer hysterical texts for the project of recuperative feminist writing. This is what I mean by *hysteria-historiography*.

Feminist Hysteria-Historiography

Hysteria-historiography, a devious proposition, can be productively divided into three approaches. First, there are feminist film histories that explicitly thematize hysteria and neurasthenia as both subjects of representation and as haywire spectator positions. Hysteria-historiography prime, let's call it, is exemplified by the work of Rae Beth Gordon, who pursues the collision between French comical performance and spectacle-based psychiatric culture from approximately 1870 to 1910, spanning the cabaret, café-concert, and movie theater. This method understands that hysteria is baked into the DNA of the medium, utterly essential to the rapid spread of its irresistible appeals. "Film's excessiveness penetrates spectators and becomes a part of them," Gordon argues, focusing on mechanisms of "incorporation" and "automatism," whereby hysterical images live on in the viewer's nerves and vascular system.[166] The depiction of magically reversible, nervous ailments—from uncontrollable hiccupping to gravity-defying epilepsy—provided abundant material for early filmmakers to feed the insatiable demands of their audiences. Mireille Berton's expansive research on psychiatric filmmaking and its relation to spirit conjuring, Elyse Singer's incisive writing on the cryptography of madwomen, and Stephanie Werder's notion of neurasthenic spectatorship all further align with the core impulses of this project.[167] They seek to rewrite the history of cinema through evocative images and embodied sensations of nervousness, hypnosis, somnambulism, and convulsive gestural anarchy.

Second, and more broadly, feminist film historiography has formatively focused on the rapidly changing social positions of women amid the pleasure factories of modernity at the turn of the last century. In a sense, the field picked up where feminist screen studies left off in the early 1990s, pivoting from the impossible female gaze cast out by classical Hollywood to forceful visions of gender mobility in the floodlights of urban modernity, with female early film viewers, amusement park riders, unruly window-shoppers, and uproarious train passengers assuming pride of place.[168] Much of that history, however, was now written long ago: Judith Mayne's *Woman at the Keyhole* (1990), Miriam Hansen's *Babel and Babylon* (1991), Giuliana Bruno's *Streetwalking on a Ruined Map* (1993), Anne Friedberg's *Window Shopping* (1993), Lynne Kirby's *Parallel Tracks* (1997), Lauren Rabinovitz's *For the Love of Pleasure* (1998), Shelley Stamp's *Movie-Struck Girls* (2000), Jennifer Bean and Diane Negra's *Feminist Reader in Early Cinema* (2002), Zhang Zhen's *An Amorous History of the Silver Screen* (2005), and Jacqueline Stewart's *Migrating to the Movies* (2006) are all touchstones of this field.

Cinema's rampant appeals to the iconography and gender anarchy of clinical hysteria remain absent presences in many of these texts, which focus instead on the cult of commodity spectacle that emancipated the body and preyed upon the soul. Modernity liberated women from the shackles of domestic confinement, galvanizing Medusan activism, but further exploited them as alienated consumers, harassed shopfloor workers, molested domestic laborers, and movie-struck enjoyers. "Women's identity as the most fanatic moviegoers led to the feminization of movie fan culture," argues Hilary Hallett in *Go West, Young Women!*, further linking the hystericization of female fandom to the dissolving divisions between leisure and work.[169] As reality recedes into spectacle, so too does labor into enjoyment, exemplified by Universal's chiasmatic tagline in 1915: "Where Work Is Play and Play Is Work."[170] The industry solicited movie idolatry as a gateway to the untapped surplus value of excess enjoyment. If women's reproductive labor invisibly kept up the home, their hypervisible recreation paved the way to the utter carnivalization of work.

Third, and above all, the field of feminist historiography is now characterized by a recuperative impulse to reveal women's abundant labor (beyond performative enjoyment) at every level of the global silent film industry. This collaborative undertaking is exemplified by the Women Film Pioneers Project (WFPP), which has compiled over 325 profiles (to date) of forgotten female filmmakers, producers, writers, editors (then known as "cutters"), stencil colorists, and multifarious "makers" whose timely resurrections now intersect with twenty-first-century movements to shatter the "celluloid ceiling."[171] As Jane Gaines put it, "to ask why these women were forgotten is also to ask why *we* forget them."[172] The repeated erasure of silent cinema's female workforce and insistent marginalization of women in the film industry today are like two sides of the same coin.

I view the core drive of hysteria-historiography as intimately aligned with the project to vindicate silent cinema's many "celluloid-ceiling" crashers. Beyond mutual appeals to the blind spots of historiographic gatekeeping, these efforts are animated by a creative longing to write while seized by the restless, undead ghosts of the archive. Alice Guy-Blaché, Lois Weber, Germaine Dulac, Marion Wong, Elvira Notari, Zora Neale Hurston, Musidora, Mabel Normand, Lotte Reiniger, and Esfir Shub are just the tip of the iceberg. The movement has now gained unstoppable momentum and elicited passionate commitment and wide cultural attention. It is "an ongoing and active process," declare Alix Beeston and Stefan Solomon in their introduction to *Incomplete: The Feminist Possibilities of the Unfinished Film*, a volume that unleashes "our ineluctably gap-ridden knowledge of the past in the terrain of the present."[173] Inexhaustibly queer, the drive-to-revive inspires inventive research into the anamorphic visibility of forgotten lesbian authorship. Key texts include Laura Horak's *Girls Will Be Boys*, Susan Potter's *Queer Timing*, Diana Anselmo's *A Queer Way of Feeling*, and Kiki Loveday's *Sapphic Cinemania!*[174] Like those of hysteria-historiography, queer archives bristle with fragments, ephemera, nonchronological time lines, surreal anecdotes, and deliciously out-of-place materials.

But where do unruly hysterical spectators fit, to quote Jennifer Bean, "as we rush forward to recover women's roles in the early industry"?[175] Hysterics have never mastered the art of transcription; that is the whole point—they writhe, wriggle, dance, hiccup, and do back flips instead. As conversion artists (or creative sublimators), they typically became novelists and performers but rarely filmmakers, producers, or even screenwriters, occupations that demanded "nerves of steel" to remain open to women. (That said, women's work in the industry often drove them to anxiety, depression, and stress-induced mental health struggles.[176])

Hysteria-historiography prompts us to understand moving pictures as multisensory outlets for nervous bodily sensations shot through with hopeful and creative longings. While feminist researchers comb the archives to reinvent cinema's mythologized origins and dominant canons, hysteria-historiography further democratizes that furious gesture of affirmation. It extends the forgotten lives, careers, and stories of female makers to the semiconscious circuits of women's performative spectatorship. And it parlays that corporeal gaze itself into a form of writing, as an impulse aligned with—but denied access to—the resource-intensive, collective work of filmmaking.

Women flooded the theaters "to satisfy their hunger for life," proclaimed Malwine Rennert in 1914. She did not mean this as a compliment: "one takes up surrogates and counterfeits when the genuine item is lacking. They filled, and fill, the cinemas, always in hope of life."[177] As hysteria historians know, there are worse places to hope for life than in the cinema. We can thus view women's insistent solicitations to hysterical spectatorship as traces of their unrealized creative productivity, rendered immediately impermanent by the flickering ephemerality of cinematic automatism and nervous projection.

Speculative Methodology and Counterfactual Experience

A hysterical medium from its inception, the cinema "let our minds fall asleep and create with our eyes whatever the soul desires," mused an anonymous German writer in 1910.[178] And "for that reason everyone streams willingly, as if hypnotized, into the cinema."[179] Hysteria—as both medical diagnosis and popular obsession—played a wildly contradictory role in relation to early film's carnival of convulsive laughter. On the one hand, hysterical excess modified laughter so it could be boiled down to a gimmick, or "a pot of beef stock," to poach Karl Strobl's "principle of the cinematograph."[180] I've already cited numerous examples, but here's another: *Tickled to Death* (Gaumont, 1909) elicited "one solid roar of hysterical laughter," especially the scene in which a wife brings her husband back from the dead by tickling his feet with a hat feather (he "flops all around the place, in an agony of involuntary laughter").[181]

On the other hand, the intense pleasures of cinema always threatened to outstrip their commercial exploitation. "The numerous cases in which cinematographic projections are able to trick the senses of mentally healthy subjects," warned Albert Hellwig, "offer exceptional illustrations of the intensity of the impression such projections make in the psyche of spectators."[182] (This translation by Michael Cowan plays on Hellwig's double meaning of the word "projection.") A hypnotic vortex of images more lifelike than reality and at the same time altogether unreal, or so its spectators were promised, early cinema demands unorthodox approaches to resurrect its wild phantasmagoria of spectator experience. How to recuperate these lost visions and wayward bodily sensations?

The Frankfurt School's attunement to "a *neurological* conception of modernity"—nervous shocks, fragmented sensations, and fleeting encounters—has long shaped the methodological agenda.[183] Epitomized by cinema, the "dialectical image" flashes up, as per Benjamin's account, empowering the bombarded subject's delirious imagination through an untapped reciprocity between human and machinic perception. (Benjamin's theory of political aesthetics hinged on the reproducible image's dialectical concurrence with rising antagonisms between fascism and communism.[184]) Hansen explores the lures and utility of Benjamin's redemptive engagement with cinema, whose scattered traces provoke us "to imagine different futures that may be buried in the past," she offers.[185] In other words, cinema commuted the harrowing ruptures that ran roughshod over the human sensorium, which now find form among the ruins and pockmarks of the silent film archive. For example, Catherine Russell focuses on found-footage filmmaking—and other practices of archival reuse, recycling, and appropriation—to make sense of the cinematic lives that were "lived fully ... in a state of perceptual dislocation."[186] Following Benjamin's *One Way Street*, Giuliana Bruno embarks on "textual journeys in a series of 'inferential walks' through novels, paintings, photographs, and architectural sites" in *Streetwalking on a Ruined Map*, in which she pursues the nonextant Neapolitan films of Elvira Notari.[187]

Silent film prints circulated all around the world, their somatic contexts indelibly marked by the "vernacular" traditions through which they were viewed.[188] Like Bruno, whose archeological gaze is incarnated by early film's "somatic topography" and the "panoramic-anatomic space of nineteenth-century vision," Zhang Zhen elaborates "the fabric of urban life" in early twentieth-century China, where reality "was lived out increasingly in cinematic terms" at "a time when many events were taking place at a head-spinning speed."[189] More recently, Debashree Mukherjee has pivoted from the thematic of "modernity" to the embodied "hustle" of "cine-ecology" to illustrate the hectic, mutating, unruly environments in which the colonial Bombay film industry ignited in the 1930s.[190]

Across these examples, the fragmented objects of early cinema give voice to the eternal ghosts of its hysterical spectators.

But these approaches tend to rewrite history from the ruins (its catastrophic remains, "exquisite corpses," sensory afterlives, etc.) rather than hazarding the counterfactual images that could never catch light. "The loss of stories sharpens the hunger for them," remarks Saidiya Hartman in "Venus in Two Acts," "so it is tempting to fill in the gaps and provide closure where there is none."[191] Hartman navigates the "death sentence" of the archive in "Venus in Two Acts," a sort of epilogue to *Lose Your Mother* (2006), in which she formulates her methodology of critical fabulation to retrieve the erasures of history "without committing further violence in my own act of narration."[192] Black feminist theory, with its driving will to imagine otherwise, fosters especially generative terrain for cultivating speculative approaches to counterfactual experience.

Hartman further brings her project of fabulation to the field of silent cinema in *Wayward Lives, Beautiful Experiments*, in which she imagines a nonexistent (which is different from nonextant) silent film about the life of lesbian, cross-dressing blues singer Gladys Bentley as directed by the Black race filmmaker Oscar Micheaux.[193] "In the film," she fabulates, "the telltale gestures, tics, and queer traits would give Bentley away: his tendency to swagger; the too-big body, the too-loud voice, the mountain of flesh, the vocal intonation . . . the preening defiance and naked display of pleasure."[194] Counterfactual objects alone can disarm the traumatic inheritances of their violent historical exclusion. That it never existed—was never allowed to materialize in delirious celluloid form—should not prevent its reconstruction through carefully researched methods in archival fictionalization.

Hysteria-historiography, if nothing else, involves the sustained movement to give evidential license to the archival realm of the unsayable. Yet it does so without relapsing into thoughtless presentism or simulacral cynicism. The impulse to fabulate has always held a special urgency for Black film studies, where the unbridgeable divide between white images and Black audiences calls for "oppositional" and "resistant" spectatorship practices, to invoke bell hooks and Manthia Diawara's crucial polemics, respectively. In this vein, Jacqueline Stewart draws on novels and short stories to "reconstruct" the "complicit and resistant possibilities for Black agency and activity" that defy both extant and nonextant film archives alike.[195]

Stewart's project of "reconstructive spectatorship" has incisive implications for the historiography of hysteria via the gaslit experience of "negated" Black viewing subjects. For example, Bigger Thomas in *Native Son* (1940) takes refuge in the movies "to hide his growing and deepening feeling of hysteria," where he laughs and shouts to negotiate his "shift between aggressive and vulnerable spectator positions."[196] (Stewart formulates a similar reading of Pauline Breedlove in Toni Morrison's *The Bluest Eye*.) What's at stake for Stewart is how cinema's migratory Black publics and mollifying white images open up ambivalent alternatives to the stone-cold negation of Black subjectivity, which she revives "on psychic, social, and public levels."[197] Her denegated Black spectator has a somewhat different orientation to the screen than the Medusan celluloid crashers whose positions I have been promiscuously elaborating. However, both figures take shape when unruly movie lovers "try to insert their physical selves, unchanged, into the fictional world" of the film.[198] Like Madame Medusa, the "reconstructed" spectator inhabits the disjuncture between living body and flickering image, between historical experience and movie fantasy.

Both are inescapably performative positions. Jayna Brown locates such activity not in the "red velvet seat" but on the Black variety stage in *Babylon Girls* (2008), looking at how "black farce and satire, often smuggled in behind the wide white mouth," reveal "the ways hierarchies breed their own instabilities."[199] Her concept of "creative disobedience" similarly arises from a certain illegibility of the unruly body, pried from its moment of misrecognition to become reinscribed as an oppositional counterimage. In contrast to "cruel optimism," where the precarity of empty enjoyment slowly tightens the noose around alienated laughers, reconstructive fabulation calls for optimism precisely in the wake of its excessive, irretrievable dislocation. For the performative spectator (as for the watchful performer), enigmatic hysteria invests laughter and enjoyment with a hazy reality that can only be conjured through its counterfactual utterance. Could this really have been?! In their empirical fugitivity, wayward spectators militate toward a spectrum of experience that resists the thoughtless pleasures of passive enjoyment.

Hysteria-historiography, I repeat, means understanding cinema as a somatic language and proxy reality for a spectator on the cusp of having a powerful voice in the world. It erupts from those curdling laughs that linger—between carnal fun and hysteric conversion—to provide tentative gateways to the cryptic, impermanent, unrealized film writing that became as much of the spectator experience as the show itself.

THE SPECTATRIX STRIKES AGAIN!

"You'll laugh your head off just at the sight" of it![200] Laugh your back teeth loose, laugh yourself sick, die laughing, roll under your seats, paralyzed with laughter.

Without that spark of hysteria, no extremity of promised or potential enjoyment could ever be enough. "But listen! I nearly fell over the pew," gushed Madame Medusa (née Mildred Irving). "Some of the girls" tried to cover their eyes with their handkerchiefs (like Perseus with his reflective shield), "but I noted that they all peeked out at one side; and then broke into a wild roar of laughter."[201] How to extract the throaty powers of Medusan laughter from the compulsive appeals of its commercial exploitation?

Feminist film scholars have looked to early cinema as a pleasure garden where the implosion of spectacle into reality could have swung any which way, toward radical freedom or savage alienation. This no longer seems to be the case in the twenty-first century, with our crisis-upon-crisis of "zany" gig workers, throttled by incitements to 24/7 fun, whose affective labor fuels the serial disavowal of mass species extinctions and looming climate apocalypse. The monstrosities of neoliberal capitalism, so it appears, have tipped the scales of hysterical laughter toward alienation and unfreedom. But perhaps we are too cynical about the potential for wild, hypnotic images to transform the material conditions of dystopian reality.

Against the tyranny of horrific gaslighting, Madame Medusa embraced the hystericization of her flickering experience. To paraphrase the echoes of her obstreperous insights, *if you surrender to enjoyment, you can destroy it.*

8

The Visual Cure?

Moving Pictures as Neurotic Trigger and Therapeutic Instrument

"Not only have the pictures made a hit," hailed *Variety* in 1910, "but as diversion is one of the chief methods for the cure of insanity, it is believed that the 'moving picture cure' will be largely introduced in other institutions for the insane."[1] While cinema rapidly infiltrated every nook and cranny of both public space and the human sensorium, it also insinuated itself in a variety of state institutions in the United States, including prisons, orphanages, and not least of all mental asylums. "Pictures are found to have a soothing and beneficial effect upon the mind," for neurological inmates as for nerve-addled city dwellers, "and the 500 patients" who attended "at the local institution [in Columbus, Ohio] have been much benefited by the shows."[2] It became common sense that film afforded vital "diversion" from "the monotony of asylum life [which] often prevented recovery."[3] Film screenings calmed "excitable patients" and commanded "the attention" of all who visited these experimental new entertainment halls.[4] From 1904, when the Dunning Asylum in Chicago adopted the Biograph Insanity Cure, hundreds of thousands of public dollars were invested in the erection of movie theaters in facilities from Washington, DC and New York to Peoria, Illinois and Lakeland, Kentucky. Whether sheer distraction from soul-sucking tedium or visual relief from perceptual symptoms, cinema posed a tantalizing tactic for the state's hazy, haphazard administration of cognitive disability.

In this chapter, I further pursue the female hysteric as an uproarious film spectator. I look to the archives of early cinema's utility for neurological research and complicity with the repressive management of mental health populations. As we know (from chapter 7), hysterical female spectatorship upped the ante on "neurological modernity," posing a visual cure in its own right for the nervous distress endemic to capitalist urban life. As I have argued, the female hysteric crash-landed into the convulsive body of the laughing film spectator, with vast implications for the theory and historiography of gender politics and early film experience.

But what about all those exploited, violated, and gaslit women who continued to toil away in the asylum? They were no longer paraded as "clownist" attractions (à la Jean-Martin Charcot's "medical muses"), but their Medusan energies demand recognition beyond the familiar frame of irretrievable pathos or unrealized social resistance.[5] Many scholars have explored the use (and abuse) of medical cinematography, exemplified by what Lisa Cartwright calls early cinema's "neurological gaze," which panoptically set its sights on patients with motion disorders such as ataxia and spastic paraparesis.[6] Cinematography allowed neurologists to control the speed, duration, and recurrence of noteworthy symptoms for the purpose of teaching and research. At the same time, as Cartwright argues, the "perverse unintelligibility" of divergent movement defied the empirical capture of psychiatric surveillance.[7] Indeed, silent cinema was enthusiastically adopted as a therapeutic instrument by medical cinematographers—from Walter Greenough Chase and Theodore Weisenburg (in the United States) to Arthur Van Gehuchten (Belgium), Albert Londe (France), Camillo Negro (Italy), and Georges Marinesco (Romania). It is well established, as Scott Curtis emphasizes, that early cinema's medical gaze forged the very "shape of spectatorship" on an international scale.[8]

NEURODIVERGENT AMUSEMENT

What has not yet received due attention is the history of neurodivergent spectatorship in state clinics and asylums.[9] True to form, the hysteria-historiography of asylum-based enjoyment is a shadowy devil—fragmented, with key details missing, and often hyperbolic, unverified, and grotesquely insensitive in its discursive reporting. For example, the *New York Clipper* parodied an overheard conversation between a typical "movie fan" and an obnoxious theater usher in 1913. "I noticed in reading one of the trade journals that motion pictures have been successfully used for the purpose of amusing the inmates of an insane asylum," commented the fan, to which the usher responded: "I wonder they had the courage ter show the loons some o' those real noxious foreign-made pitchers" because "good-night if they ever do; they will never be able to control them!"[10] Loosely paraphrased, don't show psychiatric patients foreign slapstick comedies because they will never again be placated in their unrest. The fan and usher joke about how "picture clowns . . . git away with" what would land most folks in the "foolish factory."[11] (Short-form comedy was reported to be the most effective genre for pleasing and appeasing asylum spectators—although not without exceptions.[12]) Silly and offensive, this caricature reveals wider curiosity about burlesque cinema's effects on the *other* of the ordinary nervous spectator: the viewer who turned to the screen as a salve for the chaos of everyday shock.

Public fascination with asylum spectatorship inflected popular subjects of representation, such as *She Wrote a Play* (Éclair, 1914), a slapstick comedy about a female writer who is finally "fortunate enough" to put on her show "at an insane asylum which is where she landed in the end."[13] In *Ham in the Nut Factory* (Thanhouser, 1915), comedy duo Ham and Bud are almost killed on the job as temporary asylum "keepers" by the "fiercest" patient, who it turns out had merely been trying to engage them in a game of tag: "expecting to be killed," Ham and Bud are instead tagged: " 'Tag, you're it.' "[14] When depicted on a collective scale, asylum recreation made for eccentric comedy, whereas cinema's psychiatric cure was reserved for bourgeois individuals in melodramas such as *Mystery of the Rocks of Kador* (Gaumont, 1912) and *Love and Science* (Éclair, 1912), both of which I will discuss later in this chapter.

Cinematic neurology, whether played for suspense or exploited as comedy, tapped into deep fears about the effects of a hypnotic medium on mass culture and the human sensorium. Movies incited intense moral panic that they would corrupt women and children, feminize virile men, assault the retina with jerky images, and thus bring about irreversible social decline. Cinema's overly vivid impression of reality (its hysteric underbelly) induced nightmares and hallucinations in the very gesture of calming the viewer's overstimulated nerves. "Great care is taken in selecting the films used," noted G. D. Crain after visiting the Central State Hospital in Kentucky, where four reels of comedy played two nights per week.[15]

Reformists and psychologists alike explored the dangerous "effects of film viewing on neurotic individuals," which allegedly ranged from imitative criminality to "acute psychotic disorder."[16] For example, one woman had nighttime delusional terrors that her little dog would "suddenly stretch out in the shape of an enormous snake" after watching a film in which "an Indian snake charmer was shown with a number of these creatures winding round his neck and arms."[17] Although unspecified, perhaps the film at hand was *The Hypnotist's Revenge* (Biograph, 1907), a "continuous laugh-produc[er]," in which a mesmerist snake charmer drives a rationalist skeptic into "the Insane Pavilion of Bellevue

> **PICTURES HELP TO SET RIGHT INSANE MINDS.**
>
> One of the most interesting uses to which motion pictures are put in Kentucky is that employed by the Central State Hospital, of Lakeland, Ky. The hospital is a large insane asylum located about twelve miles from Louisville. About two years ago the officials of the hospital purchased a Standard machine and introduced comedy films. Every Tuesday night four reels of comedy are shown in the big auditorium for the benefit of the white patients. Every other Wednesday night four reels of comedy are shown to the colored inmates. It has been discovered that high grade comedy is more interesting to the patients than feature material, but great care is taken in selecting the films used. These films are being supplied by the S. & P. Film & Supply Company, of Louisville. Feature material in

FIGURE 8.1 "Pictures Help to Set Right Insane Minds." *Moving Picture World*, February 27, 1915, 1320. Image courtesy of Lantern (Media History Digital Library).

Hospital."[18] Cinema capitalized on the spectacle of hysteria, and the prognosis for neurological patients increasingly drew on the medium's therapeutic powers. As we will see, the "moving picture cure" dangerously threatened to outstrip its instrumental aims.

THE "INVISIBLE PATIENT'S" VISUAL CURE; OR, *ZANDORI'S SECRET*

The spread of cinema to U.S. psychiatric hospitals overlapped with the rise of the mental hygiene movement, which sought to improve conditions within these dismal and dehumanizing facilities.[19] New humanitarian efforts extended from nineteenth-century advocacy for "moral treatment" in asylums, "in which the insane had been chained in unheated/unfurnished rooms and subjected to painful and humiliating 'treatments'/punishments," as Emily Godbey details in her study of the magic lantern's therapeutic uses in mid-nineteenth-century clinics.[20] (Precinematic projections allegedly helped "repair [patients'] diseased pathways in the brain," according to Godbey.[21]) By the early twentieth century, however, state-funded institutions had become overpopulated to the breaking point and were again riddled with corruption scandals, as local almshouses and eldercare centers rapaciously pawned off their residents on the state by declaring them mad.

As we know, so-called madwomen were locked up by their husbands and fathers throughout the nineteenth century for reasons ranging from "over-taxing mental powers" and "political excitement" to "women's trouble" and "menstrual derangement."[22] Asylum demographics shifted significantly around the turn of the twentieth century as dependency became further pathologized for the sake of fiscal expedience. Out with the madwoman, in with the indigent other. Increased federal funding for psychiatric institutions and the deployment of elderly and "incurable" patients from local facilities all tipped the scales.

The explosion of migrant populations further colored rising xenophobic perceptions of neurodivergence, which were brazenly promoted by eugenic pseudoscientists. Organizations such as the American Breeder's Association (founded in 1903) made empirical pretenses for stripping neurodivergent people of their legal rights, especially as cognitive divergence intersected with racial and ethnic biopolitics. Mass campaigns for forced sterilization continued to prey on mental health inmates throughout the twentieth century, extending ideologically from long-standing obsessions with curing hysterical white women of their alleged reproductive "derangement."[23] As Lennard Davis has put it in a very different context (that of the COVID-19 pandemic), "The urge to let live and the urge to let die morph nicely into each other."[24] To that point, rehabilitation efforts worked hand in glove with campaigns for mass sterilization, legal disenfranchisement, and "pedigree" registration.[25] There was often a thin line separating moral progressivism from white supremacist domination as these projects were being inflicted on neurodivergent populations.

Yet the flush fever dreams of reformist optimism posed unresolvable tensions for the cruel machinations of mental health biopolitics. "Patients became, in effect, virtually invisible entities," remarks Gerald Grob, populations to manage rather than human beings to rehabilitate.[26] Mounting crises of asylum recidivism steamrolled state facilities "with a class of patients, very few of whom could ever be benefited by curative treatment," per dominant therapeutic methods at the time.[27] (These ranged from enforced inactivity to rigorous exercise and experimental drug cocktails to brain electrocution.[28]) A new notion of "cure" was needed to bring progressive reform efforts to bear on the bleak institutional realities of overcrowding, abuse, maltreatment, exploitation, and sheer human misery.

A Cure for the Incurable

Enter, cinema—whose universal address and nerve-soothing appeals squared the circle of moral progressivism's biopolitical embarrassment. In other words, films promised to placate the "invisible patient's" diagnostic incoherence when mapped onto a larger body of inmates—a remedy for the irremediable. The commercial film industry, ever hungry to court new audiences, could not have been more eager to participate. Power's Cameragraph No. 6A machines were installed in asylums in Raleigh, North Carolina; Greenpoint, Long Island; and Concord, New Hampshire, whose "board of trustees [found] that moving pictures, when properly projected, have a very beneficial effect upon the patients."[29] The Enterprise Optical Manufacturing Company "expect[ed] a big increase in sales" after the "Iowa Institution for Feeble Minded Children" adopted its Motiograph equipment, as *Moving Picture World* (*MPW*) boasted, proving "a value beyond the most sanguinary anticipations of those who expected great things from the secret powers ... of the moving picture."[30] In this context, the psychology wing of the industry trade press seized on cinema's neurological advantage. The "close relationship between physical sensations and mental capacity" mediated by moving pictures, *MPW* argued, would standardize pedagogic methods and uplift "diseased minds" to the great benchmark of the American norm.[31]

The very end point or objective of "cure," as neurodiversity scholars strongly emphasize, inflicts immense harm by imposing typicality as a gold standard for care. The mad rights movement[32] shows pride and celebrates deviance by embracing the free play of "neurodivergent sensory experience."[33] The point is not to correct divergence but to "jostle" the norm, as David Jackson-Perry et al. affirm in their "Travels in Normate Sensory Worlds."[34] Invoking Georg Simmel's call for a new "sociology of the senses" (1908), they argue that over a century later this field is still "so new that it barely even exists," particularly in its attunement to the "stranger's [sensory] experience of late-onset synesthesia."[35] An inheritance of the missed potentials of neurological modernity—to regard mental divergence otherwise—Jackson-Perry et al. pursue the fluidity between pictures and sound to transmogrify a "biomedical deficit" into a "sensorially different self."[36] Early film publicity for asylum spectatorship made recourse to a similar cinematic promise, highlighting the medium's radical phantasmagoric powers to shatter rigid empirical norms.

Beyond mere distraction or diversion, moving pictures collectivized treatment for allegedly "incurable" subjects by harnessing cinema's transformation of human perception. "Excitable patients seemed to be quieted and calmed," reported the *Kansas City Star*, "those suffering from chronic melancholia appeared to be stimulated and aroused from their brooding over imaginary wrongs and showed an unusual interest in what was going on."[37] The "movie cure" pandered to a one-size-fits-all nosology. How else could it ratify cinema's psychiatric utility while encompassing such a sprawling range of afflictions? "*On-going* experiences of madness or mental diversity" demand nuanced senses of diagnostic heterogeneity, argue disability scholars Nev Jones and Timothy Kelly.[38] They further distance their own tack from Michel Foucault's genealogical method and its wide-reaching influence on critical approaches to madness, which they claim pay inadequate attention "to the varieties of [divergence] and their implications."[39] Expressing strong "discontent or dis-ease" with the vast scope of genealogy, they contend that any concept of atypicality needs to begin from a place of disorder and difference.

Can madness exist as a general category without doing irreparable violence to the diversity of divergent experience? This was precisely the premise of the movie cure—not only that madness can be radically depersonalized, but that its visual remedy provided proof of the universal powers of cinema. The silent film industry's self-serving thesis on madness, however, does not map neatly onto the visibility logistics of Foucault's notorious panopticon, whereby the asylum represents one among many repressive institutions that discipline the teeming population into anxious self-watchers. (The panopticon provides a metaphor for how inmates learn to monitor themselves in looming fear of being surveilled at any moment by a faceless authority.)

More specifically, madness is the other of reason in Foucault's account, who at once pursues it as a transhistorical concept and painstakingly outlines its precise genealogies and mutating variants. In its radical heterogeneity, madness "made possible a [total] structure of perception" that converged on "the visible presence of the truth."[40] At last, "symptoms could attain their significant value" uncovering a greater "truth to which we had too long remained blind," proclaims Foucault.[41] Like the surveillant logistics of the panopticon, "truth" here operates as a knowledge effect in that the ascension of reason becomes propped upon the exposure and classification of madness. In particular, the "resonance" of mad bodies (with their "musical fidelity of the fibers to the sensations which make them vibrate") gave animate flesh to the soulless biopolitics of a depersonalized state apparatus.[42]

In the context of asylum viewing experiments, the mad person's Medusan "resonance" met its match in the shape-shifting absurdities of the cinematic image. Archiving the "movie cure," I argue, helps bring the heterogeneity of madness to bear on the persistence of its spectacle-based exploitation. Cinema's visual cure was not just a panoptic technique in Foucault's sense—a biopolitical regime for surveilling the subject, disciplining the body, and controlling the population. (It also served those ends, but they often arose in tension with the more proximate aim of halting madness in its tracks by manipulating the temporality of its symptoms.) In other words, "the cure" could never be substantiated by the medical mastery of its corresponding expressions. It needed to own those symptoms—to play them like a fiddle and melt them away through the crazy mirror of the indexical camera eye.

The Latest and Greatest Cure

Asylum film screenings further sought to counter the multiplicities of madness with the jolting immediacy of cinema. In these efforts, they were backed by public earmarks and exploited as private commercial capital. One institution in Washington, DC received $125,000 from the federal government; the institution was named Hitchcock Hall after the Secretary of Interior when Congress approved the appropriation in 1911.[43] Illinois invested $90,000 in the entertainment hall at Peoria State Asylum to seat 1,200 viewers, and California apportioned $75,000 for Agnew State Hospital for the Insane in San Jose, which also featured live stage burlesque acts such as *The Gay Café; or, a Parisian Salad* (1914). As the superintendent preached, "amusements are the best remedies for insanity."[44] The industry trade press could not have agreed more! If hysterical women were liberated to raise a ruckus at filmed boxing matches and equine ingestion farces, neurodivergent spectators expanded the medium's remedial powers to the walls of the asylum.

As Alison Griffiths remarks, "one could easily play fill-in-the-blank with the phrase 'Cinema as a . . .'—with hyperbolic titles like "Motion Pictures as a Cure for Insanity."[45] Or, as Charles Gibson upped the ante in 1910, "Motion Pictures, *the latest and best cure* for insanity" [emphasis mine].[46] Gibson details his observations at the St. Louis Insane Asylum, where a movie apparatus had been in use for just over a year, "and since that time the improvement has been remarkable, even in cases which had been given up as hopeless."[47] Gibson's exaggerated language bears closer examination, especially in its exhaustive attempts to account for film as an ideal complement to "the hallucinations, fears and phantoms that grope in the brain of the madman."[48] Cinematic subjectivity, after all, was in itself rather mad—a "shock to the nervous system" and pageant of the "incomprehensible" and "occult," as Giuseppe d'Abundo testified in 1911.[49] But the stakes of the state's unfettered adoption of this "cure for insanity!" were nothing short of a humanitarian credo, according to Gibson. They held out hope for depathologizing mental illness—not with voyeuristic sentimentality but with contagiously mutual hilarity. Movies would reverse "the very wrong picture of the insane" that "the public could correct if [only] they had backbone enough," implored Gibson.[50]

The basis for Gibson's argument is twofold. First, it hinges on an understanding of entertainment as a zone of indistinction between madness and sanity. "It was at the weekly socials and other forms of diversions that the mania-ridden inmates appeared more nearly like normal beings," he claimed.[51] Of course, the reverse of this claim is the premise of anarchic slapstick, which relies on the infectious spirit of madcap to foil any pretense of decorum or objective reason. For example, in *Two of a Kind* (Edison, 1909), two neurotypical tourists attend a "mad ball" at an "insane asylum," where they misrecognize each other as inmates and engage in playful flirtation. The end point of their seduction appears less erotic than neurotic, aimed at the affective license to be silly and unruly, thus raising the stakes of their mutual misrecognition.

The punch line arrives with the entry of the superintendent and his wife, who disabuse the pair of their illusions by exposing their true "mental status." Reimposing the gap between inanity and insanity, the finale provides a weak cover for the film's solicitation of madness to certify play and enjoyment, in a picture that self-advertised as "chock full of fun."[52] Simply put, reason is no fun, but the line between work and play has to be drawn somewhere. In a similar vein, Gibson details the "employment" of inmates as purely recreational, not "for the profit of anyone else," such as the tramp who's "given free reins to roam the grounds as a true knight of the road."[53] He also mentions a once "lucid" civil engineer who's "allowed to direct the building of miniature dams." Gross inaccuracies notwithstanding (asylum inmates were savagely exploited in their physical labor[54]), the implication becomes clear: the difference between madness and sanity hinged on one's capacity to resume real work in the aftermath of the festum.

I repeat, the first premise of Gibson's cine-madness analogy rests on the nutty ethos of comedic entertainment. Second, the formal dissonance of mental

FIGURE 8.2 Rosalie (Sarah Duhamel), a housemaid, is hosed with water and assaulted by noise after failing to wake up from her "sleeping sickness." Her employers want her to go back to work. Frame enlargement from *Rosalie a la maladie du sommeil* [*Rosalie Has Sleeping Sickness*] (1911; Paris: Pathé). Courtesy of EYE Filmmuseum.

unreason met its match in the rapid movement and shadowy tangibility of cinematic imagery. "The flitting figures that marched before the canvas" could "subdue the chaotic mind" with "quiet fascination." Gibson claimed that movement and variation are "essential" to "cast out devils" and quell "the fevered torrent of the maniac's thoughts." The roving "eye of the camera" aligned with "the restless eye of the lunatic" to forge a new "medium through which insanity may be cured."[55] And if cinema soothed the frazzled sensorium of the excitable masses (which is a formative thesis of classical film theory[56]), the visual cure to madness assumed a similar reciprocity between cognitive anarchy and the catharsis of mediated perception.

To give a cinematic example, *An Auto Maniac* (Vitagraph, 1909) depicts an escaped asylum inmate who steals a child's motorized toy car and destructively wreaks havoc cruising it around town. Docile upon his initial fugitivity, "immediately he becomes excited, cranks up the machine . . . and dashes wildly down the street."[57] The hotwired vehicle enlivens his alertness while speeding up the inevitable climax of his arrest and recapture. In film comedy, the spectacle of madness is what authorizes uproarious enjoyment, whereas in the asylum, moving pictures projected a "home" to "to come and go and enjoy as [the] best place to live," with "the ludicrous and comic pictures proving the most beneficial," according to the industry trade press and its psychiatric ambassadors.[58] In Ohio's state asylum in Columbus, as *Variety* noted, comedies had pride of place "with a few dramatics in use occasionally."[59] St. Louis superintendent Dr. Henry S. Atkins preached the potency of films like *The Unlucky Trousers* (Éclipse, 1907), a French farce about an amiable gentleman who repeatedly damages and repairs and then damages (and then repairs) his ill-fated trousers. Eventually he gives up. (Atkins was also an evangelist for the "Department Store Shopping Cure," which involved taking large groups of women shopping at St. Louis department stores during the Yuletide season.[60]) A pity the unlucky trouser wearer could not simply have gone shopping.

The easy reading would be to say that inmates learned to take their punches by savoring the comical torments of others. How many people have "lost it" over similar material crises of repeatedly fixing a problem only for it to flare up anew! As Atkins put it, depressives "whose faces have portrayed nothing but suffering for months" began to "show a faint smile and awaken . . . their feelings," while "over-talkative, abusive and noisy" patients "have been quieted by the immediate distraction of their elusive thoughts."[61] A brief escape from abject misery or formal validation of one's inner dissonance? If only cinema could engulf the entire world, then no one would ever need to go mad.

The Revolving Screen: In-Patient/"Airship Fugitives"

The ubiquity of cinema itself was enough to make anyone doubt their own sanity. "Films can tap into deep currents of feeling," remarks Sarah Keller, who theorizes "anxious cinephilia" as a wild feedback loop between passionate attachment and nervous self-fragmentation.[62] In her account, to love cinema intensely is to feel extremely anxious about its solidity and therefore to risk unraveling at its loss or implosion. Take the "peculiar case" of George Opdyke, who "was removed to the Essex County Hospital for the Insane" in 1908 after "suffering from the hallucination that he was confronted everywhere with moving pictures."[63] His floating visions drove him headlong into a plate-glass window, on which he "cut himself badly."[64] If cinema's cure assumed a certain bond between madcap illusions and the mental life of neurodivergent spectators, then its damnation erupted precisely from their dangerous overspill into ordinary experience.

Many early film genres—comedies, trick films, sensational melodramas, adventure travelogues—riffed on the revolving screen between cinema and the asylum. For the most part, these films either exploited madness as a device for ginning up suspense or carnivalized it as a silly sight gag to elicit wild, convulsive laughter. The latter category is obscenely exemplified by Dot Farley's antics in *The Accidental Parson* (Albuquerque, 1915), in which she plays an escaped patient with a mania for marrying people. Just before her identity is exposed, "she tied four knots for cupid, and was busy with the preliminaries for the fifth couple."[65] Similarly, the cartoonist R. F. Outcault built a $50,000 corporation by adapting his "Buster Brown" comics for the screen, with titles such as *Buster Brown in the Insane Asylum* (Outcault, 1914), thus inflating his income to "twice that of the President of the United States," as *Motion Picture News* declared.[66] Outcault outearned President Woodrow Wilson, while Edison's delusional Napoleon character commanded "a highly amusing effect" in *Maniac Chase* (Edison, 1904), in which an inmate incognito as the deposed/deceased French emperor flees from an asylum to create "the most exciting and ludicrous situations" in "rapid succession."[67]

In a very different vein, illicit lovers elope in a Zeppelin dirigible and are then institutionalized by the bride's father in the exciting thriller, *The Airship Fugitives* (Great Northern, 1913).[68] The newlyweds plot their escape by feigning forced abduction (even though the affair was consensual) so that the bride can assert her innocence and abet her lover's jailbreak from what's depicted as a brutal asylum. The rightness of internment—from benevolent rehabilitation to violent abuse—hinged on the neurotypicality of the presumed patient. If the inmate was deemed insane within the diegesis, then cinema's institutional screen could proceed apace, particularly within the comedy genre. Chase scenes traversing hotwired automobiles and hot air balloons swung from pathos to burlesque depending on the mental health status of the escapee; slapstick madcaps always made their way back to confinement (like "Napoleon" at the end of *Maniac Chase*). But wronged patients prolonged the chase to prove their reason and lucidity. Genre thus provided a container for refereeing the mental "fitness" of mad persons—melodrama sensationalized innocence and cure, while comedy carnivalized the irresistible contagions of nuttiness.

A comedic precursor to *The Cabinet of Dr. Caligari* (Robert Wiene, 1920), *The Colonel of the Nutts* (Frontier, 1914) lampoons a hypnotist's efforts to recruit an army of new patients for his self-run insane asylum. (As a genre, slapstick is both broadly offensive and anti-ableist at its core.) The film apparently did not go over well with the trade press: "there is no definite plot and the humor [fails to] hold very strongly," bemoaned *MPW*.[69] In their 1915 study of "The Cinematograph in the Field of Mental Illness and Criminality," Mario Masini and Giuseppe Vidoni insist that of all "today's inventions, cinematography takes the cake for having the most profound and intense impact on psychic life . . . After reality, [it] remains the most faithful and effective source of emotions."[70] As Hugo Münsterberg warned, the "intensity with which" the medium "takes hold of the audience cannot remain without strong social effects."[71] Cinematic impressions rival the reality of firsthand sensations, resulting in visual hallucinations and other "disturbance[s] in consciousness."[72] Masini and Vidoni further detail the hazards that cinema unleashes on the nervous system among "those predisposed to sensory disorders."[73] Ever primed to visualize its own pathological resonance, film widely depicted the revolving screen between soothing catharsis and nervous fragmentation.

Comedy especially capitalized on blurring that line between mental illness and enjoyment, such as when Betty (Clara Kimball Young) powders her gloves with a mysterious Brazilian extract to drive a group of celebrity artists temporarily insane in *Betty in the Lions' Den* (Vitagraph, 1913). It's her ploy to coax her pretentious aunt to allow her to marry just an ordinary guy, a "manly country sweetheart" named Tom. In effect, "Betty demoralizes the whole place, and the ambulance, the police patrol, the insane asylum wagon, and a force of policemen are needed to handle the crazy celebrities."[74] If the arts are already a bit loony, their excess provides a foil for the cultural redemption of Tom, the normative "country bumpkin." In a very different vein, *The Cabinet of Dr. Caligari* allegorizes cinema's collective incitements to madness, as Rae Beth Gordon argues, wherein the somnambulist is a proxy and "metaphor for the *force* of the film's pull on the spectator."[75] (Gordon similarly approaches the theme of hypnosis across genres as a metaphor for the cinematograph.[76])

Caligari depicts the rise of a tyrannical psychiatrist who preys on members of a shell-shocked society, escalating the popular pathos of asylum fugitivity to the threshold of existential horror. Stylistically and narratively, normality becomes indecipherable in order to render madness collectively irreversible, thus paving the way "from Caligari to Hitler," as Siegfried Kracauer paraphrased the slippery slope from popular hypnotism to warmongering fascism.[77] This is precisely the question of neurodivergent spectatorship in its tantalizing proximity to neurological modernity. In other words, the visceral hallucinations core to cinematic experience always risked mistaking the symptom for the cure, a danger that the industry exhaustively represented and ruthlessly exploited.

To invoke a cautionary French example, *Zandori's Secret* (Éclair, 1914) follows the apocalyptic fallout of a well-meaning doctor who invents a new serum to cure madness, which is transmitted contagiously through biting and scratching. While testing the remedy on a particularly violent patient, the doctor himself is bitten and thus contracts the disease, which he spreads to his daughter (played by Renée Sylvaire). He scratches her "in his delirium and she too is doomed."[78] Allegorizing the collective tolls of insanity's eugenic eradication (with a pandemic twist), *Zandori's Secret* imagines the tipping point between well-meaning research and world-ending psychosis. That threshold turns out to be none other than sheer will to power: the daughter's vengeful admirer conceals and hoards the cure so he alone can reap its financial rewards and claim scientific credit. But the virus threatens to spread uncontrollably before he will have had time to shore up its dividends.

What is the message behind the medium's spectacle of universal madness? At its most conservative, the movie cure simply discouraged viewers from losing their minds over cinema. For example, the titular spouse in *The Prodigal Wife* (Solax, 1912) hallucinates that she "dies a raving maniac in an insane asylum . . . overcome with remorse" after driving her husband to ruin with her extravagant spending habits. With the bogeyman of delirium projected to her as if on a cinematic screen, she "shakes off this nightmare" and "resolve[s] to change [her] mode of life."[79] The moral motif of female insanity encircled the twin dangers of modernity and consumerism in many such films, including *Phantom* (Selig, 1913), *Two Mothers* (Pathé, 1913), *Two Up a Tree* (Pathé, 1913), and *The Devil of a Time* (Punch, 1912), in which an escaped inmate steals the costume of "his Satanic Majesty" to persecute poor Mrs. Sprat by destroying all her prized possessions and sneaking into the bedroom with her husband.[80] (This film is no longer extant; I would very much like to see it.) As in *The Prodigal Wife*, cinema's cure for madness turns on its evocative depiction of moral truisms revamped for freewheeling consumer capitalism.

Drawing the Color Line

Is madness a cognitive condition or collateral damage from the hopeless disconnect between social reality and wishful thinking? The sight gag of wrongful insanity assigned to neurotypical bodies often stemmed from the sudden reversal of biopolitical fortunes, epitomized by *Drawing the Color Line* (Edison, 1909).[81] "The problem of the twentieth century is the problem of the color line,"

W. E. B. DuBois famously remarked in 1903. As I have argued, the "double conscience" of white female hysteria differed fundamentally from the "double consciousness" wrought by American racism—in too many ways to recount here—not least of all, for the latter's grueling simultaneity. The Black subject had to inhabit two contradictory psyches at once (animate and dehumanized), while hystericized women notoriously tag-teamed dueling libidinal positions, like Jekyll and Hyde, or Miss Esther and Mistress Wakefield (see chapter 4). In *Drawing the Color Line*, a good old boy taking a nap at his club becomes an unwilling biosocial experiment when two merry pranksters blacken his face with burnt cork.

Jack slowly loses his mind as he's denied entry to local shops, refused transport by a cab driver, assaulted by an acquaintance he'd attempted to greet, snubbed by society women, and beaten with a broom by his personal cook, then causing his wife and child to faint and scream hysterically when he returns home. "Jack is in a fair way to land in an Insane Asylum," *The Film Index* observed, "when he runs into a mirror in the hands of a furniture mover, and the mystery is explained."[82] Cured by the vision of his own defamiliarized reflection, Jack's temporary "derangement" is washed away with a little soap and water.

To "*derange* is to throw off, to cast askew," muses La Marre Jurelle Bruce, quoting Hortense Spillers: "'to disturb the order or arrangement of an entity.' The Middle Passage literally deranged and threw millions of Africans askew."[83] In *How to Go Mad Without Losing Your Mind*, Bruce explores the doubleness of *derangement* as both a record of incommensurable trauma and a signal of unruly divergence. Their duality persists and recurs as an inheritance from "the Atlantic slave trade, and the antiblack modernity it inaugurated, [which] framed black people as always already wild, subrational, pathological, mentally unsound, mad."[84] Therefore, madness for Bruce flickers between the lived realities of anti-Black violence and the wayward potentials of radical creativity, "confounding dominant logics, subverting normative aesthetics, and eroding oppressive structures of feeling."[85] In *Drawing the Color Line*, apparently, creative divergence congeals into the stark aesthetics of slapstick white supremacy.

If the minstrel stage solicited white spectators to feast on the somatic spectacle of racist antebellum caricatures, burnt cork entraps the "double consciousness" of Black madness when Jack accidentally dons his black mask in this 1909 Edison film. Like the fugitive pianist in *The Mad Musician* (Selig, 1908), whose "gesticular remonstrance" terrorizes a Black flute musician (whom he briefly encounters on the road), Jack restores his previous blinders and is again happily immune to the structural insanity of his social position. Or, as *MPW* puts it, "For a short run this picture is a run for the money. Hot off the reel with everything that is needed to make it a winner."[86] We might say, heads you lose, tails they win.

NEUROLOGY GOES TO THE MOVIES

For more precise depictions of the symptomology and diagnosis of neurodivergence, it is helpful to consult the archives of medical cinematography. As we have seen, commercial films about madness were extremely broad, lavishly offensive, and spasmodically exploitative. Asylum-bound characters ranged from the wrongly imprisoned (thus motivating suspense) to the suggestively convulsive: the "mad musician," "raving" artists in Betty's "lions' den," Dot Farley as the "accidental parson" with a "mania for marrying people," and so forth. Movies channeled madness as a sight gag or plot device but certainly did not regard mental health as an issue for ethical representation or diagnostic fidelity, at least not in popular fictionalizations.

The cinematic "cure" to madness, unlike Zandori's secret serum, boiled down to the form of the medium not the content of its ingredients. Again, it was all about the cathartic sensations of rapid-fire movement and flickering collective hallucinations. The industry's rhetoric about mad spectatorship in mental health asylums, however, to use exactly the wrong metaphor, was riddled with blind spots. For example, there is no discussion of cinema's multisensory appeals for blind or low-vision viewers, as Robert McRuer notes (invoking Georgina Kleege), while "dominant media representations of blindness invariably both construct a spectacle for blind viewers and unconsciously imagine that blind audience members have no place in the cinema."[87] Early films with sight gags about blindness include *The Faithful Dog* (Éclipse, 1907), *Only Kids* (Lubin, 1907), *Hank and Lank* (Essanay, 1910), and *Animal Lover* (Pathé, 1912). Nor were there efforts to make the theater a physically accessible space for patients with motor disabilities or nervous paralysis, again, even as early film sight gags cashed in on the spectacle of limb dismemberment and involuntary gestural spasms.

When specified, the apt neurodivergent spectator suffered from "melancholia," "stupor," "delusional hallucinations," "mania," "epilepsy," "mental disturbance," or simply blanket "insanity." Conditions that involved moody affect, unbearable anxiety, or unwilled apparitions were especially ripe candidates for cinematic therapy. In many ways, the industry's curative mandate resonates with recent critiques of Big Pharma and profit-based Western psychiatry elaborated by "crip" activists and disability studies scholars. For example, in their introduction to "Cripistemologies" (2014), Merri Lisa Johnson and Robert McRuer "crip" the critique of neoliberalism, focusing on capitalist pharmaceutical approaches to "impairment" that merely throw money at divergence from the gold standard of ableism. "We argue that all too many ways of knowing disability are beholden to the debility or crip dollar," which ignore the unruliness of disability to monetize an ever-elusive remedy.[88] To view disability and neurodivergence as "impairments" thus presumes ability and neurotypicality as the end points of (expensive, endless, often actively harmful) treatments.

Mid-twentieth-century antipsychiatry movements pioneered by R. D. Laing—and taken up in a very different vein by Gilles Deleuze and Félix Guattari in their two-volume *Capitalism and Schizophrenia* (1980)—demanded nothing less than the total liquidation of psychosocial madness and its separation from aspirational normalcy. As Laing famously put it with a materialist twist, "the condition of alienation, of being asleep, of being unconscious, of being out of one's mind, is the condition of the normal man."[89] The silent film trade press proceeded from a similar thesis but with dollar signs in its eyes regardless of whether the goalpost was instantaneous cure or the very democratization of madness.

As I have discussed, asylum spectatorship was multiply profitable for the film industry—a publicly funded cash cow and powerful publicity engine for promoting cinema as an antidote to endemic modern neurosis. It was also a windfall for the state management of mental institutions, which grappled with rising populations, treatment methods in no way equipped to attend to the diverse needs and experiences of patients, and acute pressure from "mental hygiene" reformists to humanize conditions in these dystopian hell houses. Cinema fit the bill both financially and ideologically.

Psychiatric Cinematography

Beyond asylum spectatorship or popular fictionalizations, neurologists and psychologists cultivated cinema as a revolutionary tool for research and teaching. The justifications for film's utility were wide-ranging. First, unlike Charcot's hypnotized medical divas, people rarely conjured symptoms on command for their observers. But "film is always 'in the mood,' " argued the German neurologist Hans Hennes, whereas many patients "show their interesting peculiarities only at times when no lectures, courses, and so on are taking place."[90] Hennes posits cinema as the "perfect solution" for capturing gait disorders (such as tabetic ataxia and spastic paraparesis) as well as catatonia, manic-compulsive movements, and Huntington's chorea. Similarly, the ability to control the temporality of symptoms—beyond the unique event of their occurrence—allowed researchers "to transform a rapid movement into a slow one," to dissect wild gestures in their chaotic escalation while comparing distant phases of the same affliction (such as the passage from excitement to depression).[91] Last but not least, the moving image's treasure trove of mimetic details converged on "living sensory reality," according to Hennes, "providing a visual dimension that the most exhaustive form of description cannot begin to attain."[92] In his presentation of recordings from the Bonn Clinic at the Berlin Congress in 1910, Hennes further called for the creation of "a cinematographic archive, similar to the phonographic archive, which would undeniably be of lasting value."[93]

Indeed, film scholars today continue to view, analyze, curate, contextualize, and engage with the extant archives of psychiatric cinematography from the early twentieth century. Neurological historians such as Geneviève Aubert, Adriano Chío, and Rita Montalcini have teamed up with film archivists to exhibit surviving prints at revival festivals and retrospectives such as the Giornate del Cinema Muto in Pordenone, Italy, which featured a program in 2017 on Camillo Negro's Turinese neurology fragments (1906–1918).[94] Lisa Cartwright, Scott Curtis, Kristen Ostherr, and Oliver Gaycken similarly take up early medical films as formative traces of visual media's multifarious uses: as tools for education, instruments of panoptic surveillance, and advents of mass commercial recreation. What did the medical expert's gaze bring to the popular power and experience of neurological cinema? The field has long posed different versions of this unresolved question—not just *what cinema is* but *what else might it have become*, particularly in its contradictory use-values.[95]

The Neurological Gaze: To Shell Shock from Clownism

The pursuit of cinema as a "cure for insanity" quickly became an American cultural obsession. Like the so-called "golf cure," which "may apply in America" but was the stuff of "continual nightmares" that "almost amounted to insanity" in the United Kingdom, however, cinema in asylums outside the United States provided entertainment without the pretense of psychiatric treatment.[96] Instead, the medium's remedial powers hinged on research-based cinematography (rather than therapeutic spectatorship) in clinical experiments in France, Italy, Britain,

FIGURE 8.3 Caricature of Professor Arthur Van Gehuchten, in *Ons Leven* (1909) nr.14. KU Leuven, Universiteitsarchief.

Germany, and elsewhere in Europe. Neurologists focused on filming patients with nervous gaits and rare motion disorders to exhibit these "interesting disease[s]" in "order to gather a collection for teaching," as the Belgian anatomist Arthur Van Gehuchten explained in his request for a grant of four thousand francs to pursue his filmmaking research.[97]

There was a showman's impulse behind these cinematic trials, which were pitched primarily to professionals in the medical establishment. Like Charcot, Van Gehuchten knew how to play to a crowd. But instead of hypnotizing women to assume impossible acrobatic poses (and then photographing them in prolonged stasis), Van Gehuchten exploited film movement to inspirit his lectures and enliven his public demonstrations. Geneviève Aubert thus describes him as an "avant-garde teacher" who innovated medical cinematography to "illustrate neurologic semiology," capturing "various neurologic diseases . . . to document [their] spontaneous evolution."[98] Just over three hours of his film studies survive, preserved by the Royal Belgian Film Archive.[99] Shot at his clinic in Louvain from 1905 to 1914, they feature sequential snippets of approximately one minute each in duration, depicting male and female patients exhibiting facial spasms, compulsive gestures, motion disorders, and nervous tics in both indoor and outdoor locations. In contrast to the photographic stasis of epileptic hypnosis orchestrated by Charcot, Van Gehuchten's subjects could not hold their poses—the film camera preyed on their disorderly, constant motion.

Multiple fragments reveal adult women smiling directly at the viewer, laughing defiantly, and executing funny facial expressions evocative of Florence Turner's competitive "face-pulling" (or "gurning") in her self-directed rest cure parody, *Daisy Doodad's Dial* (Turner, 1914).[100] In one excerpt, an unnamed woman in a white cotton shirt jerks her head compulsively while staring aggressively into the lens; she smiles, as if signaling a private joke, and appears energized by the unruliness of her own gestures despite their grueling repetition. She sustains a wily smirk, apparently pleased by the idiosyncratic precision of her actions, but she is interrupted while physically approaching the camera by a jump cut to the next fragment: a middle-aged white man in a black loincloth modeling his limb spasms.

In another fragment, a blind woman in tight close-up rotates her eyeballs in intense synchronization with her furious head gestures, gazing uncannily into the lens just at the end of the clip. The visible tension between her joyful unruliness and unwilled repetition—performative defiance versus invasive surveillance—shapes the viewer's neurological gaze at these ethically uncomfortable archives. Ethical discomfort is ostensibly their mode of address, if not then, now—it would be spine-chilling to think of viewing them today without critiquing their exploitative dimensions. They sensationalize the visible agitation of people suffering epileptic seizures; neuromuscular disease; and the psychosomatic effects of untold, uncontextualized trauma. That the patients are all unidentified, nameless, anonymous—snatched from their biographies by their cinematic afterlives—only compounds the discomfort of playing witness to their ghostly automatisms.

These archives are not boring. They display Van Gehuchten's appetite for the art of cinematic spectacle. For example, the dynamic tension between unwilled convulsion and individual rebellion, which is evident on repeat viewing, appears savvily orchestrated by cinematography and editing as much it was incidental or even authentic to the conditions of visual capture. Their mystery is precisely what makes these images so entrancing, despite their pedagogic monotony and viscerally difficult aesthetics.

Van Gehuchten's advocacy for neurologic cinematography arrived on the heels of intense scandal about the lurid exploitation of research-based medical filmmaking. The French surgeon Eugène Louis-Doyen had hired two camera operators to film him performing various surgeries (including a craniotomy) at his private

FIGURE 8.4 An unidentified woman exhibits facial spasms. King Baudouin Foundation coll., Germaine Van Gehuchten Fund, entrusted to CINEMATEK—Royal Film Archive of Belgium.

clinic in Paris, which he then controversially exhibited at the British Medical Association in Edinburgh in 1898. His film crew bootlegged the graphic actualities and pedaled them all over Europe, where they played at fairgrounds, carnivals, traveling shows, and other seedy venues. Their screening "in nonmedical circles," Aubert notes, "brought cinematography into disrepute among the official medical community and froze further attempts in France for almost ten years," when Pierre Marie began filming patients with chorea and athetosis at the Bicêtre Hospital in 1909.[101] Other physicians outside France explored the pedagogic, therapeutic, and commercial capacities of cinema. The Romanian doctor Georges Marinesco, who trained with Charcot at the Salpêtrière, extensively documented his patients with locomotor ataxia, gait disorders, and hysteria from 1899 to 1902.[102] (None of his films survive unfortunately, and their nonextant properties remain uncatalogued.)

The Italian neurologist Camillo Negro yields a rich reserve that poses further questions about the continued resonance of medical cinematography. Film archivists at the Museo del Cinema and neuroscience faculty members at the University of Torino recently worked to restore and curate Negro's medical studies for revival festivals around the world. Negro's neurologic fragments of hysteric patients (1906–1908) and shell-shocked soldiers (1915–1918) assume "the structure of an anthology," claims Claudia Gianetto, "organized into chapters or episodes, which he modified several times in the 1910s and 20s."[103] One thousand meters of footage remain as visible evidence of the devastating effects of war, patriarchy, and capitalism on the human sensorium, ranging from glimmers of a masked hysterical woman undergoing epileptic fits to images of a shell-shocked soldier "reliving the horror of the trenches" in a military hospital.[104] (In his reverse engineering of shell shock, the head of the Cork Lunatic Asylum in Ireland espoused military service as a "cure for insanity," alleging that escaped patients "often joined the Army, and turned up at the Asylum in khaki, better mentally after six months in the trenches."[105])

While Negro's films are consistently less spectacular (and more anthropological) than Van Gehuchten's, similar problems adhere to the ghost of the masked hysteric in particular. "It is a powerful image that is often mistaken for an act due to the painted backdrop," observe Chío, Gianetto, and Dagno, "unfortunately printed on a film stock in very bad conditions."[106] They link this scene to another snippet of the doctors speaking to an unmasked woman. But "what was this scene? Had Negro prepared other cases of hysteria for the film? . . . Is this the same woman who wore a mask later to remain anonymous?"[107] They speculate that the lost footage would provide necessary answers to all these conundrums, which are "now destined to remain unresolved."[108] The incompletion of figments of hysteria-historiography is precisely what commands wider attention and solicits our gazes into the present. Who were these women whose hysterical convulsions at once magnetized the camera and belied its clinical capture amid the throes of neurological modernity? We can only imagine.

Epilepsy Biographs

American physicians also adopted cinema as a research instrument, sometimes in tandem with experiments in clinical spectatorship but more often in tension with them. The film industry trade press put its thumb on the scale in 1909, just after The National Association for the Study of Epilepsy (NASE) issued a report about the popular exploitation of medical cinematography. "But that portion of the public which crowds around the fake epileptic" on "the sidewalk and usually contributes money 'for a doctor,' " *The Film Index* opined, "would take a similar morbid interest in a pictured seizure, and it is to be hoped that the films of the national association do not fall into the hands of the moving picture men.' "[109] Of course, there were no lack of fictionalized epilepsy escapades in popular slapstick comedies, ranging from *That Fatal Sneeze* (Hepworth, 1907) and *Contagious*

Nervous Twitching (Pathé, 1908) to *Hungry Hank's Hallucination* (Kalem, 1909) and *The Unlucky Trousers*; the latter two played in asylum movie programs.[110]

The Film Index made a cynically patriotic appeal in their unofficial rebuttal to the NASE, conceding that "some gruesome films, intended only for educational purposes, have found their way before the public abroad" (epitomized by the Doyen scandals), "but we know that such would not be the case here."[111] It can't happen here! Dr. Theodore Weisenburg, a Philadelphia neurologist who teamed up with the Lubin Company to record epileptic seizures, aired the matter clumsily in 1913 when he boasted of the "twelve hundred feet of [filmed] epileptic fits" in his personal possession that he "could now throw a fit on the screen any time [he] wished."[112] In a similar spirit, Reverend E. Boudinot Stockton described a large private screening of medical pictures for the "Learned Society" where the meeting room was so "overflowing with the members themselves and their invited guests" that "late comers were obliged to stand on the radiators and window sills in order to obtain a view of the pictures."[113] (A convenient solution would have been to move the event to the nearby theater at the Schuylkill County Insane Asylum, which could seat over five hundred viewers.)

What was the wider allure of witnessing these decontextualized fits and spasms, specifically as they appeared in nonfiction medical research pictures? There were plenty of spasmodic sight gags already on display in popular comedies, which were chock full of contagious sneezes, yawns, laughs, winks, itches, twitches, and seizures. Beyond their uncanny resemblance to the carnival of epileptic slapstick, these early medical views bear on the powers of cinema (as well as its disturbing limits) to make visible the unknown dimensions of the neurological body. In theorizing the "neurological gaze," Lisa Cartwright emphasizes the "perverse unintelligibility" and "incomprehensible sequences of movement" that confront surveillant medicine with "the impossibility of controlling disorderly bodies that populated their field of vision."[114] For Cartwright, this point is explicitly polemical because it reveals the futility of the surveillant medical gaze to divine scientific truth from the spectacle of madness. In other words, Foucaultian critiques (of biopolitical discipline) only go so far toward reckoning with the "surplus of meaning" that attends to the scene of neurodivergence.

Cartwright focuses on Walter Greenough Chase's *Epilepsy Biographs* (AM&B, 1905), filmed at the Craig Colony for Epileptics in upstate New York. The Craig Colony's profit-driven asylum temporarily sacrificed the agricultural labor of over one hundred inmates to accrue the equally valuable capital of medical evidence: spotlighting the spasms of their worker/inmates for a national audience. "However, what emerges from this account," argues Cartwright, "is an image of the epileptic body's structural resistance within this particular disciplinary technique."[115] Loosely paraphrased, the epileptic image obfuscates its empirical transparency and medical utility with a Medusan overflow of illegible signs. As Cartwright argues, the hysteric women as well as one Black man at the Craig Colony are depicted as innately divergent and incurable, whereas the naked white men are framed as convulsive but "potentially self-correcting."[116] This contrast is not immediately apparent, however, which has vivid methodological stakes for Cartwright. All that which exceeds visual transparency thus requires psychoanalytic approaches to reading and interpretation—extending medical power beyond the realm of the sensible or mappable (i.e., beyond the discourse of biopolitical discipline). Film may have been celebrated as a "visual cure" by the trade press (as opposed to Freud's "talking cure"), but the transparency of its neurological signs could never be taken at face value.

Libidinal curiosity further enfolds the project of medical cinematography. In his discussion of the "Use of the Biograph in Medicine," Chase often struggles to separate the medium's pedagogic vocation from its corporeal pageantry.[117] Fetishism creeps in through the backdoor of psychiatric expertise. Chase notes the convenience of how photography had automated hand-drawn illustrations for medical textbooks and then lingers on cinema's magnification of epileptic images: "by the biograph projection to life size" so "the very action of the muscles may be studied," which he then attempts to transcribe from reel to print.[118] The implied spectator/reader is, of course, not the nervous, exploding masses but dignified, learned neurologists, who might adapt these "instrument[s] used in the one-cent vaudeville parlors now common in most cities," as Chase suggests, "for showing . . . rare cases to students." If medicine sought to repurpose the apparatus of commercial enjoyment for prophylactic means, the film industry was quick to explore the flip side of this proposition.

Or why not just point the camera at the nickelodeon audience? "The best behaved audience I ever saw was at Bloomington Insane Asylum," raved Epes Winthrop Sargent (using the cheeky pseudonym, Chicot). "Come to think of it you might make the sound proofs [i.e., asylum quarantine cells] the private boxes for the sane where you can shut out the merry cut-outs and the sound of the piano at one and the same time."[119] Reluctantly paraphrased, the gist of Chicot's joke is that sanity and unreason become indistinguishable in the context of film exhibition. Here "you'll find the factory worker elbow to elbow with an elegant young lady," as Giovanni Fossi optimistically described movie theater audiences in 1908. "Members of one social class mixed with the other. It is, therefore, a bit of democracy that spreads into their behaviour. Or rather, it is the new behaviour, the new invention, that invites the spreading of a democratic spirit."[120] But the license to madness, as we know, was inextricable from that spirit of democratization.

MADAME MEDUSA AT THE MOVING PICTURE ASYLUM

"Crazy about the movies" is a common expression these days. However, it is taking on new meaning out in California, where a moving-picture theater has been fitted up at the State Hospital for the Insane at Patton, and will be operated as a possible cure for insanity.

—Dean Bowman[121]

The behavior women exhibited at early film screenings would have been ample grounds to have them committed in the mid-nineteenth century, revealing how quickly the gendered lines between reason and madness were shifting during the popular explosion of cinematic modernity. Commoditized enjoyment liberated Medusan unreason from the abyss of psychiatric abjection (even while exploiting it as a compulsory recreational affect). But where did that leave the Medusan film spectator in the asylum—who, I repeat, might have endured any range of afflictions: from social banishment to chronic melancholia to involuntary muscle spasms?

In 1911, our allegorical friend Madame Medusa (MM) finally brought the fever dream of a "motion picture cure" to the public sphere's red velvet seat. "One of the strangest audiences that ever gathered in a theater . . . attended a moving picture show" at the City Opera House in Frederick, Maryland, reported *MPW*.[122] The group consisted of "about 200 insane persons, inmates of Montevue Insane Hospital," who traveled together by rail before "the queer party marched down Market Street" to the theater.[123] This story is most unusual in its anecdotal details about the scene of spectatorship itself. Typically, reports on psychiatric screenings were grossly exaggerated but lacked even basic context about individual patient diagnoses, courses of treatment, biographical background, and so forth—let alone the conditions of viewing.

The following item (from "Crazy People Entertained with Moving Pictures"), although equally unverified and deeply offensive, yields unique demographic traces of neurodivergent experiences at the movies:

> Silence was maintained almost unbroken throughout the performance, though a picture of a negro chasing a chicken caused loud chuckles and a few "aa ha's" in the section of seats occupied by the colored men. Keen interest was

manifested in the pictures and when a party of women in a cart which was whirled across the screen waved their hands to the audience, a whole row of the female patients waved back at the picture.[124]

"Crazy People Entertained with Moving Pictures" presents a clear view of what was meant to separate neurodivergent spectatorship from the metaphorical "madness" of popular movie enjoyment. Female viewers wave back at the pushcart women on-screen, and spectators of color ventriloquize the implied shouts of a Black man chasing after a chicken. "One of the ways we apprehend the movements of others is by vicariously enacting these movements at pre-conscious and conscious levels," observes Stanton B. Garner in *Kinaesthetic Spectatorship in the Theatre*.[125] Garner explores the potentials of visual embodiment (such as professional ballet dancing) to dislodge and trouble normative benchmarks for internalized, empathetic perceptions of movement. "Moving differently," in his neurological and phenomenological account, demands "a willingness to engage what eludes—and, to some extent, will always elude—the normalizing eye."[126]

Notions of kinesthetic mimesis (or automatism) in the late nineteenth and early twentieth centuries, in contrast, did not assume empathy as much as unwilled imitation that sprang from an inadmissible side of oneself. Neurotypical spectators might embark on somatic adventures in response to their convulsive doubles on-screen but presumably would not cross that threshold from imagined movement to full-fledged enactment. To fall prey to imitation was seen as an effect of hypnosis and thus a sign of hysteria: "Society is imitation, and imitation is a kind of somnambulism," warned Gabriel Tarde in *The Laws of Imitation*.[127] As Henri Bergson put it in the context of involuntary laughter, all automatic social gestures slip through "despite or separated from the total personality."[128] At the scene of the Frederick Opera House, however, imitative automatism claimed "the total personality," at least according to *MPW*'s neuro-tourism snippets.

Medusan madwomen waved back at the screen so the neurotypical spectator's cathartic automatisms could remain safely within the realm of the norm. After all, noted Tarde, "what society would last for a single day without the general and continuous circulation" of unreasoned compulsions?[129] To exist in constant awareness of both sides of oneself (intentional and unconscious) was stigmatized as the very apex of madness or social abjection and therefore to be avoided at all costs.

Madame Medusa walked the line between ebullient enjoyment and divergent enactment. Unlike her fellow traveler Uncle Josh (the cinephobic rube who tears down the screen in disbelief of his double[130]), MM always thrived on a certain excess proximity to the moving image. She inhabited both worlds at once—without having to deny that rich duality from the scope of her experience. True to her name, Madame Medusa petrified the predatory gazes of medical cinematographers and voyeuristic audience ethnographers alike.

Women's Asylum Spectatorship

It is unfortunate that so few accounts survive of women's neurodivergent spectatorship in asylum-based movie theaters. The opera house scene was exceptional, both in its popular visibility and its audience diversity. Despite the enforcement of segregated seating, the Frederick Opera House outing differed from the usual conditions in asylum venues, where patient access rotated inequitably by race and gender. For example, at the Central State Hospital in Kentucky (a facility riddled with abuse and overcrowding), "every Tuesday night four reels of comedy are shown . . . for the benefit of white patients" and "*every other Wednesday night four reels of comedy are shown to the colored inmates.*"[131] (Note also the use of "patient" versus "inmate" and recession of "benefit" with the raced marking of the spectator.)

The gender dynamics of asylum screenings varied by institution. Some facilities showed the same program alternately to male and female patients. For example, the State Insane Asylum in Pueblo, Colorado, which installed a "moving picture apparatus" in 1911, held two exhibitions per week: one for the 550 female patients and one for the 650 male patients.[132] Although the institution housed minority Black and Latino populations, it is unclear whether these screenings were racially segregated or open only to white occupants.[133] Whenever the color line superseded the gender divide, one can only speculate on female access given the lack of extant records or documentation. As in Kentucky, there is no evidence of female patients being included in these racially prohibitive screenings or if more infrequent screenings were programmed for women only and if those occasions were also racially restrictive.

American women's prisons systematically barred female inmates from the pleasures of cinema. As Alison Griffiths details in *Carceral Fantasies*, women in state prisons "suffered inequity not only in sentencing policies but in their access to modern media," for example, with no recorded exposure to cinema until 1920 at New York State's Prison for Women at Auburn.[134] Punitive moral austerity shaped the reformist agenda for female prison populations, whereas therapeutic enjoyment resonated with broader public experiences of cinema and instrumentally boosted psychiatric claims of universal rehabilitation and cure. Yet as Griffiths reminds us (via prisons), dreamy viewings within the walls of the penitentiary were "by no means isomorphic with the film-going experience of a free man or woman."[135] Of course, neither were asylum viewings, although the medical field could not resist promoting them as such. Due to "the benefits of entertainment being recognized by alienists," opined the esteemed Atkins, "it is not a too far distant time when institutions of this kind will no longer be asylums or sanitariums, but a home where most of its inmates will come and go and enjoy as their best place to live."[136] It is a wonder that Atkins did not attempt to sell tickets.

A Haze of Hysterical Visions

Cinema was not the only game in town when it came to multisensory experiments in the up-to-date rehabilitation of madwomen. "The Color Cure," for example, adapted the chromopathic science of bile-based "humorism" to the neurologic obsessions of cinematic modernity.[137] Patients at the Ward Island's Women's Hospital in New York were "surrounded by an atmosphere of a particular colour deemed best for her particular mania": black to counter "acute mania," red to ease melancholia, and so forth—the intense "atmosphere of this colour" would "have a [supposed] soothing effect on the patient."[138] Early films likewise developed an affective grammar of colors, using tinted, toned, hand-drawn, and mechanically stenciled dyes.[139] Unfortunately, I can find no mention of film color in its potential deployment toward the cinematic cure.

Asylums often screened older, deteriorated prints: recycled after their commercial shelf life and then funneled between various state institutions, including orphanages, reformatories, and hospitals. There is very little surviving documentation of which films were programmed, let alone the conditions of circulating copies. Short comedies and scenic actualities would be prioritized over "tragedies, or highly exciting events," which might "have a bad effect to show insane patients," according to *The Film Index*.[140] This is interesting in the context of color therapy because trick films and travelogues were used as canvases for displaying the vibrant dyes and intense hues that enhanced cinema's wondrous visual appeals. I therefore cannot help but recall the St. Louis Asylum screenings of *Ancient Egypt* and *The Lakes of Killarney*, which may have involved color prints. Did chromotherapy ever inflect practices of the cinematic cure despite the paucity of extant evidence on the subject?

Color effects were widely associated with film's hypnotic powers to seduce and bewitch ordinary perception. In the asylum context, such hypnosis was indeed the seat of film's miraculous powers to break through any unspecified affliction. The patient "who is habitually shown certain styles of motion pictures can be affected as through hypnotism," commented Dr. M. E. White (Milwaukee Asylum superintendent) to *The Film Index* in 1910.[141] White claimed that movies "suggest mental processes to the maniac, who can gradually be led to use his mind in a manner that will relieve the diseased cells, and thus eventually result in a cure."[142] Loosely paraphrased, you have to look at the picture itself to understand what is going on in one's delirious brain in the grip of cinematic hypnosis.

Jules Romains described the visual play and emotional atmosphere at a French cinema in 1911: "A haze of visions which resemble life hovers before them . . . They have changed color, outline, and gesture . . . What controls their rhythm is not ordinary time, which occupies most people when they are not dreaming . . . Causes produce strange effects like golden eggs."[143]

Did readers of *The Film Index* envision White's "cure"—"weak" brain cells parlayed into cognitive sense-agents—through such kaleidoscopic imagery? Given the predominance of nutty comedies in asylum programs, it is too tempting not to speculate on how physicians may have explained brain-based divergence through the analogue of slapstick madcap. "The photoplay obeys the laws of the mind rather than those of the world," observed the psychologist and film theorist Hugo Münsterburg in 1916. In his chapter on "Memory and Imagination," Münsterburg focuses on specific film techniques such as the close-up, cutback (or flashback), and the visual rhythms of juxtaposition that can hold the audience "spellbound" in "a state of heightened suggestibility . . . ready to receive suggestions."[144] In other words, the vindicating realism of film form stemmed from its appeals to unruly inner thought, which could "result disastrously to the patient" upon screening "the incorrect picture."[145]

But why was comedy the prime vehicle for impressing "sanity" on the anarchy of thousands of "disordered minds"?[146] It is often difficult to disentangle audience demands (as comedy films "so delighted the inmates they wanted to see more of them") from hypotheses about cure, which explicitly went beyond catharsis or escapism.[147] The same article specifies *Micro-Cinematography of Recurrent Fever* (Pathé, 1910) as an attraction not for patients but for physicians, for example, when Shelby County in Tennessee prepared to install motion picture equipment in their asylum after several promising test runs. It further compares neurologists viewing a documentary about epidemic brain fever to screening Edison's *Boy Scouts of America* for local troops or Gaumont's *Pharaoh, or Israel in Egypt* for members of the clergy. By that logic, it would be hard to imagine a better choice for the Shelby County occupants than *Devil of a Time*, in which a mad person escapes from an asylum and steals a devil's costume, or better yet, *The Hypnotist's Revenge*, about a learned psychiatrist who is driven by a mesmerist to commit himself to a mental institution. (Not to be confused with the lost Méliès film of this title, in which a magician uses rapid-fire prestidigitation to cheat at a card game and then flee by way of hypnosis.)

Medusanal Hallucinations

There is an odd resonance between early cinema's haze of hysterical visions and ongoing calls by disability scholars and mad rights activists to engage with the wider spectrum of divergent perceptions and experiences. These rallying cries go well beyond the familiar antinormative credo to depathologize divergence. Rather, they seek to understand extrasensory impressions as embodied archives of rupture and trauma, both individual and biosocial (such as dwelling in a community or location afflicted by poverty, police violence, water poisoning, toxic exposure, and other crises of environmental racism). In this vein, allies and activists of the twenty-first-century Hearing Voices Movement (HVM) redeem auditory hallucinations not as symptoms of psychosis but as affective emanations from particular events and community situations—"a meaningful response to traumatic life experiences," as Akiko Hart puts it.[148] Hallucinatory affirmation carries a communicative power that turns feelings "into pictures and sounds" and creates "a vocabulary in my head" mediated by "pictures and sounds (not words) ... attached to sensory experiences," as one interviewee diagnosed with autism testified.[149]

In a similar spirit, Shelley Briggs and Fiona Cameron emphasize the "stigma and psycho-emotional dis-ablism" inflicted by labeling responses to trauma as illness rather than as "adjustments that open up possibilities for alternative reactions on the part of services and communities."[150] The analogy between early film experience and mad rights activism in the climate-combusting, neoliberal hellscape of the twenty-first century only goes so far. Yet the Medusan anarchy of the former—liberating divergent sensations of rupture and shock from the belly of the beast of consumerist industrial capitalism—bears a vital resonance to the current conjuncture, where the collective fight against authoritarian gaslighting fuels the popular urgency of mad rights consciousness raising. Similarly, it has long been a truism of feminist scholarship on early cinema that endemic hysteria and radical democratization were like two sides of the same coin.

But Medusa herself has inspired very different lessons for the history and trajectory of film theory. Although celebrated by feminists from Hélène

Cixous to Mary Beard and Barbara Creed, the unwatchable Gorgon has been a bit of a dog whistle across the field of film studies at large. Above all, she raises the specter of unrepresentable reality that the cinematic shield/mirror must conquer and dissolve into an aesthetic image. This has been the gist of Medusa's resurrection: from Kracauer's "The Head of Medusa" in his epilogue to *Theory of Film: The Redemption of Physical Reality* to Hal Foster's "Medusa and the Real," which compiles Medusan allegories of "the power of the gaze and the capacity of representation to control it."[151] "For Foster," as Genevieve Yue argues in *Girl Head*, "the vanquishing of Medusa is nothing less than the foundation of art," whereby her severed head "becomes the occasion for a theory of the unassimilable" in painting, literature, photography, and film.[152]

A far cry from Cixous's antipatriarchal manifesto, Kracauer's version of Medusa is a sad foil for slaying the beast of modernity's senseless horrors by dissipating it into a mere reflection (by way of Perseus' metaphorical shield). "We redeem horror from its invisibility behind the veils of panic and imagination," wrote Kracauer after watching filmic evidence of Nazi atrocity: "the real face of things too dreadful to be beheld in reality."[153] Medusan metaphors, whatever else they might do, charge cinema with an interventionist obligation. Rather than straitjacketing Medusa under the realist auspices of digestible horror, as per Kracauer, why not liberate her madness as a vestige of multisensory trauma, in dialogue with the work of mad rights methodology?

In that spirit, it is time for us to turn the question of Medusan spectatorship on its head, or we might say, to decapitate it (because my theory of puns is that they are almost never inappropriate). There is a reason why these fishy reports on asylum movie screenings became so uncontainably prolific. Though sinister and exploitative, they depict the asylum as a kind of carnivalesque laboratory for the wider redemption of neurodivergent perception. This was the crux of the medium's Medusan vocation in its flickering instability between neurologic catharsis and eye-gouging crisis.

Toward the latter extreme, film "severely shakes the nervous system," warned Robert Graupp, "without giving us the means by which to defend our psyches against these attacks."[154] A member of the *kinogegner* ("enemies of cinema"), Graupp frequently mixes metaphors between the medium's physical and figurative hazards to the eye. As Scott Curtis notes in *The Shape of Spectatorship*, the fear of eye injury from the projector's jerky "flicker effects" posed an "outward symptom of a deeper, psychic damage caused by the temporal push of cinema."[155] Curtis emphasizes the "general medicalization of cinema" in reformist rhetoric at the time, where neurologic symptoms and moral anxieties spun together in an unending loop.

All Medusa and no Perseus, Graupp's figments of film madness "intensifie[d] the pleasurable tension" of rapid-fire images "to an unbearable level; there is no time for contemplation and thus no time to compensate psychologically."[156] Jouissance beyond the threshold of sensible enjoyment? It's a miracle that spectators didn't spontaneously combust at the sight of it. Cinema's "technical artistry" invested "an apparent reality" in "fantastic events" that were "generally creepy and stupid, and seldom tasteful," according to Graupp.[157] Locating its Medusan dangers in the false reproduction of reality, in contrast to Kracauer's call for mediated perception to lift the veil of the unwatchable, Graupp kept his eyes on the prize. But perhaps if he had stared at the screen for just a bit longer, he would have glimpsed Medusa head-on.

NARRATIVIZING THE CURE: META-MAD MOVIE SPECTATORS

Movie fans too might have lost their heads if not for witnessing the cathartic spectacle of their volatile attachments on-screen. In that vein, filmmakers widely portrayed film itself as a definitive cure to hysteria. The archives of meta-mad cinema run the gamut from melodramas about suspenseful neurology to short little larks, such as *Dr. Max in Spite of Himself* (Pathé, 1917), in which Max Linder accidentally becomes an amateur physician after curing his own neurasthenia by going to the movies. Similarly, *Tontolini Is Sad* (Cines, 1911) vanquishes the sad clown's sadness by sending him to a screening of one of his own films: a metafictional encounter at which he laughs his head off to regain his sanity.[158]

Tontolini initially fails to slay his despair at the opera or variety theater, but other characters have better luck with live entertainment. The title of *The Clown and the Neurasthenic Pasha* (Pathé, 1910), like that of *The Anti-Neurasthenic Trumpet* (Éclair, 1914), is rather self-explanatory. A depressed Ottoman ruler relieves his melancholia by watching the antics of a silly little circus clown, who stirs him to hysterical laughter after even Mistinguett had failed to do so with her mesmerizing ballet dance.

A variation on "the laughing cure"—adopted by phonograph parlors, vaudeville spielers, and carnival barkers—movies promoted their own powers to "provide a sure cure for the blues."[159] It is no surprise that popular depictions of meta-film solutions to madness often played on vividly cinematic themes such as doubleness, hypnosis, and uncanny self-recognition. In *Love and Science* (Éclair, 1912), a crazed inventor (Max) devises a surveillant machine through which he monitors his fiancée Daisy. In the process, he tragically mistakes Daisy's cross-dressed female friend for her adulterous male lover. Max loses his mind, having short-circuited the distance between his libidinal and technological fantasies of mastery and control. Therefore, he can restore his sanity only by dispelling his illusion (that Daisy is cheating on him with another man) through the eye of his own device. Daisy and her friend film a reenactment of the traumatic scene but with one sneaky twist: a gender reveal, proving that the "other man" is really just a woman in disguise! "Amused by the situation, Max is instantly cured," as Doron Galili describes the finale in *Seeing by Electricity*.[160] Galili compares Max's invention to a "visual telephone" (Zoom avant la lettre), which must be destroyed in order for cinema to emerge as the superior, antihysterical medium.

Other meta-mad movies expressed deeper ambivalence about the hypnotic powers of cinema itself to seduce and deceive. *A Representation of the Cinema* (Pathé, 1910) satirizes credulous movie fanatics who are paralyzed by the gun violence in a melodrama, convulsed into laughter by a slapstick comedy, and then sickened during a thunderstorm scene. The rocking boats "tug at the heart and gnaw at the stomach of less experienced viewers," according to Pathé's catalog summary, which concludes: "Silently, the spectators withdraw in groups, overjoyed to regain their footing on the solid Parisian asphalt."[161] Of course, Parisian ordinary life often felt far from "solid" circa 1910. *Only film* could afford a cure to the madness of its own making.

Movies about movies in which characters unexpectedly confront themselves in the cinema offered imaginary resolutions to unresolvable social tensions. Take sexuality, divorce, and infidelity, the ABCs of narrative cinema. *New Cure for Divorce* (Thanhouser, 1912) lambastes modern marriage as an open frontier for heterosexual panic. In the film, a newlywed couple has a "foolish silly quarrel" on their honeymoon, but "just as their matrimonial bark was on the verge of being hopelessly shipwrecked," they attend a public screening of a home movie about the halcyon days of their early engagement, which stirs their happy memories and miraculously reunites the couple.[162] "It's the Film Cure," proclaimed *MPW*, "See a Moving Picture in a Moving Picture. A Fine Novelty for the Heated Spell. It Boosts the Whole Picture Institution."[163]

Candid camera snafus often served disciplinary ends in early films about marital cuckoldry. For example, the exposure of adulterous affairs to shocked moviegoing spouses provides corrective evidence in comedies such as *The Story the Biograph Told* (AM&B, 1904), *Willie Visits a Moving Picture Show* (Nordisk, 1910), *Romeo Pays for the Cinema* (Pathé, 1914), and *The Little Devil*

(Rosa Porten, 1917): all films about the dangers of film to expose the unseen world of illicit attraction. *The Cameraman's Revenge* (Władysław Starewicz, 1912), a masterpiece of Russian stop-motion animation, stages a similar scenario in which the characters in a libidinal triangle are all played by anthropomorphized, dead bugs. (It's a scream!)

Filmmakers latched onto the congruence between empirical neurology and the iconography of cinema, thematizing the triangulation between body, mind, and screen as a productive premise for image-based storytelling. Léonce Perret's *Mystery of the Rocks of Kador* (Gaumont, 1912) represents perhaps the most remarkable example of a meta-film about the belief in cinema as a visual cure for madness and for female hysteria in particular. Released in the United States with the title, *In the Grip of the Vampire* (1912), *Kador* depicts the plight of an orphaned heiress, Suzanne (Joy in the U.S. version), whose insolvent cousin schemes to murder her and steal her inheritance. Failing that, he can still reap the reward if she goes insane before her eighteenth birthday, which is exactly what happens after she witnesses (or so she believes) the violent death of her lover, Captain Jean, by a gunshot wound at the seaside. As it turns out, Jean miraculously survives, although Suzanne remains oblivious to her good fortune, consumed by dissociative amnesia and hysterical catatonia.

Her family and friends enlist the medical expertise of a psychotherapist, Herr Williams, who has been experimenting with cinematographic treatments for hysterical automatism. He directs them all to reenact the events surrounding Suzanne's traumatic break, which he then records with a film camera and screens for Suzanne in a private viewing. It is not the calling to memory of repressed trauma that cures her but the temporal alignment between traumatic latency and cinematic projection. Only by reenacting the scene of her shock and then watching it played before her in a cinema (in the company of a world-renowned psychoanalyst) can she stir her memory and identify the would-be assassin: her guardian, Count Fernand (who is actually played by the filmmaker, Perret). Yet again, the medium outstrips the presence of its maker.

As in *Zandori's Secret*, madness is a mere bargaining chip in the gendered struggle for legal property rights.[164] But thanks to cinema, madwomen can pose as rational agents over their own estate and affairs (at least within the bonds of bourgeois marriage, à la *Mystery of the Rocks of Kador*). "Cinematography is represented in this film, for the first time to our knowledge, as an aid to the restoring of sanity," opined the *Moving Picture News*. "This point carries, no doubt, more than a fictionary truth behind it."[165] As Freud remarked twelve years later, "If I distrust my memory—neurotics, as we know, do so to a remarkable extent, but normal people have every reason to do so as well—I am able

FIGURE 8.5 Suzanne (Suzanne Grandais) faints after watching a cinematic reenactment of her own hysterical trauma. Frame enlargement from *Le mystère des roches de Kador* [*Mystery of the Rocks of Kador*] (Léonce Perret, 1912). Image courtesy of Kino Lorber.

to supplement and guarantee its working by making a note in writing."¹⁶⁶ In "A Note Upon the 'Mystic Writing-Pad,'" Freud pursues the antihysterical function of writing machines to relieve the impossible burdens of memory on the nerve-addled psyche. Published almost three decades after his *Studies on Hysteria* with Josef Breuer, Freud ignores the complex mechanisms of cinema, opting instead to allegorize the simple apparatus of a child's toy: the mystic writing pad. But perhaps there was something personal at stake for Freud in refusing cinema's hypnotic appeals. As we know, *talking* (not *seeing*) provides the basis for psychoanalytic treatment, whereby impossible memory attains cathartic relief through the analyst's sensemaking imperative. Images may lie but their deception can be unmasked once transcribed into words—if refereed by the analyst.

The "movie cure" made a very different kind of multisensory appeal to achieve its antihysterical potency. "So I claim there's more health stored in one reel of thrills than in all the quack doctors and all the pink pills!" kvelled Milo Ray

Phelps in "The Movie Cure," a fan poem published by *Motion Picture Magazine* in 1920.[167] His rhymes are delicious:[168]

> Well, six reels of Fairbanks brought back my left lung
> And when I saw Theda my last fling was flung...
> The Mack Sennett 'squabs' fixed my bum appetite,
> And the insomnia left with [Olga] Petrova one night.

Hyperbolic and self-aggrandizing verse notwithstanding, "the movie cure" depended on a certain immediacy and reciprocity between film movement and modern neurosis—between the lucid fever dreams of cinematography and the mass collectivity of nerve-shattered absurdity. After all, don't we often make our way to the movies in hopes of experiencing sensations as fragmented and unfamiliar as we also find ourselves?

9
From Mouth to Screen

Laughing Heads in the History of Film

Dear Sir—

Do you care to state which is the originator of the subject "Laughing Gas" and which the copier—Edison or Vitagraph? I recommended one to a prominent vaudeville house, and they received the other, which contained certain things which they cut out. I did not suppose either house would be guilty of such a practice.

—Yours truly,
John H. Thurston
Moving Picture World (1907)[1]

Two films with the title *Laughing Gas* were released in 1907—one enthusiastically celebrated and the other furiously banned. Both comedies depict the exploits of women who wreak havoc by spreading laughter contagiously through public space. As we know, hysterical laughter was the lifeblood of early cinema and a lightning rod for the euphoric experience of destructive mass culture. No longer a mirthless symptom of emotional crisis, the hysterics of uncontrollable laughter fueled the catharsis of women's explosion into capitalist modernity as consumers, laborers, streetwalkers, and activists. The cinematic screen reflected these rapid and often divisive social upheavals. My final chapter will zero in on the history of female facial close-ups of hysterical laughter, focusing on frontal views of uproarious women who directly address and confront the spectator.

From one-off funny face-making shorts (known as facials), hysterical close-ups were banished to the edges of the reel—as the novelty of recording zany motion gave way to the commercial necessity of telling longer stories that helped establish cinema as a "seventh art" (or at the very least, a respectable pastime). Women's decapitated close-ups bookended narrative films that otherwise contained only distant long shots. They occupied that liminal, uncanny realm between movie fiction and reality mirror. Early cinema, among other things, was a hotbed for hysterical, Medusan, enlarged female faces! But as the close-up itself yielded a canvas for projecting emotional depth and character psychology, its dramatic muses displaced their hysterical antecedents, whose joyful convulsions vanished into the archive.

LAUGHING GAS ×2: EDISON VERSUS VITAGRAPH

Edison and Vitagraph—two of the leading U.S. film companies at the time—each produced comedies with the title *Laughing Gas* in 1907.[2] In Edison's version, a Black woman named Mandy Brown (Bertha Regustus) opens her mouth and laughs hysterically at the camera. For the last seventeen seconds, she commands the screen—unleashing her tumultuous enjoyment onto the viewer. To end a film with the close-up of a woman's face in the throes of laughing ecstasy was an utterly conventional practice by 1907, when Edison tweaked the formula to celebrate the contagions of Black joy. Indeed, the film itself thematizes contagious joy: Mandy goes to the dentist to have her tooth pulled, where she's given nitrous oxide (aka laughing gas), which sends her into laughing hysterics that she transmits irresistibly to the public sphere at large.[3] "She causes a series of accidents and disruptions," notes Jacqueline Stewart, "only to laugh herself out of trouble every time."[4] Mandy's insuppressible laughter actively desegregates white spaces: from the streetcar to the town square to a police station. "Merry, mirthful Mandy laughs on to the end," *Moving Picture World* (*MPW*) enthused, "[b]elieving that he who laughs last, laughs best."[5] As we know, early movie theaters were ostensibly laughing sanitoria for a volatile, nerve-addled populace. "That is why people go to the cinema," declared Kurt Pinthus in 1914, "desiccated souls love it when the last wild and sweet juices remaining in them come to a boil."[6] If Mandy Brown's fellow travelers succumbed to her rhapsodic *fou rire*, film audiences at the time were just as susceptible as the white dentist, the white cop, and the Black church congregants burlesqued in this film.[7]

FIGURE 9.1 Mandy Brown (Bertha Regustus) laughs in the last shot of *Laughing Gas* (Edison, 1907). This screening took place on October 3, 2022, in the Teatro Verdi at the Giornate del Cinema Muto in Pordenone, Italy, in a program titled "Nasty Women 3: Contagious Revenge." Photograph by Valerio Greco and courtesy of Valerio Greco Photography.

Of the two comedies titled *Laughing Gas* in 1907, one might justifiably suspect that Edison's carnival of interracial, uncontrollable, hysterical laughter would be on the chopping block. John H. Thurston details in his disgruntled letter to *MPW* (quoted in the chapter-opening epigraph): "I recommended one to a prominent vaudeville house, and they received the other, which contained certain things which they cut out."[8] What did they cut? Was it the scene in the police station when Mandy's promiscuous laughter liberates her from forced detention? Or was it the dinner party where she accidentally drops a bucket of soup on her white boss's head and then breaks all the dishes? Or perhaps when she falls into a white male passenger's lap on the streetcar as all the passengers convulse "in an uproar"?[9] Before we speculate further on the unarchived extrication of Black cinematic transgression, let us look at Vitagraph's version of the offending title—now a lost film, which is "entirely different in subject and staging," as *MPW* notes in its response to Thurston—"only the name is similar."[10]

The gas itself becomes a red herring in Edison's version, which appeals to imitative automatism and instantaneous bodily contagion: *You laugh; I begin to laugh; Now we're all laughing*! Vitagraph's *Laughing Gas*, in contrast, weaponizes the chemical compound in a sadistic spree perpetrated by a boy prankster, who turns out to be played by a woman in drag. (Since the film is lost, I have no way of determining the identity of this performer; perhaps she was the same actor who stars in *The Boy Detective*, where she is revealed as a woman only in the final close-up.[11]) The *New York Clipper* describes Vitagraph's *Laughing Gas*: "A boy procures a tank containing compressed laughing gas. He opens the tank upon every possible occasion. No matter where he is, whenever the gas escapes everybody within range commences to laugh uproariously."[12] Anticipating the lethal toxins deployed by the German army in the trenches of Lorraine circa 1915—that caused "its victims [to die] flapping their arms like the wings of a decapitated fowl and with hysterical laughter on their lips;" Vitagraph's half-reel farce lambastes laughter as a chemical hazard, whereas Edison's film embraces it as an unruly biosocial experiment.[13]

Is it possible that an early film about Black female laughter could be embraced as "high class comedy" while the one about a white, cross-dressing prankster would be banned from U.S. theaters?[14] The evidence that Vitagraph's *Laughing Gas* (not Edison's) was the "copier" (although a very different film, Thurston discards it as a mere knockoff) speaks for itself. *Variety* skewered the Vitagraph version: "A flimsy idea unmercifully padded out into a series of rather less than regulation length ... The laughter was all on the sheet."[15] In other words, laughter did not break the screen barrier by infecting the audience—unless anyone had thought to release nitrous oxide into the theater. In contrast, the trade press hailed Edison's *Laughing Gas* as an exemplary "good laugh-raiser" (along with Biograph's *Dr. Skinum* and Georges Méliès's *Channel Tunnel*) that "would not travesty the good taste of a people's religion, or of a race."[16] It is unlikely that Vitagraph's cross-gender casting is what "debarred" its version from the dictums of "good taste."[17] Actresses played boy characters in numerous prestige pictures across genres, as Laura Horak establishes in *Girls Will Be Boys*.[18] *Variety* further griped that the "mischievous youngster—a woman in boy's clothing—does some very fair pantomime, but the film is a frost" (a dud, failure, fiasco).[19] There was clearly something else amiss. But what was it? An unspecified gag in particular? The coercive use of chemical gas rather than letting contagious laughter roam free? Whatever the reason, these two dueling faces of *Laughing Gas* reveal the fault lines of laughter's cinematic license to upend racial, gender, and class hierarchies with the spectacle of wild enjoyment.

As we will see, women's laughing heads often held the line between commercial recreation and social transformation. By 1907, it was typical to open and close film comedies with enlarged facial views of female characters laughing, smiling, winking, and spasming at the camera—frontally posed for direct address to the viewer. Their hovering automatisms occupied that fragile divide between cinematic fantasy and physical experience. Laughter could *never* stay "all on the sheet."[20] This chapter, among other things, will rewrite the history of film from the position of female hysterical laughter—from mouth to screen, all suggestive images have sociopolitical consequences.

TOWARD A THEORY OF THE LAUGHING HEAD

Few qualities have been as essential to the aesthetic theory and social potentials of cinema as its capacity to visualize the human face. "Close-ups are film's true terrain," claimed the Hungarian film critic Béla Balázs, who exalted them as "the technical precondition for the art of facial expression and hence of the higher art of film in general."[21] For instance, "a statement can be retracted or reinterpreted, but no statement is as utterly revealing as a facial expression."[22] Although Balázs had high melodrama in mind when detailing the gestural vocabulary of spasmodic facial cinematography—such as D. W. Griffith's *Way Down East* (1920) and Reinhold Schunzel's *Fortune's Fool* (1921)—his observations resonate vividly with early film's carnival of laughing heads *en gros plan* ("in close view"). From the very first films, giant faces bombarded the screen. Fred Ott "achooed" into the kinetoscope in 1894's four-second *Record of a Sneeze* and then all hell broke loose.

Kissing films, funny face-making films, stop-motion decapitation films: no extremity of the human face could ever satisfy the hungry gaze of the hysterically laughing early film spectator—who is even swallowed alive by the poser in James Williamson's mouthy farce, *The Big Swallow* (1901). "I won't! I won't! I'll eat the camera first."[23] In this digestive classic, a hostile photophobic subject engorges the camera operator, who leads the viewer on a journey down the man's throat, pulling back just in time to retreat by way of his gob-smacking lips! Meanwhile, "G.A.S. Film Subjects" (a double entendre on the initials of Brighton showman, George Albert Smith) launched a series of "Humorous Facial Expression" comedies, epitomized by *Grandma Threading Her Needle* (1900), in which grandma (Eva Bailey) excruciatingly attempts to place a thread in the eye of her needle. "The facial contortions engaged in are ludicrous to say the least," as Edison's catalog publicized this British "G.A.S. Subject" for the U.S. film market.[24] *Whiskey or Bullets* (1901) was concisely summarized as "a very fine facial study with a surprise at the end," which in the case of *At Last! That Awful Tooth* (1902) results in a grotesque close view of a human dental cavity.²⁵ *That Awful Tooth* in many ways anticipates Mandy's opening close-up in Edison's *Laughing Gas*—head wrapped in gauze, grimacing over her painful toothache.

True to form, *Scandal Over the Tea Cups* (1900) depicts "two maiden ladies at afternoon tea [who] relate shocking secrets of society with mingled horror and pleasure depicted by their expressions."²⁶ If eyes are the window to the soul, spasmodic blinking provides a pipeline to deliciously juicy gossip. "Many a face surprises us with a deeper look, as if gazing out at us through the eyes of a mask," mused Balázs in his discussion of morality and facial physiognomy in silent cinema.²⁷ Early face-making farces such as *Grandma* and *Scandal* do not indicate psychological depth (from behind society's laughing masks) as much as they evoke intense visual curiosity about the magnified extremities of the image's surface. They bespeak a "concept of 'depth' . . . hiding in plain sight," as Karen Redrobe and Jeff Scheible navigate surface and depth turns in *Deep Mediations*, a volume that follows the ever "shifting and uncertain boundaries" of film theory in the thick of rapidly mutating media interfaces.²⁸ How can the frisky free play of mouthy images give vivid visual form to cinema's volcanic transformations of physical reality? This is precisely the question posed by early cinema's rogues' gallery of glorious Medusan laughing heads!

They further bear witness to the enduring critical powers of early film objecthood, which will always remain timely and resonant for the exploding crises of the present: because, really, what is *it*? "Under the camouflage of comedy," early cinema "fulfills desires and dreams by projecting images of liberation, equality, and revenge," proclaims the archivist Mariann Lewinsky—in the context of a French comedy in which an angry kitchen maid rapturously breaks dishes for two and a half minutes.²⁹

From blowing up the kitchen to gurning (i.e., making grotesque silly faces) at the audience members, that cathartic impulse toward physiognomic mischief is further exemplified by *A Bucket of Cream Ale* (AM&B, 1904), in which a Black woman pours a bucket of cream ale over the head of a white Dutch man who harasses her.³⁰ Though it's a lost film with an unidentified lead, perhaps this woman was played by Bertha Regustus (of *Laughing Gas*), who we know also headlined in other sexual revenge comedies such as *The Servant Girl Problem* (Vitagraph, 1905) and *What Happened in the Tunnel* (Edison, 1903), where she tricks a white male masher into kissing her and then laughs in his face.

Female funny heads served as stand-ins for a larger social vortex in which the still burning critical question—now what *else* can film do?—was promiscuously explored and obsessively pursued. Curiosity about human faces and their relation to gender trickery sparked the desire to crash-land into the surface of the

FIGURE 9.2 Victoire (the actress is unidentified) breaks all the dishes in a burst of anger over the course of several minutes. Frame enlargement from *Victoire a ses nerfs* [*The Nervous Kitchen Maid*] (Pathé, 1907). Image courtesy of the British Film Institute.

screen, unleashing the contradictory politics of the medium's unruly aesthetics. The "Medusa-like gaze," offers Noa Steimatsky in *The Face on Film*, "is not altogether disenchanting. In roundabout ways, it can stir our subjectivity, awakening archaic desires and modern anxieties."[31] In that spirit, *Lettie Limelight in Her Lair* (G.A.S., 1903) displays "on a very clear scale" the "final abandon" of an aging actress "who removes her wig with joy" upon receiving a love note in her dressing room before a big performance.[32] Her sudden elation precipitates her physical exposure as these two events converge on the enlarged canvas of her face. At once a celebration of frontal laughter and punitive betrayal of Medusan faciality (i.e., the star "out of the limelight"), *Lettie Limelight in Her Lair* projects conflicting desires to inhabit the "the skin of the film" (as Laura U. Marks poses this temptation) while maintaining a critical distance through mockery—to experience laughter as simultaneously solicitous and supercilious.[33] The humorous close-up reaches its corporeal limit when something unseemly is divulged: a human eye, a broken tooth, a scandalous secret, or the sheer gymnastics of attempting to shave with a dull razor (as in *A Dull Razor*) or to smoke a spoiled cigar (as in *The Bad Cigar*).[34]

Early films could have gone anywhere—why zero in on the grotesquerie of the unruly face? Tom Gunning nicely encapsulates this impulse as the medium's "gnostic mission" (its revelatory visual drive), which became "especially evident in the conjunction between the cinematic device of the close-up and the subject of the human face."[35] To probe the face promised to disclose the true person—as Steimatsky paraphrases Georg Simmel, "the human face at once veils *and* unveils the soul."[36] Emblematic facials drew on a long line of aesthetic models in expressive physiognomy: from Johann Kaspar Lavater's woodcuts to Guillaume Duchenne de Boulogne's "neuropathologic photographs" (see chapter 1).[37] The art and technology of facial portraiture sought to establish a universal grammar for linking specific expressions to the assorted emotions behind them, further entangling itself with eugenic projects to divine racial superiority by way of cranial measurement. Early cinema's "gnostic mission" inherited these pernicious ideologies and blew them to smithereens through the spectacle of hysterical laughter.

To embrace or to destroy—to seize or to liberate? Early film's funny faces wore those conflicting impulses on their sleeves, exemplified by *The Four Troublesome Heads* (Star-Film, 1898) in which Georges Méliès literally wears his head on his sleeve after decapitating, duplicating, and juggling his own face.[38] But that voracious curiosity (to collide into the facial image) also belied an overwhelming sense of "instability and perversion of magnitude, of bodily scale," as Mary Ann Doane argues in *Bigger Than Life*, further posing "the problem of the threshold, of the surface or screen as limit, as barrier."[39] As Doane notes—via *The Man with the Rubber Head* (Star-Film, 1901), in which Méliès inflates his own head until it explodes—the encroaching confrontation between the camera and its subject put "into crisis the distance between screen and spectator."[40] Watch out for that laughing mouth, hysterical spectator, lest you fall down its throat!

Was there any limit to the film spectator's desire to merge with the spasmodic surface of the image? Close-ups carry "the threat of a certain monstrosity," adds Doane, "a face or object filling the screen and annihilating all sense of scale," such as the chastised masher who "runs toward the camera" at the end of *The Drenched Lover* (R. W. Paul, 1900).[41] But laughter also marks an exception to that anxiety about cine-sensorial boundaries, I would insist, because violating the screen barrier was precisely the point. Remember *Variety*'s skewering of Vitagraph's *Laughing Gas*, which left the sight gag of irresistible laughter "all on the sheet."[42] Unlike Méliès's exploding head or Sam Dalton's ravenous mouth (in *The Big Swallow*), we want to be infected by the hysterical image of unruly hilarity; otherwise, its visibility risks becoming uncanny or simply a failure.

EMBLEMATIC LAUGHTER AND HYSTERICAL POSING

What happened to the laughing head between 1900 and 1907—from funny face-making larks such as *Grandma* and *Scandal* to the dueling hysterics of the two *Laughing Gas* titles? The head started to shrink into the formations of the diegesis, foretold by *Come Along, Do!* (R. W. Paul, 1898), which Ian Christie heralds as "the earliest surviving fiction film to create narrative continuity between successive shots."[43] In an age-old tale of libidinal comeuppance, a rural couple visits a museum where their modern encounter with ancient nude sculpture results in a violent conflict between a voyeuristic husband and his angry wife, whose "most amusing expression" is pictured in a long shot across two consecutive tableaux.[44] (The couple is played by the filmmaker and his wife Ellen Paul, a retired dancer who also oversaw daily operations for the company.[45]) It is odd that such an ardent evangelist for facial close-ups like R. W. Paul would hold his own wife's amusing expressions at a visual distance (in order to keep the nude Venus statue and ambient artwork in view). Evicted from its outlandish proportions by the steamy mise-en-scène, the funny face migrates elsewhere.

It "wanders around the diegesis, with no fixed abode," Noël Burch remarks cheekily in reference to the rise of the emblematic shot. Livio Belloi further connects the facial genre's obsolescence (displaced by multishot continuity) to its spectacular resurrection at the extremities of the reel.[46] Around 1903, the frontal head was decapitated from the world of the film (the diegesis), affixed to "close-ups or semi-close-ups of faces [that] were used as introductory or ending shots in the early story films, shots that are 'about' the story but not integral to it," as Eileen Bowser explains in *The Transformation of Cinema*.[47] If physiognomy regarded human faces as emblematic signifiers of the totality of a person, early 1900s filmmaking paraded them as "metonymy for the whole film," according to Susan Hayward, when "placed at the end of the film to sum up what had just been seen."[48] Like a visual "punctuation point," adds Richard Abel, "sometimes still a full-figure shot, sometimes a waist-up or bust-shot," its emphasis remains on the face's spasmodic convulsion.[49]

Burch attributes the earliest "emblematic shot" (his coinage) to *The Great Train Robbery* (Edison, 1903), a Western holdup sensation that closes with a ghoulish, enlarged view of the Bandit shooting his gun directly at the viewer (after he is killed in the last scene of the narrative).[50] The *New York Clipper* advertised this film as a "faithful imitation of the genuine 'Hold Ups' made famous by various outlaw bands in the far West... which fact will increase the popular interest in this great HEADLINER."[51] Bald puns aside, the emblematic shot became a guarantor of both physical immediacy and topical significance. As a novel device, it allowed films to pivot smoothly from diegetic distance to thrilling proximity—from the narrative frame of the film into the world beyond the screen, which its frontal posers were assumed to inhabit. Big heads bookended reels (such as *Laughing Gas*) that otherwise contain only long views without alterations in scale, angle, or camera placement, let alone inserts of facial reactions.

Female laughing heads—decapitated from their respective bodies by the encroaching proximity of the close-up—differed in crucial ways depending on the context, especially when woven into the narrative thread of the film. For example, *Mary Jane's Mishap* (G.A.S., 1903) depicts the facial mischief of a kitchen maid who pours too much paraffin wax on the fire and spontaneously combusts through the chimney. The film integrates close-ups of Mary Jane's funny expressions into the arc of her catastrophic self-immolation.[52] After winking at the viewer, Mary Jane (Laura Bayley) explodes through the chimney, her dismembered body pieces rain down from the sky, and then she rises up briefly as an ectoplasmic ghost to haunt her own grave, which reads: "Here lies Mary Jane ... Rest in Pieces." The film does not circle back to Mary Jane's emblematic face making (as do many other G.A.S. comedies from this time) but concludes with her bodily disappearance, as she vanishes into her own burial plot. Are her frisky close-ups really emblematic shots when absorbed so seamlessly into the film's piecemeal diegesis?

Rather than put my thumb on the scale, I would emphasize the enlarged head's emblematic trajectory: from smoking gun (in *The Great Train Robbery*) to female laughing face. Burch notes that, by 1906, "the smiling face of the heroine" dominated the practice, which film historians have lamented as a woeful symptom of incipient screen fetishism.[53] Scott Bukatman further claims (with reference to Laura Mulvey) that "the emblematic shot of early cinema quickly becomes gendered, presenting the spectacle of the woman existing apart from the diegesis."[54] However, the Medusan laughers who headlined early film comedies were a far cry from the decontextualized eroticism of classic Hollywood's sparkly vixens and scantily clad torch singers.[55] Let us explore!

High Ladders and Low-Hanging Fruit

To describe what I view as an emblematic example, *When Cherries Are Ripe* (Rossi & Co, 1907) enacts a familiar scenario of a working woman harassed by a male masher. She climbs a ladder to pick ripe cherries from a tall tree, which a male bystander exploits by threatening to remove the ladder unless she "permit[s] him to 'pick a cherry' from her lips."⁵⁶ Unimpressed, she tricks the masher by luring him up a tree to retrieve *more cherries*, at which point she seizes the ladder and saunters away, "leaving him up in the air, wildly gesticulating for relief."⁵⁷ Released the same month as Edison's *Laughing Gas*, the film ends with a frontal image of the woman's victorious laughter. In the wake of her own barely averted assault, the last scene presents a "colored and close view of [her] munching cherries and mischievously winking and smiling at the audience as she decorates her ears and neck with ripe cherries."⁵⁸ Tinted or stenciled presumably with bright red dye, the cherries symbolize her "ripe" sexuality, which she happily ingests with metaphorical abandon.

Indeed, why end the film there rather than up the tree with the exasperated masher? His frantic gestures are certainly evocative of many holdover facials, such as *Hair Soup, or The Disappointed Diner* (R. W. Paul, 1903), in which "a man expresses his disgust in a most vivid manner" at discovering a rogue hair in his hot soup.⁵⁹ Or *A Shave By Installments on the Un-Easy System* (R. W. Paul, 1905), which ends with a man "making hideous grimaces" (face plastered in blotchy cream) while spasmodically attempting to shave.⁶⁰ In contrast, *When Cherries Are Ripe* summarizes itself with the scene of female oral revelry—not kissing in submission (as in *Spooning* or *Cohen's Fire Sale*⁶¹) or enacting punitive revenge (à la *Tramp and the Typewriter*⁶²), but with celebration and enjoyment: "mischievously winking and smiling at the audience."⁶³ As an image that stands apart, the emblematic shot asserts its power to affirm or reframe all that precedes it. In that spirit, the woman in *When Cherries Are Ripe* eats up the easy metaphor of the film's own suggestive title.

Feminist film scholars might raise the objection, as Judith Mayne does (in a different context) in *The Woman at the Keyhole*, that "'resistance' here should not be read as an alternative female-centered vision."⁶⁴ Mayne refers to *A Subject for the Rogue's Gallery* (AM&B, 1904), a short lark in which a female criminal's spastic facial contortions defy her visual exposure by cinema's "gnostic mission"—here, to equate expressive physiognomy with inveterate criminality. By female-centered vision, Mayne specifies films made by women, representing women's ambitions and desires, and that align the camera's look with female gazes within the diegesis (with the camera eye rather than the frontal mouth). As Linda Williams describes the last shot included in some prints of *Rogue's Gallery*, there is a "remarkable moment in which the grimacing and then crying woman, thinking that her role in the film is over, resumes a more normal, relaxed expression and then smiles."⁶⁵ An early iteration of the emblematic addendum, *A Subject for the Rogue's Gallery* portrays the Medusan face as "more normal" by comparison to its prior, wayward mug shot. Whereas *Rogue's Gallery* climaxes with a track onto the grimacing woman (before her improvised outtake), most emblematic views append films that contain no other close-ups.

What did it feel like to encounter these wild gazes exploding on-screen? To be confronted by an excessive view of laughter is to be infected by the visual sensorium of cinema—not an evil eye but a "carnal thought," to invoke Vivian Sobchack's phenomenological account of how "our lived bodies" are "always also mediated and qualified by our engagement with other bodies and things."[66] This is precisely what Sobchack means by "embodiment" as opposed to direct sensory experience; embodied viewers defy the illusion of self-continuity with allegedly unmediated movements and objects. Short-circuiting the "binary split between image and body," Sobchack highlights the "*somatic intelligibility*" of the film image via the "*somatic intelligence* of the spectator's body that is more than primitive reflex" in "What My Fingers Knew."[67] In that vein, the spectator's body becomes a treasure trove of somatic knowledge—in contrast to the passive certainty ensured by the classical screen image—when faced with such evocative encounters as the woman erotically munching her cherries.

The libidinal symbolism of *When Cherries Are Ripe* is rather low-hanging fruit, so let us pivot to the spectacle of eating, which Kyla Wazana Tompkins associates with the racial formations of political subjecthood. In her book *Racial Indigestion*, open mouths "speak, eat, and laugh with the energy generated by suppressed political affect" as sites "*to which* and *within which* various political values unevenly adhere."[68] Early cinema's emblematic mouth attempted to speak as a political subject but not in the vein of those wise-cracking lips of later narrative talkies, whereby the audible word is always subordinated to the transparent truth of the eye. (The gendered gaze here is understood as an ideological effect of the visual relations that attend to material realities of social power.) To return to *Laughing Gas*, Mandy's hysterical laughter intervenes between the sight gag of the film and its contagious appeals to the material world. To see her face is not to know her but to become somatically involved with her, an irresistible gamble of early cinema's laughing carnival.

I'll Eat Your Funny Face!

When did the laughing face of "humorous expression films" recede into the animated photography of the emblematic shot? We might date the split to around 1901, the year when *Big Swallow* took sweet cinematic revenge against its own camera operator by supposedly eating him in a trick jump cut. In fact, commercial photographers often tempted posing subjects with images of food (and other "happy objects") to compel their cheerful attention, as Tanya Sheehan details in "Look Pleasant, Please!"[69] Sheehan recounts the racist practices deployed to gin up affective warmth during the long, grueling exposure times of mid-nineteenth-century photography. For example, Charles Gallup promised to "make you look happy" (despite not feeling happy), which he advertised with a racist image of three Black male teenagers eating "a generous slice of the succulent watermelon," allegedly stolen from a white farmer.[70] Dehumanizing caricatures of Blackness thus served to invest photographic images of whiteness with joyful animacy and emotional versatility.

Early cinema's emblematic head bears an uncanny resemblance to that of the slow-burn daguerreotype poser, whose exposure time "ran anywhere from several seconds to several minutes," as Sheehan notes, "depending on the light conditions and materials used."[71] It's almost as if the laughing head had time traveled back to the 1870s, when iodine-sensitized copper plates rendered "transient (e)motions nearly impossible to record," making "good feelings especially difficult to conjure up and fix under the skylight."[72] If only sitting subjects could have recharged their batteries with unruly face making rather than holding that pose in near hypnotic stasis—to avoid scrambling their likeness during its gradual inscription. Sitters were thus forced to suspend their spontaneous animation, lest the camera capture an unsightly transition between gestures.

We might say that the emblematic shot offered a retroactive corrective to the daguerreotype's agonizing tedium. Facial gestures frozen in anticipation could at last unspool at length, as celebrated by Florence Turner's comical grimacing at the finale of *Daisy Doodad's Dial* (Florence Turner, 1914)—a film that thematizes the feminist politics of humorous face making.[73] Quarantined in her room like many a "hysterical woman," Daisy (Florence Turner) has vivid nightmares that a procession of her decapitated heads wanders over her supine body; the film then concludes with a satisfying emblematic close-up of Turner's own skillful facial mimicry and gestural spasms. (Turner was famous for her raucous impersonations as a beloved stage performer.[74]) In a relatively late and self-reflexive use of this technique, *Daisy Doodad's Dial* juxtaposes the film's emblematic end to its decapitated middle, meditating on its own narrative digestion of animated portraiture. Just after Daisy awakens in isolated terror, Turner herself assumes the screen with her defiant "dial" (British slang for "face"), entrancing the spectator with her skillful gurning (face-making).

But where do we draw the line between emblematic laughter and integrated posing? In its aesthetic autonomy, the emblematic shot allowed performers to

FIGURE 9.3 Daisy Doodad (Florence Turner) gurns at the spectator. Frame enlargement from *Daisy Doodad's Dial* (Florence Turner, 1914). Image courtesy of the British Film Institute.

indulge in taboo behaviors, even after their characters had been disciplined for those very antics within the frame of the narrative. Look no farther than Léontine, our favorite teenage miscreant and pseudonymous French series clown![75] After acquiring a massive bouquet of inflated balloons, Léontine (Titine) "takes flight" (in *Léontine Takes Flight*[76]) and cruises airborne over Nice trailed by a frantic mob of angry onlookers. Eventually, they shoot down her balloons with loaded pistols, popping enough of them to deflate her crazy joy ride. Titine is forcefully chastised for her destructive exploits, evoking the farcical violence that curtails many comical escapades such as *Explosion of a Motor Car* (Hepworth, 1900), *The Gay Shoe Clerk* (Edison, 1903), and *Humorous Phases of Funny Faces* (Vitagraph, 1906). These films always devolve into miniature apocalypse: the car explodes, the masher is beaten with an umbrella, and an animated portrait is violently defaced (literally rubbed out) by the hand of a cartoonist, respectively. In contrast, Léontine's emblematic close-up has the last laugh: she poses with her payload of balloons, restored to their glorious aeration, encircling her head like Medusan tresses as she sticks out her tongue, thumbs her nose, kisses her loot, and appears *entirely unchastised*.

FIGURE 9.4 Léontine (the actress is unidentified) laughs at the spectator as her beloved helium balloons encircle her head like Medusan tresses. Frame enlargement from *Léontine s'envole* [*Léontine Takes Flight*] (1911; Nice: Pathé). Image courtesy of Gaumont-Pathé Archives.

The final seconds of *Daisy Doodad* can likewise be read as a token of reassurance for its Medusan laughing spectator—female face making can now proceed apace without risk of being hystericized. In contrast, Daisy's compulsive convulsions are called into question by both the film's cinematography (in its use of multiple exposures to depict her ghoulish "dial") and its cohort of male characters, who gaslight Daisy with their relentless sanism. The emblematic closer, however, does not entirely negate the film's social message that female faces (and bodies) will continue to pose unresolvable crises for a male-dominated public sphere. When it comes to the politics of Medusan laughter, as Léontine and Daisy remind us, it seems one can never have enough heads.

Medusa's Extra Head: Emblematic or Diegetic?

Medusan close-ups exhibited two divergent impulses at the crossroads of cinema's spectacle-based visibility versus its narrative assimilation. First, the head was emblematized, as we have seen, and decapitated from the world of the film. *The Whole Dam Family* (Edison, 1905) celebrates the unmotivated views of all eight Dam family members, who laugh, chew gum, smile, smoke, bark, and sneeze into the lens, their mug shots adapted from popular lithographs and comic postcards.[77] The whole damn Dam family's crazy heads enframe the film's narrative antics but do not permeate them—they remain unintegrated and visually distinct, much like the two tramps "floating through the clouds" (as viewed through a magician's telescope) at the finale of *Fakir and the Footpads* (R. W. Paul, 1906).[78] Nor do their heads explode onto the place of the spectator, as in so many of R. W. Paul's early frivolities such as *The Egg-Laying Man* (1896), *Artistic Creation* (1901), The *Muddled Bill Poster* (1901), and *Chinese Magic Extraordinary* (1900), in which a Chinese magician's "head grows larger and larger, and his body smaller, as he flies towards the spectator."[79] What makes it emblematic rather than integrated or even endemic is that the head itself stands apart.

Second, the laughing head swallows up the diegesis, often episodically. To explain what I mean, I will describe an irrefutable example. *Madame's Cravings* (Alice Guy-Blaché, 1906) burlesques the amusing maternity cravings of a pregnant woman who wanders around a public park stealing and ingesting various treats, including a child's lollipop, a wino's glass of absinthe, a beggar's pickled herring, and so forth. After each scene of oral arousal, the film cuts to a close view of Madame eagerly devouring her illicit snack. Like the emblematic shot, these views *look different* from the rest of the film—mise-en-scène falls by the wayside, the location becomes indistinct, and visual depth is flattened. Madame here appears in front of a white background, sitting in medium close-up so her purloined pleasures remain visible under her chin as she slurps and noshes. In fact, *Madame's Cravings* does not end emblematically but reproductively: Madame gives birth to her new baby in a trick cut, harvesting it from a cabbage patch in a throwback to Alice Guy's *The Cabbage Fairy* (Gaumont, 1896?). No longer pregnant, she saunters away—spouse and offspring in tow.

We might say that the film eats its own tail: Madame's laughing head bears a logical connection to each preceding image, which she engorges. If the close-up's earliest iterations were taken as "monstrous, grotesque, or castrating," according to Doane, they began to provide "crucial element[s] of characterization in the service of the narrative" by around 1907.[80] We see those expressive tensions at work already in *Madame's Cravings*, whose Medusan close-ups threaten to eat the patriarchy alive! The example of *Laughing Gas* is a bit more complicated because the contagious mouth becomes visually solicitous to the spectator only at the end of the film. Stewart views it as part of a "brief but important moment of disruption, in which a Black presence challenges—at thematic and stylistic

FIGURE 9.5 Pregnant Madame (the actress is unidentified) drinks absinthe in an orally evocative medium close-up. Frame enlargement from *Madame a ses envies* [*Madame's Cravings*] (Alice Guy-Blaché, 1906). Image courtesy of the Library of Congress.

levels—the expectations of white characters and audiences across separate lines of action."[81] The segregation of Mandy's laughing head from the contagious exploits of her roving body encapsulates these two divergent paradigms of cinema, which often became interwoven by way of the mouth.

In that vein, *Madame's Cravings* mobilizes the mouth in order to displace the eye, straying from its visual roots in the feminist "keyhole" film: naughty views intended for arcade machines (rather than theatrical projection) that were sometimes addressed to a female look.[82] Breaking the mold, *Indiscreet Bathroom Maid* (Pathé, 1902) appeals to the visual pleasures of a mischievous working woman who sneakily spies on her customers in a Turkish bathhouse. It is a voyeuristic exercise in sexual curiosity, presented from the vantage point of a Medusan employee. Her unsuspecting victims include an older lady undressing, a man getting his toenails clipped, and a portly gentleman who shoves an attendant into the tub—all pictured at a distance in long shots. Less pornographic than certain male "keyholes," the real visual payoff comes with the cut back to the maid, who laughs hysterically and then energetically pantomimes the naughty scenes we've just witnessed: the unrobing, toenail clipping, and tub splash. A spasmodic embodiment of reactive narration, her full-bodied laughter elongates the visual joke (in lieu of enlarging it); she reveals to us how even crude slapstick gags might inhabit our flesh—from eye to limb.

Madame's Cravings, in contrast, vacuums the eye into the spectacle of the mouth. An "occasion for establishing the difference between the powers of the visual and the powers of the poetic," the mouth speaks to unresolvable tensions between the "figural" and the "textual."[83] Andrea Gyenge locates "something so unlikely as a mouth" at the heart of the problem of aesthetic philosophy because its "fleshy, corporeal" materiality often stands in the way of its utility as a vehicle for language and abstract expression.[84] To chomp or to chat? To emote or to articulate? The laughing, eating, twitching, spasming mouth posed a threshold orifice for filmmaking's dual imperative to narrate stories through discontinuous images and to revel in the madness of sheer oral mayhem. When the laughing head looks back at the spectator, what does it see—beyond the digestion of its own image? Two Medusan lips, interfacing together, with no end in sight.[85]

INTERREGNUM—FACES AND PLACES

Laughing, winking, gurning heads ran roughshod over the surface of the early film screen. As facials rapidly faded in their initial popularity, their gleeful grimaces continued to crop up in the most unlikely places. What is a sun or a moon if not also a hysterical cranium? Iconized by the mouthy satellite who has its left eye gouged by the explorers' rocket ship in *A Trip to the Moon* (Star-Film, 1902), a moon face enjoys celestial intercourse with a compulsively winking sun in *The Eclipse* (Star-Film, 1907), and even catches Mandy's contagious laughter from outer space in *Laughing Gas*. But it's the "grinning and grimacing moon face" who has the last laugh in *The Thieving Umbrella* (Gaumont, 1907), throwing lunar shade at a penniless organ grinder whose "athletic wife" beats him for arriving home late (and still penniless).[86] Before dissolving into a moon face, the "thieving umbrella" makes away with a gamut of ill-gotten goods (a baby carriage, a basket of food, a billboard), leaving the hapless organ grinder to take the rap—condemned as a thief but ever bereft.

The mystic umbrella seems to be a promising object at first, with its chaotic potential to redistribute wealth and raise hell on behalf of the working class. But all it wreaks in the end is further marital violence, containing its astronomic appeals (to fly away with the loot) to the taunting surface of a mischievous crescent.

(In a very different vein, a "magic umbrella" creates a crisis of overproduction for an unfortunate housemaid played by Little Chrysia in a 1913 French comedy, *Zoe's Magic Umbrella*.[87]) An emblematic mouth par excellence, the umbrella is also a vestige of cinema's own double-edged appetite to capture "the unknown and previously unseen" and to exploit those views as pretenses for colonial and materialist expropriation. Such thieving instruments will soon render planet Earth "an uninhabitable wasteland and Mars the site of real-estate speculation," as James Leo Cahill and Luca Caminati foretell in *Cinema of Exploration*.[88]

Anthropomorphized beaming objects served as ominous indications across a variety of early film locations and genres. The façade of an unoccupied cottage is struck by lightning and transforms into a grotesque, eye-rolling scowler in Segundo de Chomón's *The Haunted House* (Pathé, 1908), bewitching several travelers in a series of uncanny happenings. The film appropriately ends with a giant demonic head who eats the visitors while they cower in bed, which spins in circles and shrinks in proportion to the visual enlargement of that monstrous mouth. "It seems to many theorists [that] to extract the face from any recognizable diegetic space [is] to in effect make it spaceless."[89] Doane poses cinema's "love affair with the face" against its "potential for a derangement of scale" by "a space that has no referent"[90]—an ambivalent fascination that aligns filmmakers as disparate as Esfir Shub and Lois Weber, or Kira Muratova and Lucrecia Martel. The uncanny antics of early cinema's laughing heads—from floating "dials" to moon-faced umbrellas—reveals just how deeply that antagonism between spatial orientation versus proximate decapitation was baked into the medium from its wily formations, epitomized by the British drivers who take a joyride around the rings of Saturn under the eye of a smirking moon in W. R. Booth's *The '?' Motorist* (R. W. Paul, 1906).

Through the vehicle of the face, mused the so-called Master of Darkness, Fritz Lang, "film reveals itself as the rhapsodic poet of our time." Lang asks, "[H]ow much can be expressed in the twitching of a closed mouth, in the rising and falling of an eyelid, in a head gently turning away?"[91] Indeed, to Lang's question, how much and *what exactly* was expressed by the facial frenzy of a monk "evidently relishing" his lunch of macaroni in reverse motion (in *The Monk's Macaroni Feast*), or the gargantuan head that "fills the entire picture and appears as though it would swallow the whole audience" at the end of *The Haunted Curiosity Shop* (R. W. Paul, 1901)?[92] In early facials and their immediate successors, the sight gag of convulsion alone sufficed, as in *A Study in Facial Expression* (R. W. Paul, 1898) when a woman reads a "naughty story" in the paper and actively struggles to square her "assumed vexation and real amusement."[93] Would the meaning of her "most laughable" contortions have been resolved by the exposure of their unseen trigger: the "naughty story" (which is never pictured)?

Or perhaps her conflicted, semi-illegible expressions go beyond the revelation of any taboo object. Unlike *Madame's Cravings*, which eats the preceding image in lieu of reacting to it, free-floating facials often withheld the offending view entirely, which would no doubt have been outmatched by the galvanic face itself. Long live cinema of the funny face!

AFTER THE FLOOD: MORE LAUGHTER

The desire to penetrate human faces as psychological gateways to alternate narrative realms courses through the history of cinema—from to the Hollywood melodrama *A Woman's Face* (George Cukor, 1941) to the horror-thriller *Eyes Without a Face* (Georges Franju, 1960) to the feminist documentary *Faces Places* (Agnès Varda, 2017). "The face is a power: it is compelling, and it confronts; it imposes and orients the gaze; it alters the world within purview," explains Steimatsky.[94] As we know, the facial largely receded into the emblematic shot by the early 1900s, typified by Rosalie's (Sarah Duhamel) taunting laughter and eye-rolling close-up in the final seconds of *Rosalie Moves In* (Pathé, 1911). After demolishing an apartment building and nearly decapitating a fellow tenant, Rosalie is hoisted up through the broken floorboard by her furious neighbors, who have her bound by the hands and suspended in midair. But her gurning close-up gets the last word: placed in front of decorative wallpaper, Duhamel makes funny cross-eyes and then bursts into hysterical laughter.

Many such "transitional" comedies—poised between early/frontal and classical/invisible styles—gave emblematic encores to their rambunctious female performers, whose characters blow up the house (if not the whole universe!). Lea (Lea Guinchi) rises from behind a stack of books and laughs at the spectator in the closing seconds of *Lea and the Ball of Wool* (Cines, 1913), following her extremely destructive spree to locate a missing ball of wool, which (as we see) had been affixed to her rear the whole time. Unflappable Titine poses demonically with her toy boat in *Léontine's Boat* (Pathé, 1911), in which she floods the entire house in a spontaneous gesture to sail her miniature fleet indoors. In countless films from this period, women rebel against their domestic confinement by making the home uninhabitable: flooding it; incinerating it (sometimes both at once, as in *Léontine Guards the House*); or simply smashing all the dishes, knocking over the cupboards, and crashing through the ceiling, as in *The Unfortunate Housemaid* (Pathé, 1913), *Pétronille's Monkey* (Éclair, 1913), and *Léontine's Vacation* (Pathé, 1910).

At the end of *Léontine's Boat*, torrents of water storm through the ceilings while all the residents seek cover under large pieces of furniture. The emblematic shot surfaces in the wake of the flood: Titine blows kisses at the spectator, laughs maniacally, and floats on a wooden barrel next to her prized vessel. The shot is both de-spatialized (is the whole house in shambles?) and unmistakably marked by the wreckage. Abstracted from any concrete location, her beaming face looks ahead in the aftermath of her self-willed apocalypse. Unlike "the angel of history" ("mouth open," eyes glued to the past as he is propelled onward), Titine faces toward the future—to something hopeful, less barbaric in its catastrophe than mere technological "progress" or (at the very least) less tedious than gendered bourgeois domesticity and unending housework.[95]

IN THE BELLY OF THE BEAST: CONTAGIOUS FACES BOMBARD THE DIEGESIS

What happens when the funny face insinuates itself in the diegesis? Its conniptions become affectively contagious! Uncontained to the emblematic edges, faces exhort bodies to endure the most ghastly physical torments, all for the pleasure of witnessing their ludicrous reactions. To that end, *Onions Make People Weep* (Gaumont, 1907) integrates close views of sobbing faces (à la "comical grimaces") with a loose narrative about the spread of contagious crying, whose agent is eventually discovered to be a hidden bag of onions.[96] Laughter and tears are not isomorphic: they exist on a spectrum, and by the end of the film every character erupts in senseless hysterics.

The contagious hilarity of facial travesty offered abundant material for early film slapstick, perfected by Mandy's transmissible laughter in *Laughing Gas* and enacted in countless other short comedies. With titles like *The Yawner* (Pathé, 1907), *That Fatal Sneeze* (Hepworth, 1907), *A Contagious Nervousness* (Gaumont, 1908), *Contagious Nervous Twitching* (Pathé, 1908), and *Cayenne Pepper in a Street Cab* (Selig, 1903), any ordinary gesture or mild symptom could easily bulldoze the whole metropolis. For example, anger germinates from a husband and wife's domestic squabble in *A Contagious Nervousness* but quickly spreads to essential workers and eventually barnyard animals. A yawning man in *The Yawner* convulses an inanimate statue into a spastic tableau-vivant, while a gentleman wearing itchy woolen skivvies transmits his hysterical scratching to his office coworkers, fellow streetcar passengers, and even movie spectators in *An All-Wool Garment* (Essanay, 1908). No facial tic or nervous spasm was off-limits for the comical sight gag of destructive contagion, further motivating the facial's traversal of vast geographic spaces and assorted narrative scenarios.

As a self-reflexive gambit, the facial promised and threatened to infect the body of the laughing spectator, an ambivalence incited by *Rosalie and Léontine Go to the Theatre* (Pathé, 1911), where our two favorite hellcats raise a ruckus at Les Capucines playhouse. A good portion of the film is simply devoted to depicting their convulsive malfeasance in a medium long shot as Rosalie and Léontine rock back and forth, flail their limbs, pound their fists, gasp with amazement, and howl with ear-splitting laughter. They would appear to be having epileptic seizures were it not for the obvious facial evidence of their cathartic enjoyment. The film reportedly "convulsed the audience" in Rhodesia, "caused screams of laughter" in Bombay, and was hailed as a "laughter-maker pabulum" in Gloucestershire, England.[97] Its strong, affective appeals exemplify the cinematic dangers of hysterical contagion, feared to "surpass the theatrical drama in suggestive power" and to exert a "demagogic influence over the masses," as a German medical scientist warned (in a differently pantomimic context).[98]

Cinema's incipient love affair with spasmodic grotesquerie became an occupational hazard of its rising popularity: a conquest to be disciplined but an unavoidable attraction all the same. *The Country School Teacher* (Lubin, 1912) provides an object lesson in the fumigation of contagious Medusan laughter. Like Titine, Molly Mason is an impossible child, idolized by her peers as a "captain of disorder." Her wild, throaty laughter gives voice to her ecstatic disobedience. When a pious new schoolteacher attempts to mollify Molly "with gentle firmness," she laughs in his face. "She continues rebellious, stubborn, and even revengeful," until "her rebellious spirit is [tragically] broken." In effect, "Molly becomes a woman," falling in love with the very man "she hated . . . for beneath her wild exterior he knew lay admirable qualities if she would only . . . allow herself to be what God had made her," per *Moving Picture News*.[99] A far cry in the end from the infernal tomboy Titine, who laughs hysterically at the climax of nearly every episode—electrocuting the police, flooding the house, uncaging a lion, igniting an indoor fireworks display—Molly submits to "fright and pity" and becomes the tender "helpmate of man."[100] Her laughter is muffled lest it give any ideas to the spectator.

LAST LAUGHS BEFORE THE END

As filmmaking began to deploy facial close-ups to cut within a scene, human faces became the connective tissue for conjoining differentiated views (from the

1910s onward). For example, Mabel (Mabel Normand) hides under a bed with her dog inside a stranger's hotel room while escaping from a drunken tramp (Charlie Chaplin) in *Mabel's Strange Predicament* (Mabel Normand, 1914), which alternates her close-up with a long shot of the bedroom to underscore Mabel's awkward immobility and comic distress. The emblematic shot, in contrast, is entirely uninterested in either the problem of spatial confinement or the potentials of cinematic mobility. It may follow on the heels of chaotic chase scenes in which vehicles explode, kitchen maids wage general strikes in the streets, and ill-fated lovers fly away to the moon. But even when the close-up has the last laugh (which it often does), it relinquishes any implication in the film's narrative trajectory or fantasy of social movement. Convulsive faces become fatally severed (if not decapitated) from the cinematic temptation to wander.

Relevant instances abound but I will limit myself to several. *The Female Cab Drivers* (Pathé, 1907) follows a destructive spree of feminist action (both professional and geographical) across a variety of urban locations when the wife of a drunkard coach driver takes up the reins after her spouse returns home "soused to the eyeballs." The film wraps in a police station, at which point order is restored. The closing emblematic shot, however, revives the collective mischief of the temporary cab drivers. Two women smoke pipes together; one tells the other a joke, and both break into hysterical laughter, which is interrupted by the film's cut to black—a vanishing snippet of their ascending hilarity. In that spirit, *Fear of Shadows* (Pathé, 1911) burlesques a typical race-to-the-rescue melodrama and its manipulative conventions. A paranoid wife trapped in a house frantically telephones for help after she spies dangerous shadows projected on the wall. Pathé's parody unfolds as a triptych split screen: the wife cowers near the phone, a blasé police commissioner does desk work, and the husband repeatedly falls off his bicycle while attempting to arrive in the nick of time. In the end, the shadows were *real* but deceptive—a woman (played by Léontine) and her sweetie had been merrily engaging in target practice with toy guns. The film's gendered crisis of movement—fueled by the misrecognition of an ominous image—falls by the wayside in the final emblematic shot, which squeezes the heads of all six characters into the frame as they laugh hysterically and make silly faces at the camera.

There are no "shadows" to fear (no disorienting angles or sinister, off-screen spaces) in the emblematic shot, which holds its curiosities to the spasmodic surfaces of the face—free to let loose in convulsive bliss as long as that desire to move remains within the rectangular guardrails of the frame. Hysterical immediacy in exchange for bodily mobility: that was the wager of the emblematic interregnum in the uneven history of gendered film narration. The racial

FIGURE 9.6 Six characters laugh and make funny faces in the film's closing emblematic shot. Frame enlargement from *La peur des ombres* [*Fear of Shadows*] (Pathé, 1911). Image courtesy of EYE Filmmuseum.

politics of that bargain were notoriously fraught—from *Laughing Gas* to *Mixed Babies* (Biograph, 1908), a chase film comedy about consumerism and maternity. Written by D. W. Griffith, *Mixed Babies* depicts the chaos unleashed by a department store's new "baby check service" during a fire sale on infants' wear. In the opening scenes, Mrs. Jones (a white woman) adopts a white baby, setting the stage for eugenic panic about racial kinship and maternal possession.

The gags in the film are nothing new; identity confusion motivates racist laughter in countless silent comedies, such as *Nellie the Beautiful Housemaid* (Vitagraph, 1908), *An Up-to-Date Squ*w* (American Kinema/Pathé, 1911), and *Squirrel Food* (Warner Bros., 1921).[101] It is unsurprising that the "Black" mother in *Mixed Babies* is played by what appears to be a white actress in blackface. "When the film ends, however," as Charlene Regester notes, "two women (one white and one actually Black) are foregrounded onscreen, both holding their rightful infants."[102] Now that racial order is restored, Blackness can finally exist on-screen. But who was this uncredited Black actress and where had she been during the rest of the film?

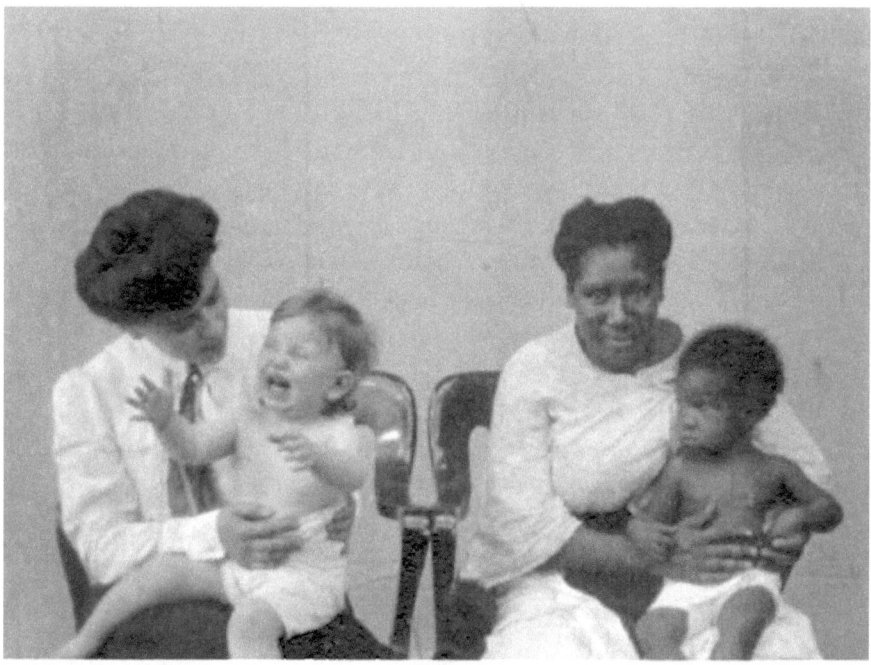

FIGURE 9.7 A white mother and a Black mother (both actresses are not identified) hold their babies in the film's closing emblematic shot. The Black woman's gaze briefly addresses the camera. Frame enlargement from *Mixed Babies* (Biograph, 1908). Image courtesy of the Library of Congress.

The closing emblematic shot of *Mixed Babies* lasts for about twenty-three seconds: the white and Black mothers sit side-by-side, each tending to their own baby.[103] Only the Black mother looks directly at the camera, which she does repeatedly, fixing her smiling gaze at the spectator for several seconds just before the film ends (per the one surviving copy preserved by the Library of Congress).[104] True to form, the final shot breaks from the aesthetic schema of the film itself, in which the full-body visibility of racial difference marks the condition of possibility for comedic action. But the Black mother's frontal gaze pulls back on the brink of hysterical absurdity, asserting her fellow humanity in lieu of indulging in silly or grotesque face making. As Elyse Singer notes, Black performers in early cinema often "resisted perpetuating" the "mad associations" between minstrelsy tropes and "carnivalesque grimaces."[105] An enigmatic (rather than emblematic?) close-up—cut off from the racial logistics of the diegesis of *Mixed Babies*—the final shot leaves no further clues as to its context.

NOW YOU SEE HER...

By the late 1910s, the emblematic shot had become obsolete (even *Daisy Doodad's Dial* was a holdover in 1914). Where did its glorious Medusan countenance go? Evicted to the outer limits of the reel, it reappeared as the so-called China Girl. Genevieve Yue places this liminal figure "at the margins of film" but at "the heart of" her book *Girl Head*. What is a China Girl? Sometimes called "a girl head," according to Yue, "a woman (despite the nomenclature, she is typically white . . .) is posed, in close-up, in front of swatches of black, white, gray, and various reference colors."[106] Adopted in the 1920s—about a decade after the initial decline of the emblematic shot—the China Girl provided a reference image for film projectionists to calibrate the color, tone, density, and other qualities of the image.

It thus exceeds the realm of representation (because it's barely detectable by the spectator) but "nevertheless has a profound effect on the look of every commercially produced film," argues Yue, " 'touching' everything a viewer sees, even if not in a way that can be readily recognized."[107] Yue expansively pursues the complex entanglement between film's gendered looking relations (which have long set the agenda for feminist film theory) and the politics of unseen female labor that undergirds film's materiality. As the field of feminist film historiography continually turns its head from "libidinal looks" and "uncanny gazes" depicted on-screen to the invisible gendered labor that props up the whole shebang, liminal specters such as the "girl head" (from Medusan emblematic shot to pro forma China Girl) have come to loom large.

Indeed, it was typical at the time for actresses to perform uncredited domestic and creative labor on the film set—everything from cooking meals and sewing costumes to concocting gags and devising scenarios.[108] We see traces of their prodigious efforts in the emblematic shot itself, reflexively depicted by *The Cook Wins* (Rossi & Co., 1907). An Italian comedy about competitive matrimony, *The Cook Wins* closes with "an enlarged view" of a kitchen maid "feeding [a] human monster," who is none other than her husband: he chooses her over an accomplished painter, a poet laureate, and a concert musician because he enjoys her cooking.[109] *The Cook Wins* "vanishes into sheer materiality," to repeat Yue's evocative word play because the film itself does not survive. We do not even know the identity of the actors, let alone who prepared the food engorged by the "confirmed bachelor" (that "tickled his palate" and goaded his libido).[110] Like *When Cherries Are Ripe* and *Madame's Cravings*, it is a comedy about cinema's desire to eat the image itself. Perhaps the uncredited prop cook was also the very actress who played the maid and whose own head may or may not have appeared alongside that of the "human monster" during his final feeding—it is unspecified whether her face is in view or only her hands.

What's a Medusan head to a laboring hand? Eat the camera, milk the baby, smoke the pipe, shoot the viewer, dismember the barber—just don't forget: (much like the ending of *Haunted Curiosity Shop*, where a ballooning head threatens to "swallow the whole audience") the emblematic reverse-shot converges onto the unsteady seat of the open-mouthed spectator.[111]

EMBLEMATIC AFTERLIVES; OR, DID SOMEBODY SAY ZOOM?

There can be no doubt that the emblematic head would feel right at home in a Zoom meeting, where the burdens of exhausted facial expressivity eat away at the desire for physical intimacy and affective immediacy. Not only is the mono-channel audio design of Zoom anathema to the sonic contagions of collective laughter (only one voice can be audible at a time), but the panoptic self-view feature ensures that everyone is habitually aware of their own sad floating mug (or "dial," British slang for face, as *Daisy Doodad* would have it). This does not make Zoom a purely dystopian throwback to the agonizing duration of the daguerreotype. After all, one can simply turn off their webcam. Even to err and gesticulate spasmodically for all to see in the Zoom room holds relatively low stakes, especially considering that Zoom is a telephonic mirror as much as a window onto other human faces—a "facial alphabet soup," as Alice Maurice describes it.[112]

Yet the Medusan afterlives of early film face making still possess and bedevil this ominous new medium, whose greatest contingencies range from "Zoombombing" to accidental self-pornography to surreal feline metamorphosis. With that last point, I refer to the infamous Zoom proceeding of a civil forfeiture case in February 2021 in which a Texas lawyer mistakenly turned on his "cat filter," a visual accessory that temporarily transforms one's human visage into that of a cat. "I'm not a cat," protested Rod Ponton, who is now simply known as "the cat lawyer."[113] The cat fiasco harkens back to early facials such as *An Over-Incubated Baby* (R. W. Paul, 1901), which exploits the "extremely humorous" expressions of a "sorrow-stricken mother" whose newborn infant prematurely ages into a "very old man" due to a haywire heat lamp that explodes in his incubator.[114] It further evokes not the cat lawyer but *The Foxy Lawyer* (Gaumont, 1910), a comedy about a criminal lawyer whose long-winded "eloquence" gives rise to "exceedingly mirth provoking examples of expressive faces," which the film depicts in an extended panorama around the courtroom.[115] And, of course, mention must be made of *The Sick Kitten* (G.A.S., 1903), *The Mouse in the Art School* (G.A.S., 1902) and *Aylesbury Ducks* (G.A.S., 1905), which end by filling the entire screen with emblematic images of a cat, a mouse, and a duck, respectively.[116]

That wild spirit of spontaneous transformation and hysterical faciality that saturated early film images and revolutionized aesthetic experience is not absent from Zoom meetings—it is simply lost on them. "I don't know of anything more superbly grotesque than the *very comical* spectacles of the Cinema," raved Ricciotto Canudo in 1908. "There are extravagant apparitions, the likes of which no magician could ever create, and sudden transformations of movement and figuration."[117] Against all odds, Zoom reveals its contradictory drive to generate unforeseen excitation in the very gesture of maintaining its grip on ordinary life, raising evocative parallels to the long obsolete emblematic shot. "Zoom promises much more than seamless video," observed Neta Alexander early in the COVID-19 pandemic, "it promises a sense of normalcy, routine, and connection during a crisis characterized by limited mobility."[118] But it has also left the door open to unannounced Zoombombers—white supremacists, misogynists, Nazis, and viral conspiracists—while sowing anxieties about intellectual property, privacy, and corporate surveillance. "We might control the frame—but we don't direct the movie," as Alexander puts it.[119]

Whereas the exhilaration of early cinema hinged on leveraging grotesque spectacle to detonate stilted tradition (from Medusan heads to demonic housemaids), the best hope for Zoom is uninterrupted transmission—with minimal fascist/facial calamity. Or is it? As the history of emblematic shots reminds us, even floating heads still dream of flying away.

Conclusion

Laughter, Hysteria, Power—Then and Now

I'm facing jail time after laughing at Jeff Sessions. I regret nothing.

—Desiree Fairooz[1]

Indelible in the hippocampus is the laughter, the uproarious laughter between the two . . . having fun at my expense. They were laughing with each other. I was underneath one of them while the two laughed.

—Christine Blasey Ford[2]

The power of hysterical laughter is that you can never be sure of its meaning. In contrast, weaponized mockery draws the battle lines of authoritarian rule and resistance, epitomized obscenely by the Donald Trump administration. In January 2017, a Code Pink protester laughed out loud during Senator Jeff Sessions's cabinet confirmation hearing and was forcibly ejected from the building. She then faced up to a year in prison and $2,000 in fines. All charges against Desiree Fairooz were eventually dropped because, as Washington, DC Judge Robert Morin decided, her laughter "would not be sufficient" grounds to bring the case to a jury, and it was "disconcerting" that the government had made such a plea in its closing arguments.[3]

A precursor to the pervasive "criminalization of the uterus," the repressive policing of feminist "hysterical" laughter did not bode well for the democratic mobility of the womb.⁴ Amid the rapid dismantling of *Roe v. Wade*, public scandal involving the gender politics of tendentious ridicule nearly derailed a Supreme Court nominee whose vote became instrumental to repealing reproductive rights.⁵ "Indelible in the hippocampus is the laughter," as Christine Blasey Ford memorably testified at Brett Kavanaugh's Supreme Court of the United States (SCOTUS) confirmation hearing in 2018, several decades after having been assaulted by two jocular, affluent, white male teenagers.⁶

Forcing women to carry a fetus to term is yet another dystopian tactic for confining the uterus and its wayward autonomy—whether out of state to secure a safe abortion, out of the body via gender-affirming surgery, or "hither and thither in the flanks" to reclaim the nonconformist behavior that has long been

FIGURE C.1 "Turkish women defy deputy PM with laughter. Bülent Arinç said women should not laugh in public, prompting backlash and highlighting state of women's rights in Turkey." *Guardian*, July 30, 2014. Screen grab by author.

abjected as "hysterical" since the ancient times of Galen, Aretaeus, and Hippocrates.[7] The hysterics of female enjoyment persist as global flashpoints of culture war struggle, exemplified by the thousands of Turkish women who posted videos of themselves laughing uproariously in 2014 after Bülent Arinç, a senior minister of Recep Tayyip Erdoğan, had attempted to outlaw women's laughter in public. Women "should know what is decent and what is not decent," Arinç admonished. "She should not laugh loudly in front of all the world and should preserve her decency at all times."[8] In response, the onomatopoeic hashtag "kahkaha" steamrolled the internet with Medusan images of Turkish women's laugh-out-loud protest.[9] Carol Williams proclaimed in the *Los Angeles Times*: "Turkish women find official's rebuke of female laughter hilarious!"[10] Or as one anti-Erdoğan candidate put it, "Our country needs our women to laugh and to hear everyone's joyful laughter more than ever."[11] Feminist jouissance against authoritarian moral repression!

DEATH OR DEFAMATION? THE FEMINIST POLITICS OF LETHAL LAUGHTER INSURANCE

To bring this book full circle, it is no longer absurd that an online insurance advertiser would prey on anxieties about exorbitant laughter by targeting comedians whose jokes allegedly "REALLY kill."[12] Though "comedians and the like thrive on making their audience members laugh," *Trusted Choice* shares, "there's always a slight chance that their material could end up doing more harm than good ... even fatally so."[13] Of course, no mention is made of the risqué material that risks inciting such dangerous extremities of unruly mirth. Would the laugh that "REALLY" kills be necessarily indigestible by a genocidal capitalist world system? Or would its taboo violence merely "punch down," further immiserating marginalized communities unsheltered from the apocalyptic wages of power? "Jokes themselves don't cause bigotry" but "they certainly help to perpetuate these prejudiced belief systems," argues Raúl Pérez in "When Bigoted Humor Isn't Just a Joke," detailing how transgressive comedy is used to justify racist, anti-trans, homophobic, and gynocidal intolerance in everyday life.[14]

Self-proclaimed "edgy" and uncensored comedians widely lament that so-called cancel culture is "killing comedy" by driving away commercial sponsors (i.e., deflating the profit margin of bigoted humor).[15] But it is the patriarchal revanchists who take feminist joke tellers to court. For example, the stand-up comedian Louise Beamont (aka Reay) faced £30,000 in damages plus legal fees after skewering her estranged husband and satirizing the collapse of their marriage in her 2017 show *Hard Mode*. He sued for libel; she defended her comedic freedom of speech, while her lawyer reportedly told the *Guardian* that "the case could rest on the judge's sense of humor."[16] As Rebecca Krefting explains, "[W]hat's notable about these new, louder [feminist] voices is that they aren't stifling free speech (that bludgeon so often used by incorrectness defenders). They're creating more."[17] Simply put, expanded free speech is actively censored in the name of regressive comedic license. Legally speaking, it is much riskier to be a woman on-stage joking about marriage or sexual intimacy than a patriarchal provocateur spewing hateful generalizations about gender, trans personhood, #MeToo, and the feminist movement.

What's so evocative about the idea of death by laughter insurance is that it isolates laughing physiology from the tendentious semantics of joke telling. Among their laundry list of potential medical complications, *Trusted Choice* covers gelastic seizures, ruptured brain aneurysms, asphyxiation, asthma attacks, cardiac arrest, and syncope, whereby "excessive laughter" triggers a lack of "proper blood flow to the brain."[18] Imagine the comedic specimen behind such a burst! Would it consist of lazy, taboo obscenities? Or perhaps existential dentistry puns? Or the jouissance of headless philosophy? *Trusted Choice* opted not to put its thumb on the scale.

But this is precisely where *hysteric laughter* holds the most promise. In cutting the tie that binds comedic gatekeeping to convulsive catharsis, the contagious spread of wild laughter—whose shared meaning defies identity, ideology, or satirical disbelief—excites affective openings for sustaining the hell-raising momentum of anti-institutional thought. Or, as a (likely fictitious) woman named Barbara Barr once put it in the throes of an eight-hour-spree of uncontrollable cachinnation, "If only humans were born without teeth!!!" (We are, you know.)

Notes

INTRODUCTION

1. Christine Lacagnina, "Does Your Stand-Up Act Need Death by Laughter Insurance?," Trustedchoice.com, August 10, 2019, https://www.trustedchoice.com/insurance-articles/opinion-variety/insurance-against-death-by-laughter/.
2. Lacagnina, "Does Your Stand-Up Act?"
3. Lacagnina, "Does Your Stand-Up Act?"
4. "Killed By a Joke," *Kalamazoo Gazette*, November 16, 1893, 2.
5. "Off the Wires for and About Women," *Trenton Evening Times*, May 29, 1916, 11.
6. "Laughed Herself to Death," *Daily People* (New York, NY), May 12, 1906, 1.
7. "Theatre Insures Patrons Against Deaths by Laughs," *Exhibitors Herald*, August 20, 1927, 47.
8. "Insurance Policy Big Help to Allan," *Moving Picture World*, May 9, 1925, 193. "Lord Chumley," *Edmonton Journal*, April 17, 1925, 10. Here and in many places throughout the book, the quoted text appears in large capitalized letters in the print advertisement, in this case from the *Edmonton Journal*.
9. Tom Kennedy, "Exploitorials," *Exhibitors Trade Review*, May 5, 1923, 1139.
10. The Week Staff, "Sunda Croonquist: A Comic Sued by Her Mother-in-Law," *The Week*, January 8, 2015.
11. Paige Gawley, "Charlize Theron Was Hospitalized for Five Days After Laughing Too Hard While Watching 'Borat,'" *ET News*, May 2, 2019.
12. Gawley, "Charlize Theron Was Hospitalized."
13. Jason Levine, "10 Crazy Insurance Policies (That Actually Exist!)," HarryLevineInsurance.com, March 26, 2019, https://www.harrylevineinsurance.com/10-crazy-insurance-policies-that-actually-exist/.
14. Lacagnina, "Does Your Stand-Up Act?"
15. Lacagnina, "Does Your Stand-Up Act?"
16. As of 2022, the estimated global net worth of the insurance industry is $5.356 trillion, which is estimated to reach $6.39 trillion by 2025. See Jennifer Ruddin, "Gross Premiums Written by the Insurance Industry Worldwide (in Trillion U.S. Dollars)", Statista, May 2, 2023, https://www.statista.com/statistics/273156/gross-premiums-generated-by-the-insurance-industry-worldwide-since-2006/
17. Neil Postman, *Amusing Ourselves to Death: Public Discourse in the Age of Show Business* (New York: Viking, 1985), 3–4.

18. Postman, *Amusing Ourselves to Death*, 16.
19. Joanna Weiss, "Reality TV Has Remade Our Politics: But Just for One Party," *Politico*, July 17, 2021.
20. See Renée Pastel and Michael Dalebout, "Truths-to-Come: Investigating Viral Rumors in 'Q: Into the Storm," *NECSUS Journal* (Spring 2022).
21. "The superego imperative to enjoy thus functions as the reversal of Immanuel Kant's *"Du kannst, denn du sollst!"* (You can, because you must!)—it relies on a "You must, because you can!" See Slavoj Zizek, *The Parallax View* (MIT Press, 2009), 310.
22. "Reconciled laughter resounds with the echo of escape from power; wrong laughter copes with fear by defecting to the agencies which inspire it. It echoes the inescapability of power." See Max Horkheimer and Theodor Adorno, "The Culture Industry," *Dialectic of Enlightenment*, trans. Edmund Jephcott (Redwood City, CA: Stanford University Press, 2002), 54.
23. Lauren Berlant, *Cruel Optimism* (Durham, NC: Duke University Press, 2011).
24. Lauren Berlant and Sianne Ngai, "Comedy Has Issues," *Critical Inquiry* 43, no. 2 (2017): 236.
25. Jared N. Champion and Peter C. Kunze, *Taking a Stand: Contemporary US Stand-Up Comedians as Public Intellectuals* (Jackson: University Press of Mississippi, 2021); Raúl Pérez, *The Souls of White Jokes: How Racist Humor Fuels White Supremacy* (Redwood City, CA: Stanford University Press, 2022); Matt Sienkiewicz and Nick Marx, *That's Not Funny: How the Right Makes Comedy Work for Them* (Berkeley: University of California Press, 2022).
26. Rachael Healy, "'I've Had Men Rub Their Genitals Against Me': Female Comedians on Extreme Sexism in Stand-Up," *Guardian*, August 5, 2020.
27. Glenda Carpio, *Laughing Fit to Kill: Black Humor in the Fictions of Slavery* (Oxford: Oxford University Press, 2008), 231.
28. Maya Angelou, "The Mask." Watch a recording of her performing "The Mask" in 1987: https://www.youtube.com/watch?v=CN9DN_PImy8.
29. Elaine Showalter, *The Female Malady: Women, Madness and English Culture, 1830–1980* (New York: Pantheon, 1985).
30. "Comments on Film Subjects. The Police Band," *Moving Picture World*, December 19, 1908, 500.
31. "An Oddity That Is The Mummy," *Moving Picture World*, March 4, 1911, 454.
32. "Killed By a Joke," *Kalamazoo Gazette*, November 16, 1893, 2; "Laughed Herself to Death: Louisville Woman's First Merriment in Months is Fatal," *The Sedan Lance* (Sedan, KS), May 18, 1906, 6; "That Denver Woman," *Dallas Morning News*, September 16, 1904, 6.
33. Georges Bataille, "The Practice of Joy in the Face of Death," *Visions of Excess: Selected Writings, 1927–1939*, ed. and trans. Allan Stoekl, with Carl R. Lovitt and Donald M. Leslie Jr. (Minneapolis: University of Minnesota Press, 1985), 236.
34. Hélène Cixous, "The Laugh of the Medusa," trans. Keith Cohen and Paula Cohen, *Signs* 1, no. 4 (Summer 1976): 878.
35. "Almost Laughed Herself to Death," *Times-Picayune* (New Orleans, LA), January 21, 1912, 13.
36. The Lexicon of Festus, *De verborum significatu* (*On the Meaning of Words*); The Festus Lexicon Project at University College London is working to make this "fragmentary and mutilated text" usable again. See https://web.archive.org/web/20130112064549/http://www.ucl.ac.uk/history2/research/festus/index.htm.
37. Mikhail Bakhtin, *Rabelais* (Bloomington: University of Indiana Press, 2009), 408. Most of his examples draw on citations from antiquity, compiled in fifteenth-century anthologies of death that were of special interest to Rabelais.
38. Bakhtin, *Rabelais*, 91.
39. François Rabelais, *Gargantua & Pantagruel* (Derby: Moray Press, 1894; Project Gutenberg, 2004), "Chapter 4. XVII.—How Pantagruel came to the islands of Tohu and Bohu; and of the strange death of Wide-nostrils, the swallower of windmills," https://www.gutenberg.org/files/1200/1200-h/1200-h.htm.

INTRODUCTION 285

40. @depthsofwiki, "just had to be there," Twitter, May 17, 2022, https://twitter.com/depthsofwiki/status/1526545363355705344. This account is run by Annie Rauwera, writer, comedian and "Wikipedia influencer."
41. Maggie Hennefeld, "Looking for Léontine: My Obsession with a Forgotten Screen Queen," *Los Angeles Review of Books*, September 24, 2019.
42. "Laughs Herself to Death Over Joke of Husband," *The Columbus Enquirer-Sun* (Columbus, GA), September 21, 1911, 2.
43. Lauren Le Vine, "Once Upon a Time in Hollywood: Women Cutting Through Bullshit for a Century," *Refinery29*, December 26, 2019; Shelley Stamp, *Movie-Struck Girls: Women and Motion Picture Culture After the Nickelodeon* (Princeton, NJ: Princeton University Press, 2000), 8.
44. "Gleanings and Gossip," *The Springfield Daily Republican*, December 23, 1891, 15.
45. "Laughed Herself to Death. Telling Funny Stories Fatal to a New York Woman," *The Savannah Tribune*, December 23, 1911, 1.
46. Margaret Atwood, "Writing the Male Character," Hagey Lecture, University of Waterloo, February 9, 1982.
47. "Editorial Comments," *The Philadelphia Inquirer*, March 22, 1911, 8.
48. Margaret I. MacDonald, "Impressions Gathered from a Visit to the Fourteenth Street Theater," *Moving Picture News*, October 14, 1911, 16.
49. Madeline Lane-McKinley, *Comedy Against Work: Utopian Longing in Dystopian Times* (Philadelphia: Common Notions Press, 2022), 4.
50. A brief note on the geographical parameters of this project, which are not strictly bounded by national or linguistic borders. I engage with the materials I have been able to access in the archive and with texts that are animating lively conversations in my field and among my interlocutors. On the question of affective contagion and global solidarity politics (especially in chapter 6), I consider a wide scale of geopolitical contexts. By "disproportionately intersectional," I mean contradictorily driven by the limits of my own subject position and the necessity of solidarity-based universalisms in ways that cannot yet be resolved in language or thought.
51. "Heart Disease from Laughter," *English Mechanic and World of Science: No. 1749*, September 30, 1898, 156–157.
52. "Heart Disease from Laughter," 157.
53. "Heart Disease from Laughter," 157.
54. "Laughs Herself to Death. Jokes of a Girl's Chums Were Too Much for Her—Heart Overtax'd and Stops Working," *The Anaconda Standard* (Anaconda, MT), April 13, 1907, 13.
55. "Death from Laughter," *New York Tribune*, October 4, 1897, 2.
56. *Isabel de Barsas: A Tradition of the Twelfth Century* (by anonymous author), vol. 1 (1823) (Nineteenth Century Collections Online, 2017), 65.
57. Charles Baudelaire, "Of the Essence of Laughter, and Generally of the Comic in the Plastic Arts," in *Baudelaire; Selected Writings on Art and Artists*, trans. P. E. Charvet (Cambridge: Cambridge University Press, 1981), 150–151.
58. Rabelais, *Gargantua & Pantagruel*, chap. 4.
59. Bataille, "The Practice of Joy in the Face of Death," 236.
60. Axel Munthe, *The Story of San Michele* (New York: E.P. Dutton, 1932), 296.
61. See the mission statement of HYSTERICAL FEMINISMS: https://hystericalfeminisms.com/about/.
62. Hélène Cixous, "Sorties: Out and Out: Attacks/Ways Out/Forays," in *The Newly Born Woman (La Jeune Née, 1975)*, trans. Betsy Wing (Minneapolis: University of Minnesota Press, 1986), 95.
63. Anna Furse, *Performing Nerves: Four Plays, Four Essays, On Hysteria* (London: Routledge, 2020).
64. Cecily Devereux, "Hysteria, Feminism, and Gender Revisited: The Case of the Second Wave," *English Studies in Canada* 40, no. 1 (March 2014): 41.

65. Sigmund Freud, *Jokes and Their Relation to the Unconscious*, trans. James Strachey (New York: Norton, 1960), 207.
66. Walter Benjamin, "A Look at Chaplin," in "Walter Benjamin and Rudolf Arnheim on Charlie Chaplin," trans. John McKay, *The Yale Journal of Criticism* 9, no. 2 (Fall 1996): 311.
67. Gustave Le Bon, *The Crowd: A Study of the Popular Mind* (1895), 2nd ed. (New York: Macmillan, 1897), xviii.
68. "Sandy McPherson's Quiet Fishing Trip," *The Film Index*, October 17, 1908, 14.
69. "A Boom in Prices," *The Birmingham Age Herald* (Birmingham, AL), October 25, 1895, 2.
70. "Play to the Ladies," *The Nickelodeon*, February 1909, 34.
71. Miriam Hansen, *Cinema and Experience: Siegfried Kracauer, Walter Benjamin, and Theodor W. Adorno* (Berkeley: University of California Press, 2012), xvii.
72. "'Skigie' Discovers a New Sort of Girl: Says She Loudly Laughed at Julius Tannen to Make Everybody Look at Her . . . ," *Variety*, February 20, 1909, 18.
73. "A Dull Knife," *Moving Picture World*, October 23, 1909, 558.
74. Ben Singer, "Modernity, Hyperstimulus, and the Rise of Popular Sensationalism," in *Cinema and the Invention of Modern Life*, ed. Leo Charney and Vanessa Schwartz (Berkeley: University of California Press, 1995), 72.
75. Charles Gibson, "Moving Pictures Curing Insanity," *The Nickelodeon*, November 1, 1910, 253.
76. "Biograph An Insanity Cure. A Chicago Asylum Experiment with Moving Pictures," *Kansas City Star*, April 9, 1904, 1.
77. Mario Umberto Masini and Giuseppe Vidoni, "The Cinematograph in the Field of Mental Illness and Criminality: Notes" (1915), in *Early Film Theories in Italy 1896–1922*, ed. Franesco Casetti with Silvio Alovisio and Luca Mazzei (Amsterdam: Amsterdam University Press, 2017), 290.
78. Masini and Vidoni, "The Cinematograph," 290.
79. Lacagnina, "Does Your Stand-Up Act?"

1. HYSTERICAL LAUGHTER ON THE BRINK OF ENJOYMENT

1. "Canadian Woman's Hysterical Laughter Is a Viral Hit," *AOL World News*, January 13, 2017, https://www.aol.com/article/news/2017/01/13/canadian-womans-hysterical-laughter-is-a-viral-hit/21654682/.
2. Rachel Bishop, "Woman's Hilarious Reaction to Daughter Struggling Across Ice Is So Funny Her Laugh Is Being Made into a Ringtone," *Mirror*, January 10, 2017, https://www.mirror.co.uk/news/world-news/womans-hilarious-reaction-daughter-struggling-9595622.
3. Bishop, "Woman's Hilarious Reaction."
4. Leitch Ritchie, "The Balance of Life," *Daily Atlas* (Boston, MA), March 19, 1850, 1; *The Gazette of the Union, Golden Rule, and Odd Fellows' Family Companion, Volume 12* (New York: Crampton and Clarke, 1850), 197–199.
5. Charles Baudelaire, "Of the Essence of Laughter, and Generally of the Comic in the Plastic Arts," in *Baudelaire; Selected Writings on Art and Artists*, trans. P. E. Charvet (Cambridge: Cambridge University Press, 1981), 150–151.
6. Baudelaire, "Of the Essence of Laughter," 150–151.
7. Baudelaire, "Of the Essence of Laughter," 154–155.
8. See also Peter Quennell, ed., *The Essence of Laughter: And Other Essays, Journals, and Letters* (Santa Cruz, CA: Meridian, 1956).
9. Sianne Ngai, *Ugly Feelings* (Cambridge, MA: Harvard University Press, 2005), 1.
10. Ngai, *Ugly Feelings*, 271.

11. Ngai, *Ugly Feelings*, 271.
12. "Warning the Vendors of Spoiled Eggs," *Evening Journal* (Jersey City, NJ), March 9, 1872, 4.
13. *Isabel de Barsas: A Tradition of the Twelfth Century* (by anonymous author), vol. 1 (1823) (Nineteenth Century Collections Online, 2017), 65.
14. *Isabel de Barsas.*
15. Maturin Charles Robert, *The Albigenses: A Romance* (London: Hurst, Robinson, 1824), 112.
16. "Married but Not Mated," *New York World*, September 13, 1870, 2.
17. "From Robert Swinhoe," August 4, 1868, via Darwin Correspondence Project, https://www.darwinproject.ac.uk/letter/DCP-LETT-6303.xml.
18. "Unwritten Music," *Cincinnati Chronicle and Literary Gazette*, May 23, 1829, 1.
19. "The Cruise of the Midge," *Blackwood's Magazine*, October 3, 1834, 1–2.
20. Oliver Optic, *Fighting Joe; Or, The Fortunes of a Staff Officer. A Story of the Great Rebellion* (Boston: Lee & Shepard, 1893), https://www.gutenberg.org/files/59429/59429-h/59429-h.htm#ch05.
21. Optic, *Fighting Joe.*
22. Optic, *Fighting Joe.*
23. Lauren Berlant, "Humorlessness (Three Monologues and a Hairpiece)," *Critical Inquiry* 43, no. 2 (Winter 2017): 308.
24. Berlant, "Humorlessness," 308.
25. James Russell Lowell, "Leaves from My Journal in Italy and Elsewhere," in *American Prose (1607–1865)*, ed. Walter C. Bronson (Chicago: University of Chicago Press, 1916), 577; Immanuel Kant, *Critique of Judgment* (Mineola, NY: Dover Publications, 2004), 133; Helmuth Plessner, *Laughing and Crying: A Study of the Limits of Human Behavior*, trans. James Churchill and Marjorie Grene (Evanston, IL: Northwestern University Press, 1970), 77; Arthur Schopenhauer, "Theory of the Ludicrous," in *The World as Will and Representation*, trans. R. B. Haldane and J. Kemp (Boston: Ticknor, 1887), 279–280; Soren Kierkegaard, "Concluding Unscientific Postscript to Philosophical Fragments," in *The Essential Kierkegaard*, ed., Howard V. Hong and Edna Hong (Princeton, NJ: Princeton University Press, 1978), 230–231.
26. Sydney Smith, *Sydney Smith's Sketches of Moral Philosophy* (London: Longman, 1850), 394.
27. Key examples of the sensation novel include: Wilkie Collins, *The Woman in White* (1860), Ellen Wood, *East Lynne* (1861), Mary Elizabeth Braddon, *Lady Audley's Secret* (1862), Ouida (Maria Louise Ramé), *Held in Bondage* (1863), Rhoda Broughton, *Cometh Up as a Flower* (1867).
28. Joan Wallach Scott, *Gender and the Politics of History* (New York: Columbia University Press, 1988), 45.
29. Margracia Loudon, *Fortune-Hunting: A Novel* (London: Henry Colburn and Richard Bentley, 1832), 230.
30. Sara Ahmed, *The Cultural Politics of Emotion* (New York: Routledge, 2004), 177; Marilyn Frye, *The Politics of Reality: Essays in Feminist Theory* (New York: Crossing Press, 1983).
31. Emily Steinlight, *Populating the Novel: Literary Form and the Politics of Surplus Life* (Ithaca, NY: Cornell University Press, 2018), 39.
32. D. A. Miller, "Cages Aux Folles: Sensation and Gender in Wilkie Collins's *The Woman in White*," *Representations*, no. 14 (Spring 1986): 107.
33. Pamela K. Gilbert, *Disease, Desire, and the Body in Victorian Women's Popular Novels* (Cambridge: Cambridge University Press, 1997), 8–9.
34. H. L. Mansel, "Sensation Novels," *Quarterly Review*, 113 (1863): 488–489.
35. Lauren Berlant, *The Female Complaint: The Unfinished Business of Sentimentality in American Culture* (Durham, NC: Duke University Press, 2008).
36. Catherine Day Haynes, *Eleanor: The Spectre of St. Michael's* (London: Minerva Press, 1821). Haynes was a prolific author of popular gothic fiction who contributed serialized stories to *Lady's Magazine*, one of which she published as a novel with Minerva Press: *The Foundling of Devonshire, or Who Is*

She? (1818), followed by *Augustus and Adeline, or, the Monk of St. Barnadine: A Romance* (1819), and then *Eleanor* (1821). Her work was widely read, and it influenced the rise of the sensation novel in the 1860s. See https://blogs.kent.ac.uk/ladys-magazine/2015/08/19/c-d-h-or-catharine-day-haynes-a-gothic-author-for-the-ladys-magazine-and-the-minerva-press/.

37. Haynes, *Eleanor*, 2.
38. Haynes, *Eleanor*, 2–9.
39. Haynes, *Eleanor*, 6.
40. Mention must be made of Sandra Gilbert and Susan Gubar, *The Madwoman in the Attic: The Woman Writer and the Nineteenth-Century Literary Imagination* (New Haven, CT: Yale University Press, 1979).
41. Lyn Pickett notes that *Lady Audley's Secret* spawned nine editions in just three months when it was published in volume form in 1862, "after first appearing as a magazine serial." Lyn Pickett, *The 'Improper' Feminine: The Women's Sensation Novel and the New Woman Writing* (London: Routledge, 1992), 6–7.
42. Gilbert, *Disease, Desire, and the Body*, 8.
43. Ann Cvetkovich, *Mixed Feelings: Feminism, Mass Culture, and Victorian Sensationalism* (New Brunswick, NJ: Rutgers University Press, 1992), 9.
44. Mary Elizabeth Braddon, *Lady Audley's Secret*, Project Gutenberg https://www.gutenberg.org/files/8954/8954-h/8954-h.htm.
45. Braddon, *Lady Audley's Secret*.
46. Braddon, *Lady Audley's Secret*.
47. Berlant, *The Female Complaint*, 40.
48. Lauren Berlant, "Genre Flailing," *Capacious: Journal for Emerging Affect Inquiry* (June 2018), https://capaciousjournal.com/article/genre-flailing/.
49. Berlant, *The Female Complaint*, 40.
50. Berlant, "Genre Flailing."
51. Kyla Schuller, *Biopolitics of Feeling: Race, Sex, and Science in the Nineteenth Century* (Durham, NC: Duke University Press), 3–4.
52. Xine Yao, *Disaffected: The Cultural Politics of Unfeeling in Nineteenth-Century America* (Durham, NC: Duke University Press, 2021), 4.
53. Yao, *Disaffected*, 6.
54. Yao, *Disaffected*, 7–8.
55. James Baldwin, "Everybody's Protest Novel," in *Notes of a Native Son* (Boston: Beacon Press, 1995), 13–23.
56. Harriet Beecher Stowe, *Uncle Tom's Cabin: Life Among the Lowly* (New York: Cosimo Classics, 2009): 311.
57. Ann Douglas, *The Feminization of American Culture* (New York: Farrar, Straus, and Giroux, 1977), 12.
58. Berlant, *The Female Complaint*, 46.
59. Baudelaire, "Of the Essence of Laughter," 157.
60. Baudelaire, "Of the Essence of Laughter," 157.
61. F. Byrdsall, *The History of the Loco-Foco; or Equal Rights Party, Its Movements, Conventions, and Proceedings* (New York: Clement & Packard, 1842).
62. "Young Men's Whig Convention at Lexington," *Louisville Journal Extra*, May 2, 1844, 3.
63. "Young Men's Whig Convention," 3.
64. "An Orphic Utterance," *Boston Courier*, November 3, 1840, 1.
65. Henry Cockton, *Valentine Vox the Ventriloquist: His Life and Adventures* (1840), 36.
66. "Young Men's Whig Convention," 3.
67. Robert Davidson, *History of the Presbyterian Church in the State of Kentucky* (1847), 156, https://archive.org/stream/historyofpresbytoodavi/historyofpresbytoodavi_djvu.txt.

1. HYSTERICAL LAUGHTER ON THE BRINK OF ENJOYMENT ❦ 289

68. Davidson, *History of the Presbyterian Church*, 157.
69. Davidson, *History of the Presbyterian Church*, 157.
70. "Sleeping in the Country," *Hartford Daily Current*, August 15, 1870, 1.
71. "Away from the World in a Utah Canyon," *Plain Dealer* (Cleveland, OH), February 27, 1887, 13.
72. "Loon-Shooting in a Thunder Storm," *Union Democrat* (Manchester, NH), April 27, 1869, 1.
73. "Stories Told by Travelers," *Olympia Daily Recorder* (Olympia, WA), February 15, 1908, 2.
74. Loudon, *Fortune-Hunting*, 230.
75. Charles Darwin, *The Expression of the Emotions in Man and Animal* (New York: D. Appleton, 1872), 196. This was Darwin's third major work, following *The Origin of the Species* (1859) and *The Descent of Man, and Selection in Relation to Sex* (1871).
76. Darwin, *The Expression of the Emotions*, 198.
77. Darwin, *The Expression of the Emotions*, 201.
78. Darwin, *The Expression of the Emotions*, 208.
79. Schuller, *Biopolitics of Feeling*, 29.
80. Schuller, *Biopolitics of Feeling*, 29.
81. Darwin, *The Expression of the Emotions*, 20.
82. Darwin, *The Expression of the Emotions*, 359.
83. Darwin, *The Expression of the Emotions*, 207.
84. Darwin, *The Expression of the Emotions*, 207.
85. Schuller, *Biopolitics of Feeling*, 137. "We find every man endowed with two inlets of impression," claimed Bushnell, "the ear ... and the sympathetic powers, the sensibilities or affections, for tinder to those sparks of emotion revealed by looks, tones, manners, and general conduct." Horace Bushnell, *Unconscious Influence: A Sermon* (London: Partridge and Oakey, 1852), 13–14.
86. Guillaume-Benjamin-Amand Duchenne de Boulogne, *The Mechanism of Human Facial Expression* (Cambridge: Cambridge University Press, 1862, 1990). The text contained over one hundred original photographic plates. It initially had very limited circulation due to the expensive costs of print production.
87. Duchenne, *The Mechanism of Human Facial Expression*, 29.
88. Duchenne, *The Mechanism of Human Facial Expression*, 30.
89. Duchenne, *The Mechanism of Human Facial Expression*, 71.
90. Duchenne, *The Mechanism of Human Facial Expression*, 71.
91. Duchenne, *The Mechanism of Human Facial Expression*, 81.
92. Duchenne, *The Mechanism of Human Facial Expression*, 72.
93. Duchenne, *The Mechanism of Human Facial Expression*, 27–28.
94. Duchenne, *The Mechanism of Human Facial Expression*, 115.
95. Duchenne, *The Mechanism of Human Facial Expression*, 115.
96. For example, he analyzes his own photographic plates of a woman whose facial expressions reveal "the muscle of aggression" through lengthy discussion of Lady Macbeth and comparison to Caravaggio's 1597 *Medusa* painting.
97. Frederic Montagu, *The Ages of Female Beauty* (London: Charles Tilt, 1838), 45.
98. Duchenne, *The Mechanism of Human Facial Expression*, 116.
99. Duchenne, *The Mechanism of Human Facial Expression*, 116.
100. Ahmed, *The Cultural Politics of Emotion*, 359.
101. Anca Parvulescu, *Laughter: Notes on a Passion* (Cambridge, MA: MIT Press, 2010), 66.
102. Darwin, *The Expression of the Emotions*, 207.
103. Darwin, *The Expression of the Emotions*, 207.
104. Darwin, *The Expression of the Emotions*, 207.
105. Frantz Fanon, *The Wretched of the Earth*, trans. Constance Farrington (New York: Grove Press, 1963), 39–40.

106. Fanon, *The Wretched of the Earth*, 35–36.
107. Fanon, *The Wretched of the Earth*, 36.
108. Fanon, *The Wretched of the Earth*, 36.
109. George Beard, *American Nervousness: Its Causes and Consequences* (New York: G.P. Putnam, 1881), 336.
110. George J. Preston, *Hysteria and Certain Allied Conditions, Their Nature and Treatment, with Special Reference to the Application of the Rest Cure, Massage, Electrotherapy, Hypnotism, Etc.* (Philadelphia: Blakiston, 1897), 31.
111. Preston, *Hysteria and Certain Allied Conditions*, 122.
112. Fanon, *The Wretched of the Earth*, 40.
113. Preston, *Hysteria and Certain Allied Conditions*, 122.
114. "In a Chinese Gambling Den," *The Grit* (Washington, DC), August 9, 1884, 1.
115. "Life at Mobile," *Weekly Picayune* (New Orleans, LA), March 8, 1841, 1.
116. Fanon, *The Wretched of the Earth*, 43.
117. The Trail of Tears refers to the forced displacements perpetrated by the U.S. government from 1830 to 1850 after President Andrew Jackson signed the Indian Removal Act in 1830. It uprooted over sixty thousand Native Americans from their ancestral homes, inflicting mass death, illness, and suffering. The trail itself spans over five thousand miles across nine U.S. states.
118. This is not to say that nineteenth-century women's sentimental literature lacked humor or wit or biting satire. See, for example, Kate Sanborn, *The Wit of Women* (New York: Funk & Wagnalls, 1885). Convulsive laughter converged on the pathos of tears while women's wit provoked mirth above cachinnation.
119. Baudelaire, "Of the Essence of Laughter," 160.
120. Baudelaire, "Of the Essence of Laughter," 161.
121. Herbert Spencer, *Illustrations of Universal Progress; A Series of Discussions* (New York: Appleton., 1875), 194–209.
122. "Religions of the People. Hinduism: Funeral Rites," *Demerara Daily Chronicle* (Georgetown, Guyana), January 7, 1883, 3.
123. E. A. de Cosson, *The Cradle of the Blue Nile: A Visit to the Court of King John of Ethiopia*, vol. 1 (London: J. Murray, 1877), 251–252.
124. de Cosson, *Cradle of the Blue Nile*, 251–252.
125. "The Scramble for Africa" (or "Rape of Africa") refers to the period of New Imperialism from 1881 to 1914, by the end of which over 90 percent of the African continent had been violently divvied up, colonized, and occupied or mined for resources by the Western European powers: Belgium, Britain, France, Germany, Italy, Portugal, and Spain.
126. bell hooks, "Eating the Other: Desire and Resistance," *Black Looks: Race and Representation* (Boston: South End Press, 1992), 21–39.
127. Ann Laura Stoler, *Race and the Education of Desire: Foucault's History of Sexuality and the Colonial Order of Things* (Durham, NC: Duke University Press, 1995), 7.
128. See also Lisa Lowe, *The Intimacies of Four Continents* (Durham, NC: Duke University Press, 2015); Rey Chow, *Primitive Passions: Visuality, Sexuality, Ethnography, and Contemporary Chinese Cinema* (New York: Columbia University Press, 1995).
129. See Michel Foucault, *The History of Sexuality, Volume 1: An Introduction* (New York: Vintage, 1990), 103–115.
130. W. Page McIntosh, "Hysteria in the Male," *Medical News* 48 (January 1886): 6.
131. Donald Fleming, "Attitude: The History of a Concept," *Perspectives in American History*, vol. 1 (Cambridge, MA: Harvard University Press, 1967), 287.
132. "Hysterical," *Oxford English Dictionary*, 3rd ed. (Oxford: Oxford University Press, 2020); "Five Reels of Hysterical, Hilarious Merriment," *Courier & Argus* (Dundee, Scotland), May 18, 1925, 6.

133. "May Irwin's Great Hit," *Boston Daily Advertiser*, September 22, 1900, 5; "May Irwin's New Play," *The New York Times*, Sept 22, 1900, 7.
134. "Hysterical," *Online Etymology Dictionary*, https://www.etymonline.com/search?q=hysterical.
135. "Hysterical," *Oxford English Dictionary*.
136. "Hysterical," *Oxford English Dictionary*.
137. "Hysterical," *Oxford English Dictionary*.
138. "Hysterical," *Online Etymology Dictionary*, https://www.etymonline.com/search?q=hysterical.
139. "Warning the Vendors of Spoiled Eggs," 4.
140. "An Episode," *Daily Evening Herald* (Stockton, CA), September 11, 1873, 3.
141. "An Episode," 3.
142. "An Episode," 3.
143. "An Episode," 3.
144. "Hysterical laughter," "laughed hysterically," "hysterical laugh," *Google Books Ngram Viewer*, http://books.google.com/ngrams. Google Ngram is a search engine that tracks word frequencies using digitized books and periodicals published from 1500 to 2008.
145. I have consulted literary and medical periodicals, including *Gale Primary Sources, Dickens Journals Online, Nineteenth Century Serials Edition, Internet Library of Early Journals, British Medical Journal, MacMillan's Magazine*, and *Contemporary Review*.
146. "Fun at the Bijou," *Boston Herald*, May 20, 1884, 2.
147. "Amusements: Nye and Riley," *Daily Nebraska State Journal*, April 3, 1889, 7.
148. A brief note on method, I used digital keyword searches to compile a broad range of relevant examples. When expedient and/or possible, I read texts in their entirety and across their juxtapositions. Context and critical understanding are essential to the art of archival "rag-picking." See also "Amusements," *Daily Bee* (San Francisco, CA), December 4, 1889, 3; "City in Brief," *Aberdeen Daily News* (Aberdeen, SD), September 6, 1892, 3; "Amusements for the Week," *Philadelphia Inquirer*, May 21, 1893, 11; "Minstrels Reopen St. James' Hall," *New York Herald*, September 30, 1894, 11; "Depew and the Dolls' Fair," *New Haven Register*, December 14, 1895, 2; "Stuart Robson," *The State* (Columbia, SC), March 8, 1899, 4.
149. "Plays and Players. Grand Opera House," *Boston Herald*, October 19, 1897, 9; "A Rollicking Farce," *The Anaconda Standard* (Anaconda, MT), October 12, 1899, 4.
150. Karl Marx, *Capital: A Critique of Political Economy, vol. 1*, ed. Frederick Engels, trans. Samuel Moore and Edward Aveling (Moscow: Progress, 1887), 285–286, https://www.marxists.org/archive/marx/works/download/pdf/Capital-Volume-I.pdf.
151. Marx, *Capital*, 127.
152. Marx, *Capital*, 113.
153. Andrew F. Jones, "The Gramophone in Shanghai," *Tokens of Exchange: The Problem of Translation in Global Circulations*, ed., Lydia H. Liu (Durham, NC: Duke University Press, 1999), 214.
154. "Burned at the Stake. Awful Deed of an Infuriated Mob at Leavenworth, Kansas," *Idaho Daily Statesman* (Boise, ID), January 16, 1901, 1.
155. Ida B. Wells, "Lynching, Our National Crime" (1909), https://www.blackpast.org/african-american-history/1909-ida-b-wells-awful-slaughter/.
156. Wells, "Lynching."
157. Wells, "Lynching."
158. The superiority theory of humor contends that one's risible burst always derives from witnessing the misfortune of others. It is the oldest theory of humor according to the humor philosopher John Morreall. See John Morreall, *The Philosophy of Laughter and Humor* (Albany, NY: SUNY Press, 1986).
159. Emily Steinlight, "Why Novels Are Redundant: Sensation Fiction and the Overpopulation of Literature," *ELH*, vol. 79, no. 2 (2012): 503.

2. FEMALE DEATH BY LAUGHTER (BEYOND ENJOYMENT)

1. "Literally Laughed Herself to Death: Lesion of Brain Caused by Kentucky Girl's Violent Fit of Mirth," *Salt Lake Telegram*, April 23, 1902, 1.
2. "Killed by a Joke," *Kalamazoo Gazette*, November 16, 1893, 2; "Laughed Herself to Death: Louisville Woman's First Merriment in Months Is Fatal," *Sedan Lance* (Sedan, KS), May 18, 1906, 6; "That Denver Woman," *Dallas Morning News*, September 16, 1904, 6.
3. "A Woman Laughed Herself to Death," *Wheeling Register* (Wheeling, WV), November 10, 1897, 4.
4. Kate Sanborn, *The Wit of Women* (New York: Funk & Wagnalls, 1885), 14.
5. "Killed by a Joke," *Kalamazoo Gazette*, November 16, 1893, 2.
6. "Laughed Herself to Death at Old Joke," *Columbus Daily Enquirer* (Columbus, GA), April 3, 1908, 2.
7. Christine Ammer, *The American Heritage Dictionary of Idioms* (Boston: Houghton Mifflin, 1997), 113.
8. "Laughed Herself to Death at Old Joke," *Columbus Daily Enquirer* (Columbus, GA), April 3, 1908, 2.
9. "This Woman Laughed Herself to Death," *Philadelphia Inquirer*, January 14, 1901, 4.
10. "This Woman Laughed Herself to Death," 4.
11. "The Oklahoma Woman," *The State* (Columbia, SC), October 19, 1915, 4.
12. Here are several among countless examples: "'Fake' News: There Are a Lot of Unconscionable Rascals in Journalistic Circles," *Cincinnati Commercial Tribune*, December 4, 1890, 1; "No Use for 'Fake' News," *New York Herald*, October 31, 1891, 3; "Real News and 'Fake' News," *New York Herald*, July 15, 1892, 11; "The Press and Its Influence: Will People Demand Loftier Journalism?", *Colorado Springs Gazette*, August 29, 1896, 2; "Is It 'Fake' News," *New Haven Register*, November 13, 1896, 5; "Genuine and Spurious News," *Arizona Weekly Journal-Miner* (Prescott, AZ), March 9, 1898, 2.
13. *New York Press* editor Ervin Wardman coined the term "yellow journalism" in late 1896 or early 1897 in reference to the escalating rivalry between William Randolph Hearst's *New York Journal* and Joseph Pulitzer's *New York World*. The phrase quickly came to designate a mode of journalism that appeals to emotional sensationalism, preposterous exaggeration, eye-popping headlines, prurient intrigue, and lavish illustrations above detached observation or fact-based reporting.
14. "What Was the Joke?", *Emporia Gazette* (Kansas), April 3, 1908, 2. The *Gazette* rose to national prominence in the early twentieth century under the ownership of William Allen White, who was a vociferous opponent of American populism. See William Allen White, "What's the Matter with Kansas?", *Emporia Gazette*, August 15, 1896.
15. Longinus, "Joy and Sorrow," *The Jewish Messenger*, August 28, 1857, 34.
16. "Laughs Herself to Death. Jokes of a Girl's Chums Were Too Much for Her—Heart Overtax'd and Stops Working," *Anaconda Standard* (Anaconda, MT), April 13, 1907, 13.
17. "Back in Lockport, N.Y.," *Olympia Daily Recorder*, April 4, 1907, 2.
18. Miriam Hansen, *Babel and Babylon: Spectatorship in American Silent Film* (Cambridge, MA: Harvard University Press, 1991), 1–2.
19. "A Beacon Light for Exhibitors! (Nestor: Carl von Gordon's Family)," *Moving Picture World*, September 28, 1912, 1238–1239.
20. "Insures Patrons for Laughing Hysteria During Comedy," *Exhibitors Herald*, May 2, 1925, 29.
21. D. Diane Davis, *Breaking Up (at) Totality: A Rhetoric of Laughter* (Carbondale: Southern Illinois University Press, 2000), 9.
22. Danielle Fuentes Morgan, *Laughing to Keep from Dying: African American Satire in the Twenty-First Century* (Champaign: University of Illinois Press, 2020), 34.
23. Cynthia Willett and Julie Willett, *Uproarious: How Feminists and Other Subversive Comics Speak Truth* (Minneapolis: University of Minnesota Press, 2019), 14.

24. "Almost Laughed Herself to Death," *Times-Picayune* (New Orleans, LA), January 21, 1912, 13.
25. "Laughed Herself to Death," *Daily True American* (Trenton, NJ), August 26, 1879, 2; "Laughed Herself to Death," *Daily Commercial* (Vicksburg, MS), August 29, 1879, 1. Both sources are reprints from *The Syracuse Standard*.
26. Davis, *Breaking Up (at) Totality*, 9–10.
27. "A Unique Heroine," *Boston Herald*, September 25, 1911, 6. They further call for "another Leonardo [to] arise who might immortalize this lovely woman's heroic laugh."
28. "Woman Laughs Herself to Death in Reading," *Evening News* (San Jose, CA), November 13, 1913, 6.
29. "Laughed to Death: Hysteria Assumes a Singular and Fatal Form," *Kalamazoo Gazette*, August 6, 1891, 3.
30. "Laughed Herself to Death: The Singular Death of a Young Girl Who Lived Near Nashville from Hysteria," *New York Herald*, December 27, 1891, 26.
31. "Weston, Field, and Carroll," *Variety*, December 9, 1911, 26.
32. "Off the Wires for and About Women," *Trenton Evening Times*, May 29, 1916, 11.
33. There are several instances of "death by laughter" obituaries that I have linked to coroner's reports that make no mention of laughter. For example, Elizabeth Courtney's death was reported in the *New York Times* in an article titled "Laughter Brought About Her Death: Mrs. Courtney's Joking Remark Has a Sad Ending in a Workshop," October 19, 1894. Coroner's Report 34275 claims Elizabeth Courtney died of cardiovascular disease (New York, NY: October 18, 1894). In Springfield, Massachusetts, an article announced: "Death from Laughter: Convulsed with Mirth a Moment Before She Expired in Theater," May 5, 1902. Coroner's Report 436 (Springfield, MA: April 28, 1902) says that Agnes E. Rogan, who was unnamed in the newspaper article, died of heart failure after a fall from her seat—a detail also included at the end of the newspaper article but omitted from the sensational headline. Mary Bofano of Pennsylvania reportedly died of laughter at age sixteen in 1916, but her death certificate (803, filed on September 4, 1916) states that she died of cardiac embolism.
34. "Laughed Herself to Death," *Kansas City Star*, July 30, 1898, 3.
35. "Laughs to Death at Caller's Story," *Boston Herald*, October 1 1915, 3; "Laughed Herself to Death," *San Francisco Chronicle*, November 17, 1897, 3.
36. George Vasey, *The Philosophy of Laughter and Smiling* (London: J. Burns, 1875), 40.
37. Vasey, *The Philosophy of Laughter and Smiling*, 41. There were a few cases of women's deaths by laughter reported in England (and elsewhere in Western Europe) during these years, but the phenomenon was much more prevalent in the United States.
38. "Last Laugh Was Not Best Laugh," *Boston Herald*, May 22, 1913, 1.
39. "Last Laugh Was Not Best Laugh," *Boston Herald*, May 22, 1913, 1.
40. "Death from Laughter," *Times-Picayune* (New Orleans, LA), February 14, 1875, 8.
41. Eloise Beaumont, "How to Laugh," *Afro-American Sentinel* (Omaha, NE), April 23, 1898, 1.
42. "Death from Excessive Laugher," *Riverside Daily Press* (Riverside, CA), May 21, 1896, 1.
43. Margaret L. Briggs, "Evils of Tight Clothing," *Philadelphia Inquirer*, April 13, 1902, 7.
44. Briggs, "Evils of Tight Clothing," 7.
45. Torstein Veblen, The *Theory of the Leisure Class: An Economic Study of Institutions* (New York: Huebsch, 1899), 79.
46. Veblen, *Theory of the Leisure Class*, 184.
47. W. Stephen Bush, "Who Goes to the Moving Pictures?," *Moving Picture World*, October 30, 1908, 336.
48. "Laughed Herself to Death: Comedy Performance Fatal to Connecticut Woman," *Plain Dealer* (Cleveland, OH), September 13, 1906, 1.
49. "Death from Laughter: Convulsed with Mirth a Moment Before She Expired in Theater," *Salt Lake Telegram-Mortuary Notice* (Salt Lake City, UT), May 5, 1902, 2.
50. "Mrs. Livermore's Lecture," *Vermont Christian Messenger* (Montpelier, VT), January 1, 1874, 3. See also "Effects of Tight Lacing," *Helena Daily Herald* (Helena, MT), September 21, 1889, 6; "Cause of

Death Was Tight Corset," *Salt Lake Telegram*, May 1, 1902, 2; "Things Wise, and Otherwise," *Alpine Miner*, August 24, 1872, 8; "What Women Will Wear," *Kansas City Times*, September 22, 1889, 16; "Stays and the Heart: Injurious Effects of Tight Clothing During Exercise," *Washington D.C. Evening Star*, January 28, 1889, 7.

51. "Laughter Brought About Her Death: Mrs. Courtney's Joking Remark Has a Sad Ending in a Workshop," *New York Times*, October 19, 1894, 1. Coroner's Report 34275 (New York, NY), October 18, 1894, reports Elizabeth Courtney died of cardiovascular disease.
52. "Laughed Herself to Death," *Washington Bee*, October 27, 1894, 1.
53. "Laughter Brought About Her Death: Mrs. Courtney's Joking Remark Has a Sad Ending in a Workshop," *New York Times*, October 19, 1894, 1.
54. Karen Graves, *Girls Schooling During the Progressive Era: From Female Scholar to Domesticated Citizen* (London: Routledge, 1998), 57.
55. See U.S. Department of Labor, "History: An Overview 1920-2021," https://www.dol.gov/agencies/wb/about/history.
56. New Jersey Bureau of Statistics of Labor and Industries, *Twelfth Annual Report of the Bureau of Statistics of Labor and Industries of New Jersey for the Year Ending October 31, 1889* (Trenton, NJ: F. F. Patterson).
57. Richard P. Weeden, "Were the Hatters of New Jersey 'Mad'?," *American Journal of Industrial Medicine* 16 (1989): 229.
58. "Here's the New Laugh" *Boston Herald* (reprinted from *New York Herald*), August 21, 1898, 32.
59. "Here's the New Laugh," 32.
60. Eloise Beaumont, "How to Laugh," *Afro-American Sentinel* (Omaha, NB), April 23, 1898, 2.
61. Beaumont, "How to Laugh."
62. "Loretta's Looking Glass: She Holds It Up to the Girl That Squeals," *Beaumont Journal* (Beaumont, TX), July 24, 1911, 3.
63. Loretta's prolific columns appeared regularly in the *Boston Journal* in 1911 and 1912 and were republished by many newspapers, such as the *Pittsburgh Gazette Times* and the *Beaumont Journal* (Beaumont, TX).
64. "Loretta's Looking Glass: She Holds It Up to the Girl Who Giggles," *Boston Journal*, February 14, 1911, 5.
65. "Loretta's Looking Glass. She Holds It Up to the Girl Who Giggles," 5.
66. "Giggling Girls," *Morning Tribune* (Tampa, FL), May 2, 1902, 4.
67. "Women's Laughter: Subtle Distinctions Cause Likes and Dislikes," *San Jose Mercury News*, February 8, 1903, 18.
68. "Women's Laughter: Subtle Distinctions Cause Likes and Dislikes," 18.
69. "Now They Say the Laugh Reveals the Character of Woman," *The Plain Dealer* (Cleveland, OH), May 8, 1904, 42.
70. "Now They Say the Laugh Reveals the Character of Woman," 42.
71. "Now They Say the Laugh Reveals the Character of Woman," 42.
72. "Now They Say the Laugh Reveals the Character of Woman," 42.
73. Abigail Moore, "How to Keep Young and Pretty: The Trick of Smiling Attractively," *Sacramento Bee* (Sacramento, CA), August 13, 1913, 6.
74. "Had It Pulled," *Salt Lake Telegram*, August 20, 1910, 13.
75. "Laughing Woman Chokes to Death on Her Bridge," *Sacramento Bee* (Sacramento, CA), September 30, 1936, 1.
76. "The Perils of Laughter," *Morning Oregonian* (Portland, OR), October 5, 1912, 10.
77. "The Perils of Laughter," 10.
78. "The Perils of Laughter," 10.

79. Beaumont, "How to Laugh," 1.
80. "Girl Laughs for Eight Hours: Gets Started and Can't Stop—Forgets the Joke," *Aberdeen American* (Aberdeen, SD), March 1, 1907, 5.
81. "A Girl Laughs Eight Hours: Two Doctors Work over Her While Friends Stand by Terrified," *Times-Picayune* (New Orleans, LA), March 24, 1907, 38.
82. Sigmund Freud, "Symbolism in the Dream," *A General Introduction to Psychoanalysis*, trans. G. Stanley Hall (New York: Boni and Liveright, 1920), 160. Freud also claims, citing Carl Jung, that "dreams of dental irritation in women signify parturition," which maps a bit too neatly onto Barbara Barr's hysterical laughter at the dentistry joke about infantile dental lack. See Sigmund Freud, *The Interpretation of Dreams*, trans. A. A. Brill (New York: MacMillan, 1913), 237.
83. Freud, *The Interpretation of Dreams*, 91.
84. Freud, *The Interpretation of Dreams*, 89.
85. Max Schur, *Freud: Living and Dying* (Madison, CT: International Universities Press, 1972), 79–87. Emma Eckstein played a formative role alongside Freud in innovating psychoanalysis, especially in theorizing daydreams. She was also a leader of the Viennese Women's Movement.
86. Rebecca Krefting, *All Joking Aside: American Humor and Its Discontents* (Baltimore, MD: Johns Hopkins University Press, 2014), 2.
87. Alenka Zupančič, *The Odd One In: On Comedy* (Cambridge, MA: MIT Press, 2008), 53.
88. Zupančič, *The Odd One In*, 38, 53.
89. Florence Hartley, *The Ladies Book of Etiquette and Manual of Politeness* (Boston: G. W. Cotrell, 1860), 248.
90. Margaret Atwood, "Writing the Male Character," Hagey Lecture, University of Waterloo, February 9, 1982.
91. Barbara Creed, *Monstrous Feminine: Film, Feminism, and Psychoanalysis* (New York: Routledge, 1993), 106.
92. Creed, *Monstrous Feminine*, 106.
93. Hélène Cixous, "Castration or Decapitation?," *Signs* 7, no. 1 (1981): 42–43.
94. "Mrs. Livermore's Lecture," *Vermont Christian Messenger* (Montpelier, VT), January 1, 1874, 3.
95. Clement of Alexandria, *Exhortation to the Greeks, the Rich Man's Salvation, and the Fragment of an Address Entitled to the Newly Baptized*, trans. G. W. Butterworth (London: G. P. Putnam's Sons, 1919).
96. Anca Parvulescu, *Laughter: Notes on a Passion* (Cambridge, MA: MIT Press, 2010), 110; Luce Irigaray, *Speculum of the Other Woman* (Ithaca, NY: Cornell University Press, 1985), 24.
97. "New York Humorist," *Cleveland Plain Dealer* (Cleveland, OH), May 22, 1903, 6.
98. Ovid, "Perseus Tells the Story of Medusa," *Metamorphoses*, Book IV, 753–803.
99. Hélène Cixous, "The Laugh of the Medusa," trans. Keith Cohen and Paula Cohen, *Signs* 1, no. 4 (Summer 1976): 885.
100. Cixous, "The Laugh of the Medusa," 888.
101. Todd McGowan, *Enjoying What We Don't Have: The Political Project of Psychoanalysis* (Lincoln: University of Nebraska Press, 2013), 116.
102. McGowan, *Enjoying What We Don't Have*, 90.
103. Jacqueline Rose explains: "The woman is implicated, of necessity, in phallic sexuality, but at the same time 'it is elsewhere that she upholds the question of her own *jouissance*'" (121). Lacan designates "this *jouissance* supplementary so as to avoid any notion of complement, of woman as a complement to man's phallic nature (which is precisely the fantasy). But it is also a recognition of the 'something more,' the 'more than *jouissance*' ... what escapes or is left over from the phallic function, and exceeds it" (51). Juliet Mitchell and Jacqueline Rose, eds., *Feminine Sexuality: Jacques Lacan and the Écoles Freudienne*, trans. Jacqueline Rose (New York: Norton, 1982).
104. Cixous, "The Laugh of the Medusa," 878.

105. "The Washington Post Says . . ." *Charlotte Daily Observer*, December 25, 1911, 4.
106. "Tampa Husbands Wish . . ." *Tampa Morning Tribune*, September 28, 1911, 6.
107. "Laughs Herself to Death: Husband's Funny Story Told at Midnight Proves Fatal," *Richmond Planet* (Richmond, VA), December 18, 1909, 5.
108. Helen Rowland, "Meditations of a Married Woman," *Charlotte News*, September 17, 1922, 6.
109. "San Francisco Girl's Laugh Almost Fatal: Violet Adams Falls out of Window While Filled with Mirth," *Seattle Sunday Times*, May 30, 1915, 10; "Laughed Herself to Death," *Omaha World-Herald*, May 27, 1906, 17.
110. "Laughed Herself to Death," *Daily People* (New York, NY), May 12, 1906, 1.
111. "Laughed Herself to Death," 1.
112. "Death from Grief," *Dallas Morning News*, October 10, 1905, 9.
113. Bambi Haggins, "Stand-up Comedy & Survival," *Quarry Farm Symposium: American Humor and Matters of Empire* (online talk), October 3, 2020, https://www.youtube.com/watch?v=PnR6J7ogKq4&t=738s.
114. For example, see Tina Campt, "The Haptic Frequencies of Radical Black Joy," in *A Black Gaze: Artists Changing How We See* (Cambridge, MA: MIT Press, 2021), 193–202; Lindsey Stewart, *The Politics of Black Joy: Zora Neale Hurston and Neo-Abolitionism* (Evanston, IL: Northwestern University Press, 2021).
115. Glenda Carpio, *Laughing Fit to Kill: Black Humor in the Fictions of Slavery* (Oxford: Oxford University Press, 2008), 197; Samuel Beckett, *Watt* (Paris: Olympia Press, 1953).
116. Carpio, *Laughing Fit to Kill*, 197.
117. "Laughed Herself to Death: Negress' Enjoyment of Show Caused Heart Attack," *Baltimore Sun*, August 28, 1909, 1.
118. "Manager Sackett," *Rockford-Register Gazette* (Rockford, IL), August 28, 1909, 4.
119. "Coming Attractions: Empire Bill Next Week," *Morning Oregonian* (Portland, OR), July 9, 1903, 9.
120. Morgan, *Laughing to Keep from Dying*, 12.
121. "News and Comment," *Augusta Chronicle* (Augusta, GA), March 15, 1914, 24.
122. "Lots of Fun but Not for Any Man: Females Only Will Be Admitted to the Annual Minstrel Show of the Y.W.C.A." *Trenton Evening Times*, February 25, 1911, 3.
123. "Lots of Fun but Not for Any Man," 3.
124. Eric Lott, "Love and Theft: The Racial Unconscious of Blackface Minstrelsy," *Representations*, no. 39 (Summer 1992): 23–34.
125. "Loretta's Looking-Glass: She Holds It Up to the Wife Who Is a Kill-Joy," *Boston Morning Journal*, February 22, 1911, 4.
126. "Loretta's Looking-Glass," 4.
127. Rebecca Wanzo, "Rethinking Rape and Laughter: Michaela Coel's 'I May Destroy You,'" *Los Angeles Review of Books* (September 22, 2020).
128. "'Sober Sue' at $15 Per," *Variety*, June 15, 1907, 8.
129. "'Sober Sue' at $15 Per," 8; "'Sober Sue.' Freak," *Variety*, June 29, 1907, 12–13.
130. "'Sober Sue' at $15 Per," 8.
131. "'Sober Sue' at $15 Per," 8.
132. "Few Cases in Police Court: Negro Woman Is Warned to Restrain Her Joy in the Future," *Macon Daily Telegraph*, November 8, 1917, 3.
133. "Few Cases in Police Court," 3.
134. Ernestina Nehring died of "heart disease, brought on by the fit of merriment over the innocent joke of her youngest son." Here's the joke: "Mamma, if you can make a rhubarb pie out of a pie plant, could you make a chicken pie out of an egg plant? [sic]," "Laughs Herself to Death over Joke of Son Aged 9," *Evening World Herald* (Omaha, NE), April 13, 1911, 4.
135. "A Woman Laughs Herself to Death," *Providence Journal* (Providence, RI), December 15, 1878, 1.
136. "Laughed Herself to Death," *Salt Lake Tribune*, January 4, 1879, 8.

137. "Minor Topics," *Evening Journal* (Jersey City, NJ), December 27, 1878, 1; "Laughed Herself to Death," *Salt Lake Tribune*, January 4, 1879, 8.
138. See my discussion of "impressibility" and sentimental biopower in chapter 1.
139. Elizabeth Abbott cites William Fox in her analysis of sugar's "bittersweet" economic history: Elizabeth Abbott, *Sugar: A Bittersweet History* (New York: Duckworth, 2009), 546.
140. *Queen Sugar*, created by Ava Duvernay, directed by Ava Duvernay and several directors, Harpo Films, aired 2016 to 2022 on the Oprah Winfrey Network; Kara Walker, "A Subtlety, or the Marvelous Sugar Baby, Sugar," art installation, Brooklyn, New York, 2014.
141. Paul Laurence Dunbar, "We Wear the Mask" (1896), Poetry Foundation, https://www.poetryfoundation.org/poems/44203/we-wear-the-mask.
142. Maya Angelou, "The Mask." Watch a recording of her performing "The Mask" in 1987: https://www.youtube.com/watch?v=CN9DN_PImy8.
143. Saidiya Hartman, *Scenes of Subjection: Terror, Slavery, and Self-Making in Nineteenth-Century American* (Oxford: Oxford University Press, 1997), 26.
144. Angelou, "The Mask."
145. "Death From Fear," *Dallas Morning News*, January 8, 1895, 6.
146. "The News in a Nutshell," *Evening Journal* (Jersey City, NJ), March 10, 1890, 2.
147. "Death from Fear," *Aberdeen Daily News*, February 2, 1901, 2.
148. "Death From Fear: Scientific Explanation of Why Dissolution Often Follows Fright—Joy, Too, Sometimes Fatal," *Salt Lake Telegram*, September 6, 1902, 11.
149. "Death From Fear," 11.
150. "Death From Fear: Scientific Explanation of Why Dissolution Often Follows Fright—Joy, Too, Sometimes Fatal," 11.
151. "Death from Laughter," *New York Tribune*, October 4, 1897, 2.
152. "Death from Anger," *Ohio State Journal*, September 22, 1858, 2.
153. "Loretta's Looking-Glass: She Holds It up to the Man-Hater," *Boston Journal*, September 4, 1911, 6.
154. In 1915, the Germans reportedly invented a fatal laughing gas that caused its victims to die "flapping their arms like the wings of a decapitated fowl and with hysterical laughter on their lips." "Laughs Selves to Death: Suffocating Gas Used by Germans Drives Men Crazy—They Die Like Maniacs," *Idaho Register*, June 15, 1915, 3. The French also experimented with weaponized laughing gas. "Tears Are Brought by Laughing Gas in French Bombs: Rheims Factory Turns Out 7,000 Bombs of All Kinds Daily," *Times-Picayune* (New Orleans, LA), June 15, 1915, 10.
155. Valerie Steele, *The Corset: A Cultural History* (New Haven, CT: Yale University Press, 2003), 151. The corset ban "released 28,000 tons of steel—'enough to build two battleships,' according to a member of the U.S. War Industries Board." The World War I armistice was signed on November 11, 1918.
156. Tom Sims, "Smile a While," *Bay City Times Tribune* (Bay City, MI), December 1, 1921, 4.
157. Roscoe "Fatty" Arbuckle was acquitted and there is no evidence that he was responsible for Virginia Rappe's death.
158. "Laughs Self to Death," *Columbia Record* (Columbia, SC), March 19, 1931, 14.
159. "Dies of Laughter," *National Labor Tribune* (Pittsburgh, PA), February 4, 1932, 2.
160. "Readers Might Doubt," *Evening Star* (Washington DC), December 17, 1931, 8.
161. "Up in Salem Mass.," *Times-Picayune*, May 8, 1932, 32.
162. "Fatal Fiction," *Evening Star*, March 5, 1934, 1; *The State* (Columbia, SC), October 26, 1934, 14; "Notes on the Margin," *San Francisco Chronicle*, January 22, 1936, 11; "Girl in West Virginia Laughing Herself to Death," *The State* (Columbia, SC), March 5, 1936, 3; "She Died Laughing," *Sunday Oregonian* (Portland, Oregon), September 1, 1935, 1. (It is unclear whether Noël Coward knew of this incident when writing *Blithe Spirit*, in which Elvira is conjured during a séance after having died of a heart attack from excess laughter.)

3. AN ALL TOO BRIEF HISTORY OF LAUGHTER AND DEATH

1. *Monty Python's Flying Circus*, episode 1, "Whither Canada?," directed by Ian MacNaughton and John Howard, aired October 5, 1969, on BBC 1.
2. It appears that Google Translate has lost its sense of humor. As of 2023, it no longer translates this phrase as "[FATAL ERROR]." See: "Anyone ever try to translate 'The Funniest Joke in the World' in Google Translate?", 2016, post on Reddit, https://www.reddit.com/r/montypython/comments/4rtvyl/anyone_ever_try_to_translate_the_funniest_joke_in/.
3. Darryn King, "Just a Concoction of Nonsense: The Oral History of *A Fish Called Wanda*," *Vanity Fair*, July 12, 2018; Stacy Conradt, "The Quick 10: 10 People Who Laughed Themselves to Death," *Mental Floss*, May 27, 2010, https://www.mentalfloss.com/article/24796/quick-10-10-people-who-laughed-themselves-death; *A Fish Called Wanda*, directed by Charles Crichton (1988; Beverly Hills, CA: Metro-Goldwyn-Mayer).
4. "Death from Excessive Laugher," *Riverside Daily Press* (Riverside, CA), May 21, 1896, 1.
5. Friedrich Nietzsche, *The Gay Science* (New York: Penguin Random House, 1974).
6. Sigmund Freud, *Beyond the Pleasure Principle*, trans. C. J. M. Hubback (London: International Psycho-Analytical, 1922); Georges Bataille, "The Practice of Joy Before Death," in *Visions of Excess: Selected Writings, 1927–1939*, ed. and trans. Allan Stoekl, with Carl R. Lovitt and Donald M. Leslie Jr. (Minneapolis: University of Minnesota Press, 1985), 235–239; Mikhail Bakhtin, *Rabelais and His World* (Bloomington: University of Indiana Press, 2009).
7. See "Of the Essence of Laughter, and Generally the Comic in the Plastic Arts," in *Baudelaire: Selected Writings on Art and Artists*, trans. P. E. Charvet (London: Cambridge University Press, 1972), 148.
8. The Lexicon of Festus, *De verborum significatu* (*On the Meaning of Words*). The Festus Lexicon Project at University College London is working to make this "fragmentary and mutilated text" usable again. For the purposes of this quote, please find the best translation available in Mary Beard, *Laughter in Ancient Rome: On Joking, Tickling, and Cracking Up* (Berkeley: University of California Press, 2014), 172.
9. Beard, *Laughter in Ancient Rome*, 173.
10. Bakhtin, *Rabelais and His World*, 53.
11. Bakhtin, *Rabelais and His World*, 407.
12. Bakhtin, *Rabelais and His World*, 91.
13. Bakhtin, *Rabelais and His World*, 91.
14. François Rabelais, *Gargantua and Pantagruel*, book 2, page 3, trans. Jacques LeClerq (New York: Modern Library Edition, 1928).
15. Rabelais, *Gargantua and Pantagruel*, book 2, page 3.
16. Bakhtin, *Rabelais and His World*, 408. Most of his examples draw on citations from antiquity, compiled in fifteenth-century anthologies of death that were of special interest to Rabelais.
17. Rabelais, *Gargantua & Pantagruel*, "Chapter 4. XVII.—How Pantagruel came to the islands of Tohu and Bohu; and of the strange death of Wide-nostrils, the swallower of windmills."
18. Rabelais, *Gargantua & Pantagruel*, chap. 4.
19. Rabelais, *Gargantua & Pantagruel*, chap. 4.
20. Bakhtin, *Rabelais and His World*, 23.
21. Bakhtin, *Rabelais and His World*, 23.
22. Karl Marx, *Capital: A Critique of Political Economy*, vol. 1, ed. Frederick Engels, trans. Samuel Moore and Edward Aveling (Moscow: Progress Publishers, 1887), 822–838, https://www.marxists.org/archive/marx/works/download/pdf/Capital-Volume-I.pdf.
23. Bakhtin, *Rabelais and His World*, 19.

24. Silvia Federici, *Caliban and the Witch: Women, The Body and Primitive Accumulation* (Chico, CA: AK Press, 2004), 11. She further argues that witch hunts were instrumental to the transition from feudalism to early capitalism, whereby common land was privatized, ruling classes seized unlimited power over the people, and the separation between labor production and social reproduction took hold. This latter aspect, according to Federici, was policed through witch hunts, that is, mass imprisonment, torture, and execution of women under allegations of "witchcraft" for straying from their assigned roles of biological reproduction, childcare, and housework.
25. Mary Russo, *The Female Grotesque: Risk, Excess, and Modernity* (London: Routledge, 1994), 56.
26. She refers to writings by Julia Kristeva, Mary Russo, Victor Turner, and Natalie Zemon Davis, but carnivalesque laughter has been deployed as a token of subversive protest by many feminist scholars, including Mary Douglas, "The Social Control of Cognition: Some Factors in Joke Perception," *Man* 3, no. 3 (September 1968): 361–376; Susan Glenn, *Female Spectacle: The Theatrical Roots of Modern Feminism* (Cambridge, MA: Harvard University Press, 2000); Alison Kibler, *Rank Ladies: Gender and Cultural Hierarchy in American Vaudeville* (Chapel Hill: University of North Carolina Press, 1999); Kathleen Rowe, *The Unruly Woman* (Austin: University of Texas Press, 2011); and others.
27. Bakhtin, *Rabelais and His World*, 50.
28. Charles Baudelaire, "Of the Essence of Laughter, and Generally of the Comic in the Plastic Arts," in *Baudelaire; Selected Writings on Art and Artists*, trans. P. E. Charvet (Cambridge: Cambridge University Press, 1981), 148.
29. Bakhtin, *Rabelais and His World*, 51.
30. "A Kentucky woman . . . ," *Tampa Morning Tribune*, 1911, 6.
31. Federici, *Caliban and the Witch*, 153. Excessive or threatening laughter could be admitted as evidence of a woman's covenant with the devil.
32. Sigmund Freud, *The Ego and the Id* (New York: Norton, 1990), 55.
33. Rabelais, *Gargantua & Pantagruel*, "Chapter 1. XX.—How the Sophister carried away his cloth, and how he had a suit in law against the other masters."
34. Rabelais, *Gargantua & Pantagruel*, chap. 1.
35. Bakhtin, *Rabelais and His World*, 12
36. Bakhtin, *Rabelais and His World*, 12
37. "Death from Laughter (from the *Louisville-Courier Journal*)," *New-York Tribune*, October 4, 1897, 2.
38. Friedrich Nietzsche, *The Joyful Wisdom*, trans. Thomas Common (London: T. N. Foulis, 1910), 168, http://www.gutenberg.org/files/52124/52124-h/52124-h.htm.
39. Nietzsche, *The Joyful Wisdom*, 168.
40. Nietzsche, *The Joyful Wisdom*, 253.
41. Nietzsche, *Birth of Tragedy*, trans. Douglas Smith (Oxford: Oxford University Press, 2000), 10.
42. Nietzsche, *The Joyful Wisdom*, 325
43. Nietzsche, *Thus Spoke Zarathustra*, trans. Thomas Common (London: T. N. Foulis, 1909).
44. Frances Nesbitt Oppel, *Nietzsche on Gender: Beyond Man and Woman* (Charlottesville: University of Virginia Press, 2005), 119.
45. See Kelly Oliver and Marilyn Pearsall, eds., *Feminist Interpretations of Friedrich Nietzsche* (University Park: Pennsylvania State University Press, 1998); Maudemarie Clark, "7. Nietzsche's Misogyny" in *Nietzsche on Ethics and Politics* (Oxford: Oxford University Press, 2015); Kelly Oliver, *Womanizing Nietzsche* (London: Routledge, 1994).
46. Ruth Abbey, *Nietzsche's Middle Period* (Oxford: Oxford University Press, 2000), 116.
47. John Lippitt, "Nietzsche, Zarathustra, and the Status of Laughter," *British Journal of Aesthetics* 32, no. 1 (January 1992): 40.
48. Nietzsche, *Zarathustra*, LX: The Seven Seals.
49. "Laughs Herself to Death over Joke of Son Aged 9," *Evening World Herald* (Omaha, NE), April 13, 1911, 4.

50. Kate Sanborn, *The Wit of Women* (London: Funk & Wagnalls, 1885), 16.
51. Nietzsche, *Zarathustra*, LX: The Seven Seals; "Laughs Herself to Death over Joke of Son Aged 9," *Evening World Herald* (Omaha, NE), April 13, 1911, 4.
52. Lippitt, "Nietzsche, Zarathustra," 40.
53. Sigmund Freud, "Humour" (1927), Scribd, https://www.scribd.com/doc/34515345/Sigmund-Freud-Humor-1927.
54. André Breton, *Anthology of Black Humor*, trans. Mark Polizzotti (San Francisco: City Lights Publishers, 2001), xix.
55. Breton, *Anthology of Black Humor*, xix; Pierre Piobb, *Les Mysteres des Dieux* (Paris: H. Daragon, 1909).
56. Breton, *Anthology of Black Humor*, xvi.
57. Both Leonora Carrington and Gisèle Prassinos were pivotally involved in the surrealist movement in France. Prassinos's humorous experiments in "automatic writing" took aim at the gender politics of the unconscious. See Gisèle Prassinos, *The Arthritic Grasshopper: Collected Stories, 1934–1944* (Cambridge, MA: Wakefield Press, 2017). Carrington was an English-born Mexican painter and novelist who collaborated frequently with Max Ernst. Her work explores themes of feminist collectivity and female sexuality. She later helped found the Women's Liberation Movement in Mexico in the 1970s.
58. Max Ernst, *The Hundred Headless Woman*, trans. Dorothea Tanning (New York: George Brazilier, 1981).
59. Georges Bataille, "The Practice of Joy in the Face of Death," *Visions*, 236.
60. Bataille, "The Practice of Joy," 236.
61. Bataille named his secret society *Acéphale*, from the Greek *akephalos*, meaning "headless." Ritual sacrifices such as decapitation were, for Bataille, morally preferable to war and organized religion. See William Pawlett, *Georges Bataille: The Sacred and Society* (London: Routledge, 2015), 92.
62. For key examples of Bataille's erotic fiction, see *Story of the Eye* (1928), *Madame Edwarda* (1941), and *L'Abbé C* (1950).
63. Georges Bataille, *Inner Experience*, trans. Stuart Kendall (Albany, NY: SUNY Press, 2014), 233.
64. Georges Bataille, *The Guilty*, trans. Stuart Kendall (Albany, NY: SUNY Press, 2011); Georges Batalille, *On Nietzsche*, trans. Stuart Kendall (Albany, NY: SUNY Press, 2015).
65. Bataille, *Inner Experience*, 233.
66. Bataille, *Inner Experience*, 233
67. Bakhtin, *Rabelais and His World*, 7.
68. Bakhtin, *Rabelais and His World*, 23.
69. David Sterritt, "Time's Timing and the Threat of Laughter in Nicolas Roeg's *Don't Look Now*," in *The Last Laugh: Strange Humors of Cinema*, ed. Murray Pomerance (Detroit, MI: Wayne State University Press, 2013), 108.
70. Jean-Luc Nancy, "Wild Laughter in the Throat of Death," *MLN* 102, no. 4 (September 1987): 722.
71. Nancy, "Wild Laughter," 723.
72. Nancy, "Wild Laughter," 722.
73. Nancy, "Wild Laughter," 724.
74. Nancy, "Wild Laughter," 723.
75. Hans Blumenberg, *The Laughter of the Thracian Woman: A Protohistory of Theory* (London: Bloomsbury, 2015), 143.
76. Michel de Montaigne, "That to Study Philosophy Is to Learn to Die" (1580).
77. "Here's the New Laugh," *Boston Herald*, reprinted from *New York Herald*, August 21, 1898, 32.
78. "Laughed Herself to Death: The Sensational Suicide of a Woman at Niagara," *Boston Herald*, September 6, 1889, 5.
79. "Laughed Herself to Death: The Sensational Suicide of a Woman at Niagara," 5.

80. "Laughed Herself to Death: The Sensational Suicide of a Woman at Niagara," 5.
81. Nietzsche collapsed in Turin on January 3, 1889, and thereafter suffered a total nervous breakdown, "diagnosed as suffering from progressive paralysis induced by syphilitic infection." See Sue Prideaux, *I Am Dynamite! A Life of Nietzsche* (Surry Hills, Australia: Tim Duggin Books, 2014), 404–405. Detailed accounts of Nietzsche's time in a Swiss asylum after his breakdown chronicle his hysterical behavior: "The flow of speech constant, confused and without logical connection. Continues throughout the night. Often a high state of manic excitement. Considerable priapic content. Delusions of whores in his room. At times he will converse quite normally but then lapse into jokes, dances, confusion, and delusion. Occasionally breaks into singing, yodeling, and screaming" (Prideux, *I Am Dynamite*, 335).
82. Bataille, *Inner Experience*, 233.

4. GASLIGHTING THE LIBIDO: FEMINIST POLITICS OF MADNESS, LAUGHTER, AND POWER

1. Hélène Cixous, "Sorties: Out and Out: Attacks/Ways Out/Forays," in *The Newly Born Woman (La jeune née, 1975)*, Hélène Cixous and Catherine Clément, trans. Betsy Wing (Minneapolis: University of Minnesota Press, 1986), 95.
2. Cixous, "Sorties," 95.
3. Catherine Clément, "The Guilty One," in Cixous and Clément, *The Newly Born Woman*, 52.
4. Cixous, "Sorties," 91.
5. Jouissance involves intense sexual pleasure beyond orgasm; it cannot be equated with "enjoyment," which is a consumerist imperative; "it is, therefore, a word with *simultaneously* sexual, political, and economic overtones," as Betsy Wing and Sandra Gilbert gloss it. Betsy Wing and Sandra Gilbert, "Glossary," in Cixous and Clément, *Newly Born Woman*, 165).
6. Cixous and Clément, "Exchange," in *Newly Born Woman*, 150. Cixous adds: "She is the hole in the social cell ... it goes through her body."
7. Cixous and Clément, "Exchange," 156.
8. Jane Gallop, *Feminism and Psychoanalysis: The Daughter's Seduction* (London: Macmillan, 1982), 135.
9. Elaine Showalter, *The Female Malady: Women, Madness and English Culture, 1830–1980* (New York: Pantheon, 1985), 160.
10. Bridget Everett, *Gynecological Wonder*, directed by Lance Bangs, written by Bridget Everett, aired July 10, 2015, on Comedy Central; Tiffany Haddish, *Black Mitzvah*, directed by Linda Mendoza, written by Tiffany Haddish, aired December 3, 2019, on Netflix; Jacqueline Novak, *Get on Your Knees*, directed by John Early, live stand-up show running since 2019.
11. Cynthia Willett and Julie Willett, *Uproarious: How Feminists and Other Subversive Comics Speak Truth* (Minneapolis: University of Minnesota Press, 2019), 12.
12. Bambi Haggins, *Laughing Mad: The Black Comic Persona in Post-Soul America* (New Brunswick, NJ: Rutgers University Press, 2007), 1–2.
13. Jenny Sundén and Susanna Paasonen, *Who's Laughing Now? Feminist Tactics in Social Media* (Cambridge, MA: MIT Press, 2020), 3.
14. Sundén and Paasonen, *Who's Laughing Now?*, 3.
15. Cixous, "Sorties," 88.
16. Linda Mizejewski and Victoria Sturtevant, "Introduction," in *Hysterical! Women in American Comedy* ed. Linda Mizejewski and Victoria Sturtevant (Austin: University of Texas Press, 2017), 2.
17. Mizejewski and Sturtevant, "Introduction," 4.

18. Cecily Devereux, "Hysteria, Feminism, and Gender Revisited: The Case of the Second Wave," *English Studies in Canada* 40, no. 1 (March 2014): 41. Devereux expands Mark Micale's declaration of a "new hysteria studies" (1995) to what "we might call the new new hysteria studies [which] is evident in academic study." She cites three feature films on the topic made in 2011 and 2012 and scholarship published between 2005 and 2012 by Christina Wald, Lilian R. Hurst, Asti Hustvedt, and Georges Didi-Huberman.
19. Hannah Gadsby, *Nanette*, directed by Jon Olb and Madeline Parry, written by Hannah Gadsby, aired June 19, 2018, on Netflix. Gadsby debuted *Nanette* as a live show in 2017 in Australia and toured with it internationally (in Edinburgh, New York City, Montreal) before it was released on Netflix. (I saw the show live in New York City on May 26, 2018!)
20. Gadsby, *Nanette*.
21. Michelle Wolf, "White House Correspondents' Dinner Speech" (April 28, 2018). The recording and transcript have been archived by C-SPAN and are accessible at https://www.c-span.org/video/?444555-1/comedian-michelle-wolf-headlines-white-house-correspondents-dinner.
22. Wolf, "White House Correspondents' Dinner Speech."
23. Margaret Cho, *Psycho*, directed by John Asher, written by Margaret Cho, aired September 9, 2015, on Showtime Networks; Wanda Sykes, *Not Normal*, directed by Linda Mendoza, written by Wanda Sykes, aired May 21, 2019, on Netflix; Maria Bamford, *Lady Dynamite*, creators Pam Brady and Mitchell Hurwitz, featuring Maria Bamford, Fred Melamed, and Mary Kay Place, aired May 20, 2016, to November 10, 2017, on Netflix; Lynne Koplitz, *Hormonal Beast*, directed by Marcus Raboy, written by Lynne Koplitz, aired August 22, 2017, on Netflix; *Hysterical*, directed by Andrea Nevins, aired April 2, 2021, on FX.
24. Ann Cvetkovich, *Mixed Feelings: Feminism, Mass Culture, and Victorian Sensationalism* (New Brunswick, NJ: Rutgers University Press, 1992), 3.
25. Jean-Martin Charcot, *Lectures on the Diseases of the Nervous System, vols. 1–2, 1877*, trans. George Sigerson (London: New Sydenham Society, 1877–1889), 195.
26. I am using "hysteric" (as opposed to "hysterical") to refer to laughter as a symptom of clinical hysteria that was not provoked by a direct impetus, such as a joke or gag or humorous incident.
27. "Is Affected with Oscularitis: Terrible Effects of the Kissing Bug on a Young Woman Stenographer," *Anaconda Standard* (Anaconda, Montana), August 13, 1899, 3. I sourced this article from the World Newspaper Archive; it appears as a reprint of a story originally published in the *Chicago Chronicle*. However, I was unable to locate the original source after searching through microfiche records of the *Chicago Chronicle* from July to August, 1899.
28. "Is Affected with Oscularitis," 3.
29. "Is Affected with Oscularitis," 3.
30. "Is Affected with Oscularitis," 3.
31. "Is Affected with Oscularitis," 3.
32. "Is Affected with Oscularitis," 3.
33. "Is Affected with Oscularitis," 3.
34. "Killed by a Joke," *Kalamazoo Gazette*, November 16, 1893, 2; "Last Laugh Was Not Best Laugh," *Boston Herald*, May 22, 1913, 1.
35. As with many of the female cachinnators who died from laughing detailed in chapter 2, I can find no verifiable information that this Esther Wakefield even existed.
36. "Is Affected with Oscularitis," 3. I presume that this story did originally appear in the *Chicago Chronicle* and that it was reprinted in other local newspapers as a curiosity item. Much like hysteric consciousness, the archive is full of holes.
37. Robert Louis Stevenson, *Strange Case of Dr. Jekyll and Mr. Hyde* (London: Longmans, Green, 1886); Joseph Robert W. Paul, "Artistic Creation," in *Catalogue of Paul's Animatographs & Films* (London, Animatograph Depot, 1903), n.p.

38. Edward Shorter, *From Paralysis to Fatigue: A History of Psychosomatic Illness in the Modern Era* (New York: Free Press, 1992), 5–10; Elaine Showalter, *Hystories: Hysterical Epidemics and Modern Media* (New York: Columbia University Press, 1997), 15.
39. Josef Breuer and Sigmund Freud, *Studies on Hysteria*, trans. James Strachey (New York: Basic, 1957), 143.
40. Sara Ahmed, *Cultural Politics of Emotion*, 2nd ed. (New York: Routledge, 2014), 66.
41. Sigmund Freud, *Jokes and Their Relation to the Unconscious*, trans. James Strachey (New York: W.W. Norton, 1960), 149.
42. Freud, *Jokes and Their Relation*, 207.
43. Breuer and Freud, *Studies on Hysteria*, 70–71.
44. Cixous, "Sorties," 95. Dora did not appear in the original *Studies on Hysteria* cowritten with Breuer. She was Freud's patient in 1900. See Sigmund Freud, *Dora: Fragment of an Analysis of a Case of Hysteria* (New York: Simon and Schuster, 1963).
45. Claire Kahane, *Passions of the Voice: Hysteria, Narrative, and the Figure of the Speaking Woman, 1850–1915* (Baltimore, MD: Johns Hopkins University Press, 1995); Toril Moi, "Representation of Patriarchy: Sexuality and Epistemology in Freud's Dora," *Feminist Review*, no. 9 (October 1981): 65. See also Charles Bernheimer and Claire Kahane, eds., *In Dora's Case: Freud, Hysteria, Feminism* (New York Columbia University Press, 1985); Dianne Hunter, "Hysteria, Psychoanalysis, and Feminism: The Case of Anna O.," *Feminist Studies* 9, no. 3 (1983): 464–488; Juliet Mitchell, *Psychoanalysis and Feminism: Freud, Reich, Laing, and Women* (New York: Pantheon, 1974); Jacqueline Rose, *Sexuality in the Field of Vision* (London: Verso, 1986).
46. Breuer and Freud, *Studies on Hysteria*, 8.
47. Teresa Brennan, *The Transmission of Affect* (Ithaca, NY: Cornell University Press, 2004), 107.
48. Sara Ahmed, *The Promise of Happiness* (Durham, NC: Duke University Press, 2010), 68.
49. Luce Irigaray, *This Sex Which Is Not One* (Ithaca, NY: Cornell University Press, 1985), 162–163.
50. Luce Irigaray, *Speculum of the Other Woman*, trans. Gillian Gill (Ithaca, NY: Cornell University Press, 1985), 60.
51. Irigaray, *Speculum of the Other Woman*, 60.
52. Julia Kristeva, *Powers of Horror: An Essay on Abjection*, trans. Leon S. Roudiez (New York: Columbia University Press, 1982), 8, 133. See also Monique Wittig, *Les Guérillères*, trans. David Le Vay (New York: Viking Press, 1971). Originally published in 1969, Wittig's novel depicts a lesbian warrior tribe whose weaponized, antiphallic laughter cuts as deep as their knives and rocket launchers.
53. Kristeva, *Powers of Horror*, 45.
54. Wing and Gilbert, "Glossary," 165.
55. Axel Munthe, *The Story of San Michele* (New York: E. P. Dutton, 1932), 296.
56. Asti Hustvedt, *Medical Muses: Hysteria in Nineteenth-Century Paris* (London: Bloomsbury, 2011), 23.
57. E. M. Thornton, *Hypnotism, Hysteria, and Epilepsy: An Historical Synthesis* (Liverpool, UK: Wilmer Brothers, 1976), 147.
58. Hustvedt, *Medical Muses*, 71, cites: Gilles de la Tourette and Paul Marie Louis Richer, "Hypnotisme," in *Dictionnaire encyclopédique des sciences médicales* (1887), 88–89.
59. Louis Aragon and André Breton, "Le cinquantenaire de l'hystérie (1878–1928)," *La Révolution surréaliste* 11, no. 4 (1928): 20–22.
60. Rae Beth Gordon, *Why the French Love Jerry Lewis: From Cabaret to Early Cinema* (Redwood City, CA: Stanford University Press, 2001), 29.
61. Michel Foucault, *Madness and Civilization: A History of Insanity in the Age of Reason* (New York: Vintage, 1988), 275.
62. Showalter, *The Female Malady*, 52.
63. Showalter, *The Female Malady*, 151.

64. Georges Didi-Huberman, *Invention of Hysteria: Charcot and the Iconography of the Salpêtrière*, trans. Alisa Hartz (Cambridge, MA: MIT Press, 2003), 17; Showalter, *The Female Malady*, 151.
65. Munthe, *The Story of San Michele*, 302.
66. "Hypnotism in Paris. Wonderful Experiments at the Hospital of La Charité," reprinted in the *Kansas City Times* (Kansas City, MO), June 8, 1890, 20, originally published in *New York Commercial Advertiser*.
67. "The Nancy School of Hypnotism," *Current Literature: A Magazine of Record and Review*, vol. VI (January–April 1891), 558.
68. "Hypnotism," the *Sunday News* (Charleston, SC), September 8, 1889, 4.
69. Hustvedt, *Medical Muses*, 74.
70. "From Our Special Correspondent," *The Mercantile Record and Commercial Gazette* (Port Louis, Mauritius), July 28, 1880, 2.
71. "Strange Case of Hysteria," *Daily Nebraska State Journal*, reprinted from *London Standard*, September 1, 1889, 11.
72. "Extraordinary Hysteria," *San Francisco Evening Bulletin*, November 25, 1884, 4.
73. Hustvedt, *Medical Muses*, 122, cites: Alfred Binet and Charles Féré, "L'Hypnotisme chez les hystériques: Le transfer psychique," *Revue Philosophique* 19 (1885): 3.
74. Claudie Massicotte, *Trance Speakers: Femininity and Authorship in Spiritual Séances, 1850–1930* (Montreal: McGill-Queen's University Press, 2017), 178.
75. Hustvedt, *Medical Muses*, 112.
76. Hustvedt, *Medical Muses*, 112–114. Hustvedt details an anecdote about a patient named Jeanne whom Tourette later encountered working as a professional somnambulist. He attempted to play a practical joke, suggesting to Jeanne: "Look, there's a man with a nose as long as a donkey." She replied: "I'm too tired. Every night I'm put under, and I no longer know what I'm doing or what I've become . . . I don't have a shred of will power left. I'm convinced I'll end up mad."
77. Gordon, *Why the French Love Jerry Lewis*, 71.
78. Gordon, *Why the French Love Jerry Lewis*, 62.
79. Henri Bergson, *Laughter: An Essay on the Meaning of the Comic*, trans. Cloudesley Brereton and Fred Rothwell (Mineola, NY: Dover, 2005), 58–60.
80. Jean-Martin Charcot, *Clinical Lectures on Certain Diseases of the Nervous System*, trans. E. P. Hurd (Detroit, MI: George S. Davis, 1888), 128–129.
81. Andrew Scull, *Hysteria: The Disturbing History* (Oxford: Oxford University Press, 2009), 115.
82. Gordon, *Why the French Love Jerry Lewis*, 62–63.
83. "Mad Mummers: Masked Ball at the Salpêtrière Lunatics Asylum," *New York Herald*, April 26, 1881, 4.
84. "Mad Mummers," 4.
85. Sara Ahmed, *Willful Subjects* (Durham, NC: Duke University Press, 2014), 118.
86. "Reasons for Admission, West Virginia Hospital for the Insane (Weston), October 22, 1864 to December 12, 1889," archived in the Weston Hospital Collection (part of the West Virginia and Regional History Center Repository at West Virginia University in Morgantown, WV).
87. Juliet Mitchell, *Mad Men and Medusas: Reclaiming Hysteria* (New York: Basic Books, 2000), 7. See also Mark S. Micale, *Hysterical Men: The Hidden History of Male Nervous Illness* (Cambridge, MA: Harvard University Press, 2008); Paul Lerner, *Hysterical Men: War, Psychiatry, and the Politics of Trauma in Germany, 1890–1930* (Ithaca, NY: Cornell University Press, 2003).
88. Charcot, *Clinical Lectures on Certain Diseases*, 101.
89. Charcot, *Clinical Lectures on Certain Diseases*, 101–102.
90. Hysteria was often referred to as "railway spine" in diagnoses of male nervousness. Whether "railway spine" could be attributed to ailments not caused directly by railroad injury was a subject of heated debate. According to one account, a man lost his "bodily energy, mental capacity, business aptitude . . . His concussion of the spine" shook "the nervous force out of him . . . [like] a magnet struck with a heavy blow of hammer loses its magnetic power." "The 'Railway Spine'—A New Disease," *Daily Constitutionalist* (Augusta, GA), October 20, 1866, 4.

91. Didi-Huberman, *Invention of Hysteria*, 68.
92. Hélène Cixous and Elisabeth Schäfer, "Via Telefaune: A Phone Call with Hélène Cixous," in *Hysterical Methodologies in the Arts: Rising in Revolt*, ed. Johanna Braun (London: Palgrave Macmillan, 2021), 370.
93. Rox Samer, "Trans Chaplin," *Journal of Cinema and Media Studies* 61, no. 2 (Winter 2022): 178–179.
94. Samer, "Trans Chaplin," 178–179.
95. Heather Findlay, "Queer Dora: Hysteria, Sexual Politics, and Lacan's 'Intervention on Transference,'" *GLQ* 1 (1994): 323.
96. Findlay, "Queer Dora," 335.
97. Findlay, "Queer Dora," 335.
98. Cixous, "Sorties," 84–85.
99. Cvetkovich, *Mixed Feelings*, 3.
100. Anne Worthington, "Beyond Queer," in *Hysteria Today*, ed. Anouchka Grose (New York: Taylor & Francis, 2016), 41.
101. Worthington, "Beyond Queer," 49.
102. Elke Krasny, "Hysteria Activism: Feminist Collectives for the Twenty-First Century," in *Performing Hysteria: Images and Imaginations of Hysteria*, ed. Johanna Braun (Leuven, Belgium: Leuven University Press, 2020), 130.
103. Xine Yao, *Disaffected: The Cultural Politics of Unfeeling in the Nineteenth-Century* (Durham, NC: Duke University Press, 2021), 115.
104. Yao, *Disaffected*, 11.
105. W. E. B. Du Bois, *The Souls of Black Folk: Essays and Sketches* (Chicago: A. C. McClurg, 1908), vii.
106. Laura Briggs, "The Race of Hysteria: 'Overcivilization' and the 'Savage' Woman in Late Nineteenth-Century Obstetrics and Gynecology," *American Quarterly* 52, no. 2 (June 2000): 250.
107. George Beard, *American Nervousness: Its Causes and Consequences* (New York: G. P. Putnam's Sons, 1881), vi.
108. Beard, *American Nervousness*, 336.
109. Beard, *American Nervousness*, 336.
110. Rae Beth Gordon, *Dances with Darwin, 1875–1910: Vernacular Modernity in France*," (Routledge, 2009), 146.
111. Gordon, *Dances with Darwin*, 5.
112. Gordon, *Dances with Darwin*, 4.
113. Saidiya Hartman, *Scenes of Subjection: Terror, Slavery, and Self-Making in Nineteenth-Century America* (Oxford: Oxford University Press, 1997), 27.
114. Hartman, *Scenes of Subjection*, 25–26.
115. Hartman, *Scenes of Subjection*, 26.
116. Du Bois, *The Souls of Black Folk*, 3.
117. Breuer and Freud, *Studies on Hysteria*, 250.
118. Breuer and Freud, *Studies on Hysteria*, 250.
119. Du Bois, *The Souls of Black Folk*, 3.
120. Lisa Guerrero, *Crazy/Funny: Popular Black Satire and the Method of Madness* (New York: Taylor & Francis, 2019), 3.
121. Danielle Fuentes Morgan, *Laughing to Keep from Dying: African-American Satire in the Twenty-First Century* (Urbana: University of Illinois Press, 2020), 91–92.
122. Guerrero, *Crazy/Funny*, 3.
123. Therí Alyce Pickens, *Black Madness :: Mad Blackness* (Durham, NC: Duke University Press, 2019), 3. The double colon is meant to unsettle the mutually constitutive relation between Blackness and madness in popular discourses as well as in Black studies and disability studies, according to Pickens (20).
124. Pickens, *Black Madness*, 3.

125. Christina Sharpe, *Monstrous Intimacies: Making Post-Slavery Subjects* (Durham, NC: Duke University Press, 2010), 48.
126. Sharpe, *Monstrous Intimacies*, 59.
127. Gayl Jones, *Corregidora* (Boston: Beacon Press, 1975), 68.
128. Hortense J. Spillers, "Mama's Baby, Papa's Maybe: An American Grammear Book," *diacritics* 17, no. 2 (Summer 1987): 67.
129. Jones, *Corregidora*, 68.
130. Sharpe, *Monstrous Intimacies*, 59–60.
131. Jones, *Corregidora*, 57, 55.
132. Jones, *Corregidora*, 15.
133. Jones, *Corregidora*, 15.
134. Jones, *Corregidora*, 104.
135. Jones, *Corregidora*, 55.
136. Jones, *Corregidora*, 150.
137. Jones, *Corregidora*, 176.
138. Fabiola Cineas, "What the Hysteria over Critical Race Theory Is Really About," *Vox*, June 24, 2021.
139. Lauren Duca, "Donald Trump Is Gaslighting America," *Teen Vogue*, December 10, 2016. See also Bonnie Honig, *Shell-Shocked: Feminist Criticism After Trump* (New York: Fordham University Press, 2021); Christine Williams, *Gaslighted: How the Oil and Gas Industry Shortchanges Women Scientists* (Berkeley: University of California Press, 2021). Williams links tactics of psychological warfare used against women to the oil and gas industry's rampage on the planet, focusing on female science, technology, engineering, and mathematics (STEM) workers.
140. Joan Copjec, *Read My Desire: Lacan Against the Historicists* (London: Verso, 1994), 141.
141. Copjec, *Read My Desire*, 141–142.
142. Copjec, *Read My Desire*, 143.
143. Laura González, "Making Ghosts Heard," in *Hysterical Methodologies in the Arts: Rising in Revolt*, ed. Johanna Braun (London: Palgrave Macmillan, 2021), 259. "g*Hosting* is a method of intersemiotic translation" involving "both verbal and non-verbal sign systems," according to González. South African artist Mary Sibande creates vivid purple sculptures of her alter-ego Sophie, using her own body as a canvas for molding the outline, which Anne Scheffer, Amanda du Preez, and Ingrid Stevens explore as a "strategy of hysterical representation," linking the traumas of South African apartheid to Charcot's hysteric iconography. Anne Scheffer, Amanda du Preez, and Ingrid Stevens, "Hysterical Representation in the Art of Mary Sibande," in *Hysterical Methodologies in the Arts: Rising in Revolt*, ed. Johanna Braun (London: Palgrave Macmillan, 2021), 204.
144. Johanna Braun, "Introduction: Searching for Methods in this Madness," in *Hysterical Methodologies in the Arts: Rising in Revolt*, ed. Johanna Braun (London: Palgrave Macmillan, 2021), 3–4.
145. This project was funded by the Austrian Science Fund (J 464-G24) from 2018 to 2020. It focused on transnational circuits of art and performance, from nineteenth-century hysteria to its twenty-first-century imprints.
146. Cixous, "Sorties," 95.

5. LAUGHTER: THE FORGOTTEN SYMPTOM

1. I expanded on this argument in a recent article: Maggie Hennefeld, "The Problem of Film Comedy in the Twenty-First Century," *New Review of Film and Television Studies* 20, no. 1 (2022), 101–118.
2. "It would be funny, if it wasn't so absurd," as Bernie Sanders once put it in reference to the procession of billionaires at Trump's presidential inauguration (Facebook post by U.S. Senator Bernie Sanders, January 2022, 2017).

3. Jordan Lauf, "Uncovering the Mad Woman," *Tufts Observer*, December 11, 2015, https://tuftsobserver.org/uncovering-the-mad-woman/.
4. José Ingenieros, "Le rire hystérique," *Journal de Psychologie Normal et Pathologique* (Paris, 1906): 501–518.
5. John F. Shepard, "Laughter. Review of Le rire hystérique," *Psychological Bulletin* 5, no. 1 (1908): 24.
6. Pierre Janet, *The Major Symptoms of Hysteria: Fifteen Lectures Given in the Medical School of Harvard University* (New York: Macmillan, 1920), 262.
7. Janet, *Major Symptoms*, 261.
8. Janet, *Major Symptoms*, 261.
9. Herman Hoppe, "The Diagnosis and Treatment of Hysteria," *The Lancet-Clinic CVIII*, no. 21 (1912): 567.
10. Josef Breuer and Sigmund Freud, *Studies on Hysteria*, trans. James Strachey (New York: Basic, 1957), 220.
11. Breuer and Freud, *Studies on Hysteria*, 220.
12. Jean-Martin Charcot, "Lecture I: Spiritism and Hysteria," in *Clinical Lectures on Certain Diseases of the Nervous System*, trans. E. P. Hurd (Detroit, MI: George S. Davis, 1888), 1–12.
13. Jean-Martin Charcot, *Clinical Lectures on Certain Diseases of the Nervous System*, trans. E. P. Hurd (Detroit, MI: George S. Davis, 1888), 4.
14. Jean-Martin Charcot, *Lectures on the Diseases of the Nervous System, vol. 1–2, 1877*, trans. George Sigerson (London: New Sydenham Society, 1877–1889), 195.
15. Charcot, *Clinical Lectures on Certain Diseases*, 5.
16. Charcot, *Clinical Lectures on Certain Diseases*, 6.
17. Charcot, *Clinical Lectures on Certain Diseases*, 7.
18. Charcot, *Clinical Lectures on Certain Diseases*, 8.
19. Charcot, *Clinical Lectures on Certain Diseases*, 8.
20. Charcot, *Clinical Lectures on Certain Diseases*, 8.
21. Henri Bergson, *Laughter: An Essay on the Meaning of the Comic*, trans. Cloudesley Brereton and Fred Rothwell (Mineola, NY: Dover, 2005), 2.
22. Bergson, *Laughter*, 87.
23. It was published as a series of three essays in the French magazine *Revue de Paris* in 1900.
24. *Le Rire* magazine launched in 1894, a year after Jean-Martin Charcot's death.
25. Axel Munthe, *The Story of San Michele* (New York: Dutton, 1932), 306.
26. Janet, *Major Symptoms*, 289.
27. Théodule Ribot, *The Psychology of the Emotions* (London: Walter Scott Publishing, 1896, 1914), 357.
28. The worker's alienation from the product of their labor due to the exploitative conditions of surplus capital production is a core tenet of Marxist theory. I invoke the concept of alienation in both its Marxist meaning and its psychoanalytic sense of estrangement from the other and the unconscious.
29. Janet, *Major Symptoms*, 262.
30. Pierre Janet was primarily interested in its clinical dimensions as a transformation of "personal consciousness" into somnambulism, "medianimic writings," and hysteric symptoms (Janet, *Major Symptoms*, xiv–xv). In a 1910 symposium on the metaphysics of subconsciousness, which also included Hugo Münsterburg and Théodule Ribot, Janet demurred that "my old studies, modest as they were, simply endeavored to throw light upon . . . certain phenomena of pathologic psychology." Pierre Janet, "Chapter Four," in *Subconscious Phenomena* (Boston: Gorham Press, 1910), 53–54. Sigmund Freud, in contrast, explicitly rejected the term "subconscious": "If someone talks of subconsciousness, I cannot tell whether he means . . . to indicate something lying in the mind beneath consciousness" or "to indicate another consciousness, a subterranean one, as it were. He is probably not clear about any of it. The only trustworthy antithesis is between conscious and unconscious." Sigmund Freud, *The Question of Lay Analysis: Conversations with an Impartial Person* (New York: Norton, 1989), 22.

31. Janet, *Major Symptoms*, xix.
32. Janet, *Major Symptoms*, 289.
33. Janet, *Major Symptoms*, xix.
34. Pierre Janet *L'automatisme psychologique* (Paris: F. Alcan, 1889, 1903). See also Pierre Janet, *The Mental State of Hystericals*, trans. Caroline Rollin Corson (New York: Putnam's Sons, 1901).
35. Rae Beth Gordon, *Why the French Love Jerry Lewis: From Cabaret to Early Cinema* (Redwood City, CA: Stanford University Press, 2001), 16.
36. Ribot, *The Psychology of the Emotions*, 353.
37. An invention of the German poet Heinrich Heine, Hirsch-Hyacinth is a lottery agent from Hamburg and "extractor of corns." His malapropisms gave Freud vital material for theorizing jokes as emanations from the unconscious. Although perhaps funny in their original German circa 1905, reading their English translations over a century later, as Freud remarked in a related context, "cannot possibly raise a laugh." Perhaps jokes age less well than other symptoms. Sigmund Freud, *Jokes and Their Relation to the Unconscious*, trans. James Strachey (New York: Norton, 1960), 16–17.
38. Freud, *Jokes and Their Relation*, 131.
39. Freud, *Jokes and Their Relation*, 101.
40. "The Philosophy of Laughter," *Alexandria Gazette*, November 14, 1832, 2.
41. Freud, *Jokes and Their Relation*, 101.
42. Freud, *Jokes and Their Relation*, 99.
43. Breuer and Freud, *Studies on Hysteria*, 53.
44. Breuer and Freud, *Studies on Hysteria*, 53.
45. Breuer and Freud, *Studies on Hysteria*, 53–54.
46. Breuer and Freud, *Studies on Hysteria*, 53.
47. Breuer and Freud, *Studies on Hysteria*, 54.
48. Breuer and Freud, *Studies on Hysteria*, 54.
49. Breuer and Freud, *Studies on Hysteria*, 180.
50. Breuer and Freud, *Studies on Hysteria*, 145.
51. Freud, *The Question of Lay Analysis*, 43.
52. Mary Ann Doane, *Femmes Fatales: Feminism, Film Theory, Psychoanalysis* (New York: Routledge, 1991), 209.
53. Charles Darwin, *The Expression of the Emotions in Man and Animals* (New York: Appleton., 1898), 155.
54. "Laughter Sometimes Disease," *Jackson Daily Citizen* (Jackson, MI), February 8, 1897, 8.
55. "Laughter a Disease," (reprinted from *The London Mail*) *Grand Rapids Evening Press*, December 2, 1896, 3.
56. "Laughter a Disease," 3.
57. "Is Affected with Oscularitis: Terrible Effects of the Kissing Bug on a Young Woman Stenographer," *The Anaconda Standard* (Anaconda, Montana), August 13, 1899, 3.
58. Allan Ropper and Brian Burrell, *How the Brain Lost Its Mind: Sex, Hysteria, and the Riddle of Mental Illness* (New York: Avery, 2019), 50.
59. David P. Moore and Basant K. Puri, *Textbook of Clinical Neuropsychiatry and Behavioral Neuroscience* (New York: Taylor & Francis, 2012), 171.
60. Mario F. Mendez, Tomoko V. Nakawatase, and Charles V. Brown, "Involuntary Laughter and Inappropriate Hilarity," *The Journal of Neuropsychiatry and Clinical Neurosciences* 11, no. 2 (May 1999): 255.
61. Mendez et al., "Involuntary Laughter," 254.
62. Mendez et al., "Involuntary Laughter," 254.
63. Stephen King, *It: A Novel* (New York: Scribner, 1986).
64. I have many anecdotal tales of just barely succeeding to inhibit my laughter, which I hope to share at some point in one format or other (but before it is too late).

65. Francisco de Assis Aquino Gondim, Florian P Thomas, Salvador Cruz-Flores, Henry A Nasrallah, and John B. Selhorst, "Pathological Laughter and Crying: A Case Series and Proposal for a New Classification," *Annals of Clinical Psychology* 28, no. 1 (2016): 12.
66. The cult of domesticity was a nineteenth-century movement that sought to contain women to the domestic sphere.
67. Edward Tilt, *A Handbook of Uterine Therapeutics and of Diseases of Women* (New York: Appleton, 1869), 84.
68. Tilt, *A Handbook of Uterine Therapeutics*, 84.
69. Karl Marx, "The Eighteenth Brumaire of Louis Bonaparte" (1851–185), trans. Saul K. Padover, from 1869 German edition, Marxists.org, https://www.marxists.org/archive/marx/works/1852/18th-brumaire/.
70. Marx, "The Eighteenth Brumaire of Louis Bonaparte."
71. Marx, "The Eighteenth Brumaire of Louis Bonaparte."
72. Marx, "The Eighteenth Brumaire of Louis Bonaparte."
73. Marx, "The Eighteenth Brumaire of Louis Bonaparte."
74. See Olivia Nuzza, "The Full(est) Possible Story of the Four Seasons Total Landscaping Press Conference," *New York Magazine*, December 21, 2020.
75. A mob of several thousand armed Trump supporters violently attacked the U.S. Capitol on January 6, 2021.
76. The "enigmatic signifier" is a message from the unconscious whose libidinal content cannot yet be metabolized (amid the scene of "primal seduction"), thus inaugurating the latent temporality of sexuality and trauma. According to Jean Laplanche, who adopts the term from Jacques Lacan's reading of Freud, it can never be fully reconciled because the infant's ignorance of sex is further mediated by the adult's misrecognition of the other's desire. It represents "the possibility that the signifier may be *designified*, or lose what it signifies, without thereby losing its power to *signify*." Jean Laplanche, *New Foundations for Psychoanalysis*, trans. David Macey (London: Basil Blackwell, 1989), 45.

6. MASS HYSTERIA, COLLECTIVE LAUGHTER, AND AFFECTIVE CONTAGION

1. Angela Mecking, "Lachen in der U-bahn—official," YouTube video, December 7, 2011, https://www.youtube.com/watch?v=EeauvE1M7qc.
2. Henri Bergson, *Laughter: An Essay on the Meaning of the Comic*, trans. Cloudesley Brereton and Fred Rothwell (Mineola, NY: Dover, 2005), 5a.
3. Bergson, *Laughter*, 5a.
4. Mecking, "Lachen in der U-bahn—official."
5. King Sisyphus, comment on Mecking, "Lachen in der U-bahn—official."
6. Walter Benjamin, "A Look at Chaplin," in "Walter Benjamin and Rudolf Arnheim on Charlie Chaplin," trans. John McKay, *The Yale Journal of Criticism* 9, no. 2 (Fall 1996): 311.
7. Walter Benjamin, "The Work of Art in the Age of Its Technological Reproducibility," in *The Work of Art in the Age of Its Technological Reproducibility, and Other Writings on Media*, ed. Michael W. Jennings, Brigid Doherty, and Thomas Y. Levin, trans. Edmund Jephcott, Rodney Livingstone, Howard Eiland, and others (Cambridge, MA: Harvard University Press, 2008), 38.
8. Gustave Le Bon, *The Crowd: A Study of the Popular Mind* (1895), 2nd ed. (New York: Macmillan, 1897), xviii.
9. Le Bon, *The Crowd*, xviii.
10. Le Bon, *The Crowd*, 12.

11. Sigmund Freud, *Group Psychology and the Analysis of the Ego* (1921) (New York: Norton: 1990), 80.
12. Wikipedia paraphrases medical and sociological definitions in its reference page: "List of Mass Hysteria Cases," https://en.wikipedia.org/wiki/List_of_mass_hysteria_cases.
13. See Steven Poole, "The Great Clown Panic of 2016: 'A volatile mix of fear and contagion,'" *Guardian*, October 31, 2016, https://www.theguardian.com/culture/2016/oct/31/the-great-clown-panic-of-2016-a-volatile-mix-of-fear-and-contagion.
14. Paul Bouissac, *Semiotics of Clowning* (New York: Bloomsbury, 2015), 19.
15. Kathleen Rowe Karlyn, "Foreword," in *Hysterical!: Women in American Comedy*, ed. Linda Mizejewski and Victoria Sturtevant (Austin: University of Texas Press, 2017), vii.
16. Karlyn, "Foreword," vii.
17. Cynthia Willett and Julie Willett, *Uproarious: How Feminists and Other Subversive Comics Speak Truth* (Minneapolis: University of Minnesota Press), 35.
18. Robert Provine, "Contagious Laughter and the Brain," in *Laughter: A Scientific Investigation* (New York: Penguin, 2001), 129–151.
19. Robert Provine, "Laughter as a Scientific Problem: An Adventure in Sidewalk Neuroscience," *The Journal of Comparative Neurology* (July 2015): 1537.
20. Julian Hanich, *The Audience Effect: On the Collective Experience of Cinema* (Edinburgh: Edinburgh University Press, 2017), 206.
21. Jacob Smith describes the contagious escalation of uncanny cachinnation archived by an early laughing record. Jacob Smith, *Vocal Tracks: Performance and Sound Media* (Berkeley: University of California Press, 2008), 20.
22. Doron Galili, *Seeing by Electricity: The Emergence of Television 1878–1939* (Durham, NC: Duke University Press, 2020), 129; William S. Paley, "Radio and the Movies Join Hands," *Nation's Business*, October 1929, 21–22.
23. See my article: Maggie Hennefeld, "Cinema's First Epidemic: From Contagious Twitching to Convulsive Laughter," *Los Angeles Review of Books* (June 23, 2020), https://lareviewofbooks.org/article/cinemas-first-epidemic-from-contagious-twitching-to-convulsive-laughter/.
24. "Bills Next Week," *Variety*, November 11, 1918, 23, editorial republished from *The Boston Evening Record* in *Variety*, November 10, 1918, 11; "The Psychology of a Smile," *Motion Picture News*, January 18, 1919, 426.
25. "Contagion of Laughter," *Motion Picture News*, June 18, 1918, 3417.
26. Alenka Zupančič, "Preston Sturges and the End of Laughter," *Crisis & Critique* 7, no. 2 (Summer 2020): 281.
27. Amelia Groom, "'Eruptions of Silence': The Unheard, the Unsaid, and the Politics of Laughter in Marleen Gorris' *A Question of Silence*," *Another Screen*, https://www.another-screen.com/silence-laughter. Groom explores motifs of laughter and silence in *A Question of Silence* (1982), a Dutch feminist film in which a group of female strangers spontaneously execute a misogynist boutique owner and then laugh hysterically during their own murder trial.
28. Groom, "'Eruptions of Silence.'"
29. Alenka Zupančič, "Stand Up for Comedy," *Fall Semester* (April 29, 2020), https://fallsemester.org/2020-1/2020/4/26/alenka-zupani-stand-up-for-comedy.
30. There has been intense debate about comedy, free speech, censorship, and so-called cancel culture or political correctness. For a summary of backlash ranging from Dave Chappelle's antitransgender jokes to James Buckley's concerns about "the joke police," see Rachel Aroesti, "Cancel Culture Killing Comedy?: What a Joke," *Guardian*, August 10, 2021, https://www.theguardian.com/tv-and-radio/2021/aug/10/cancel-culture-killing-comedy-what-a-joke.
31. Willett and Willett, *Uproarious*, 35.
32. Benjamin, "A Look at Chaplin," 311.
33. Benjamin, "A Look at Chaplin," 311.

34. Benjamin, "The Work of Art in the Age," 38.
35. Benjamin, "The Work of Art in the Age," 38.
36. When the German Reichstag building went up in flames on February 27, 1933, Hitler blamed Communist saboteurs. "The Reichstag Fire" now indicates any historical flashpoint at which a crisis is exploited to consolidate undemocratic political power.
37. "Sustaining Alternative Worlds: On Comedy and the Politics of Representation. A Roundtable Discussion with Lauren Berlant, Sianne Ngai, and Alenka Zupančič, Moderated by the Editors," *Texte zur Kunste*, no. 121 (March 2021): 78.
38. "Laughing Epidemics," *The Evening Press* (Grand Rapids, MI), February 16, 1903, 3.
39. "Ah There, Singultus: A Wily Foe to Mankind Not to be Regarded Lightly," *Morning News* (Savannah, GA), May 21, 1898, 7.
40. Basil Lambert, "Munich Savant Writes Book That Stirs Debate: Calls Hysteria an Infectious Disease," *Salt Lake Tribune*, May 14, 1911, 20.
41. Hermann Aub, *Hysterie des Mannes* (München: Reinhardt, 1911).
42. Le Bon, *The Crowd*, 20.
43. "Communal Insanity," *Morning Oregonian* (Portland, OR), January 20, 1896, 4; Adolph Moses, "Popular Insanity," *The American Magazine of Civics* 7 (July–December, 1895), 599–607.
44. "Communal Insanity," 4; Moses, "Popular Insanity."
45. "The Old Story," *Crisis: A Record of the Darker Races* (New York, NY), February 1, 1911, 20.
46. "The Old Story," 20.
47. "Hard Times, More Lynching," *Plaindealer* (Topeka, KS), January 16, 1931, 2.
48. Claudia Breger, "Different Crowds, Layered Affects: Spike Lee's Audiovisual Storytelling in *BlacKkKlansman*," Society of Cinema and Media Studies Conference, March 20, 2021, online presentation.
49. "Riot in E. St. Louis: A Disgrace to American Civilization That American Citizens Should Be Mobbed Simply Because They Seek to Improve Their Industrial Condition," *The Forum* (Springfield, IL), June 2, 1917, 1.
50. "Riot in E. St. Louis: A Disgrace to American Civilization."
51. J. M. Buckley, *A History of Methodists in the United States* (New York: Christian Literature, 1896), 218.
52. "Getting the Power," *Times Republican Marshalltown* (Iowa), June 26, 1907, 4.
53. "Women as Wage Earners," *Times Republican Marshalltown* (Iowa), June 26, 1907, 4.
54. "Negro Camp-Meetings. Woman Evangelist Speaks," *The Sun* (Baltimore, MD), August 17, 1900, 8.
55. Florence Spearing Randolph was one of the first women ordained as a deacon in the African Methodist Episcopal Zion Church. See Bettye Collier-Thomas, *Daughters of Thunder: Black Women Preachers and Their Sermons, 1850–1979* (San Francisco: Jossey-Bass, 1998).
56. "A.M.E. Zion Mission Workers in Session: Rev. Florence Randolph, Noted Woman Preacher, Is in Attendance," *Trenton Evening Times*, October 16, 1906, 2.
57. "Raids by Suffragettes Epidemic of Hysteria: Excitable Women Join Violence Movement as Sort of Holy Crusade," *The Sun* (Baltimore, MD), March 17, 1912, 12.
58. "Raids by Suffragettes Epidemic of Hysteria."
59. "No Place for a Fight," *Times-Republican* (Iowa), April 2, 1920, 6.
60. L. J. Donaldson, J. Cavanaugh, and J. Rankin, "The Dancing Plague: A Public Health Conundrum," *Public Health* 111, no. 4 (July 1997): 201–204.
61. Ernest Jones, "The Relation Between the Anxiety Neurosis and Anxiety-Hysteria," in *Papers on Psycho-Analysis* (London: Baillière, Tindall and Cox, 1913), 500.
62. Juliet Mitchell, *Mad Men and Medusas* (New York: Basic), 36.
63. Sigmund Freud, *Totem and Taboo*, trans. James Strachey (Taylor & Francis, 2012), 41.
64. Judith Butler, *Excitable Speech: A Politics of the Performative* (New York: Routledge, 1997), 114.
65. Butler, *Excitable Speech*, 114.

66. Butler, *Excitable Speech*, 114.
67. Jaye McBride performs this joke in the documentary, *Funny Women of a Certain Age*, directed by Cat Solen (2019; New York: Showtime).
68. Simon Wessely, "Mass Hysteria: Two Syndromes?," *Psychological Medicine* 17 (1987): 109–110.
69. William Burnham describes this incident as "an epidemic of tickling," whereby long-handled feather dusters advertised at "a tickle for a nickel" caused an "astonishing... demoralization of the manners of Worcester people," as "if Satan had come to the city in person." William Burnham, *The Normal Mind: An Introduction to Mental Hygiene and the Hygiene of School Instruction* (New York: Appleton Century, 1924), 538.
70. Or do we? A. Brad Schwartz raises doubts about the scale of the panic, claiming that media coverage oversampled frightened listeners in 1938, making the narrative of Martian-invasion hysteria a "cultural touchstone." A. Brad Schwartz, *Broadcast Hysteria: Orson Welles's War of the Worlds and the Art of Fake News* (New York: Hill and Wang, 2015), 8.
71. Hilary Evans and Robert E. Bartholomew, *Outbreak!: The Encyclopedia of Extraordinary Social Behavior* (San Antonio, TX: Anomalist, 2009), 360–361.
72. Wessely, "Mass Hysteria," 114.
73. Silvan S. Tomkins, "The Quest for Primary Motives: Biography and Autobiography of an Idea," *Journal of Personality and Social Psychology* 41, no. 2 (1981): 322.
74. Sianne Ngai, *Ugly Feelings* (Cambridge, MA: Harvard University Press, 2005), 210.
75. Carol Becker, *The Invisible Drama: Women and the Anxiety of Change* (New York: Macmillan, 1987), 30.
76. Elaine Showalter, *Hystories: Hysterical Epidemics and Modern Media* (New York: Columbia University Press, 1997), 15.
77. "Nervous Phenomena," *Sacramento Daily Record-Union*, October 29, 1888, 2.
78. Evans and Bartholomew, *Outbreak!*, 362.
79. A. M. Rankin and P. J. Philip, "An Epidemic of Laughing in the Bukoba District of Tanganyika," *The Central African Journal of Medicine* 9 (1963): 167–170.
80. Evans and Bartholomew, *Outbreak!*, 309; Manohar Dhadphale and S. P. Shaikh, "The Mysterious Madness of Mwinilunga," *British Journal of Psychiatry* 142, no. 1 (January 1983): 85–88.
81. Evans and Bartholomew, *Outbreak!*, 310.
82. Congregants frequently participated in group rituals that had all the trappings of mass motor hysteria: "Many people began experiencing this uncontrollable shaking of their bodies. Many fell on the floor roaring and screeching. Some were laughing, hilariously." One man "became intoxicated by the Holy Spirit," according to Pastor Howard-Browne, and "laughed uncontrollably for 3 days." An anonymous adherent testified: "And for the first time ever, holy laughter came over me, and I was laughing, and shaking, and laughing, and shaking, and laughing... for at least 30 minutes, maybe for an hour." Evans and Bartholomew, *Outbreak!*, 311.
83. The East Africa Groundnut Scheme was a failed attempt by the British Empire to cultivate peanuts on 3 million acres of land in Tanganyika to justify postwar, continued colonial occupation and to bolster margarine supplies in the United Kingdom. The project was plagued by hasty implementation and lack of arable land or adequate infrastructure in the region, whose long-term flourishing Britain had no financial or ideological interest in supporting.
84. See chapter 2 of this book for extensive discussion of "Death by Laughter" obituaries.
85. Robert Holden, *Laughter: The Best Medicine* (London: Thorsons, 1993), 82. It feels exigent to mention that Holden addresses his theories to an imaginary field of "anthropolojests."
86. Provine, "Contagious Laughter and the Brain," 131–132.
87. Provine, "Contagious Laughter and the Brain," 132.
88. Christian F. Hempelmann, "The Laughter of the 1962 Tanganyika 'Laughter Epidemic,'" *Humor* 20, no. 21 (2007): 67.

89. Showalter, *Hystories*, 5.
90. Showalter, *Hystories*, 4.
91. Contemporary reviews expressed concerns about Showalter's psychosomatic diagnoses of wide-ranging phenomena through the lens of hysteria and psychoanalysis. For example, Mary Schweitzer focuses on chronic fatigue syndrome in her critical book review: Mary Schweitzer, "Chronic Fatigue Syndrome and the Cynics," *Life with ME/CFS: Essays by Mary Schweitzer* (1997), https://www.cfids-me.org/marys/elaine.html.
92. Elaine Showalter, "Hystories Revisited: Hysterical Epidemics and Social Media," in *Performing Hysteria: Images and Imaginations of Hysteria*, ed. Johanna Braun (Leuven, Belgium: Leuven University Press, 2020), 31–32.
93. Elke Krasny, "Hysteria Activism: Feminist Collectives for the Twenty-First Century," in *Performing Hysteria: Images and Imaginations of Hysteria*, ed. Johanna Braun (Leuven, Belgium: Leuven University Press, 2020), 125.
94. Johanna Braun, "Introduction," *Performing Hysteria: Images and Imaginations of Hysteria*, ed. Johanna Braun (Leuven, Belgium: Leuven University Press, 2020), 12.
95. "Precession of simulacra" refers to Jean Baudrillard's critical term for the postmodern condition whereby the image precedes reality. There is no more reality, only simulation (of simulation, and so on).
96. See Michael Savage, *Stop Mass Hysteria: America's Insanity from the Salem Witch Trials to the Trump Witch Hunt* (New York: Hachette, 2018); Danielle Pletka, "The Anti-Trump Hysteria Isn't Helping," *Atlantic*, July 27, 2018; Gene Lyon, "How to End Border Wall Hysteria: Get Real," *Chicago Sun Times*, January 4, 2019.
97. See the mission statement of Hysterical Feminisms: https://hystericalfeminisms.com/about/.
98. Krasny, "Hysteria Activism," 138.
99. Braun, "Introduction," 12.
100. See the mission statement of Hysterical Feminisms: https://hystericalfeminisms.com/about/.
101. Disability justice scholars and activists have appropriated negative signifiers, such as "crip" and "madness," with justifiable caution about the scope, intention, and utterance of retooled ableist language. See Lydia X. Z. Brown, "Violence in Language: Circling Back to Linguistic Ableism," *Autistic Hoya Blog* (February 2014), https://www.autistichoya.com/2014/02/violence-linguistic-ableism.html.
102. Anouchka Grose, "Introduction: Reclaiming Hysteria," in *Hysteria Today* (London: Routledge, 2016), xxix.
103. Grose, "Introduction," xxix.
104. Jenny Sundén and Susanna Paasonen, *Who's Laughing Now?: Feminist Tactics in Social Media* (Cambridge, MA: MIT Press, 2020).
105. Kathleen Rowe Karlyn, *The Unruly Woman: Gender and the Genres of Laughter* (Austin: University of Texas Press, 1995); Mary Russo, *Female Grotesque: Risk, Excess, and Modernity* (New York: Routledge, 1995); Bambi Haggins, *Laughing Mad: The Black Comic Persona in Post-Soul America* (New Brunswick, NJ: Rutgers University Press, 2007); Glenda Carpio, *Laughing Fit to Kill: Black Humor in the Fictions of Slavery* (New York: Oxford University Press, 2008).
106. To this list, I would add Katelyn Hale Wood's *Cracking Up: Black Feminist Comedy in the Twentieth and Twenty-First Century United States* (Iowa City: University of Iowa Press, 2021) and Bambi Haggins's recent work on stand-up comedy and emotional survival. She presented some of these ideas in her keynote talk, "Stand-Up Comedy & Survival," *Quarry Farm Symposium* (online only), Center for Mark Twain Studies, October 3, 2020, https://www.youtube.com/watch?v=PnR6J70gKq4.
107. Lisa Guerrero, *Crazy/Funny: Popular Black Satire and the Method of Madness* (New York: Taylor & Francis, 2019), 17.
108. Guerrero, *Crazy/Funny*, 1.
109. Guerrero, *Crazy/Funny*, 146.

110. Danielle Fuentes Morgan, *Laughing to Keep from Dying: African American Satire in the Twenty-First Century* (Champaign: University of Illinois Press, 2020), 3.
111. In *Get Out*, protagonist Chris is "phenomenally banished" to a "sunken place," where "he finds himself *horrified*, looking on at his life 'as a passenger' . . . but unable to make any decisions or determinations of his own," as Jared Sexton describes it, invoking Hortense Spillers: "Peele's visual concept-metaphor dramatizes for contemporary viewers the central mechanism of enslavement, a situation marked by a 'severing of the captive body from its motive will, its active desire.'" Jared Sexton, "The Flash of History: On the Unwatchable in *Get Out*," in *Unwatchable*, ed. Nicholas Baer, Maggie Hennefeld, Laura Horak, and Gunnar Iversen (New Brunswick: Rutgers University Press, 2019), 117; Hortense Spillers, *Black, White, and in Color: Essays on American Literature and Culture* (Chicago: University of Chicago Press, 2003), 206.
112. Morgan, *Laughing to Keep from Dying*, 2.
113. La Marr Jurelle Bruce, *How to Go Mad Without Losing Your Mind: Madness and Black Radical Creativity* (Durham, NC: Duke University Press, 2021), 6–8.
114. Bruce, *How to Go Mad*, 10.
115. Nick Marx and Matt Sienkiewicz, *That's Not Funny: How the Right Makes Comedy Work for Them* (Berkeley: University of California Press, 2022). They compare the "robust, growing, and profitable" network of far-right media to "a different kind of complex—one of a psychological variety—that leaves the collective liberal world defensive and eager to repress the influence of right-wing comedy today," 4. Liberal psychosis is thus understood as a by-product of far-right media consolidation.
116. Viveca S. Greene, "'Deplorable' Satire: Alt-Right Memes, White Genocide Tweets, and Redpilling Normies," *Studies in American Humor* 5, no. 1 (2019), 31–69; Julia Rose DeCook, "Trust Me I'm Trolling: Irony and the Alt-Right's Political Aesthetic," *M/C Journal* 23, no. 3 (2020), https://journal.media-culture.org.au/index.php/mcjournal/article/view/1655.
117. Oliver Morrison, "Why There's No Conservative Jon Stewart," *Atlantic*, February 14, 2015; Sophie Quirk, "Where Are All the Right-Wing Comedians?," in *The Politics of British Stand-Up Comedy: The New Alternative*, ed. Roger Sabin and Sharon Lockyer (London: Palgrave Macmillan, 2018), 11–43.
118. See Amber Day, *Satire and Dissent: Interventions in Contemporary Political Debate* (Bloomington: Indiana University Press, 2011); Jonathan Gray, Jeffrey P. Jones, and Ethan Thompson, ed. *Satire TV: Politics and Comedy in the Post-Network Era* (New York: New York University Press, 2009).
119. Claudia Breger, *Making Worlds: Affect and Collectivity in Contemporary European Cinema* (New York: Columbia University Press, 2020), 3.
120. Breger, *Making Worlds*, 6.
121. Brian Massumi, *Politics of Affect* (Cambridge: Polity Press, 2015), 39.
122. Sara Ahmed, *Cultural Politics of Emotion*, 2nd ed. (New York: Routledge, 2014), 50–51.
123. Anna Gibbs, "Contagious Feelings: Pauline Gibson and the Epidemiology of Affect," *Australian Humanities Review*, no. 24 (December 2001), https://australianhumanitiesreview.org/2001/12/01/contagious-feelings-pauline-hanson-and-the-epidemiology-of-affect/.
124. Gibbs, "Contagious Feelings."
125. Jodi Dean, *Crowds and Party* (London: Verso, 2016), 4.
126. Jackie Wang, "Oceaning Feeling and Communist Affect," Tumblr (December 3, 2016), https://loneberry.tumblr.com/post/153995404787/oceanic-feeling-and-communist-affect.
127. Eve Kosofsky Sedgwick, *Touching Feeling: Affect, Pedagogy, Performativity* (Durham, NC: Duke University Press, 2003), 146.
128. Mira Nair has made a fascinating documentary, *The Laughing Club of India*, directed by Mira Nair (2001; New York: Mirabai Films), which follows the international phenomenon of laughing clubs from their origins in Bombay, where Doctor Madan Kataria established contagious laughter exercises that attempted to transcend caste, gender, race, and class divisions.

129. Angela Mecking, "Laughing in Berlin Metro—With 3 Million Viewers on YouTube!!," *Laughter Yoga University* (2011), https://laughteryoga.org/laughing-in-berlin-metro-with-3-million-viewers-on-youtube/.
130. A group of Black women had a very different experience of contagious laughter on a Napa Valley wine train in 2015; they successfully settled a lawsuit accusing the company of racial bias after they were ejected from the train for "#LaughingWhileBlack," inciting the viral hashtag. See Brandy Monk-Payton, "#LaughingWhileBlack: Gender and the Comedy of Social Media Blackness," *Feminist Media Histories* 3, no. 2 (2017): 15–35.
131. Mecking, "Laughing in Berlin Metro."
132. I have selected and briefly detailed a range of examples from Hilary Evans and Robert Bartholomew's expansive compendium, *Outbreak!: The Encyclopedia of Extraordinary Social Behavior* (2009). For longer descriptions, I encourage you all to consult this intriguing volume. For more nuanced contexts and narratives, I suggest research well beyond it. It is indeed beyond the scope of this book to undertake that research.
133. Evans and Bartholomew, *Outbreak!*, 23–25, 32, 46–47, 51–53, 58–62, 67–68, 83–86, 90–91, 97–98, 111, 143–144, 170, 182, 213, 224, 249–250, 277–278, 360, 463, 64, 501, 505, 508, 546, 592, 623–624, 672–674, 728–730, 753–754.
134. Evans and Bartholomew, *Outbreak!*, 62, 68–69, 116–121, 155–159, 194–203, 211–212, 248–249, 260, 284, 300–304, 309–311, 317–324, 423–430, 71–72, 503–504, 260–262, 555–566, 577–579, 588, 627–630, 680, 683–685, 752–753.

7. LAUGHTER UNLEASHED: HYSTERICAL WOMEN AT THE MOVIES

1. "A Beacon Light for Exhibitors! (Nestor: Carl von Gordon's Family)," *Moving Picture World*, September 28, 1912, 1238–1239.
2. "A Beacon Light for Exhibitors!" 1238–1239.
3. Eleanor Brewster, "Taylor Holmes Has Struck Twelve: The New Laugh-Maker Is Making a Strong Appeal for Supremacy in the Shadow World," *Motion Picture Magazine*, May 1918, 72.
4. "A Boom in Prices," *Birmingham Age Herald* (Birmingham, AL), October 25, 1895, 2.
5. "Boston," *Variety*, November 21, 1913, 26.
6. "A Tribute to Moving Picture Shows" (reprinted from *Galvestone Texas Tribune*), *Moving Picture World*, March 28, 1908, 265.
7. Vanessa R. Schwartz, *Spectacular Realities: Early Mass Culture in Fin-de-Siècle Paris* (Berkeley: University of California Press, 1998), 2.
8. Miriam Hansen, *Babel and Babylon: Spectatorship in American Silent Film* (Cambridge, MA: Harvard University Press, 1991), 17.
9. Jacqueline Najuma Stewart, *Migrating to the Movies: Cinema and Black Urban Modernity* (Berkeley: University of California Press, 2005), xiii–xiv.
10. Jennifer M. Bean and Diane Negra, "Introduction: Toward a Feminist Historiography of Early Cinema," in *A Feminist Reader in Early Cinema*, ed. Jennifer M. Bean and Diane Negra (Durham, NC: Duke University Press, 2002), 7.
11. Slavoj Žižek, *For They Know Not What They Do: Enjoyment as a Political Factor* (London: Verso, 1991), 237.
12. "Apply to Drive with Lyft," Lyft, https://www.lyft.com/drive-with-lyft.
13. Lauren Berlant and Sianne Ngai, "Comedy Has Issues," *Critical Inquiry* 43, no. 2 (2017): 236.

14. Lauren Berlant, "Humorlessness (Three Monologues and a Hairpiece)," *Critical Inquiry* 43, no. 2 (2017): 305–340.
15. Sara Ahmed, *Living a Feminist Life* (Durham, NC: Duke University Press, 2017), 63.
16. "The Colonial Ladies' Matinee," *Moving Picture World*, October 26, 1907, 540.
17. Nina Peterson is currently writing an excellent dissertation on feminist avant-garde art and absurdist laughter: *Ridiculous Contraptions: American Art, Humor, and Machine Technology During an Era of Social Change, 1954–1975* (Minneapolis: University of Minnesota Press), forthcoming. See also Kate Blackmore, *The One Hour Laugh* (2009), https://www.mca.com.au/artists-works/works/2011.18. The Museum of Contemporary Art San Diego curated an exhibit in 2015, "Laugh-In: Art, Comedy, Performance" (https://www.mcasd.org/exhibitions/laugh-art-comedy-performance), that explores "the recent turn toward comedic performance in contemporary art" and its resonances with "the cultural moment of the late 1960s and early 1970s." "Non-Knowledge, Laughter, and the Moving Image" is a three-year artistic research project led by Annika Larsson and in collaboration with HFBK Hamburg and the Royal Institute of Art Stockholm (2019–2022).
18. Karl Ritter, "Mass-Man in the Cinema" (1929), trans. Alex H. Bush, in *The Promise of Cinema: German Film Theory, 1907–1933*, ed. Anton Kaes, Nicholas Baer, and Michael J. Cowan (Berkeley: University of California Press, 2016), 367.
19. Sydney Herald, "Lydia Yeamans-Titus, the Peerless Lyric Actress, Artist, Ttravesty Queen, and the Most Brilliant Character Vocalist on the American Stage," *New York Clipper*, February 28, 1903, 17.
20. "At the Local Theaters: The Alcazar," *San Francisco Dramatic Review*, October 7, 1899, 6.
21. "American Roof," *Variety*, September 26, 1914, 19.
22. All film citations in this chapter mention the production company rather than the film director.
23. "Three Imps on 2 Reels," *Moving Picture World*, October 22, 1910, 909.
24. Walt, "Vanity Fair," *Variety*, February 5, 1910, 18.
25. Lauren Rabinovitz, *Electric Dreamland: Amusement Parks, Movies, and American Modernity* (New York: Columbia University Press, 2012) 7.
26. Lynne Kirby, *Parallel Tracks: The Railroad and Silent Cinema* (Durham: NC: Duke University Press, 1997); Anne Friedberg, *Window Shopping: Cinema and the Postmodern* (Berkeley: University of California Press, 1994); Asli Ozgen-Tuncer, "Walking in Women's Shoes: Feminism and Pedestrian Acts in Cinema," *Feminist Media Histories* 7, no. 3 (2021), 135–153.
27. "When 'Music' Is a Nuisance," *Moving Picture World*, December 28, 1907, 702.
28. "Warm Spieling," *Variety*, July 15, 1908, 17.
29. "Arrested for Laughing," *Jackson Citizen* (Jackson, MI), July 14, 1899, 1.
30. "A Phonograph Studio. Where Voices of Noted Artists Are Stored," *Phonoscope*, December 15, 1896, 5.
31. "Advance List: 10081 Ev'rything's Funny to Me," *Edison Phonograph Monthly*, January 1909, 16.
32. Sallie Strembler, "Ev'rything's Funny To Me," Edison Standard Record: 10081 (1909), https://cylinders.library.ucsb.edu/search.php?queryType=@attr+1=1020&num=1&start=1&query=cylinder3529.
33. "His Laugh Is Echoing All Over the World," *Edison Phonograph Monthly*, March 1906/February 1907, 12.
34. "Sandy McPherson's Quiet Fishing Trip," *The Film Index*, October 17, 1908, 14.
35. "Newspaper Comments on Film Subjects," *Moving Picture World*, August 29, 1908, 156.
36. "Phonograph Jingles," *Edison Phonograph Monthly*, December 1907, 13.
37. "A Boom in Prices," 2.
38. "A Boom in Prices," 2.
39. Brewster, "Taylor Holmes Has Struck Twelve," 72.
40. Brewster, "Taylor Holmes Has Struck Twelve," 72.
41. "Weston, Field, and Carroll," *Variety*, December 9, 1911, 26.
42. "Playing the Picture," *Moving Picture World*, February 20, 1915, 1128.
43. "New Films for 'Screen' Machines," *Phonoscope*, November 1898, 15.

44. "Moving Picture Advertising," *Phonoscope*, May 1898, 14.
45. Walter Benjamin, "The Work of Art in the Age of Mechanical Reproduction," trans. Harry Zohn, in *Illuminations*, ed. Hannah Arendt (New York: Shocken, 1969), 223.
46. "The Chutes," *San Francisco Dramatic Review*, January 27, 1900, 11.
47. Hansen, *Babel and Babylon*, 1.
48. "'Picture Projecting' Devices," *Phonoscope*, July 1897, 10.
49. "Vitascope Mob at the Hanging," *Phonoscope*, November/December 1897, 8.
50. "Vitascope Mob at the Hanging," 8.
51. "Vitascope Mob at the Hanging," 8.
52. Schwartz, *Spectacular Realities*, 3.
53. "Varied Uses of the Kinetoscope," *Phonoscope*, September 1899, 12.
54. "Furious Storm of Hail and Rain: Trenton Treated to a Novel Spectacle and Pavement Littered with Hail Stones," *Trenton Evening Times* (Trenton, NJ), June 24, 1906, 1.
55. Tom Gunning famously adopted "attractions" from Sergei Eisenstein's notion, which "aggressively subjected the spectator to 'sensual or psychological impact.'" As Gunning explains, "I pick up this term partly to underscore the relation to the spectator that this later avant-garde practice shares with early cinema: that of exhibitionist confrontation rather than diegetic absorption." Tom Gunning, "The Cinema of Attraction: Early Film, Its Spectator, and the Avant-Garde," *Wide Angle* 8, no 3–4 (Fall 1986): 66.
56. Corinna Müller, "Exhibition," in *Encyclopedia of Early Cinema*, ed. Richard Abel (London: Routledge, 2005), 395.
57. Schwartz, *Spectacular Realities*, 5, 178.
58. Hansen, *Babel and Babylon*, 2.
59. Rae Beth Gordon, *Why the French Love Jerry Lewis: From Cabaret to Early Cinema* (Redwood City, CA: Stanford University Press, 2002), xvii.
60. You can stream *Charming Augustine* on Zoe Beloff's website: http://www.zoebeloff.com/pages/augustine.html.
61. Matilde Serao, "A Spectatrix Is Speaking to You" (1916), in *Red Velvet Seat: Women's Writings on the First Fifty Years of Cinema*, ed. Antonia Lant with Ingrid Períz, trans. Giorgio Bertellini (London: Verso, 2006), 97–99.
62. Serao, "A Spectatrix Is Speaking to You," 97–99.
63. Serao, "A Spectatrix Is Speaking to You," 97–99.
64. W. Stephen Bush, "Who Goes to the Moving Pictures?," *Moving Picture World*, October 30, 1908, 336.
65. Bush, "Who Goes to the Moving Pictures?," 336.
66. Louise De Koven Bowen, "Five and Ten Cent Theatres (1909 and 1911), in *Red Velvet Seat: Women's Writings on the First Fifty Years of Cinema*, ed. Antonia Lant with Ingrid Períz (London: Verso, 2006), 303–308.
67. "An Oddity That Is the Mummy," *Moving Picture World*, March 4, 1911, 454.
68. Mary Heaton Vorse, "Some Picture Show Audiences" (1911), in *Red Velvet Seat: Women's Writings on the First Fifty Years of Cinema*, ed. Antonia Lant with Ingrid Períz (London: Verso, 2006), 69.
69. Vorse, "Some Picture Show Audiences," 73.
70. Carl Forch, "Thrills in Film Drama and Elsewhere" (1912–1913), trans. Sara Hall, in *The Promise of Cinema: German Film Theory, 1907–1933*, ed. Anton Kaes, Nicholas Baer, and Michael J. Cowan (Berkeley: University of California Press, 2016), 37; Karl Hans Strobl, "The Cinematograph" (1910), trans. Dan Reneau, in *The Promise of Cinema: German Film Theory, 1907–1933*, ed. Anton Kaes, Nicholas Baer, and Michael J. Cowan (Berkeley: University of California Press, 2016), 26.
71. Jane Addams, "The House of Dreams" (1909), in *Red Velvet Seat: Women's Writings on the First Fifty Years of Cinema*, ed. Antonia Lant with Ingrid Períz (London: Verso, 2006), 297.

72. Kathy Lee Peiss, *Cheap Amusements: Working Women and Leisure in Turn-of-the-Century New York* (Philadelphia: Temple University Press, 1986), 5.
73. Malwine Rennert, "The Onlookers of Life at the Cinema" (1914–1915), in *Red Velvet Seat: Women's Writings on the First Fifty Years of Cinema*, ed. Antonia Lant with Ingrid Períz (London: Verso, 2006), 93.
74. Aurel Wolfram, "Cinema" (1931), trans. Michael Cowan, in *The Promise of Cinema: German Film Theory, 1907–1933*, ed. Anton Kaes, Nicholas Baer, and Michael J. Cowan (Berkeley: University of California Press, 2016), 249.
75. Film scholars have periodized the "transitional era" from about 1908 to 1917, when the impulses of early cinema coexisted with the rise of narrative techniques such as continuity editing before the standardization of classical production models. See Charlie Keil and Shelley Stamp, eds., *American Cinema's Transitional Era: Audiences, Institutions, Practices* (Berkeley: University of California Press, 2004).
76. Olivia Howard Dunbar, "The Lure of the Films" (1913), in *Red Velvet Seat: Women's Writings on the First Fifty Years of Cinema*, ed. Antonia Lant with Ingrid Períz (London: Verso, 2006), 77–78, 80.
77. "Comments on Film Subjects: Everything Sticks but Glue," *Moving Picture World*, November 28, 1908, 423.
78. "Comments on Film Subjects. The Results of Eating Horse Flesh," *Moving Picture World*, October 24, 1908, 318.
79. "Geo. Méliès 'Star' Films," *New York Clipper*, July 1906, 596.
80. "Released Sept. 24: The Suicidal Poet," *Variety*, September 26, 1908, 33.
81. "Released Sept. 24: The Suicidal Poet," 33.
82. "Stories of the Films: The Mock Baronets," *Moving Picture World*, November 7, 1908, 364.
83. W. Stephen Bush, "The Place and Province of Humor in the Moving Picture," *Moving Picture World*, November 8, 1908, 420–421.
84. John E. Henshaw, "Comedy," *Variety*, December 20, 1912, 20.
85. "Play to the Ladies," *Nickelodeon*, February 1909, 34.
86. W. Stephen Bush, "Comments on Film Subjects. The Soul Kiss—Beg Pardon," *Moving Picture World*, October 10, 1908, 279.
87. The quoted synopsis is provided by a film memorabilia collector in his post about purchasing trimmed sheet music from the Ziegfeld show (2016): "1908 Ziegfeld Production, 'The Soul Kiss,' with Lucifer! I'm the Human Night Key of New York," Collectors Weekly, 2018, https://www.collectorsweekly.com/stories/242554-1908-ziegfeld-production-the-soul-kiss.
88. "Essanay. The Soul Kiss," *The Film Index*, September 26, 1908, 10.
89. "Essanay. The Soul Kiss," 10.
90. "Betty Rolls Along (Pathe)," *Moving Picture World*, February 11, 1911, 315.
91. "Betty Rolls Along," *The Nickelodeon*, January 28, 1911, 116.
92. I. L. Epstein, "Brooklyn Exhibitor Praises 'Tale of Twenty Stories,' Universal Comedy," *Motion Picture News*, October 16, 1915, 91.
93. "'Mustang' Pete's Love Affair (Essanay)," *Moving Picture World*, July 8, 1911, 1590.
94. "Pointed Paragraphs," *Augusta Chronicle* (Augusta, GA), June 21, 1907, 6.
95. Ricciotto Canudo, "The Birth of a Sixth Art," in *French Film Theory and Criticism: A History/Anthology, 1907–1939, Volume 1: 1907–1929*, ed. Richard Abel (Princeton, NJ: Princeton University Press, 1988), 62.
96. "Business Outlook Good, Says Horkheimer," *Motion Picture News*, November 14, 1914, 25.
97. "The Trading Stamp Mania," *Moving Picture World*, April 22, 1911, 900.
98. The Skirt, "Twilight Sleep," *Variety*, November 5, 1915, 23.
99. "Comments on the Films. Dear, Kind Hubby," *Moving Picture World*, May 27, 1911, 1200.
100. "William Lord Wright's Page," *Moving Picture News*, 1912, 12.

101. Karl Ritter, "Mass-Man in the Cinema" (1929), trans. Alex H. Bush, in *The Promise of Cinema: German Film Theory, 1907–1933*, ed. Anton Kaes, Nicholas Baer, and Michael J. Cowan (Berkeley: University of California Press, 2016), 367.
102. Leo Witlin, "On the Psychomechanics of the Spectator" (1929), trans. Michael Cowan, in *The Promise of Cinema: German Film Theory, 1907–1933*, ed. Anton Kaes, Nicholas Baer, and Michael J. Cowan (Berkeley: University of California Press, 2016), 138.
103. Gordon, *Why the French Love Jerry Lewis*, 132.
104. Jean Epstein, "Magnification" (1921), in *French Film Theory and Criticism: A History/Anthology, 1907–1939, Volume 1: 1907–1929*, ed. Richard Abel (Princeton, NJ: Princeton University Press, 1988), 238. See *Fred Ott's Sneeze*, directed by William K. L. Dickson (1894; West Orange, NJ: Edison Manufacturing Company).
105. Despite the film industry's damage control, film's infectious popularity triggered moral panic that it would corrupt young girls, incite feminist activism, and distract women from their traditional domestic duties. For example, the *Birmingham Herald* condemned the "degrading picture shows" in 1908, which it warned would lure "young women who always have a loose nickel in their purse . . . [they] go to these places to see a moving picture, but they often see a good deal more than a picture and hear a good deal more than what's good for them." "Editorial: Exhibitors Keep Up the Standard of the Show," *Moving Picture World*, March 14, 1908, 203.
106. Max Grempe, "Against a Cinema That Makes Women Stupid" (1912), trans. Eric Ames, in *The Promise of Cinema: German Film Theory, 1907–1933*, ed. Anton Kaes, Nicholas Baer, and Michael J. Cowan (Berkeley: University of California Press, 2016), 231.
107. "Triangle Program: Excellent Production on View at the Knickerbocker Theater, New York," *Moving Picture World*, December 4, 1915, 1848.
108. "Special Film Reviews," *Motion Picture News*, January 24, 1914, 37.
109. Jane Gaines questions the consensus that Alice Guy made *Cabbage Fairy* in 1896, pointing to a frame enlargement dated to 1900 archived by the Collection Musée Gaumont. Jane Gaines, *Pink-Slipped: What Happened to Women in the Silent Film Industries?* (Urbana: University of Illinois Press, 2018), 51–70.
110. "In the Year 2000," *Moving Picture News*, May 4, 1912, 34.
111. Emilie Altenloh, "A Sociology of the Cinema: The Audience," *Screen* 42, no. 3 (Autumn 2001), 275.
112. I refer to the following films: *The Nursemaid's Strikes* (Pathé, 1907), *The Nervous Kitchen Maid* (Pathé, 1907), and *Rosalie Has Sleeping Sickness* (Pathé, 1911)—all filmed in France and exhibited internationally. They are included in *Cinema's First Nasty Women*, various directors (2022; New York: Kino Lorber).
113. Edoardo Coli, "Cinematic Psychology," trans. Siobhan Quinlan, in *Early Film Theories in Italy 1896–1922*, ed. Franesco Casetti with Silvio Alovisio and Luca Mazzei (Amsterdam: Amsterdam University Press, 2017), 113; original publication: "Psicologia cinematica," *Fanfulla della Domenica* 24 (August 1917): 3.
114. Giuseppe d'Abundo, "Concerning the Effects of Film Viewing on Neurotic Individuals," in *Early Film Theories in Italy 1896–1922*, ed. Francesco Casetti with Silvio Alovisio and Luca Mazzei (Amsterdam: Amsterdam University Press, 2017), 280, original publication: 'Sopra alcuni particolari effetti delle proiezioni cinematografiche nei nevrotici', Rivista italiana di neuropatologia, psichiatria ed elettroterapia 4/10, trans. National Museum of Cinema, Turin (October 1911): 433–442.
115. I use the phrase "going postal" anachronistically. It originated in the late 1980s in response to a series of violent incidents in U.S. post offices, particularly a mass shooting in 1986 perpetrated by a postal worker, Patrick Sherrill, who killed 14 of his colleagues.
116. "Jennie Postal," *Variety*, January 22, 1910, 14.
117. "Tale of a Leg," *Variety*, January 22, 1910, 14.
118. "Jennie Postal," 14.

119. I find Pamela Hutchinson's notion of "young cinema" very generative. Rather than regard silent films as "old movies," Hutchinson emphasizes their fresh, unruly, and energetic qualities, whereas so-called new films that deploy old-hat stylistic norms and conventions epitomize "old cinema." Pamela Hutchinson, "Philip French Memorial Lecture," July 28, 2021, https://silentlondon.co.uk/2021/07/30/young-cinema/.
120. David Bordwell, Janet Staiger, and Kristen Thompson have influentially defined classical Hollywood cinema as a system that dominated commercial filmmaking from 1917 to 1960, codifying a particular division of labor and set of stylistic norms that functioned to immerse the viewer cognitively by prioritizing narrative causality, that is, "distinguishing significant information from 'noise,' sorting the film's stimuli into the most comprehensive patterns." David Bordwell, "An Excessively Obvious Cinema," *The Classical Hollywood Cinema: Film Style & Mode of Production to 1960*, ed. David Bordwell, Janet Staiger, and Kristen Thompson (New York: Routledge, 1985), 7. Many scholars have challenged this paradigm, such as Linda Williams who argues that "the very concept of the classical can often provide a very questionable norm against which far too many deviations are measured." Linda Williams, *Hard Core: Power, Pleasure, and the 'Frenzy of the Visible,'* expanded ed. (Berkeley: University of California Press, 1999), 335.
121. "Across the Silver Sheet," *Motion Picture Magazine*, January 1917, 111.
122. "'Skigie' Discovers a New Sort of Girl: Says She Loudly Laughed at Julius Tannen to Make Everybody Look at Her . . .," *Variety*, February 20, 1909, 18.
123. Jolo, "Hammerstein's," *Variety*, April 29, 1911, 17.
124. "Kate Elinore in 'My Aunt from Utah,'" *Variety*, January 26, 1917, 41.
125. Louise Reeves Harrison, "Studio Saunterings," *Moving Picture World*, March 30, 1912, 1143.
126. "Would Bar Women's Hats from Theaters: Mayor Looking for Alderman Willing to Incur Wrath of Women of Macon," *Macon Daily Telegraph* (Macon, GA), May 3, 1912, 11.
127. "Musings of 'The Photoplay Philosopher,'" *Motion Picture Story Magazine*, March 1912, 137.
128. "Contagion of Laughter," *Motion Picture News*, June 18, 1918, 3417.
129. "Gay Scenes in Cafes," *New York Clipper*, September 6, 1913, 17.
130. Margaret I. MacDonald, "Impressions Gathered from a Visit to the Fourteenth Street Theater," *Moving Picture News*, October 14, 1911, 16.
131. "Dr. Herman's Act Novel and Funny," *Variety*, January 28, 1911, 32.
132. "Bernhardt Conquers New World: Says Her Immortality Will Depend Upon the Record of the New Films," *Moving Picture World*, March 9, 1912, 874–875.
133. "Playing the Picture" *Moving Picture World*, February 20, 1915, 1128.
134. *Betty and the Brook [La Tête de loup]* (1911; Nice: Pathé).
135. Guy Debord, "Separation Perfected": 6 and 12, *Society of the Spectacle* (1967), Marxists Internet Archive, https://www.marxists.org/reference/archive/debord/society.htm.
136. Key feminist accounts associate cinema's expansive transformations of experience with various nineteenth-century practices that commodified new ways of looking, modalities of spatial and temporal mobility, and affective fluidities that fostered the gendered integration of public spheres. See also Mary Ann Doane, *The Emergence of Cinematic Time: Modernity, Contingency, the Archive* (Cambridge, MA: Harvard University Press, 2002); Alison Griffiths, *Wondrous Difference: Cinema, Anthropology, and Turn-of-the-Century Visual Culture* (New York: Columbia University Press, 2002); Patrice Petro, *Joyless Streets: Women and Melodramatic Representation in Weimar Germany* (Princeton, NJ: Princeton University Press, 1989).
137. Friedberg, *Window Shopping*, 3.
138. Jean-Martin Charcot, *Lectures on the Diseases of the Nervous System: Delivered at La Salpêtrière* (Philadelphia: Lea, 1879), 194–195, 279–282.
139. "A Dull Knife," *Moving Picture World*, October 23, 1909, 558.
140. "An International Heart-Breaker," *Moving Picture World*, December 9, 1911, 828.

141. *Rosalie et Léontine vont au théâtre*, directed by Roméo Bosetti (1911; Nice: Pathé).
142. "Enlivened the Play: Sentiment and Impromptu Humor at a Moving Picture Show," reprinted from *New York Sun*, 1914.
143. "Chicago Film Brevities," *Moving Picture World*, October 26, 1912, 328.
144. "Wouldn't Let Her Laugh at Movies," *Kalamazoo Gazette*, May 22, 1917, 3.
145. "An Oddity That Is the Mummy," 454.
146. "Comments on Film Subjects. The Police Band," *Moving Picture World*, December 19, 1908, 500.
147. "Insures Patrons for Laughing Hysteria During Comedy," *Exhibitors Herald*, May 2, 1925, 29.
148. "Insurance Policy Is Stunt on 'The Hottentot,'" *Motion Picture News*, April 28, 1923, 2051.
149. Frederick M. McCloy, "Burlesque. Walt Leslie's New One," *Variety*, September 26, 1914, 12.
150. "Vaudeville. The Orpheum," *San Francisco Dramatic Review*, November 4, 1899, 7.
151. Sianne Ngai, *Theory of the Gimmick: Aesthetic Judgment and Capitalist Form* (Cambridge, MA: Belknap Press of Harvard University Press, 2020), 173.
152. "Howard Theatre Has Big Lloyd Campaign," *Moving Picture World*, June 2, 1923, 395.
153. "Across the Silver Sheet," 117.
154. "Laughter Insurance," *Moving Picture World*, March 4, 1916, 1523.
155. As Karen Ward Mahar notes, Keystone's merger with the Triangle Film Corporation in 1915 put an end to "the autonomy enjoyed by the Keystone Production units" and likely influenced Mabel Normand's decision to go independent, fearing a loss of creative control at Keystone. Karen Ward Mahar, *Women Filmmakers in Early Hollywood* (Baltimore, MD: Johns Hopkins University Press, 2006), 122.
156. "Pictorial Theatre News," *Exhibitors Herald*, March 18, 1922, 52. Thanks to Jennifer Bean for sharing this tidbit with me.
157. "Legal Matinee at Belasco Theatre: 'Tainted Philanthropy,' on Which Plagiarism Suit Rests, Brings Screams of Laughter," *New York Times*, November 27, 1912, 13.
158. "Roars of Derision Greet Goldknopf's Masterpiece," *Variety*, November 29, 1912, 12.
159. "The Following Editorial on the Closing of the Theatres Appeared in the *Boston Evening Record*, Oct. 21," *Variety*, November 1, 1918, 11.
160. "Chaplin? Pah! He Iss Not Fonny! Iss Sadt, with Troubles So Much I Should Die to Have, Says Smileless Winner of Griffith Tenspot," *Motion Picture World*, December 28, 1918, 1504.
161. "Chaplin? Pah! He Iss Not Fonny!," 1504.
162. The Wages for Housework campaign was launched in the early 1970s by the International Feminist Collective and has gained renewed urgency during the "gendered pandemic" of COVID-19, which has placed a disproportionate burden on women to exit the professional workforce in order to take up the mantle of reproductive care work (cooking, cleaning, parenting, homeschooling, etc.). Many early film comedies burlesque the gendered division of labor, such as *The Nursemaids' Strike* (Pathé, 1907), *Nervous Kitchen Maid* (Pathé, 1907), and *When Women Win* (Lubin, 1909).
163. Nancy Fraser, *Fortunes of Feminism: From State-Managed Capitalism to Neoliberal Crisis* (London: Verso, 2013), 228.
164. Fraser, *Fortunes of Feminism*, 5, 228.
165. "The Installment Collector," *Moving Picture World*, December 12, 1908, 484.
166. Gordon, *Why the French Love Jerry Lewis*, 156.
167. See Mireille Berton, *Le corps nerveux de spectateurs: Cinéma et sciences du psychisme autour de 1900* (Lausanne: L'Age d'Homme, 2015); Elyse Singer, "Strike a Pose: Performing Gestures of the Madwoman in Early Cinema," *Feminist Media Histories* 7, no. 1 (2021): 147–171; Stephanie Werder, "Perils of Cinema? The German Cinema Debate and the 'Nerve-Wracking' Medium," in *Corporeality in Early Cinema: Viscera, Skin, and Physical Form*, ed. Marina Dahlquist, Doron Galili, Jan Olsson, and Valentine Robert (Bloomington: Indiana University Press, 2018), 240–248.
168. The historical turn in feminist film studies (as in the field of film studies at large) has been ambivalent in its critical use of psychoanalysis, which was formative for feminist film theory, exemplified

by the scholarship of Laura Mulvey, Teresa de Lauretis, Mary Ann Doane, E. Ann Kaplan, Kaja Silverman, Annette Kuhn, and many others.

169. Hilary Hallett, *Go West, Young Women! The Rise of Early Hollywood* (Berkeley: University of California Press, 2013), 14.

170. Hallett, *Go West, Young Women!*, 12. See also Mark Garrett Cooper, *Universal Women: Filmmaking and Institutional Change in Early Hollywood* (Urbana: University of Illinois Press, 2010): 45–90.

171. See Kate Saccone, "Research Update: Alice Guy Blaché at Columbia University," in Women Film Pioneers Project, ed. Jane Gaines, Radha Vatsal, and Monica Dall'Asta (New York: Columbia University Libraries, 2021), https://doi.org/10.7916/d8-hwn3-2928.

172. Jane M. Gaines, "Film History and the Two Presents of Feminist Theory," *Cinema Journal* 44, no. 1 (Fall 2004): 113.

173. Alix Beeston and Stefan Solomon, "Pathways to the Feminist Incomplete: *An Introduction, a Theory, a Manifesto*," in *Incomplete: The Feminist Possibilities of the Unfinished Film*, ed. Alix Beeston and Stefan Solomon (Berkeley: University of California Press, 2023), 10.

174. Laura Horak, *Girls Will Be Boys: Cross-Dressed Women, Lesbians, and American Cinema, 1908–1934* (New Brunswick, NJ: Rutgers University Press, 2016); Susan Potter, *Queer Timing: The Emergence of Lesbian Sexuality in Early Cinema* (Urbana: University of Illinois Press, 2020); Diana W. Anselmo, *A Queer Way of Feeling: Girl Fans and Personal Archives in Early Hollywood* (Berkeley: University of California Press, 2023); Kiki Loveday, *Sapphic Cinemania!* (PhD diss., University of California Irvine, 2022).

175. Bean and Negra, "Introduction: Toward a Feminist Historiography," 2.

176. A comprehensive study of the relation between accusations of madness and the creative power of women in the silent film industry is long overdue. In a different context, Jennifer Bean excavates the early film industry's promotion of "'nervy movie ladies,' as they were often called" (36), epitomized by Pearl White, Helen Holmes, Ruth Roland, Marie Walcamp, Grace Cunard, and Texas Guinan. Bean theorizes the female action star's discursive body as a "catastrophe machine," connecting their "blithe *jouissance*" (34) with an "alarming" prevalence of nervous disorders (36). Jennifer Bean, "Technologies of Early Stardom and the Extraordinary Body," *Camera Obscura* 16, no. 3 (2001): 8–57.

177. Malwine Rennert, "The Onlookers of Life at the Cinema" (1914–1915), in *Red Velvet Seat: Women's Writings on the First Fifty Years of Cinema*, ed. Antonia Lant with Ingrid Períz (London: Verso, 2006), 93.

178. Anonymous, "New Terrain for Cinematographic Theaters," 1910, 22.

179. Anonymous, "New Terrain," 22.

180. Strobl, "The Cinematograph," 26.

181. "Tickled to Death," *Moving Picture World*, October 23, 1909, 579; "Tickled to Death," *Variety*, October 30, 1909, 11.

182. Albert Hellwig, "Illusions and Hallucinations During Cinematograph Projections" (1914), trans. Michael Cowan, in *The Promise of Cinema: German Film Theory, 1907–1933*, ed. Anton Kaes, Nicholas Baer, and Michael J. Cowan (Berkeley: University of California Press, 2016), 47.

183. Ben Singer, "Modernity, Hyperstimulus, and the Rise of Popular Sensationalism," in *Cinema and the Invention of Modern Life*, ed. Leo Charney and Vanessa Schwartz (Berkeley: University of California Press, 1995), 72. "For Kracauer, Benjamin, and their many predecessors," Singer explains, "this broad escalation of sensational amusement was clearly a sign of the times . . . Sidestepping a more strictly socioeconomic explanation, they framed the commercialization of the thrill as a reflection and symptom (as well as an agent or catalyst) of neurological modernity. The increasing intensity of popular amusements, they argued, corresponded to the new texture of daily life," 91.

184. As Walter Benjamin explains in *Theses on the Philosophy of History* (1940), the dialectical image "flashes up at a moment of danger" (VI) "at the instant when it can be recognized and is never seen

again" (V). It distills the possibilities of the historical conjuncture into a revolutionary image that jolts the masses into political awakening. "In every era the attempt must be made anew to wrest tradition away from a conformism that is about to overpower it" (VI)—to disrupt historical repetition with hopeful, fleeting possibilities that mass experience will explode into collective politics. When Benjamin wrote this essay in 1940 (which in many ways parallels our own moment), the contradictions of capitalism concretized by cinema's many dialectical images converged on the struggle between communism and fascism. Walter Benjamin, *Illuminations*, ed. Hannah Arendt (New York: Shocken, 1969), 255.

185. Miriam Hansen, *Cinema and Experience: Siegfried Kracauer, Walter Benjamin, and Theodor W. Adorno* (Berkeley: University of California Press, 2012), xvii.
186. Catherine Russell, *Archiveology: Walter Benjamin and Archival Film Practices* (Durham, NC: Duke University Press, 2018), 3. This quotation is in reference to Walter Benjamin's concept of "experience."
187. Giuliana Bruno, *Streetwalking on a Ruined Map: Cultural Theory and the City Films of Elvira Notari* (Princeton, NJ: Princeton University Press, 1993), 3. A number of Notari's films have been discovered and restored since the publication of Bruno's book on Notari in 1993. In 2018, Daniela Currò and Maria Assunta Pimpinelli curated these surviving films in a program at the Bologna Ritrovato, "Song of Naples: Tribute to Elvira Notari and Vittorio Martinelli." "Song of Naples: Tribute to Elvira Notari and Vittorio Martinelli," Il Cinema Ritrovato, 2018, https://festival.ilcinemaritrovato.it/en/sezione/napoli-che-canta-omaggio-a-elvira-notari-e-vittorio-martinelli/.
188. See Miriam Bratu Hansen, "Fallen Women, Rising Stars, New Horizons: Shanghai Silent Film as Vernacular Modernism," *Film Quarterly* 54, no. 1 (2000): 10–22.
189. Zhen Zhang, *An Amorous History of the Silver Screen: Shanghai Cinema, 1896–1937* (Chicago: University of Chicago Press, 2005), xiii.
190. Debrashree Mukherjee focuses on the transition to talkies in 1930s Bombay. For her, "*cine-ecology* describes a material reality as well as a method for a processual and nondualist approach to film ... Cine-ecologies emerge out of the energetic entanglements of practices, symbols, infrastructures, ideologies, actors, and climates that swirl around the film image in locations where filmmaking and film consumption are prominent aspects of everyday life." Debrashree Mukherjee, *Bombay Hustle: Making Movies in a Colonial City* (New York: Columbia University Press, 2020), 2–3.
191. Saidiya Hartman, "Venus in Two Acts," *Small Axe 26* 12, no. 2 (June 2008): 8. The eponym for this essay is an African girl named Venus who died aboard the slave ship *Recovery* in 1792. As in *Lose Your Mother*, "Venus" aims to "tell an impossible story and to amplify the impossibility of its telling" (11) in order to forge a history written against the grain of the archive. Hartman follows the modal verb of unrealized past possibility to pursue "what might have happened or might have been said or might have been done" (11) as a way of "listening for the unsaid" and "redressing the violence that produced numbers, ciphers, and fragments of discourse" (2–3) in lieu of narrative evidence.
192. Hartman, "Venus in Two Acts," 2.
193. Saidiya Hartman, *Wayward Lives, Beautiful Experiments: Intimate Histories of Riotous Black Girls, Troublesome Women, and Queer Radicals* (New York: Norton, 2019), 193–202.
194. Hartman, *Wayward Lives, Beautiful Experiments*, 194.
195. Stewart, *Migrating to the Movies*, 104.
196. Stewart, 98.
197. Stewart, 98.
198. Stewart, 105.
199. Jayna Brown, *Babylon Girls: Black Women Performers and the Shaping of the Modern* (Durham, NC: Duke University Press, 2008), 5.
200. "Algy's Awful Auto," *Reel Life*, October 25, 1913, 26.
201. "Algy's Awful Auto," 26.

8. THE VISUAL CURE? MOVING PICTURES AS NEUROTIC TRIGGER AND THERAPEUTIC INSTRUMENT

1. "Pictures for Insane," *Variety*, March 9, 1910, 13.
2. "Pictures for Insane," 13.
3. "Pictures for Asylum Is Grand Jury Idea," *Exhibitors Herald* (Chicago, IL), December 15, 1917, 34.
4. "Biograph An Insanity Cure: A Chicago Asylum Experiment with Moving Pictures," *Kansas City Star* (Kansas City, MO), April 9, 1904, 1.
5. Archival work on nineteenth-century gender and madness in the field of critical disability studies often adopts a narrative frame that amplifies the pathos of historical experience but defers the redemption of neurodivergent knowledges until the material conditions of social consciousness and legal reform can allow them to be articulated.
6. Lisa Cartwright, "An Etiology of the Neurological Gaze," in *Screening the Body: Tracing Medicine's Visual Culture* (Minneapolis: University of Minnesota Press, 1995), 47–80.
7. Cartwright, "An Etiology of the Neurological Gaze," 48.
8. Scott Curtis, "Between Observation and Spectatorship: Medicine, Movies, and Mass Culture," in *The Shape of Spectatorship: Art, Science, and Early Cinema in Germany* (New York: Columbia University Press, 2015), 90–141.
9. Neurodiversity simply refers to the vast range of cognitive processes that regulate learning, perception, attention, sociability, and behavior—beyond what is considered "normal," "typical," or "neurotypical." Sociologist Judy Singer coined the term in 1998 to challenge the pathologization of cognitive difference or disability by medical practices and society at large. See Judy Singer, *NeuroDiversity: The Birth of an Idea* (Author, 2017).
10. Quizz, "The Moving Picture Fan and the Usher," *New York Clipper*, November 15, 1913, 8.
11. Quizz, "The Moving Picture Fan and the Usher."
12. According to Janus Films, an original print of Carl Theodor Dreyer's *The Passion of Joan of Arc* (1929) was discovered while someone cleaned out a closet at the Dikemark Sykehouse (a mental asylum outside Oslo, Norway) in 1981. "How did the film end up in a closet? Harald Arnesen, the director of the institute at the time, may have wanted to screen it for staff and patients." Although the print had been projected several times, there are no records of its exhibition in the asylum. "Lost and Found: The Passion of *The Passion of Joan of Arc*," Janus Films, press release, 2017.
13. "Comments on the Films: She Wrote a Play," *Moving Picture World*, January 17, 1914, 290.
14. "Interesting Film Reviews: Ham in the Nut Factory," *Motion Picture News*, June 5, 1915, 76. All film citations in this chapter include the production company in lieu of the film director.
15. G. D. Crain Jr., "Pictures Help to Set Right Insane Minds," *Moving Picture World*, February 27, 1915, 1320.
16. Giuseppe d'Abundo, "Concerning the Effects of Film Viewing on Neurotic Individuals" (1911), in *Early Film Theories in Italy 1896–1922*, ed. Franesco Casetti with Silvio Alovisio and Luca Mazzei (Amsterdam: Amsterdam University Press, 2017), 278.
17. d'Abundo, "Concerning the Effects of Film Viewing," 281.
18. "Film Review: The Hypnotist's Revenge. Biograph," *Moving Picture World*, July 27, 1907, 331.
19. See Gerald Grob, "The Mental Hygiene Movement," in *Mental Illness and American Society, 1875–1940* (Princeton, NJ: Princeton University Press, 1983), 144–178.
20. Emily Godbey, "Picture Me Sane: Photography and the Magic Lantern in a Nineteenth-Century Asylum," *American Studies* 41, no. 1 (Spring 2000): 35.
21. Godbey, "Picture Me Sane," 64.
22. "Reasons for Admission, West Virginia Hospital for the Insane (Weston), October 22, 1864, to December 12, 1889." A long list of varied, often scandalous justifications for admission to the hospital was published in a pamphlet by Marjorie E. Carr in 1993 and is now archived in the Weston Hospital Collection.

23. The United States has a long, sordid history of perpetrating forced sterilizations against neurodivergent people, often targeting women and immigrants. Eugenic progressivism embraced involuntary hysterectomies in the early twentieth century, provoking Indiana to enact the first eugenic sterilization law in 1907, which was upheld by the U.S. Supreme Court in 1927. See Philip R. Reilly, "Eugenics and Involuntary Sterilization: 1907–2015," *Annual Review of Genomics and Human Genetics* 16, no. 1 (2015): 351–368.
24. Lennard Davis, "In the Time of Pandemic, the Deep Structure of Biopower Is Laid Bare," *Critical Inquiry* 47, no. 2 (June 26, 2020), https://www.journals.uchicago.edu/doi/10.1086/711458.
25. The Race Betterment Foundation established a "pedigree registry" in 1911, which was administered by a eugenics record office. Genetic traits were selectively monitored and subjectively interpreted to advance the racist theory that immigrants and racial minorities lacked genetic fitness.
26. Gerald N. Grob, *Mental Illness and American Society, 1875–1940* (Princeton, NJ: Princeton University Press, 1983), 179.
27. Grob, *Mental Illness and American Society*, 77.
28. Grob, *Mental Illness and American Society*, 77. Silas Weir Mitchell, the American neurasthenia specialist and "rest cure" evangelist, also advocated the use of electricity (in addition to seclusion, rest, fatty diet, and massages) to restore nervous women to "active useful life." Silas Weir Mitchell, "Electricity," in *Fat and Blood: An Essay on the Treatment of Certain Forms of Hysteria* (Philadelphia: J. B. Lippincott , 1877), https://www.gutenberg.org/files/16230/16230-h/16230-h.htm.
29. "Power's No. 6A Installation," *Moving Picture World*, March 1, 1913, 890; "Power's Cameragraph in the Hospital and School," *Moving Picture News*, December 13, 1912, 17.
30. "Moving Picture Educator: Unusual Motiograph Installation," *Moving Picture World*, February 7, 1914, 665.
31. "Moving Picture Educator: Reading the Mind by Kinematography," *Moving Picture World*, February 7, 1914, 665.
32. Mad Pride is an international mass movement that celebrates the identity and experience of current and former "users" (that is, patients, consumers, survivors) of mental health services. Its redemptive rhetoric further seeks to recuperate negative signifiers and slurs such as "mad," "nuts," "crazy," and so forth. The movement originated in Toronto in 1993 to combat social stigmas against people with psychiatric histories living in boarding houses in the Parkdale neighborhood. See Ted Curtis and Robert Dellar, *Mad Pride: A Celebration of Mad Culture* (London: Spare Change Books, 2000).
33. David Jackson-Perry, Hanna Bertilsdotter Rosqvist, Marianthi Kourti, and Jenn Layton Annable, "Sensory Strangers: Travels in Normate Sensory Worlds," in *Neurodiversity Studies: A New Critical Paradigm*, ed. Hanna Rosqvist, Nick Chown, and Anna Stenning (New York: Routledge, 2020), 125, 127.
34. Jackson-Perry et al., "Sensory Strangers," 130.
35. Jackson-Perry et al., "Sensory Strangers," 130.
36. Jackson-Perry et al., "Sensory Strangers," 130.
37. "Biograph An Insanity Cure," 1.
38. Nev Jones and Timothy Kelly, "Three Inconvenient Complications: On the Heterogeneities of Madness and Their Relationship to Disability," in *Madness, Distress, and the Politics of Disablement*, ed. Helen Spandler, Jill Anderson, and Bob Sapey (Bristol, UK: Policy Press, 2015), 49.
39. Jones and Kelly, "Three Inconvenient Complications," 44.
40. Michel Foucault, *Madness and Civilization: A History of Insanity in the Age of Reason* (New York: Vintage, 1961/1988), 135.
41. Foucault, *Madness and Civilization*, 135, 241.
42. Foucault, *Madness and Civilization*, 127.
43. "Open Theater for Washington Insane," *National News Association*, December 1, 1911, 8.
44. "Theatre for Insane," *New York Clipper*, December 12, 1914, 2.

45. Alison Griffiths, *Carceral Fantasies: Cinema and Prisons in Early Twentieth-Century America* (New York: Columbia University Press, 2016), 134.
46. Charles Gibson, "Moving Pictures Curing Insanity," *Nickelodeon*, November 1, 1910, 253.
47. Gibson, "Moving Pictures Curing Insanity."
48. Gibson, "Moving Pictures Curing Insanity."
49. d'Abundo, "Concerning the Effects of Film Viewing," 284.
50. Gibson, "Moving Pictures Curing Insanity," 254.
51. Gibson, "Moving Pictures Curing Insanity," 253.
52. "Two of a Kind," *The Film Index*, January 16, 1909, 7.
53. Gibson, "Moving Pictures Curing Insanity," 253.
54. As Benjamin Reiss notes, "some state-funded asylums made labor compulsory for all but the 'furiously mad,' and although the New York State Lunatic Asylum—among others—prided itself upon the voluntary nature of patient labor there, work was always a key component of the moral treatment movement in asylum medicine." Benjamin Reiss, *Theaters of Madness: Insane Asylums and Nineteenth-Century American Culture* (Chicago: University of Chicago Press, 2008), 32.
55. Gibson, "Moving Pictures Curing Insanity," 253.
56. See chapter 7 of this book for my discussion of early film theory and neurological modernity.
57. "An Auto Maniac," *Film Index*, January 16, 1909, 4.
58. Gibson, "Moving Pictures Curing Insanity," 254.
59. "Pictures for Insane," 13.
60. "Cure for Insanity: Patients of Insane Asylum are Taken to Department Store Shopping as Treatment," *Jonesboro Weekly Sun* (Jonesboro, AK), January 1, 1907, 1.
61. Gibson, "Moving Pictures Curing Insanity," 254.
62. Sarah Keller, *Anxious Cinephilia: Pleasure and Peril at the Movies* (New York: Columbia University Press, 2020), 189.
63. "Moving Picture News from Everywhere," *Views and Films Index*, January 11, 1908, 6.
64. "Moving Picture News from Everywhere," 6.
65. "M-R Forms a Fishing Club," *Motion Picture News*, May 22, 1915, 53.
66. "'Buster Brown' Comedy Series Coming," *Motion Picture News*, December 27, 1914, 18.
67. This film has been preserved by the Library of Congress. You can view it on their website: https://www.loc.gov/item/00694242/.
68. "The Airship Fugitives," *Motion Picture World*, July 5, 1913, 53. For more on early film's aerial vision, see Patrick Ellis, *Aeroscopics: Media of the Bird's-Eye View* (Berkeley: University of California Press, 2021).
69. "The Colonel of the Nutts," *Moving Picture World*, March 14, 1914, 1386.
70. Mario Umberto Masini and Giuseppe Vidoni, "The Cinematograph in the Field of Mental Illness and Criminality: Notes" (1915), in *Early Film Theories in Italy 1896–1922*, ed. Franesco Casetti with Silvio Alovisio and Luca Mazzei (Amsterdam: Amsterdam University Press, 2017), 290.
71. Hugo Münsterberg, *The Photoplay: A Psychological Study*, 221, https://www.gutenberg.org/files/15383/15383-h/15383-h.htm.
72. Masini and Vidoni, "The Cinematograph," 290.
73. Masini and Vidoni, "The Cinematograph," 292.
74. "Betty in the Lions' Den," *Moving Picture World*, November 22, 1913, 898.
75. Rae Beth Gordon, *Why the French Love Jerry Lewis: From Cabaret to Early Cinema* (Redwood City, CA: Stanford University Press, 2002), 143.
76. Gordon, *Why the French Love Jerry Lewis*, 141.
77. Siegfried Kracauer, *From Caligari to Hitler: A Psychological History of the German Film* (Princeton, NJ: Princeton University Press, 2019).
78. "'Zandori's Secret': A Cure for Madness Has Been Found; but the Finder Has Gone Mad and the Villain Won't Use It to Help Him," *Moving Picture World*, November 28, 1914, 1220.

79. "Solax: The Prodigal Wife," *Moving Picture News*, November 7, 1912, 32.
80. "Punch: The Devil of a Time," *Moving Picture News*, December 14, 1912, 29.
81. For further discussion of racism, disability, and American history, see Dennis Tyler, *Disabilities of the Color Line: Redressing Antiblackness from Slavery to the Present* (New York: New York University Press, 2022).
82. "Edison Co. 'Drawing the Color Line,'" *Film Index*, January 16, 1909, 9.
83. La Marr Jurelle Bruce, *How to Go Mad Without Losing Your Mind: Madness and Black Radical Creativity* (Durham, NC: Duke University Press, 2021), 4.
84. Bruce, *How to Go Mad*, 2.
85. Bruce, *How to Go Mad*, 4.
86. "The Mad Musician (An Escape from an Insane Asylum)," *Moving Picture World*, March 7, 1908, 195.
87. Robert McRuer, "In Focus: Cripping Cinema and Media Studies," *JCMS* 58, no. 4 (2019): 136. See also Georgina Kleege, *Sight Unseen* (New Haven, CT: Yale University Press, 1999), 43–66.
88. Merri Lisa Johnson and Robert McRuer, "Cripistemologies," *Journal of Literary and Cultural Disability Studies* 8, no. 2 (2014): 128.
89. R. D. Laing, "Persons and Experience," in *The Politics of Experience* (New York: Pantheon, 1967), 28.
90. Hans Hennes, "Cinematography in the Service of Neurology and Psychology, with a Description of Some Rarer Motion Disorders" (1910), in *The Promise of Cinema: German Film Theory, 1907–1933*, ed. Anton Kaes, Nicholas Baer, and Michael Cowan (Berkeley: University of California Press 2016), 521.
91. Hennes, "Cinematography in the Service of Neurology and Psychology," 522.
92. Hennes, "Cinematography in the Service of Neurology and Psychology," 522.
93. Hennes, "Cinematography in the Service of Neurology and Psychology," 522.
94. Claudia Gianetto, "Antologia Filmati Neuropatologici Realizzati dal Prof. Camillo Negro con Roberto Omegna: Camillo Negro (IT 1906–1919)," Le Giornate del Cinema Muto, online program notes, http://www.giornatedelcinemamuto.it/anno/2017/en/antologia-filmati-neuropatologici-realizzati-dal-prof-camillo-negro-con-roberto-omegna-2/index.html.
95. The subfield of film scholarship on medical uses of early cinema is further aligned with ongoing research about useful cinema, orphaned media, and educational and nontheatrical films. See *Useful Cinema*, ed. Charles Acland and Haidee Wasson (Durham, NC: Duke University Press, 2011); *Learning with the Lights Off: Educational Film in the United States*, ed. Devin Orgeron, Marsha Gordon, and Dan Streible (Oxford: Oxford University Press, 2011); Orphan Film Symposium: https://wp.nyu.edu/orphanfilm/.
96. "Munitions of War," *The Globe*, July 24, 1900, 1.
97. Geneviève Aubert, "Arthur van Gehuchten Takes Neurology to the Movies," *Neurology* 59, no. 10 (2002): 1616. Quoted from July 16, 1911, in a letter written by Van Gehuchten to the rector of his university: only 1,000 francs were granted according to surviving records.
98. Aubert, "Arthur van Gehuchten Takes Neurology," 1616.
99. I visited the Royal Belgian Film Archive from October 10–12, 2017, where I watched (and rewatched) digital scans transferred from 35mm copies of the surviving three hours of footage in the Arthur Van Gehuchten Collection.
100. Preserved by the British Film Institute, *Daisy Doodad's Dial* (1914) is included in *Cinema's First Nasty Women*, various directors (2022; New York: Kino Lorber), a four-disc DVD/Blu-ray set cocurated by Maggie Hennefeld, Laura Horak, and Elif Rongen-Kaynakçi.
101. Aubert, "Arthur van Gehuchten Takes Neurology," 1615.
102. O. Buda, D. Arsene, M. Ceausu, D. Dermengiu, and G.C. Curca, "Georges Marinesco and the early research in neuropathology," *Neurology* 72, no. 1 (2009): 90.
103. Gianetto, "Antologia Filmati Neuropatologici Realizzati dal Prof. Camillo Negro."
104. Gianetto, "Antologia Filmati Neuropatologici Realizzati dal Prof. Camillo Negro."

105. "Trench Cure for Insanity," *Sunderland Daily Echo and Shipping Gazette* (Sunderland, Durham, England), September 12, 1916, 3.
106. Adriano Chío, Claudia Gianetto, and Stella Dagna, "Professor Camillo Negro's Neuropathological Films," *Journal of the History of the Neurosciences* 25, no. 1 (2016): 46.
107. Chío et al., "Professor Camillo Negro's Neuropathological Films."
108. Chío et al., "Professor Camillo Negro's Neuropathological Films."
109. "Would We?," *Film Index*, Feb 27, 1909, 3.
110. "Pictures for Insane," 13.
111. "Pictures for Insane," 13.
112. E. Boudinot Stockton, "Pictures in Learned Society," *Moving Picture World*, May 24, 1913, 799.
113. Stockton, "Pictures in Learned Society," 799.
114. Cartwright, "An Etiology of the Neurological Gaze," 48.
115. Cartwright, "An Etiology of the Neurological Gaze," 57.
116. Cartwright, "An Etiology of the Neurological Gaze," 66–67.
117. Walter Greenough Chase, "The Use of the Biograph in Medicine," *Boston Medical and Surgical Journal* 153, no. 21 (1905): 571–572.
118. Chase, "The Use of the Biograph in Medicine," 572.
119. Chicot, "The Short Talk Man," *Film Index*, March 25, 1911, 12.
120. Giovanni Fossi, "The Movie Theatre Audience" (1908), in *Early Film Theories in Italy 1896–1922*, ed. Franesco Casetti with Silvio Alovisio and Luca Mazzei (Amsterdam: Amsterdam University Press, 2017), 58.
121. Dean Bowman, "Film Flams," *Picture-Play Weekly*, November 6, 1915, 7.
122. "Crazy People Entertained with Moving Pictures," *Moving Picture World*, February 4, 1911, 233.
123. "Crazy People Entertained with Moving Pictures."
124. "Crazy People Entertained with Moving Pictures."
125. Stanton B. Garner Jr., *Kinesthetic Spectatorship in the Theatre: Phenomenology, Cognition, Movement* (London: Palgrave Macmillan, 2016), 1.
126. Garner, *Kinesthetic Spectatorship in the Theatre*, 82.
127. Gabriel Tarde, *The Laws of Imitation* (New York: Henry Holt, 1903), 87, https://archive.org/details/lawsofimitation00tard/.
128. Henri Bergson, *Laughter: An Essay on the Meaning of the Comic* (Paris: Revue de Paris, 1900), 109–110, https://archive.org/details/laughteranessay00berggoog.
129. Tarde, *The Laws of Imitation*, 87.
130. See my discussion of Uncle Josh in chapter 7.
131. "Pictures to Help Set Right Insane Minds," *Motion Picture World*, February 27, 1915, 1320.
132. G. F. Blaisdell, "Notes of the Week," *Moving Picture News*, August 26, 1911, 19.
133. I consulted the Colorado Mental Health Institute at Pueblo (CMHIP) Museum, which was unable to provide further information about the institute's early silent film screenings.
134. Griffiths, *Carceral Fantasies*, 191.
135. Griffiths, *Carceral Fantasies*, 149.
136. Gibson, "Moving Pictures Curing Insanity," 254.
137. The theory of the four humors (or fluids) shaped medical treatments for bodily ailments from Ancient Greece and Islam to medieval Europe. It was largely displaced by germ theory and pathogenic understandings of disease in the mid-nineteenth century. According to Hippocrates, the four humors/temperaments include: black bile (melancholic), yellow bile (choleric), phlegm (phlegmatic), and blood (sanguine).
138. "Colours to Cure Insanity," *Cornubian and Redruth Times* (Cornwall, England), November 21, 1902, 4.
139. "Colours to Cure Insanity," 4. See also Barbara Flueckiger, "Timeline of Historical Film Colors," https://filmcolors.org/.

140. "More Pictures for Insane: Inmates at Dunning Institution to See Comic Pictures," *Film Index*, April 22, 1911, 9. Dunning was officially closed the following year after multiple public exposés of its "joyless" atmosphere, insanitary conditions, and "sickening odor," as detailed by Katherine Reed, "A Day at the Poor House," *The Graphic*, September 24, 1892.
141. "Believes in Motion Pictures," *Film Index*, December 24, 1910, 5.
142. "Believes in Motion Pictures," 5.
143. Jules Romains, "The Crowd at the Cinematograph" (1911), in *French Film Theory and Criticism: A History/Anthology, 1907–1939*, ed. Richard Abel (Princeton, NJ: Princeton University Press, 1988), 53.
144. Münsterberg, *The Photoplay*, 111.
145. "Believes in Motion Pictures," 5.
146. G. F. Blaisdell, "Notes of the Week," *Moving Picture News*, August 26, 1911, 24.
147. "Motion Pictures Help Insane: Majestic Amusement Co. Give Performance at Shelby County Insane Asylum—Dr. Anderson Pleased with Results," *Film Index*, December 24, 1910, 9.
148. Akiko Hart, "A New Alliance? The Hearing Voices Movement and Neurodiversity," in *Neurodiversity Studies: A New Critical Paradigm*, ed. Hanna Bertilsdotter Rosqvist, Nick Chown, and Anna Stenning (New York: Routledge, 2020), 221.
149. Jackson-Perry et al., "Sensory Strangers," 130.
150. Shelley Briggs and Fiona Cameron, "Psycho-emotional Disablism, Complex Trauma and Women's Mental Distress," in *Madness, Distress, and the Politics of Disablement*, ed. Helen Spandler, Jill Anderson, and Bob Sapey (Bristol, UK: Policy Press, 2015), 115.
151. Siegfried Kracauer, "The Head of Medusa," in *Theory of Film: The Redemption of Physical Reality* (Princeton, NJ: Princeton University Press, 1960/1997), 305–306; Hal Foster, "Medusa and the Real," *RES: Anthropology and Aesthetics* 44 (Autumn 2003): 181.
152. Genevieve Yue, *Girl Head: Feminism and Film Materiality* (New York: Fordham University Press, 2020), 21, 18.
153. Kracauer, "The Head of Medusa," 305.
154. Robert Graupp, "The Dangers of the Cinema" (1911–12), in *The Promise of Cinema: German Film Theory, 1907–1933*, ed. Anton Kaes, Nicholas Baer, and Michael Cowan (Berkeley: University of California Press, 2016), 225.
155. Curtis, "Between Observation and Spectatorship," 130.
156. Graupp, "The Head of Medusa," 224–225.
157. Graupp, "The Head of Medusa," 225.
158. *Tontolini* was a popular series produced by the Cines company in Rome. Ferdinand Guillaume (widely known by his stage name Polidor) appeared in over 100 short films from 1910 to 1919. Tontolini is frequently depicted as a neurotic or neurasthenic, such as in *Tontolini and Hypnotism* (1910) and *Tontolini the Sleep-walker* (1913).
159. "Ohio: Dr. Dippy's Sanitorium," *New York Clipper*, November 16, 1907, 1081.
160. Doron Galili, *Seeing by Electricity* (Durham, NC: Duke University Press, 2020), 100. For more on this remarkable film, see Katharina Loew's 2020 video essay, "Split-Screen Effects and Early Cinema," Domitor 2020, https://domitor2020.org/en-ca/split-screen-effects-and-early-cinema/.
161. For more information on this film, see the online database of the Foundation Jérôme Seydoux-Pathé: http://filmographie.fondation-jeromeseydoux-pathe.com/7458-une-representation-au-cinema.
162. "A New Cure for Divorce," *Moving Picture News*, July 27, 1912, 25.
163. "The Thanhouser Three-a-Week," *Moving Picture World*, August 27, 1912, 302.
164. The pretense of inherited madness plays a similar role in *Feel My Pulse*, directed by Gregory La Cava (1928; Hollywood: Paramount Pictures), a screwball comedy film about a neurasthenic woman who asserts her sanity—and thus claims her inheritance—after falling in love with a fake bootlegger who's really an undercover reporter but is pretending to be a psychiatric attendant in a rum-running sanitorium.

165. "In the Grip of the Vampire (Gaumont Three-Reel Production)," *Moving Picture News*, December 21, 1912, 13.
166. Sigmund Freud, *The Standard Edition of the Complete Psychological Works of Sigmund Freud*, vol. XIX *(1923–1925)*, trans. James Strachey (London: Hogarth Press, 1966), 227.
167. Milo Ray Phelps, "The Movie Cure," *Motion Picture Magazine*, January 1920, 74.
168. Phelps, "The Movie Cure," 74.

9. FROM MOUTH TO SCREEN: LAUGHING HEADS IN THE HISTORY OF FILM

1. "Correspondence: Coincidence," *Moving Picture World*, December 11, 1907, 687.
2. All film citations in this chapter include the production company in lieu of the film director.
3. Kyla Wazana Tompkins notes: *Laughing Gas* was made when "the criminalization of narcotics in relation to African-Americans is starting to take hold in the state and in the law." Video introduction for *Laughing Gas*, included in *Cinema's First Nasty Women*, various directors (2022; New York: Kino Lorber). Eileen Bowser claims that "medicine shows and carnivals" sold nitrous oxide "to customers to inhale as a cheap high," linking the film's "joke of non-stop laughter that spreads like contagion" to earlier vaudeville acts and minstrel shows. "Movies and the Expansion of the Audience," in *American Cinema 1890–1909: Themes and Variations*, ed. André Gaudreault (New Brunswick, NJ: Rutgers University Press, 2009), 196.
4. Jacqueline Stewart, "What Happened in the Transition? Reading Race, Gender, and Labor Between the Shots," in *American Cinema's Transitional Era: Audiences, Institutions, Practices*, ed. Charlie Keil and Shelley Stamp (Berkeley: University of California Press, 2004), 119.
5. "Film Review. Laughing Gas," *Moving Picture World*, December 11, 1907, 671.
6. Kurt Pinthus, "The Photoplay: A Serious Introduction for Those Who Think Ahead and Reflect" (1914), trans. Don Reneau, in *The Promise of Cinema: German Film Theory, 1907–1933*, ed. Anton Kaes, Nicholas Baer, and Michael J. Cowan (Berkeley: University of California Press, 2016), 201.
7. *Fou rire* ("crazy laughter") is a common colloquial expression in French that would have been familiar to American laughers at the time. For example, "Le Fou Rire" (1907), a laughing song performed by Mme Rolini (of the Folies Bergère), was an international hit recorded by Cylindres Edison Moulés the same year of Edison's *Laughing Gas*. You can hear a recording at http://www.library.ucsb.edu/OBJID/Cylinder9454. But it also evoked the "fou rire prodromique," a serious medical condition diagnosed by Charles Féré in 1903 as an affliction of uncontrollable laughter before an apoplectic event. See also F. A. A. Gondim, F. P. Thomas, G. R. Oliveira, S. Cruz-Flores, "Fou Rire Prodromique and History of Pathological Laughter in the XIXth and XXth Centuries," *Revue Neurologique* 160, no. 3 (March 2004): 277–283.
8. "Correspondence. Coincidence," 687.
9. "Film Review: Laughing Gas," 671.
10. "Correspondence. Coincidence," 687.
11. *The Boy Detective, or the Abductors Foiled*, directed by Wallace McCutcheon (1908; New York: Biograph), is included in *Cinema's First Nasty Women*, various directors (2022; New York: Kino Lorber).
12. "Vitagraph Films. Laughing Gas," *New York Clipper*, December 7, 1907, 1180.
13. "Laugh Selves to Death: Suffocating Gas Used by Germans Drives Men Crazy—They Die Like Maniacs," *Idaho Register* (Idaho Falls, ID), June 5, 1915, 3.
14. "Health, Happiness and Success for 1908," *Moving Picture World*, January 4, 1908, 4.
15. Rush, "Moving Picture: 'Laughing Gas' (Comedy)," *Variety*, December 21, 1907, 10.

16. "Health, Happiness and Success for 1908," 4. *Dr. Skinum*, directed by Wallace McCutcheon (1907; New York: Biograph), depicts the efforts of an ambitious dermatologist who invents a "Cabinet of Beauty" to cure women of physical deformities. *Channel Tunnel*, directed by Georges Méliès (1907; France: Star Film Company), also known as *Tunneling the English Channel*, envisions the Chunnel over eight decades avant la lettre.
17. "Health, Happiness and Success for 1908," 4.
18. Laura Horak, *Girls Will Be Boys: Cross-Dressed Women, Lesbians, and American Cinema, 1908–1934* (New Brunswick, NJ: Rutgers University Press, 2016).
19. Rush, "Moving Picture: 'Laughing Gas,'" 10.
20. Rush, "Moving Picture: 'Laughing Gas,'" 10.
21. Béla Balázs, *Béla Balázs: Early Film Theory, Visible Man and the Spirit of Film*, ed. Erica Carter, trans. Rodney Livingstone (New York: Berghan, 2010), 37, 38.
22. Balázs, *Béla Balázs*, 37.
23. "4142 . . . A Big Swallow," *We Put the World Before You by Means of the Bioscope and Urban Films*, November 1903, 115.
24. "3501 . . . Grandma Threading Her Needle," *We Put the World Before You by Means of the Bioscope and Urban Films*, November 1903, 104.
25. "3509 . . . Whiskey or Bullets," *We Put the World Before You by Means of the Bioscope and Urban Films*, November 1903, 105.
26. "3502 . . . Scandal over the Tea Cups," *We Put the World Before You by Means of the Bioscope and Urban Films*, November 1903, 104.
27. Balázs, *Béla Balázs*, 36.
28. Karen Redrobe and Jeff Scheible, "Preface," in *Deep Mediations: Thinking Space in Cinema and Digital Culture*, ed. Karen Redrobe and Jeff Scheible (Minneapolis: University of Minnesota Press, 2021), xviii.
29. Mariann Lewinsky, commentary track for *The Nervous Kitchen Maid [Victoire a ses nerfs]* (1907; Paris: Pathé Frères), included in *Cinema's First Nasty Women*, various directors (2022; New York: Kino Lorber).
30. Gurning is a centuries-old English tradition that involves making grotesque comic faces by projecting the lower jaw upward while covering the upper lip with the lower lip. The World Gurning Championship is held annually at the Edgemont Crab Fair, which began in 1267. For more on gurning, see Rebecca Brill, "On Gurning," *Colorado Review* 47, no. 2 (Summer 2000): 147–152.
31. Noa Steimatsky, *The Face on Film* (Oxford: Oxford University Press, 2017), 3.
32. "3525 . . . Lettie Limelight in Her Lair," *We Put the World Before You by Means of the Bioscope and Urban Films*, November 1903, 107.
33. Laura U. Marks, *The Skin of the Film: Intercultural Film, Embodiment, and the Senses* (Durham, NC: Duke University Press, 2000). Skin serves as a broad metaphor for "how film signifies through its materiality" and "the way vision itself can be tactile," which Marks theorizes as its "haptic visuality." Marks also uses this term polemically "to suggest . . . that film (and video) may be thought of as impressionable and conductive, like skin . . . I want to emphasize the tactile and contagious quality of cinema as something we viewers brush up against like another body," xi–xii.
34. *A Dull Razor*, directed by Edwin S. Porter (1900; New York: Edison); *A Bad Cigar*, directed by George Albert Smith (1900; United Kingdom: G.A.S. Films).
35. Tom Gunning, "In Your Face: Physiognomy, Photography, and the Gnostic Mission of Early Film," *Modernism/modernity* 4, no. 1 (1997): 1.
36. Steimatsky, *The Face on Film*, 6.
37. Johann Kaspar Lavater believed that one's moral character or inner soul could be deduced from their countenance: "The eye, the look, the cheeks, the mouth, the forehead, whether considered in a state of entire rest, or during their innumerable varieties of motion, in fine, whatever is

understood by physiognomy—are the most expressive, the most convincing picture of interior sensation, desires, passions, will." Johann Kaspar Lavater, *Physiognomy; or, The Corresponding Analogy Between the Conformation of the Features and the Ruling Passions of the Mind* (London: Cowie, Low, 1826), 25.

38. Georges Méliès experimented with self-decapitating laughter in his stage act, as Matthew Solomon evocatively describes it in "Laughing while Decapitated": "First staged in 1891, Méliès recalled 'the mad hilarity that shook spectators during this extra-burlesque scene' . . . adults laughing so hard that tears came to their eyes and children stomping their feet enthusiastically." Matthew Solomon, *Méliès Boots: Footwear and Film Manufacturing in Second Industrial Revolution Paris* (Ann Arbor: University of Michigan Press, 2022), 105–106.

39. Mary Ann Doane, *Bigger Than Life: The Close-Up and Scale in the Cinema* (Durham, NC: Duke University Press, 2022), 2.

40. Doane, *Bigger Than Life*, 3.

41. Doane, *Bigger Than Life*, 2; Robert W. Paul, "The Drenched Lover," *Catalogue of Paul's Animatographs & Films* (London: Animatograph Depot, 1903), n.p.

42. Rush, "Moving Picture: 'Laughing Gas,'" 10.

43. Ian Christie, *Robert Paul and the Origins of British Cinema* (Chicago: University of Chicago Press, 2019), 170. Christie's book on Paul provides extensive context about the family's business operation, patent applications, lost works, extant films, and their historiographic importance to the development of cinema.

44. The early film popularity of tableaux vivants provides an interesting counterpoint to the emblematic shot: one emphasizes physical distance and durational stasis, the other jarring proximity and excess movement. See Valentine Robert, "Performing Painting: Projected Images as Living Pictures," in *Performing New Media, 1890–1915*, ed. Kaveh Askari, Scott Curtis, Frank Gray, Louis Pelletier, Tami Williams, and Joshua Yumibe (Bloomington: Indiana University Press, 2014), 282–292; Daniel Wiegand, "Tableaux Vivants, Early Cinema, and Beauty-as-Attraction," *Film and Media Studies*, no. 15 (2018): 9–32.

45. Ellen Paul (née Daws) appeared in numerous films such as *A Soldier's Courtship*, directed by R. W. Paul (1896; United Kingdom). According to Paul's obituarist, W. H. Eccles, she was "the business brain" of the whole operation, and acted as "producer, stage manager, or principal lady in many a playlet" (Christie, *Robert Paul and the Origins of British Cinema*, 107).

46. Livio Belloi, "La fiction de la vue attentoire," in *Le Regard Retourné: Aspects du cinéma des premiers temps*, ed. Frank Kessler, Sabine Lenk, and Martin Loiperdinger (Québec: Nota Bene, 2001), 77–181.

47. Eileen Bowser, *The Transformation of Cinema, 1907–1915* (Berkeley: University of California Press, 1994), 96.

48. Susan Hayward, *Cinema Studies: The Key Concepts* (New York: Routledge, 2012), 98.

49. Richard Abel, ed., *The Encyclopedia of Early Cinema* (New York: Routledge, 2010), 247.

50. Strictly speaking, *The Great Train Robbery*'s emblematic shot is only ghoulish when placed at the end, which was not always the case.

51. "Edison Films: The Great Train Robbery," *The New York Clipper*, December 12, 1903, 1016.

52. I also discuss *Mary Jane's Mishap*, directed by George Albert Smith (1903: United Kingdom: G.A.S. Films), at length in chapter 2, "Female Combustion and Feminist Film Historiography," of *Specters of Slapstick and Silent Film Comediennes* (New York: Columbia University Press, 2018), 54–82.

53. Noël Burch, *Life to Those Shadows* (Berkley: University of California Press, 1990), 196.

54. Scott Bukatman, "Spectacle, Attractions and Visual Pleasure," in *Cinema of Attractions Reloaded*, ed. Wanda Strauven (Amsterdam: Amsterdam University Press, 2006) 79–80.

55. Marlene Dietrich's "supreme moments of erotic meaning" serve as "the ultimate example" of Laura Mulvey's paradigm of fetishistic scopophilia (in contrast to voyeurism), whereby the diegetic looker's gaze becomes "one with, not standing in for, that of the audience." Laura Mulvey, "Visual Pleasure

and Narrative Cinema" (written in 1973 and first published in 1975), in *Visual and Other Pleasures* (London: Palgrave, 1989), 21–23.

56. "Film Review: When Cherries Are Ripe," *Moving Picture World*, December 7, 1907, 652.
57. "Film Review: When Cherries Are Ripe," 652.
58. "Film Review: When Cherries Are Ripe," 652.
59. Paul, "Hair Soup," *Catalogue of Paul's Animatographs & Films* (London: Animatograph Depot, 1903), n.p. Early film facials drew on stage and magic lantern practices of facial mimicry, pantomime, and animated portraiture. For example, the mimic Monsieur Pitrot would project larger-than-life lantern slides while "assum[ing] the facial expression of the individual depicted on the screen." "Music Halls and the Lantern," *Optical Magical Lantern Journal and Photographic Enlarger*, October 1, 1890, 38. Songs, recitations, and phonograph records also frequently accompanied the projection of magic lantern "facial expression slides." "Notes," *Optical Magical Lantern Journal and Photographic Enlarger*, November 15, 1889, 41.
60. R. W. Paul, "A Shave by Installments on the Un-Easy System," in *Catalogue of Selected Animatograph Films* (London: Animatograph Depot, 1906–1907), 26.
61. "A pretty girl and a gentleman making fierce love to each other, with rather more than the usual proportion of kisses." Paul, "Spooning," *Catalogue* (1906–1907), 12. *Cohen's Fire Sale*, directed by Edwin S. Porter (1907; New York: Edison Manufacturing Company), is an anti-Semitic comedy about a man named Cohen whose millinery store burns down the same day that he holds a "fire sale." Luckily, he has a good insurance policy. "The closing picture shows a close view of Cohen and his wife ... Cohen looks for his reward in a kiss, and after several attempts, in which their noses seem to be in the way, they at last succeed." *Moving Picture World*, July 20, 1907, 314.
62. *The Tramp and the Typewriter*, directed by J. H. Martin (1905; United Kingdom: R. W. Paul) depicts the plight of a tramp who attempts to steal a typewriter and is then tied to a cart hitched to an automobile that drives away "while the unfortunate tramp is dragged behind ... Exceedingly funny throughout." Paul, "Tramp," *Catalogue* (1906–07), 31.
63. "Film Review: When Cherries Are Ripe," 652.
64. Judith Mayne, *The Woman at the Keyhole: Feminism and Women's Cinema* (Bloomington: Indiana University Press, 1990), 173.
65. Linda Williams, *Hard Core: Power, Pleasure and the 'Frenzy of the Visible'* (Berkeley: University of California Press, 1989), 67.
66. Vivian Sobchack, *Carnal Thoughts: Embodiment and Moving Image Culture* (Berkley: University California Press, 2004), 4.
67. Vivian Sobchack, "What My Fingers Knew: The Cinesthetic Subject, or Vision in the Flesh," *Senses of Cinema* (April 2000), https://www.sensesofcinema.com/2000/conference-special-effects-special-affects/fingers/.
68. Kyla Wazana Tompkins, *Racial Indigestion: Eating Bodies in the 19th Century* (New York: New York University, 2012), 4–5.
69. Tanya Sheehan, "Look Pleasant, Please! A Social History of the Photographic Smile," in *Study in Black and White: Photography, Race, Humor* (University Park: Pennsylvania State University Press, 2018), 74–101.
70. Sheehan, "Look Pleasant, Please!," 88–89; C. H. Gallup & Co., *The Melon Story*, ca. 1890.
71. Sheehan, "Look Pleasant, Please!," 75.
72. Sheehan, "Look Pleasant, Please!," 75.
73. I also discuss *Daisy Doodad's Dial*, directed by Florence Turner (1914; United Kingdom: Turner Film Company), at length in *Specters of Slapstick*, 67, 90, 93–94, 107–110, 116, 265.
74. Florence Turner headlined as a stage and film impersonator throughout her career, touring British music halls in 1913 (after leaving Vitagraph) until returning to New York in 1916. See Jon Burrows, "Florence Turner: Her British Career," in *Women Film Pioneers Project*, ed. Jane Gaines, Radha

Vatsal, and Monica Dall'Asta (New York: Columbia University Libraries, 2013). As Steve Massa notes, she was a "wicked mimic" who burlesqued "Mabel Normand, Ford Sterling, Sarah Bernhardt, Broncho Billy Anderson, and even Larry Semon." Steve Massa, Facebook post, "Orphan Film Symposium" public group, May 6, 2023.

75. I have written extensively about my obsession with the comic figure Léontine, whose identity remains a complete mystery. Pathé Nizza/Comica produced 24 episodes of this series from 1910 to 1912, half of which can be viewed in the collection, *Cinema's First Nasty Women*, various directors (2022; New York: Kino Lorber).

76. *Léontine s'envole* [*Léontine Takes Flight*] (1911; Nice: Pathé).

77. Each Dam member's emblematic portrait bears their name at the bottom of the frame, a direct visual reference to the comic souvenir postcards from which the film was adapted. It also spawned an acclaimed vaudeville act and various memorabilia. As advertised in *Popular Mechanics*, you could purchase a 7- × 15¼-inch Dam postcard for only 25 cents. "New McNally Skit," *Billboard*, July 8, 1905, 7; "Everybody Has Heard of the Whole Dam Family," *Popular Mechanics*, April 1906, 488.

78. Paul, "The Fakir and the Footpads," *Catalogue* (1906–07), 18.

79. Paul, "Chinese Magic Extraordinary," *Catalogue* (1903), n.p.

80. Doane, *Bigger Than Life*, 67.

81. Stewart, "What Happened in the Transition?," 122.

82. Mayne's *Woman at the Keyhole*, "which takes as its most obvious point of reference those early films . . . in which mostly men, but occasionally women, peek through keyholes," remains a definitive reference on the gender politics of this genre. Mayne, *The Woman at the Keyhole*, 9.

83. Andrea Gyenge, "Laocoön's Scream; or, Lessing Redux," *New German Critique* 48, no. 1 (2021): 43.

84. Gyenge, "Laocoön's Scream," 43.

85. With "two Medusan lips," I of course invoke Luce Irigaray's antiphallic model of the vulva (women's second pair of lips), which doubles the facial lips of the mouth to assert a counterdiscourse for feminist articulation that dethrones the master signifier. See Luce Irigaray, "When Our Lips Speak Together," trans. Carolyn Burke, *Signs* 6, no. 1 (Autumn 1980): 69–79; Luce Irigaray, *This Sex Which Is Not One*, trans. Catherine Porter (Ithaca, NY: Cornell University Press, 1985).

86. "Film Review," *Moving Picture World*, November 9, 1907, 582.

87. *Zoe's Magic Umbrella* (1913; Pathé). This film is included in *Cinema's First Nasty Women*, various directors (2022; New York: Kino Lorber), with an original score by Gonca Feride Varol. Elif Rongen-Kaynakçi and I found a 28mm copy in an untitled cannister at the EYE Film Museum in 2019. For more on its star, see Rongen's spotlight essay on Little Chrysia in the DVD booklet: https://www.dropbox.com/s/0cwexgqm052bhhz/NastyWomen_Booklet_Integrated_v1.pdf.

88. James Leo Cahill and Luca Caminati, "Cinema of Exploration: An Adventurous Film Practice and Theory," in *Cinema of Exploration: Essays on Adventurous Film Practice*, ed. James Leo Cahill and Luca Caminati (New York: Routledge, 2021), 7, 2.

89. Doane, *Bigger Than Life*, 18.

90. Doane, *Bigger Than Life*, 18.

91. Fritz Lang, "The Art of Mimic Expression in Film" (1929), trans. Michael Cowan, in *The Promise of Cinema: German Film Theory, 1907–1933*, ed. Anton Kaes, Nicholas Baer, and Michael J. Cowan (Berkeley: University of California Press, 2016), 142.

92. *The Monk's Macaroni Feast*, directed by George Albert Smith (1902; United Kingdom: G.A.S. Films); "3550 The Monk's Macaroni Feast (Reversing)," 111; Paul, "The Haunted Curiosity Shop," *Catalogue* (1903), n.p.

93. Paul, "A Study in Facial Expression," *Catalogue* (1903), n.p.

94. Steimatsky, *The Face on Film*, 1.

95. Walter Benjamin, "IX," *On the Concept of History* (1942), https://www.marxists.org/reference/archive/benjamin/1940/history.htm.

96. "Onions Make People Weep," *Moving Picture World*, November 2, 1907, 563.
97. "Excelsior Cinematograph," *The Times of India* (Bombay, India), June 17, 1911, 12; "Posada Roller Rink," *The Rhodesia Herald* (Harare, Zimbabwe), August 11, 1911, 11; "Arrivals and Departures," *Gloucestershire Echo* (Gloucester, United Kingdom), June 13, 1911, 3.
98. Hermann Duenschmann, "Cinematograph and Crowd Psychology: A Sociopolitical Study," trans. Eric Ames, in *The Promise of Cinema: German Film Theory, 1907–1933*, ed. Anton Kaes, Nicholas Baer, and Michael J. Cowan (Berkeley: University of California Press, 2016), 257.
99. "The Country School Teacher," *Moving Picture News*, November 9, 1912, 29–30.
100. "The Country School Teacher," 29–30.
101. *Squirrel Food*, directed by Gilbert Pratt (1921; Burbank, CA: Warner Bros.), is an especially intriguing example of the clichéd, racist sight gag where an alluring veiled figure is revealed to be a woman of color (much to the visible horror of her white male assaulter) because it includes a brief (uncredited) cameo by Madame Sul-Te-Wan: pioneering Black actress who appeared in at least sixty films over the course of her fifty-year career. For more on Sul-Te-Wan, see Charlene Regester, "Madame Sul-Te-Wan: The Struggle for Visibility," *African American Actresses: The Struggle for Visibility, 1900–1960* (Bloomington: Indiana University Press, 2010), 19–40.
102. Charlene Regester, "Bertha Regustus and the Black Women of Silent Comedy," *Cinema's First Nasty Women*, various directors (2022; New York: Kino Lorber), booklet, ed. Maggie Hennefeld, Laura Horak, Alana Skwarok, pp. 25–32.
103. Filming and projection speeds varied at the time, as the camera was hand-cranked at an average speed of sixteen to eighteen frames per second (fps), as opposed to today's standard of twenty-four fps. The total length of *Mixed Babies*, directed by Wallace McCutcheon (1908; New York: Biograph), was measured in feet (550 feet), not in duration (approximately 8 minutes as per the extant 35mm scan by Library of Congress). The emblematic shot lasts for about 5 percent of the film's total length.
104. This film is also included in *Cinema's First Nasty Women*, various directors (2022; New York: Kino Lorber), with catalog notes written by Charlene Regester and an original score composed by Renée C. Baker.
105. Elyse Singer, "Mad Faces: Coding Features and Expressions of Female Madness in Physiognomy Texts, Asylum Photographs and Early Cinema," in *Faces on Screen: New Approaches*, ed. Alice Maurice (Toronto: University of Toronto Press, 2022), 36. See also Allyson Nadia Field, "The Cinema of Racialized Attraction(s): *The John C. Rice—May Irwin Kiss* and *Something Good—Negro Kiss*," *Discourse* 44, no. 1 (2022): 3–41.
106. Genevieve Yue, *Girl Head: Feminism and Film Materiality* (New York: Fordham University Press, 2020), 3.
107. Yue, *Girl Head*, 3.
108. In a rare exception, Black actress Madame Sul-Te-Wan parlayed her underpaid labor as a cook and a maid (for white stage and screen actors) into a prolific film career, after hiring an NAACP attorney to defend her against false accusations of theft on the film set of *Birth of a Nation*. Regester, "Bertha Regustus and the Black Women of Silent Cinema," 28.
109. "The Cook Wins," *Moving Picture World*, March 21, 1908, 244.
110. Yue, *Girl Head*, 4; "The Cook Wins," 244.
111. Paul, "Haunted Curiosity Shop," *Catalogue* (1903), n.p.
112. Alice Maurice, "Introduction: Facing Forward, Facing Back," in *Faces on Screen: New Approaches*, ed. Alice Maurice (Toronto: University of Toronto Press, 2022), 1.
113. Daniel Victor, "'I'm Not a Cat,' Says Lawyer Having Zoom Difficulties," *New York Times*, February 9, 2021.
114. Paul, "An Over-Incubated Baby," *Catalogue* (1903), n.p.
115. "The Foxy Lawyer," *Film Index*, July 23, 1910, 14.
116. "Magnified view of mouse's head protruding from hole." "3536 . . . The Mouse in the Art School," *We Put the World Before You by Means of yhe Bioscope and Urban Films*, November 1903, 108.

117. Ricciotto Canudo, "The Triumph of the Cinema," trans. Siobhan Quinlan, in *Early Film Theories in Italy 1896–1922*, ed. Francesco Casetti with Silvio Alovisio and Luca Mazzei (Amsterdam: Amsterdam University Press, 2017), 72.
118. Neta Alexander, "The Zoombie Apocalypse," *In Media Res: A MediaCommons Project*, April 11, 2020, http://mediacommons.org/imr/content/zoombie-apocalypse.
119. Alexander, "The Zoombie Apocalypse."

CONCLUSION: LAUGHTER, HYSTERIA, POWER— THEN AND NOW

1. Desiree Fairooz, "I'm Facing Jail Time After Laughing at Jeff Sessions. I Regret Nothing," *Vox*, May 8, 2017.
2. "Christine Blasey Ford Says Her Strongest Memory of Attack is 'Uproarious Laughter,'" YouTube video of Senate testimony, *PBS NewsHour*, September 27, 2018, https://www.youtube.com/watch?v=MsKo3KyyypA.
3. Camila Domonoske, "Judge Throws Out Conviction of Woman Who Laughed at Jeff Sessions," *NPR News*, July 14, 2017.
4. Roe v. Wade was officially overturned by U.S. Supreme Court on June 24, 2022.
5. Robin Levinson-King, "US Women Are Being Jailed for Having Miscarriages," *BBC News*, November 12, 2021.
6. "Christine Blasey Ford Says."
7. Aretaeus (of Cappadocia), *The Extant works of Aretaeus, the Cappadocian*, trans. Francis Adams (London: Printed for the Sydenham Society, 1856), 285, https://archive.org/details/aretaioukappadoko0aret.
8. Elahe Izadi, "Turkish Deputy Prime Minister Says Women Shouldn't Laugh Out Loud," *Washington Post*, July 29, 2014.
9. Constanze Letsch, "Turkish Women Defy Deputy PM with Laughter," *Guardian*, July 30, 2014.
10. Carol J. Williams, "Turkish Women Find Official's Rebuke of Female Laughter Hilarious," *Los Angeles Times*, July 29, 2014.
11. Reuters Staff, "Turkish Women Laugh Online to Protest Deputy PM's Remark," *Reuters*, July 30, 2014.
12. Christine Lacagnina, "Does Your Stand-Up Act Need Death by Laughter Insurance?," Trustedchoice.com, August 10, 2019, https://www.trustedchoice.com/insurance-articles/opinion-variety/insurance-against-death-by-laughter/.
13. Lacagnina, "Does Your Stand-Up Act?"
14. Raúl Pérez, "When Bigoted Humor Isn't Just a Joke," *Zócalo*, September 19, 2016.
15. Rachel Aroesti, "Cancel Culture Killing Comedy? What a Joke," *Guardian*, August 10, 2021.
16. Haroon Siddique, "Stand-Up Comedian's Husband Sues for Defamation over 'Provocative' Show," *Guardian*, February 19, 2018.
17. Rebecca Krefting, "Political Correctness Isn't Killing Comedy, It's Making It Better," *Zócalo*, September 19, 2016, https://www.zocalopublicsquare.org/2016/09/19/political-correctness-isnt-killing-comedy-making-better/ideas/nexus/.
18. Lacagnina, "Does Your Stand-Up Act?"

Index

Abbey, Ruth, 82
Abel, Richard, 259
d'Abundo, Giuseppe, 197, 223
Abyssinia, 41–42
Accidental Parson, The (film), 226
activism, hysteria, 114, 162
acute psychotic disorder, 217
Adams, Violet, 64
Addams, Jane, 192
Adorno, Theodore, 4
Adrienne Lecouvreur (play), 108
affect alien, 103–104
affective contagion, 147
African Immortals series (Duo), 118
African slave trade, 70
"Against a Cinema That Makes Women Stupid" (Grempe), 196
Ages of Female Beauty (Frederic Montagu), 38
Agnew State Hospital for the Insane, 222
Ahmed, Sara, 29, 38–39, 93, 103, 105, 112, 168, 183
Akademische Burschenschaft Hysteria, 162
Albigenses, The (Robert), 26
Alexander, Fred, 46
Alexander, Neta, 278
alien abductions, 157–159
Alkili Ike's Auto (film), 195
Alkili Ike's Pants (film), 202
All-Wool Garment, An (film), 271
Altenloh, Emilie, 197
alt-right insult comedy, 167
American Breeder's Association, 219
American Horror Story: Asylum (TV series), 123
American Nervousness (Beard, G.), 115

Amorous History of the Silver Screen, An (Zhen), 208
Amusing Ourselves to Death (Postman), 4
amygdala, 145
Anaconda Standard, 12, 49, 101, 103
ancient Greek mythology, 61–63
Andree Balloon Mania (1896), 171
Angelou, Maya, 70–71
anger, 29, 72
Animal Lover (film), 230
animal magnetism (mesmerism), 108
Anna O. (Bertha Pappenheim), 103–104
Anselmo, Diana, 209
Anthology of Black Humor (Breton), 14, 84
anti-Black racism, 166, 229
Anti-Neurasthenic Trumpet, The (film), 246
antipatriarchal language, 94
anxiety, contagious, 154–157
anxiety-hysteria, 152
anxious cinephilia, 225
Appalachians, 33–34
Aragon, Louis, 14, 108
Arendt, Hannah, 88
Aretaeus, 281
Arinç, Bülent, 281
Armisted, Mary, 55, 73
Arndt, Mrs. Charles A., 51
Artistic Creation (film), 103, 266
Association of Hysteric Curators, The (coalition group), 114, 162
asylum spectatorship, 217, 241–242
Atkins, Henry S., 225, 242
Atlanta (TV series), 166
At Last! That Awful Tooth (film), 19, 255–256
Attitude (Fleming), 42

"Attitudes Passionelles" (Bourneville and Régnard), *107*
attractions (concept), 189, 317n55
Atwood, Margaret, 10, 60, 64
Aub, Hermann, 149, 235
Aubert, Genevieve, 232–233
audience effect, 146
auditory hallucinations, 244
Augusta Chronicle, 67, 195
Augustine, 108, 113
Augustine (Big Hysteria) (Furse), 15
Augustine (film), 113
Aurora End-of-the-World Panic (1938), 171
Auto Maniac, An (film), 18, 224
automatism, 127–129, 129–132, 240
Aylesbury Ducks (film), 278

Babel and Babylon (Hansen), 180, 188, 208
Babylon Girls (Brown), 213
Bad Cigar, The (film), 258
Bailey, Eva, 255
Baker, Mrs. George A., 55
Bakhtin, Mikhail, 8, 76, 78–81, 89
Balance of Life, The (print melodrama), 24–25
Balázs, Béla, 255–256
Bals des Folles, 110
Baptists, 33, 150
Barr, Barbara, 7, 59–60, 83, 102, 282, 295n82
Barsas, Isabel de, 25–26
Bartholomew, Robert, 155, 156
Bataille, Georges, 7, 14, 76, 84–86, *85*
Baubo, 61–62
"Baubo" (statuette), *62*
Baudelaire, Charles, 13, 25, 32, 41, 80, 84, 88, 201
Baudrillard, Jean, 313n95
Bauer, Ida (Dora), 94–95, 104, 136
Bayley, Laura, 9, 260
BBC Radio Hoax (1923/1926), 155, 171
Beamont, Louise, 281–282
Bean, Jennifer, 10, 182, 208–209, 322n176
Beard, George, 40, 115
Beard, Mary, 77, 245
Beatty, Paul, 166
Beaumont, Eloise, 53, 58
Becker, Carol, 156
Beckett, Samuel, 66
Beeston, Alix, 209
Belle of Bridgeport, The, 43
Bellevue, Elizabeth, 35
Belloi, Livio, 259
Beloff, Zoe, 15, *29*, 121, 190
Benedetta (film), 16, 124

Benjamin, Walter, 143, 148, 167, 211
Bentley, Gladys, 212
Bentzen, Ole, 8
Bergson, Henri, 110, 129, 141, 240
Berlant, Lauren, 5, 26, 29–32, 68, 93, 182
Bernhardt, Sarah, 108
Berry, Ace, 202
Berton, Mireille, 208
Betty in the Lions' Den (film), 227
"Beyond Queer" (Worthington), 114
Bicetre Hospital, 235
Bigger Than Life (Doane), 258
Big Pharma, 230
Big Swallow, The (film), 255, 263–263
Bijou Theatre, 44
Binet, Alfred, 109, 125
Biograph Company, 205, 254
"Biograph Insanity Cure," 18
biopolitics, racial, 115–116
Biopolitics of Feeling (Schuller), 35
bird flu pandemic scare (2005), 171
Birth of a Nation (film), 335n108
Birth of Tragedy (Nietzsche), 81
bisexuality, 114
Black Americans, 67, 180–181, 229
blackface, 67, 116
Black feminism, 13
Black flesh, 119
Black hysteria, 116
Black laughter, 66–67, 69
Black Madness :: Mad Blackness (Pickens), 118
Black Mitzvah, 96
Blackness, 116–118, 166, 263
Black satire, 6, 96, 117, 166
Black Swan (film), 16, 124
Black women, 42, 274–275, 315n130
blindness, 230
Bluest Eye, The (Morrison), 213
Blumenberg, Hans, 88
bodily language, 121
Bodomo, Nuotama, 5
Bofano, Mary, 68
Bolley, Ida, 12, 72, 81
Bombay film industry, 211
Bonaparte, Louis-Napoléon, 139
Bonn Clinic, 232
Booth, W. R., 269
Borat (film), 3
borderline personality disorder, 124
Bornean women, 39
Boston Courier, 33
Boston Daily, 43

Boston Globe, 33
Boston Herald, 49, 51, 53
Bouissac, Paul, 145
Boulogne, Guillaume Duchenne de, 258
Bourneville, D. M., *107*, *111*
Bowen, Louise De Koven, 192
Bowman, Dean, 239
Bowser, Eileen, 259
Boy Detective, The (film), 254
Braddon, Mary Elizabeth, 30
Braun, Johanna, 15, 121, 162–163
Breaking Up (at) Totality (Davis, D.), 51
Breger, Claudia, 150, 168
Brennan, Teresa, 105
Breton, André, 14, 84, 88–89, 108
Breuer, Josef, 102–103, 117, 125–126, 132, 249
Brice, Fanny, 116
Brigand Great Fear (1789), 171
Briggs, Laura, 115
Briggs, Margaret, 54
Briggs, Shelley, 244
Briquet, Paul, 125
Britain, 33, 39, 84
British Journal of Psychiatry, The, 159
British Medical Association, 235
British military fainting epidemics (1951), 157, 173
"broken heart," 66
Brooklyn Bridge Panic (1883), 155, 171
Brouillet, André, 107
Brown, Jayna, 49, 213
Bruce, La Marr Jurelle, 166–167, 229
Bruegel the Elder, Pieter, *77*
Bruno, Giuliana, 208, 211
Bucket of Cream Ale, A (film), 256
Buckley, James, 310n10
Buckley, J. M., 150
Bukatman, Scott, 260
Burch, Noël, 259
Bureau of Labor, U.S., 56
Burnham, William, 312n69
Bush, W. Stephen, 191–192
Bushnell, Horace, 36
Buster Brown in the Insane Asylum (film), 226
Butler, Judith, 153–154, 156
Butler, Octavia, 118

cabaret, French, 116
Cabbage Fairy, The (film), 197, 266, 319n109
Cabinet of Dr. Caligari, The (film), 226
Cäcilie M. (Anna von Lieben), 104, 136
Cahill, James Leo, 269
Calchas, 75

California telephone illness (1984), 171
Cambrai convent outbreak (1491), 157, 173
Cameragraph No. 6A machines, 220
Cameraman's Revenge, The (film), 248
Cameron, Fiona, 244
Caminati, Luca, 269
"Canadian Driveway Ice Hysterics" (video), 23, *24*
cancel culture, 5, 281, 310n10
Canudo, Ricciotto, 278
Capital (Marx), 45
capitalism, 4, 45, 64, 79, 183, 214
Capitalism and Schizophrenia (Deleuze and Guattari), 231
Carceral Fantasies (Griffiths), 241
carnival, 78–79, 182–183
carnival somnambulism, 106–116
Carpio, Glenda, 6, 66, 165
Carr, William, 188
Carrington, Leonora, 300n57
Carroll, Jean, 99
Cartwright, Lisa, 216, 232, 237–238
Cayenne Pepper in a Street Cab (film), 271
Central State Hospital, 217, 241
Central West Casualty Company, 202
Chadwick, Ida May, 186
Channel Tunnel (film), 254
Chaplin, Charlie, 5, 148, 206, 273
Chappelle, Dave, 166, 310n10
Chappelle, Edythe, 198
Charcot, Jean-Martin, 15, 93, 106, 124–130, 179, 190, 201, 231, 233; clownism and, 101, 110; *Iconographie photographique de la Salpêtrière*, 108; living subject of, 109; medical muses of, 216; on sexual division of hysteria, 112; "Spiritism and Hysteria," 127
Charlotte Daily Observer, 64
Charming Augustine (film), 114, 190, *191*
Charter, Caroline, 23
Chase, Walter Greenough, 216, 237–238
Châtelet Théâtre, 116
chattel slavery, 71
Cheap Amusements (Peiss), 180, 192
Chicago Chronicle, 102
childbirth, 38
Child-Eating Scare (Middle Ages), 171
Chile, 155
Chilon, 80
China, 211
China Girl, 276
Chinese Magic Extraordinary (film), 266
Chinese Needle Scare (2001–2002), 171
Chío, Adriana, 232, 236

Cho, Margaret, 15, 98–99
Chomón, Segundo de, 269
Christie, Ian, 259
chromotherapy, 242
Chrysippus of Soli, *8*, 8–9, 75, 78, 80, 86
Cicero, 88
Cineas, Fabiola, 120
Cinema of Exploration (Cahill and Caminati), 269
"Cinematograph in the Field of Mental Illness and Criminality, The" (Masini and Vidoni), 227
cinematography: medical, 216; psychiatric, 231–232
Circle Theatre, 202
Circus, The (film), 148
Cixous, Hélène, 7, 14–15, 61–63, 93–97, 105, 113–114, 122, 244
Clarke, Edward H., 114
Clausnitz incident (2016), 168
Clément, Catherine, 14, 93
clinical neuropsychiatry, 137–138
Clown and the Neurasthenic Pasha, The (film), 246
clownism, 101, 106–112, 127–129, 201, 216
Coca-Cola Scare (1999), 171
Cockton, Henry, 33
Code Pink, 279
coercive enjoyment, 182
cognitive psychology, 168
Cohen, Sasha Baron, 3
Coli, Edoardo, 197
collective closures, 167–169
collective laughter, 146–151
Colonel of the Nutts, The (film), 226
colonialism, 33, 39–42
"Color Cure, The," 242
color effects, 243
Come Along, Do! (film), 259
comic meaning, 147
commodity capital, 50
communicative capitalism, 183
communist affect, 169
compulsory enjoyment, 182
Connecticut Yankee, A (film), 205
contagion: affective, 147; hysterical, 16–17, 141; redintegrative, 168–169
contagious anxiety, 154–157
"Contagious Feelings" (Gibbs), 168
contagious fun, 42–46
contagious glossolalia, 173
contagious laughter, 144–146, 314n128, 315n130
Contagious Nervousness, A (film), 271
Contagious Nervous Twitching (film), 237, 271
convalescent humor, 204–207
conversion hysteria, 115, 148, 152, 154, 156

conversion therapy, 114
"Coochie Hygiene" (Haddish), 96
Cook Wins, The (film), 276
Copjec, Joan, 121
Corbett-Fitzsimmons Fight (film), 188
Cork Lunatic Asylum, 236
Corregidora (Jones, G.), 118–120
corsets, 53–55
Cossonde, Emilius Albert de, 41–42
Country School Teacher, The (film), 272
Courtney, Elizabeth, 55–56, 76
COVID-19 pandemic, 219, 278, 321n162
Cowan, Michael, 211
Craig Colony for Epileptics, 237–238
Crain, G. D., 217
cranial anatomy, 138
Crassus, 80
Crawford, Joan, 123
Crazy Funny (Guerrero), 117, 166
crazy laughter (*fou rire*), 10–11, 16, 125, 252
"Crazy People Entertained with Moving Pictures," 239–240
Creed, Barbara, 61, 245
"Cripistemologies" (Johnson, M., and McRuer), 231
Crisis, The (newspaper), 149
Critical Inquiry, 182
critical race theory, 120
Crooked to the End (film), 196
Croonquist, Sunda, 3
Crowd, The (Le Bon), 143
crowd psychology, 148, 167–169
crowds, 143–144, 149–151
Crowds and Party (Dean), 169
Crowe, Mrs. Thomas D., 26
Crush, The (film), 124
"cult of domesticity," 139
Curtis, Scott, 216, 232, 245
Cvetkovich, Ann, 29, 100
Cyber Ghost Scare (2003), 171
Czechoslovakia, 84

Daily Nebraska State Journal, 44
Daisy Doodad's Dial (film), 234, 263, *264*, 265, 276
Dallas Morning News, 47, 72
Dalton, Sam, 258
"Dance at Molenbeek," *152*
Dances with Darwin (Gordon), 116
dancing manias (1100s–1600s), 173–174
dancing plagues, 151, 157–159
"dark continent," 136
Darwin, Charles, 26, 35–36, 38–39, 137
Darwinism, 116

Davidson, Robert, 34
Davis, Bette, 123, *124*
Davis, D. Diane, 51
Davis, Lennard, 219
Dean, Jodi, 169
Dear, Kind Hubby (film), 195
Death of the Last Black Man in the Whole Entire World, The (Parks), 66
Debord, Guy, 200–201
decolonization, 40
DeCook, Julia Rose, 167
Deep Meditations (Redrobe and Scheible), 256
deindividualization, 169
Deleuze, Gilles, 168, 231
Demeter, 61
deMille, William C., 205
Democratic Party, 33
dentistry, 58–60
"'Deplorable' Satire" (Greene), 167
@depthsofwiki, 8, *8*
Descartes, Rene, 46
Devereux, Cecily, 15, 97, 302n18
Devil of a Time, The (film), 228, 244
Diawara, Manthia, 212
dictionaries, 42–43
Didi-Huberman, Georges, 108, 113
Dietrich, Marlene, 332n44
Diller, Phyllis, 99
Disaffected (Yao), 114
Disappearing Act (film), 197
divided selves, 103
divorce, 247
Doane, Mary Ann, 136, 258, 269
Dodge, Mary Mapes, 47
Domino Sugar factory, 70
"Donald Trump Is Gaslighting America" (*Teen Vogue* article), 120
Don César de Bazan (Massenet), 43–44
doppelgänger, 103
Dora (Ida Bauer), 94–95, 104, 136
double conscience, 103, 117–118, 229
double consciousness, 117–118, 229
Douglas, Ann, 32
Drawing the Color Line (film), 228–230
Drenched Lover, The (film), 258
Dreyer, Carl Theodor, 324n12
Dr. Mabuse, der Spieler (*Dr. Mabuse, the Gambler*) (film), *128*
Dr. Max in Spite of Himself (film), 246
Dr. Skinum (film), 254
Du Bois, W. E. B., 117, 149, 229
Duchenne de Boulogne, Guillaume, 36, *37*, 38, 41

Duhamel, Sarah, 9, 270
Dulac, Germaine, 209
Dull Knife, The (film), 17, 201
Dull Razor, A (film), 258
Dunbar, Olivia Howard, 193
Dunbar, Paul Laurence, 70–71
Dunning Asylum, 18, 215
Duo, Tananarive, 118
Duvernay, Ava, 70

East Lynne (Wood), 27
Eckstein, Emma, 59, 295n85
Eclipse, The (film), 268
écriture féminine ("writing women"), 63
Ecuador, 155
Ecuador Martian Panic (1949), 172
Edison, 252–255
Edison Phonograph Monthly, 186
Egg-Laying Man, The (film), 266
Eisenstein, Sergei, 317n55
Eleanor, 29–30
Electric Theatre, 189
"Électro-Physiologie Photographique" (Duchenne de Boulogne), *37*
Elinore, Kate, 198
Eliot, George, 29
emblematic laughter, 259–268
"emblematic shot, the," 19
Emmy von N. (Fanny Moser), 104, 135
"Emotions Go to Work" (Beloff), *29*
Encyclopedia of Extraordinary Social Behavior (Evans and Bartholomew), 155
Enjoying What We Don't Have (McGowan), 63
Enterprise Optical Manufacturing Company, 220
epilepsy, 236–238
Epilepsy Biographs (Chase), 237–238
epileptic clownism, 110–112
Epstein, Jean, 196
Erdoğan, Recep Tayyip, 281
Ernst, Max, 14, 84, *87*
Espionage Act, 73
Etchevery, Justine, 108
Eudemon, 80, 81
eugenics, 219
Evans, Hilary, 155–156
Everett, Bridget, 96
Everybody Dies! (film), 5
Everything Sticks but Glue (film), 193
"Ev'rything's Funny to Me" (Strembler), 186
Excitable Speech (Butler, J.), 153
Exhibitors Herald, 202
Exhibitors Trade Review, The, 3

Explosion of a Motor Car (film), 187, 264
Expression of Emotions in Man and Animals, The (Darwin), 35
Eyes Without a Face (film), 270

Face on Film, The (Steimatsky), 257
fainting Vietnamese schoolgirls (2004), 174
Fairooz, Desiree, 19, 279
Faithful Dog, The (film), 230
Fakir and the Footpads (film), 266
Fanon, Franz, 39–41
farce, 139–140
Farley, Dot, 226
far-right humor, 5
Fatal Attraction (film), 16, 124
Fear of Shadows (film), 273, 274
feather tickling fad (early 1900s), 172
Federici, Silvia, 79, 299n24
feeling blue, 133–136
Feel My Pulse (film), 329n164
Feilchenfeld, Dr., 12
Feimster, Fortune, 99
Feinstein, Rachel, 99
Female Cab Drivers (film), 273
Female Complaint (Berlant), 29, 31
Female Grotesque (Russo), 165
Female Malady, 161
female sexuality, 94, 136
femininity, traditional, 89
feminist comedy, 94–101, 165
feminist hysterical laughter, 100–101
Feminist Reader in Early Cinema (Bean and Negra), 208
femme 100 têtes, La (The Hundred Headless Woman) (Ernst), 84, *85*, *87*
Féré, Charles, 109, 125
Ferrer, Anna, 48, 76
"Fight Between Carnival and Lent, The" (Bruegel the Elder), *77*
Film Index, The, 186, 229, 236, 242–243
filming speeds, 335n103
Findlay, Heather, 113
Fish Called Wanda, A (film), 8, 75
Fledgling (Butler, O.), 118
Fleming, Donald, 42
Fliess, Wilhelm, 59
flu pandemic (1918), 147, 205
Folies Bergère, 116
forced sterilization, 219, 325n23
Forch, Carl, 192
Ford, Christine Blasey, 19, 279, 280
For the Love of Pleasure (Rabinovitz), 180, 208

Fortune Hunting (Loudon), 28
Fortune's Fool (film), 255
Fortunes of Feminism (Fraser), 206
Fossi, Giovanni, 238
Foster, Hal, 245
Foucault, Michel, 42, 108, 221
four humors theory, 328n137
fou rire (crazy laughter), 10–11, 16, 125, 252
Four Seasons Total Landscaping, 140
Four Troublesome Heads, The (film), 103, 187, 258
Fox, Mrs. A., 7, 51
Fox, William, 70
Foxy Lawyer, The (film), 277
fragmented language, 95
France, 73, 84, 89, 116, 139, 158, 190, 232
Frankfurt School, 211
Frankie Avalon mania (1959), 172
Franklin, Marina, 99
Fraser, Nancy, 206
Frederick Opera House, 240
freedom-to-enjoy, 182
French phantom hat pin stabber (1923), 155
Freud, Sigmund, 15, 93, 125, 135, 143, 155, 168, 248, 295n82; anxiety-hysteria and, 152; Dora and, 94–95, 104, 136; *The Interpretation of Dreams*, 133; "Irma's Injection," 59; *Jokes and Their Relation to the Unconscious*, 84, 133; "A Note Upon the 'Mystic Writing-Pad,'" 249; "On Humour," 84; psychoanalysis and, 59, 101, 132–133, 136; *Studies on Hysteria*, 132, 249; subconscious and, 131, 307n30; talking cure, 101, 105; *Totem and Taboo*, 153
Friedberg, Anne, 49, 185, 201, 208
Frye, Marilyn, 29
Fumudoh, Ziwe, 5
Funke's opera house, 44
"Funniest Joke in the World, The" (TV skit), 75
Furse, Anna, 15

Gadsby, Hannah, 15, 19, 98, 302n19
Gaines, Jane, 209, 319n109
Galen, 281
Galili, Doron, 146, 247
Gallop, Jane, 95
Gallup, Charles, 263
Gargantua, 86
Gargantua and Pantagruel (Rabelais), 8, 77, 78, 80
Garner, Stanton B., 240
"G.A.S. Film Subjects," 255
gaslighting, 33, 95, 99, 120–122
Gay Café, The (film), 222
Gaycken, Oliver, 232

Gay Science (Nietzsche), 81
"gay science," 14, 76
Gay Shoe Clerk, The (film), 264
Genee, Adelade, 194
Geneviève, 15, 108, 130
genital shrinking scares, 174
genre flailing, 30–31
Germany, 73, 75, 233
Get on Your Knees (Novak), 96
Get Out (film), 6, 166, 314n111
Gianetto, Claudia, 235, 236
Gibbs, Anna, 168–169
Gibson, Charles, 18, 222–224
gig workers, 182, 214
Gilbert, Pamela K., 30
Giornate del Cinema Muto, 232
Girl, Interrupted (film), 124
Girl Head (Yue), 245, 276
Girls Will Be Boys (Horak), 209, 254
Giunchi, Lea, 9
Gleizes, Augustine, 15, 108, 190
Godbey, Emily, 219
Gold, Judy, 99
goldfish swallowing fad (1939), 172
Goldknopf, Abraham, 205
golf cure, 232
González, Laura, 15, 121, 306n143
Goodies, The (comedy sketch show), 8
Google Ngram, 44, 291n144
Gordon, Rae Beth, 110, 116, 131, 190, 196, 207–208, 227
Go West, Young Women! (Hallett), 208
Grandais, Suzanne, *249*
grande hystérie, 106–109
Grandma Threading Her Needle (film), 19, 255, 259
Grau, Matt, 170
Graupp, Robert, 245–246
Graves, Karen, 55
Great Clown Panic (2016), 144, 155
Great Depression, 73
Great Dictator, The (film), 5
Great Train Robbery, The (film), 259
Greek mythology, ancient, 61–63
Greek telephone panic attacks (1975), 172
Greeley, Horace, 44
Greene, Viveca, 167
Grempe, Max, 196
Griffin, Kathy, 99
Griffith, D. W., 255
Griffiths, Alison, 10, 222, 241–242
Grob, Gerald, 219
Groom, Amelia, 147
Grose, Anouchka, 164

groundnut scheme (1946–1951), 159, 312n83
Guardian, The, 280, 282
Guattari, Félix, 231
Guerrero, Lisa, 117–118, 166
Guilty, The (Bataille), 86
Guinchi, Lea, 270
Gunning, Tom, 189, 258, 317n55
Guy-Blaché, Alice, 197, 209, 266, 319n109
Guzzle, Ida, 73
Gyenge, Andrea, 268
Gynecological Wonder (Everett), 96

Haddish, Tiffany, 96
Haggins, Bambi, 66, 165
Hair Soup, or The Disappointed Diner (film), 261
Hallett, Hilary, 208
hallucinatory fascination, 196–198
Ham in the Nut Factory (film), 18, 217
Hammerstein, William, 69
Hammond, William, 42
Handbook of Uterine Therapeutics, 139
Hanich, Julian, 146
Hank and Lank (film), 230
Hansen, Miriam, 10, 17, 49–50, 180, 188, 190, 208, 211
Harlow, Sage, 121
Harrington, Louis Reeves, 198
Hart, Akiko, 244
Hartley, Florence, 60
Hartman, Saidiya, 71, 116, 212
Haunted Curiosity Shop, The (film), 269, 277
Haunted House, The (film), 269
Haupstadt Lacht, 170
Haynes, Catherine Day, 287n36
Hayward, Susan, 259
Hearing Voices Movement (HVM), 244
"Hee-Haw Girl" (Chadwick), 186
Hegel, Georg Wilhelm Friedrich, 139
Held in Bondage (Ouida), 13, 27
Hellwig, Albert, 211
Hempelmann, Christian, 160
Hendrickson, Mary, 72
Hennefeld, Maggie, 9
Hennes, Hans, 231, 232
He Who Laughs Last Laughs Best (film), 186
High, Lucy, 66
Hill, Gus, 185
Hill, Lauryn, 166
Hindu funeral rites, 41
hippocampus, 145
Hippocrates, 281, 328n137
His Musical Soul (film), 195
"History of Methodists" (Buckley), 150

History of the Presbyterian Church in the State of Kentucky (Davidson), 34
histrionic personality disorder, 124
Hitchcock Hall, 222
Hobbes, Thomas, 46
Hobble Skirt, The (film), 184
Hochardel, Josephine, 12, 50
Hoffmann, E. T. A., 25
Holden, Robert, 159
Holmes, Taylor, 179
Holy Laugh Movement, 159
homophobia, 98, 153, 154
Hong Kong, 40
hooks, bell, 212
Hoorn Orphanage possession (1673), 157, 174
Hopkinson, Nalo, 118
Hoppe, Herman, 126
Horak, Laura, 209, 254
Horkheimer, Max, 4
Hormonal Beast (comedy special), 99
Hottentot, The (film), 203
House (TV series), 123
Howard-Browne, Rodney, 159
How Bridget Made the Fire (film), 187
How to Go Mad Without Losing Your Mind (Bruce), 166, 229
Hula-Hoop Fad (1958), 172
Human Squib, The (film), 199
humorism, 242
humorlessness, 68–69
"Humorous Facial Expression" comedies, 255
Humorous Phases of Funny Faces (film), 264
Hundred Headless Woman, The (La femme 100 têtes) (Ernst), 84, *85*, 87
Hungry Hank's Hallucination (film), 237
Hurston, Zora Neale, 209
Hustvedt, Asti, 109, 110
Hutchinson, Pamela, 320n119
HVM. *See* Hearing Voices Movement
hypnotism, 108–109
Hypnotist's Revenge, The (film), 217, 244
Hypnotizing the Hypnotist (film), 190
Hypochondriac, The (Molière), 25
Hysteria (coalition group), 114, 162
Hysteria (feminist collective), 15
hysteria activism, 114, 162
"Hysteria and Democracy in America" (Copjec), 121
HysteriaFemCon (coalition group), 114, 162
hysteria-historiography, 207–213, 216
Hysteria in Men (Aub), 149
Hysteria Today (Grose), 164

Hysterical! (Mizejewski and Sturtevant), 97, 145, 165
Hysterical (documentary), 15, *99*, 99–100, 115
Hysterical Boredom (1972), 174
hysterical contagion, 16–17, 141
Hysterical Feminisms, 163–164, *164*
hysterical laughter. *See specific topics*
hysterical posing, 259–268
hysterical spectatorship, 196–198
hysterical visions, 242–244
"Hysteric As Conceptual Operator, The" (Braun), 121
hysteric openings, 167–169
hystero-epilepsy, 15
Hystories (Showalter), 161

Iconographie photographique de la Salpêtrière (Charcot and Londe), 108
Idle, Eric, 75
Illinois bus bedlam (2000), 172
Incomplete (Beeston and Solomon), 209
Indian Removal Act (1830), 290n117
Indigenous displacement, 41
Indiscreet Bathroom Maid (film), 267
infidelity, 247
Ingenieros, José, 125
inherited madness, 329n164
Inner Experience (Bataille), 86
insanity, 108
Insecure (TV series), 166
Installment Collector, The (film), 206–207
International Feminist Collective, 321n162
International Heart-Breaker, An (film), 201
International Laughter Yoga University, 170
Internet Archive, 44
Interpretation of Dreams, The (Freud), 133
"Intervention on Transference" (Lacan), 113
In the Consommé (film), 199
In the Grip of the Vampire (film), 248
In the Year 2000 (film), 197
invisible patients, 218–230
"Involuntary Laughter and Inappropriate Hilarity" (study), 138
Irigaray, Luce, 61, 105, 334n85
"Irma's Injection" (Freud), 59
Irradiated Mail Scare (1992), 172
Irving, Mildred, 183
Irwin, May, 43
Isabel de Barsas (anonymous), 12
Isabelle B. (Trusted Choice service representative), 3
It (King), 138
Italian Fatigue Outbreak (1978), 157, 174
Italy, 232

Jackson, Andrew, 290n117
Jackson, Polly Ann, 2, 47, 64, 102
Jackson-Perry, David, 220
Jane Eyre, 30
Janet, Pierre, 125–126, 130–131, 307n30
Janotus de Bragmardo (fictional character), 80–81
January 6, 2021, U.S. Capitol attacks, 140
Jarry, Alfred, 84
Jazz Age, 73
Jerry's Uncle's Namesake (film), 197
jeune née, La (The Newly Born Woman) (Clément), 95
Jezebel (stock character), 67
Jim Crow, 151
Johnson, Merri Lisa, 231
Johnson, Mrs. Bailey, 71–72
Joker (film), 16, 123–124
Jokes and Their Relation to the Unconscious (Freud), 84, 133
"joking addiction" (*witzelsucht*), 138
Jones, Andrew F., 45
Jones, Ernest, 152
Jones, Gayl, 118–120, 166
Jones, Nev, 221
jouissance, 63–64, 68, 95, 246, 295n103
Journal of Neuropsychiatry and Clinical Neurosciences, The, 138
Joyful Wisdom, The (Nietzsche), 81
joylessness, 66–71, 68–69
"Joyous Smile of Friendly Recognition, The," 65
Jung, Carl, 295n82

Kaffir tribes, 39
Kafka, Franz, 84
Kalamazoo Gazette, 49
kaleidoscopic Blackness, 166
Kansas City Star, 221
Kant, Immanuel, 27
Karlyn, Kathleen Rowe, 145, 165
Kavanaugh, Brett, 19, 280
Keller, Sarah, 225
Kelly, Timothy, 221
keyhole film, 267
Key & Peele (TV series), 166
Kierkegaard, Soren, 27
Kinaesthetic Spectatorship in the Theatre (Garner), 240
kinesthetic mimesis (automatism), 240
King, Stephen, 138
Kirby, Lynne, 185, 208
Kirson, Jessica, 99
Kitchen Maid's Dream, The (film), 187
Klikuschestvo shouting mania (1861), 157, 174

Kluge, Alexander, 180
Koln outbreak of erotic convulsions (1564), 174
Koplitz, Lynne, 98–99
Kracauer, Siegfried, 227, 245–246
Krasny, Elke, 114, 162
Krefting, Rebecca, 60, 282
Kristeva, Julia, 105, 106

Lacan, Jacques, 61, 113, 295n103, 309n76
La Cava, Gregory, 329n164
"Lachen in der U-bahn" (video), 141–142, *142*
Lady Audley's Secret (Braddon), 13, 27, 30
Laing, R. D., 231
Lake, Ellen, 48–49
Lane-McKinley, Madeline, 11
Lang, Fritz, 269
language: antipatriarchal, 94; bodily, 121; fragmented, 95
Laplanche, Jean, 309n76
late capitalism, 4
"Laugh and the World Laughs with You" (Smith, B., and Walker, K.), 186
laughing affects, 167–169
Laughing Club of India, The (documentary), 314n128
laughing cure, 147, 246
laughing epidemics (1960s–1970s), 157–159, 175
Laughing Fit to Kill (Carpio), 66, 165
Laughing Gas (film), 251, 252–255, *253*, 259, 262, 266, 268, 271
"Laughing Girl" (Strembler), 186
laughing head, 255–258, 266
Laughing Mad (Haggins), 165
"Laughing Song" (Smith, B., and Walker, K.), 186
"Laughing Spectator, The" (Smith, B., and Walker, K.), 186
laughing spectatorship, 183
Laughing to Keep from Dying (Morgan), 51, 166
"Laugh of the Medusa" (Cixous), 61–62, 97
Laughter (Bergson), 129
"laughter of emotional survival," 66
Lavater, Johann Kaspar, 258, 331n37
Lawrence, Mrs., 89
Laws of Imitation, The (Tarde), 240
Lea and the Ball of Wool (film), 270
Leaking Glue Pot, The (film), 193
Leathers, Margaret, 55, 66, 70, 76
Le Bon, Gustave, 16, 143, 149, 168, 189
leçon clinique à la Salpetrière, Une (Brouillet), 107
Leisslie, Josie, 14, 53, 76
Léontine, 9, 10, 130, 200, 201, 264, 265, 272, 273
Léontine's Boat (film), 270–271
Léontine Takes Flight (film), 264, *265*

Lerroux, Rosalie, 15, 108
lesbian authorship, 209
lesbian feminism, 113
Lettie Limelight in Her Lair (film), 257
Lewinsky, Mariann, 256
Lexicon of Festus, The, 7
Lieben, Anna von (Cäcilie M.), 104, 136
Life and Adventures of Valentine Vox, the Ventriloquist, The (Cockton), 33
Life of the Mind, The (Arendt), 88
limbic system, 145
Linder, Max, 246
Lippitt, John, 82, 83
Little Devil, The (film), 247
Livermore, Mary, 61
Lloyd, Harold, 204
Lloyd's of London, 1
Locofocos, 32–34
Loew, Katharina, 329n160
Londe, Albert, 15, 108, 110, 216
Lord Chumley in Canada (1925), 2
Loretta (etiquette guru), 57, 67, 68, 72
Los Angeles Times, 281
Loudon, Margracia, 28
Loudun outbreak of possessed nuns (1632–1638), 175
Louis-Doyen, Eugène, 234
Louisiana twitching epidemic (1939), 157, 175
Love and Science (film), 217, 246–247
Loveday, Kiki, 209
Lowell, James Russell, 27
Lubin Company, 237
Lubitsch, Ernst, 5
Lutker, Shana, 121
lynchings, 45–46, 150

Mabel's Strange Predicament (film), 273
Mabley, Moms, 99
Macbeth (Shakespeare), 193
MacDonald, Margaret I., 10–11, 199
Madame Medusa, 17, 62–63, 95–96, 198–202, 214, 239–241, 244–245
Madame's Cravings (film), 197, 266–268, *267*, 270
Mad Love (film), 124
Mad Men and Medusas (Mitchell), 112
Mad Musician, The (film), 18, 229
madness, 166–167, 223, 227–228, 329n164
Mad Pride, 325n32
mad rights movement, 220
madwoman, 123–124, 126, 219
Mad Women's Ball, The (film), 114
"Mae Gordon's Original Insane Moving Pedestal," *181*
Maggie Jolly, 68–69
Maher, Annie, 53, 68

Making Worlds (Breger), 168
Mammy (stock character), 67
Mandingo (stock character), 67
Maniac Barber, The (film), 187
Maniac Chase (film), 226
Mannequin, The (film), 200, *200*
Mansel, H. L., 29
Man With the Rubber Head, The (film), 258
Marie, Pierre, 235
Marinesco, Georges, 216, 235
Marks, Laura U., 257
Mars earthquake panic (1939), 155, 172
Martin, Vivian, 205
Martyrdom of St. Agnes, The (Zampieri), 38
Marx, Karl, 45, 79, 139–140
Marx, Nick, 167
Marxism, 307n28
Mary Jane's Mishap (film), 187, 260
Masini, Mario, 18, 227
"Mask, The" (Angelou), 70–71
Massachusetts feather tickling fad (early 1900s), 155
mass anxiety hysteria, 155, 156–157, 171–173
Massenet, Jules, 43–44
mass enjoyment, 42–46
mass hysteria, 143, 144, 148, 149–151, 156, 159–160
"Mass Hysteria" (Wessely), 154
mass motor hysteria, 157–158, 173–176, 312n82
mass psychogenic illness (MPI), 144, 160
Massumi, Brian, 168
Maurice, Alice, 277
Mayne, Judith, 208, 261
McBride, Jaye, 153
McCutcheon, Wallace, 335n103
McGinnis, Mrs. Abelarde, 58
McGowan, Todd, 63
McMahon, Tim, 198
McRuer, Robert, 230, 231
Mecking, Angela, 170
medical cinematography, 216
medical filmmaking, 234–235
medicalized madness, 166
Medical Muses (Hustvedt), 109
Méliès Boots (Solomon), 332n38
Méliès, Georges, 254, 258
Melrose, Bert, 184
Mendez, Mario, 138
mental hygiene movement, 218–219, 231
mesmerism (animal magnetism), 108
meta-mad movie spectators, 246–250
Methodists, 33, 150
Micheaux, Oscar, 212
Micro-Cinematography of Recurrent Fever (film), 243
Midnight Robber (Hopkinson), 118

INDEX

Migrating to the Movies (Stewart), 180, 208
Miller, D. A., 29
Mill on the Floss, The (Eliot), 29
minstrelsy, 66–71, 116, 229
Mirandy Smiles (film), 205
Mitchell, Juliet, 14, 112, 152
Mixed Babies (film), 274–275, *275*, 335n103
Mixed Feelings (Cvetkovich), 29, 100
Mizejewski, Linda, 97
mob hysteria, 149–150
Mock Baroness, The (film), 193
modernity, 180–181, 208, 211, 215
Mohr, Mrs. Charles, 67
Moi, Toril, 104
Molière, 25
Monk's Macaroni Feast, The (film), 269
Monstrous-Feminine, The (Creed), 61
Monstrous Intimacies (Sharpe), 118
Montaigne, Michel de, 88
Montalcini, Rita, 232
Monty Python, 75, 80
Morgan, Danielle Fuentes, 6, 51, 67, 117–118, 166
moria ("pathologic giddiness"), 138
Morin, Robert, 279
Morning Oregonian, 58, 66
Morrison, Toni, 213
Morzine Outbreaks (1857–1864), 158
Moser, Fanny (Emmy von N.), 104, 135
Moses, Adolph, 149
Motiograph equipment, 220
Motion Picture Magazine, 250
Motion Picture News, 147, 195, 204–205, 226
Motion Picture Story Magazine, 199
Mouse in the Art School, The (film), 278
mouth, management of, 57
movie cure, 215; for invisible patients, 218–230; meta-mad movie spectators and, 246–250; neurodivergent spectatorship and, 216–218
Movie-Struck Girl (Stamp), 10, 208
Moving by Electricity (film), 186
Moving Picture News, 11, 199, 248
Moving Picture World (*MPW*), 50, 54, 179, 191, 194, 196, 206–207, 220, 251
MPI. *See* mass psychogenic illness
MPW. *See Moving Picture World*
Muddled Bill Poster (film), 266
Mukherjee, Debashree, 211, 323n190
Müller, Corinna, 189
Mulvey, Laura, 260, 332n44
Mummy, The (film), 192
Münsterberg, Hugo, 227, 243
Munthe, Axel, 15, 106, 130
Murphy, Ryan, 123

Museo del Cinema, 235
Musidora, 209
Mystery of the Rocks of Kador (film), 217, 248, *249*

Nair, Mira, 314n128
Nancy, Jean-Luc, 14, 84, 87–88
Nancy School, 109
Nanette (comedy special), 19, 98, 302n19
Napoléon III, 140
narcissistic personality disorder, 124
National Association for the Study of Epilepsy (NASE), 236–237
Native Son (Wright), 212
Nazis, 5, 75, 84, 148, 167, 245
Negra, Diane, 208
Negro, Camillo, 18, 216, 232, 235–236
Negt, Oskar, 180
Nehring, Ernestina, 7, 51, 70, 76, 83, 296n134
Nellie the Beautiful Housemaid (film), 274
neurodivergent spectatorship, 216–218
neurodiversity, 220, 324n9
neurological gaze, 216, 232–237
neurological modernity, 215
neuropsychiatry, clinical, 137–138
New Cure for Divorce (film), 247
"New Laugh, The," 56–60
Newly Born Woman, The (*La jeune née*) (Clément), 95
"New New Hysteria Studies, The," 15, 97
New York Times, 49, 205
New York World, 49, 72
Ngai, Sianne, 5, 25, 156, 182, 204
Nickelodeon, The, 17, 194
Nietzsche, Friedrich, 8, 14, 75–76, 81–85, 88, 149, 301n81
Nietzsche on Gender, 82
nonagricultural workforce, 55–56
Nordstrom, Marie, 179
Normand, Mabel, 9, 209, 273
Norworth, Jack, 204
Notari, Elvira, 209
"Note Upon the 'Mystic Writing-Pad,' A" (Freud), 249
Not Normal (comedy special), 98
Novak, Jacqueline, 96
Nuclear Disaster Hoax (1982), 172
Nye, Bill, 44
Nyerere, Julius, 158

obituaries, 50–52, 64
Obstinate Tooth, The (film), 193
Occupy movement, 169
oceanic feeling, 169
One Way Street (Benjamin), 211
"On Humour" (Freud), 84

Onions Make People Weep (film), 271
Only Kids (film), 230
On Nietzsche (Bataille), 86
Ontario Equitable Life and Accident Insurance Company, 2
"On the Essence of Laughter" (Baudelaire), 13, 25
"On the Physiology of Laughter" (Spencer), 41
Opdyke, George, 225
Oppel, Frances Nesbitt, 82
optimism, 182–184
orbicularis oculi, 36
Orissa cat calls (2004), 158, 175
Ostherr, Kristen, 232
Ott, Fred, 255
Outcault, R. F., 226
Ozgen-Tuncer, Asli, 185

Page of Madness, A (film), 123
Paley, William, 146
Palmer, Mrs. Joe, *9*, 9–10
panopticon, 221
Pappenheim, Berta (Anna O.), 103–104
Parallel Tracks (Kirby), 185, 208
Parasite (film), 16, 123, 124
Parks, Suzan-Lori, 66, 166
Parvulescu, Anca, 39, 61
Passion of Joan of Arc, The (film), 324n12
pathological laughter, 123, 137–138
"pathologic giddiness" (*moria*), 138
Paul, Ellen, 259
Paul, R. W., 259, 266
PBA. *See* pseudobulbar affect
Pearl (film), 124
Peele, Jordan, 6, 166
Peiss, Kathy, 49, 180, 192
Pérez, Raúl, 5, 271
Performing Hysteria (Braun), 163
Performing Nerves (Furse), 15
"Periode de Clownisme" (Bourneville and Régnard), *111*
permanent carnival, 182–183
Perret, Léonce, 248
Perry, Mrs., 51
Peterson, Nina, 316n17
Petro, Patrice, 10
Pétronille's Monkey (film), 270
Phantom (film), 228
Phantom Hat Pin Stabber (1923), 172
Phelps, Milo Ray, 249–250
Philippine Devil Hysteria (1994), 157–158, 175
phonography, 185–186
Phonoscope, The, 188, 189

Pickens, Therí Alyce, 118
"Pictures Help to Set Right Insane Minds," *218*
Pietro Aretino, 75
pigsty hysteria (1972), 172
Pinthus, Kurt, 252
Piobb, Pierre, 84
Plato, 46
"Play to the Ladies," 17
Plessner, Helmuth, 27
Pokémon Illness (1997), 173
Poland, 84, 155, 173
Police Band, The (film), 202
Ponocrates, 80–81
Postal, Jennie, 197
Poster Girls and the Hypnotist, The (film), 187
Postman, Neil, 4
Potter, Susan, 209
Poussin, Nicolas, 38
"Practice of Joy in the Face of Death, The" (Bataille), 14, 84
Prassinos, Gisèle, 84, 300n57
Pratt, Gilbert, 335n101
prefrontal cortex, 145
Presbyterian religious revivals, 33–34
Preston, George, 40
Priest, Helen, 64
Princess Brambilla (Hoffmann), 25
Prison for Women at Auburn, 241
Prodigal Wife, The (film), 228
professional workforce, 55–56
projection speeds, 335n103
Promise of Cinema, The, 196
Providence Journal, 70
Provine, Robert, 145, 160
Pruett, Bertha, 1, 14, 47, 48, 76, 102
Pryor, Richard, 166
pseudobulbar affect (PBA), 123, 124, 137, 138
psychiatric cinematography, 231–232
Psycho (comedy special), 98
psychoanalysis, 59, 63, 101, 114, 132–133, 136, 144
Psychological Automatism (Janet), 131
Psychologie des foules, 189
Psychology of Emotions, The (Ribot), 132
psychosocial madness, 167
Public Sphere and Experience (Kluge and Negt), 180
Pullman Maids, 198

Qawa Hysterical Schoolgirls (1968), 175
Queen Sugar (TV series), 70
queer theory, 113–115
Queer Timing (Potter), 209
queer utterance, 153

Queer Way of Feeling, A (Anselmo), 209
"Question of Lay Analysis, The," 136
Question of Silence, A (film), *165*
Quick Change Mesmerist, A (film), 190

Rabelais, François, 8, 77–78, 80
Rabinovitz, Lauren, 10, 180, 185, 208
"Race of Hysteria, The" (Briggs, L.), 115
racial biopolitics, 115–116
Racial Indigestion (Tompkins), 262
racism, 39–42, 117–118, 166, 229, 274
rage, 166–167
"railway spine," 304n90
Randolph, Florence Spearing, 151
Rappe, Virginia, 73
Reagan, Ronald, 121
"reality-TV-to-electoral-politics pipeline," 4
"Reclaiming Hysteria" (Grose), 164
reconstructive spectatorship, 212
Record of a Sneeze (film), 255
recreational capital, 45
redintegrative contagion, 168–169
Redrobe, Karen, 256
"Reducing the Surplus. 'Now Pull Hard!,'" *54*
Regester, Charlene, 274
Régnard, P., *107*, *111*
Regustus, Bertha, 9, 252, *253*, 256
Rehm, Cindy, 121
Reichstag Fire (1933), 148, 311n36
Reiniger, Lotte, 209
Reiss, Benjamin, 326n54
"Relation Between the Anxiety Neurosis and Anxiety-Hysteria, The" (Jones, E.), 152
religious revivalism, 150–151
Rennert, Malwine, 210
Representation of the Cinema, A (film), 247
research-based medical filmmaking, 234–235
Results of Eating Horse Flesh, The (film), 193, 202
Resurrection of a Young Japanese Girl, The (Poussin), 38
Ribot, Théodule, 130
Rice, Catherine Maude, 47
Richer, Paul, 110
Riley, James Whitcomb, 44
Rire, Le (magazine), 130, *134*
rire hystérique, 125–127
risible mortis, 2
Ritter, Karl, 184, 196
Rivers, Joan, 99
Roaring Lions and Wedding-Bells (film), 198
Roe v. Wade, 280
Rolland, Romain, 169

Romains, Jules, 243
Romanticism, 80
Romeo Pays for the Cinema (film), 247
Rosalie a la maladie du sommeil (*Rosalie Has Sleeping Sickness*) (film), 224
Rosalie and Léontine Go to the Theatre (film), 272
Rosalie Moves In (film), 270
Rose, Jacqueline, 295n103
Rowland, Helen, 64
Royal Belgian Film Archive, 233
Rubin, Gayle, 113
Russell, Catherine, 211
Russia, 89
Russian Poland balloon scare (1892), 155, 173
Russo, Mary, 79, 165

Sade, Marquis de, 84
Safety Last! (film), 204
Saint-Médard Convulsionnairies (1730s), 175
Salem Witch Trials (1692–1693), 156–157
Salpêtrière Hospital, 108, 110
Salt Lake Telegram, 49, 55
Sambo (stock character), 67
Samer, Rox, 113
Sanborn, Kate, 83
Sanders, Bernie, 306n2
Sandy McPherson's Quiet Fishing Trip (film), 17, 186
San Francisco Dramatic Review, 188
sanity, madness *versus*, 223
Sapphic Cinemania! (Loveday), 209
Sapphire (stock character), 67
Sargent, Epes Winthrop, 238
satire, Black, 6, 96, 117, 166
Savannah Morning News, 149
Scandal Over the Tea Cups (film), 19, 256, 259
Scheible, Jeff, 256
School Writing Tremors (1880s–1910s), 175
Schopenhauer, Arthur, 27, 149
Schuller, Kyla, 31, 35, 39
Schunzel, Reinhold, 255
Schur, Max, 59
Schuylkill County Insane Asylum, 237
Schwartz, Vanessa, 10, 49, 180, 189–190
Scott, Joan Wallach, 27
Second Great Awakening, 33–34
"second self," 16, 127
Sedgwick, Eve, 169
Seeing by Electricity (film), 247
Sellout, The (Beatty), 166
Semiotics of Clowns and Clowning, The (Bouissac), 145
sensation literature, 27–32, 287n27
sentimentalism, 32, 39

Serao, Matilde, 191
Serna, Laura Isabel, 10
Servant Girl Problem, The (film), 256
Sessions, Jeff, 19, 279
Sex in Education (Clarke), 114
Sexton, Jared, 314n111
sexual harassment, 105
sexuality, female, 136
Shakespeare, William, 193–194
Shange, Ntozake, 166
Shape of Spectatorship (Curtis), 245
Sharpe, Christina, 118, 119
Shave By Installments on the Un-Easy System, A (film), 261
Sheehan, Tanya, 263
Shepherd, Sherri, 99
Sherman, Cindy, 121
She Wrote a Play (film), 217
Shimp, Daniel F., 64, 68
SHOCKS (Furse), 15
Shooting the Chutes (film), 187
Shorter, Edward, 103
Shoulder Arms (film), 206
Showalter, Elaine, 95, 103, 108, 157, 161
Shub, Esfir, 209
Sibande, Mary, 121
Sick Kitten, The (film), 278
Sienkiewicz, Matt, 167
Silas Marner (Eliot), 29
Simmel, Georg, 220, 258
Simone, Nina, 166
Singapore factory hysteria (1970s), 175
Singer, Elyse, 208, 275
Single White Female (film), 16, 124
Skipped by the Light of the Moon (play), 44
Skunked Workers (Ohio), 173
slapstick, 18, 30–31, 226
slavery, chattel, 71
slave trade, African, 70
Smith, Andrew, 39
Smith, Belle, 185–186
Smith, George Albert, 255
Smith, Jacob, 146
Smith, Sydney, 27
Snake Pit, The (film), 123
Sobchack, Vivian, 262
Sober Sue, 68–69
social death by laughter, 66–71
social transformation, 86–87
Solomon, Matthew, 332n38
Solomon, Stefan, 209
somnambulism, carnival, 106–116
Somnambulist, The (film), 190

Soul Kiss, The (film), 194, 195
Souls of White Jokes (Pérez), 5
South Africa, 39
Soviet Union, 89
spectatorship, 196–198, 212, 216–218, 217
Specters of Slapstick and Silent Film Comediennes (Hennefeld), 9
Speetzen, Louise, 14, 53–54, 76
Spencer, Herbert, 35, 41
Spillers, Hortense, 119, 229, 314n111
spiritism, 127–129
"Spiritism and Hysteria" (Charcot), 127
split personality disorder, 117
Springfield Daily Republican, The, 10
Squirrel Food (film), 274, 335n101
Stamp, Shelley, 10, 208
"Stand-Up Comedians as Public Intellectuals," 5
Stanley, Myrtle, 72
Steimatsky, Noa, 257–258, 270
Steinlight, Emily, 29, 46
stereotypes, 41, 67
Sterritt, David, 86
Stevenson, Robert Louis, 103
Stewart, Jacqueline Najuma, 10, 180, 208, 212–213, 252
Stiller, Mauritz, 200
St. Louis Insane Asylum, 222–223
stock characters, 67
Stockton, E. Boudinot, 237
Stoler, Ann Laura, 42
"Stop Being Poor" (parody), 5
Stowe, Harriet Beecher, 31–32
Strange Case of Dr. Jekyll and Mr. Hyde (Stevenson), 103
Strasbourg Dancing Plague (1518), 157
Strawberries with Sugar Virus (2006), 173
Streetwalking on a Ruined Map (Bruno), 208, 211
Strembler, Sallie, 186
Strobl, Karl, 210
Strouse, Ethel M., 202
Stuber, Charles S., 2, 52, 55
Studies on Hysteria (Breuer and Freud), 132, 249
Study in Facial Expression, A (film), 269
Sturtevant, Victoria, 97
subconscious, 131, 307n30
Subject for the Rogue's Gallery, A (film), 261–262
Suffragette's Dream, The (film), 197
Suicidal Poet, The (film), 193–194
Sul-Te-Wan, Madame, 335n101, 335n108
Sun Tse, 61
superiority theory of humor, 291n158
Supreme Court, 280
Sure Cure, A (film), 199
surrealist movement, 300n57

Sutherland, Donald, 86
Swedish Preaching Epidemic (1841), 157, 175
Swift, Jonathan, 84
Swinhoe, Robert, 26
Sykes, Wanda, 15
Sylvaire, Renée, 228

tableaux vivants, 332n44
taboos, 5, 7, 151–154
Tainted Philanthropy (Goldknopf), 205
Tale of a Leg (film), 197
talking cure, 101, 105
Tammany Hall, 33
Tampa Morning Tribune, 57, 80
Tanganyika African National Union (TANU), 158, 159
Tanganyika laughter epidemic (1962), 146, 157–160
Tannen, Julius, 17, 198
tarantism, 151
Tarde, Gabriel, 240
Taylor, Alf, 186
Taylor, Bob, 186
Teen Vogue (magazine), 120
teeth, 58–60
Tempest, The (Shakespeare), 193
Textbook of Clinical Neuropsychiatry, 138
Thales of Miletus, 88–89
That Fatal Sneeze (film), 1, 202, 236, 271
That's Not Funny (Marx, N., and Sienkiewicz), 167
That to Study Philosophy Is to Learn to Die (Montaigne), 88
Theory of Film (Kracauer), 245
Theory of the Gimmick (Ngai), 204
Theory of the Leisure Class (Veblen), 54
Theron, Charlize, 3
Thieving Umbrella, The (film), 268
Thirteen (film), 124
Thirteenth Amendment, 70
Thurston, John H., 251, 253
Thus Spake Zarathustra (Nietzsche), 82–83
Tickled to Death (film), 1, 210
tickling, 155, 172, 312n69
To Be or Not to Be (film), 5
Tomkins, Silvan, 155, 168
Tompkins, Kyla Wazana, 262
Tontolini Is Sad (film), 246
toothed vaginas (vagina dentata), 61–64
Toronto Airport Church, 159
Totem and Taboo (Freud), 153
Tourette, Gilles de la, 110
Trading Stamp Mania, The (film), 195
tragedy, 139–140
Trail of Tears, 41, 290n117

Tramp and the Mattress Makers, The (film), 193
Tramp and the Typewriter (film), 261
Transformation of Cinema, The (Bowser), 259
Transmission of Affect, The (Brennan), 105
trans phenomenology, 113
transphobia, 153
"Travels in Normate Sensory Worlds" (Jackson-Perry et al.), 220
Trelkald, Mary, 53, 76, 204
Trenton Evening Times, 189
Treumann, Wanda, 9
Triple Lady, The (film), 103
Trip to the Moon, A (film), 268
Truman, Jane, 58
Trump, Donald, 120–121, 279
Trusted Choice, 1, 2, 3, 271, 282
"Trust Me I'm Trolling" (DeCook), 167
Tucker, Sophie, 116
Tulip Mania (1634–1637), 173
"Turkish women defy deputy PM with laughter," *280*
Turner, Florence, 9, 234, 263, *264*, 333n74
Twilight Sleep (film), 195
Twitter, 8, 43
Two Mothers (film), 228
Two Up a Tree (film), 228

Ugandan Running Sickness (2002), 175–176
Ugly Feelings (Ngai), 156
Uncle Josh at the Moving Picture Show (film), 199
Uncle Josh in a Spooky Hotel (film), 199
Uncle Josh's Nightmare (film), 199
Uncle Tom (stock character), 67
Uncle Tom's Cabin (Stowe), 31–32
Unconscious Influence (Bushnell), 36
Unfortunate Housemaid, The (film), 270
Universal Film Company, 195
University of Torino, 235
University of Toronto, 9
Unlucky Trousers, The (film), 225, 237
Unruly Woman (Karlyn), 165
Unterzell Outbreak (1738), 176
"Unwritten Music," 26
Uproarious, 165
Up-to-Date Squ*w, An (film), 274
"Use of the Biograph in Medicine" (Chase), 238
U.S. War Industries Board, 73

vagina dentata, 61–64
Van Gehuchten, Arthur, 18, 216, *233*, 233–234, 236
van Gogh, Vincent, 149
Vanishing Lady, The (film), 187
Variety (magazine), 69, 185, 197, 204–205, 215, 225, 254, 258

Vasey, George, 53
Veblen, Thorstein, 54, 55
Veillette, Mary, 206
"Venus in Two Acts" (Hartman), 212
Vénus noire, La, 116
Victoire a ses nerfs (film), *257*
Victoria (queen), 61
Vidoni, Giuseppe, 18, 227
Vitagraph, 252–255
Vorse, Mary Heaton, 192

Wages for Housework campaign, 321n162
Wakefield, Esther, 15, 101–104, 117, 137
Walker, Kara, 70, 76, 185–186
Walker, Rosa, 7, 14, 51, 70
Wang, Jackie, 169
Wanzo, Rebecca, 69
Ward Island's Women's Hospital, 242
War of the Worlds (radio broadcast), 155
Washington Post, 64
Way Down East (film), 255
Wayward Lives, Beautiful Experiments (Hartman), 212
Weber, Lois, 209
Weisenburg, Theodore, 18, 216, 237
Welles, Orson, 155
Wells, Ida B., 46
Werder, Stephanie, 208
Wessely, Simon, 154
"We Wear the Mask" (Dunbar), 70–71
WFPP. *See* Women Film Pioneers Project
Whatever Happened to Baby Jane? (film), 123, *124*
What Happened in the Tunnel (film), 256
"When Bigoted Humor Isn't Just a Joke" (Pérez), 271
When Cherries Are Ripe (film), 260–261, 262
Whiskey or Bullets (film), 255
White, M. E., 243
White, William Allen, 292n14
White House Correspondents' dinner (2018), 98
white nervousness, 39–42
white supremacy, 115, 118, 136, 229
"Who Goes to the Moving Pictures?" (Bush), 191
Whole Dam Family, The (film), 266
Who's Laughing Now? Feminist Tactics in Social Media, 165
Why the French Love Jerry Lewis (Gordon), 190
"Wild Laughter in the Throat of Death" (Nancy), 87
Willett, Cynthia, 51, 96, 145, 147
Willett, Julie, 51, 96, 145, 147
Willful Subjects (Ahmed), 112
Williams, Carol, 281
Williams, Linda, 261
Williamson, James, 255
Williamson, Nellie, 55

Willie Visits a Moving Picture Show (film), 247
Wilson, Woodrow, 226
Window Shopping (Friedberg), 185, 208
windshield pitting scare (1954), 173
Winnipeg balloon mania (1896), 155
Witlin, Leo, 196
Wit of Wisdom, The (Sanborn), 83
Wittig, Monique, 303n52
Wittman, Blanche, 15, 107, 143
witzelsucht ("joking addiction"), 138
Wolf, Michelle, 15, 98
Wolfram, Aurel, 193
Woman, The (play), 205
Woman at the Keyhole, The (film), 208, 261
Woman in White, The (Collins), 13, 27
"woman laughed herself to death in a Pittsburg theatre, a" (headline), *48*
Woman's Face, A (film), 270
Women Film Pioneers Project (WFPP), 209
women's work, 206
Wong, Marion, 209
workforce, professional, 55–56
World Newspaper Archive, 44
World War I, 83–84, 148
World War II, 86
Worthington, Anne, 114
Wretched of the Earth, The (Fanon), 39
"writing women" (*écriture féminine*), 63

X-Ray Fiend, The (film), 187

Yao, Xine, 31, 114–115
Yawner, The (film), 271
Yeamans-Titus, Lydia, 184
yellow journalism, 49
Young, Clara Kimball, 227
young cinema, 320n119
Young Women's Christian Association, 67
Yue, Genevieve, 245, 276

Zampieri, Domenico, 38
Zandori's Secret (film), 228, 248
Zeuxis (ancient Greek artist), 7, 14, 80, 86
Zhen, Zhang, 10, 50, 208, 211
Ziedner, Lili, 200, *200*
Ziegfield, Florence, 194
Zimbabwe zombie school (2002), 176
Zip Coon (stock character), 67
Zizek, Slavoj, 182
Zoe's Magic Umbrella (film), 269
Zoom, 277–278
Zoot Suit Riots (1942–1943), 155, 173
Zupančič, Alenka, 60–61, 147, 169

GPSR Authorized Representative: Easy Access System Europe, Mustamäe tee 50, 10621 Tallinn, Estonia, gpsr.requests@easproject.com

www.ingramcontent.com/pod-product-compliance
Lightning Source LLC
Chambersburg PA
CBHW022027290426
44109CB00014B/784